Elizabeth
and Michael

Center Point
Large Print

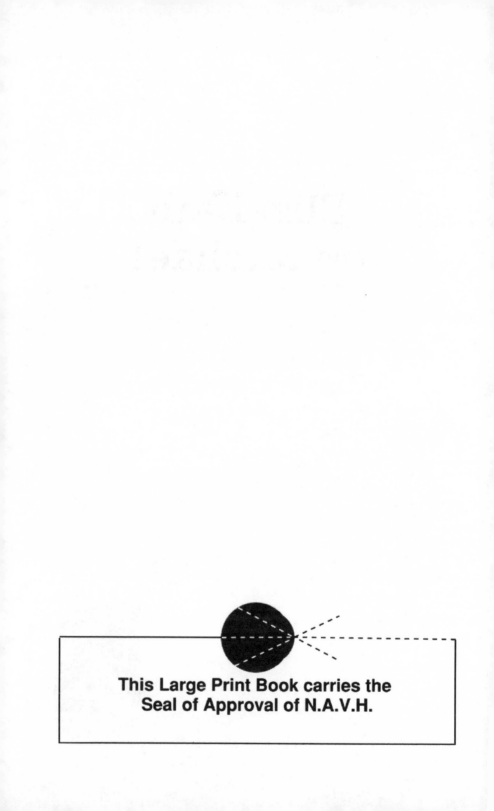

**This Large Print Book carries the
Seal of Approval of N.A.V.H.**

Elizabeth
and Michael

THE QUEEN OF HOLLYWOOD
AND THE KING OF POP
—A LOVE STORY

Donald Bogle

CENTER POINT LARGE PRINT
THORNDIKE, MAINE

This Center Point Large Print edition is published
in the year 2016 by arrangement with Atria Books,
a division of Simon & Schuster, Inc.

Photographs are from Photofest (1 through 14)
and ImageCollect

The text of this Large Print edition is unabridged.
In other aspects, this book may vary
from the original edition.
Printed in the United States of America
on permanent paper.
Set in 16-point Times New Roman type.

ISBN: 978-1-68324-129-4

Library of Congress Cataloging-in-Publication Data

Names: Bogle, Donald, author.
Title: Elizabeth and Michael : the queen of Hollywood and the
  king of pop : a love story / Donald Bogle.
Description: Center Point Large Print edition. | Thorndike, Maine :
Center Point Large Print, 2016.
Identifiers: LCCN 2016028056 | ISBN 9781683241294
  (hardcover : alk. paper)
Subjects: LCSH: Taylor, Elizabeth, 1932–2011. | Taylor, Elizabeth,
1932–2011—Friends and associates. | Actors—United States—
Biography. | Jackson, Michael, 1958–2009. | Jackson, Michael,
1958–2009—Friends and associates. | Rock musicians—United
States—Biography. | Large type books.
Classification: LCC PN2287.T18 B64 2016b |
  DDC 791.4302/8092 [B] —dc23
LC record available at https://lccn.loc.gov/2016028056

To Emery Wimbish and Grace Frankowsky
To Marie Dutton Brown
To the memory of Marie Kanalas Bogle
To the memory of my agent Bob Silverstein
And to my parents, Roslyn and John;
my brother John; and Carol Bogle

Elizabeth
and Michael

February 16, 1997

IN SOME RESPECTS, it was just another Hollywood night, another of those big affairs with a gallery of glamorous stars, overeager publicists, agents, managers, and immaculately groomed industry executives—as well as a surge of pushy photographers and reporters who snapped pictures and shouted out questions. Barricaded on the sidelines were the fans, pumped up with excitement at seeing so many famous faces. On such occasions, everyone was accustomed to the star glow, the sparkling jewels, the designer gowns, the brilliant smiles, the air kisses, and the funny chatter that didn't mean much of anything. On such nights, it was almost hard for anyone else to be really impressed. Glamour was, of course, valued, appreciated, held to high standards. Yet glamour in Hollywood was almost second nature.

But then in the midst of all the expected fanfare, all the lights and cameras and cries of joy, all the gilded chaos, there was a hush in the air. Something miraculous seemed to have happened. Suddenly, *they* were there. Exiting from a limousine was Elizabeth Taylor, perhaps the greatest movie star of the twentieth century, and there wasn't one person who did not strain to see her. She still elicited the kind of awe that was seldom seen, the kind that had vanished long ago with the demise of the classic Old Hollywood and the old studio system. But no sooner had the great Liz come into view than another wave of excitement roared through the crowd as a second star, the elusive Michael Jackson, no doubt the greatest entertainer of the twentieth century, stepped out of the same limousine.

Elizabeth and Michael. A dazzling pair. Every eye was on them. "Michael and Elizabeth's combined celebrity was just so incredibly intense," Carrie Fisher once recalled. "And in a way it may have been comforting for each of them to have found someone with equivalent unimaginable celebrity. A rare species—endangered, protected, shiny."

The event that night was ABC's televised tribute to Elizabeth Taylor's sixty-fifth birthday. In a short time, she was scheduled to enter the hospital for brain surgery. Doctors were optimistic, but no one could say for sure how the operation would go. Because the tribute had been scheduled long before she knew she'd have the surgery, Elizabeth Taylor decided to go ahead with it. And Michael Jackson knew he wanted no one else to escort her but himself. So there *they* were.

Elizabeth Taylor and Michael Jackson were hooked on each other. Not too long after their first meeting, a deep friendship had blossomed: a true kind of love affair, frankly unlike any relationship either had had before. They were eager to share secrets, to express their ways of looking at the world, to enter a private realm all their own. At his Neverland Valley Ranch in Los Olivos, California, Michael constructed a room in Elizabeth's honor. Taylor, in turn, saw that he was one of those misunderstood, sensitive souls to which she had long been attracted.

But, frankly, what added to the crowd's fervor at seeing the two together on this special night in February 1997 was the fact that no could quite figure them out. Both within and outside the entertainment industry, among the public at large and among other stars, some thought the relationship was flat-out weird. Incomprehensible. What went on with these two? What was this friendship all about? They were Hollywood's Odd Couple. Old enough to be Michael Jackson's mother, Elizabeth Taylor was a woman of the world who had been on the scene for decades, from the time she was a little girl, then through her youthful reign as the town's dark-haired princess until her ascension as Hollywood's Queen Elizabeth (and eventually, Dame Elizabeth). Why was a woman who looked as if she had been everywhere and done everything spending time with *him?* He was something of a strange bird, an asexual enigmatic Peter Pan, also on the scene since his childhood, now looking fearful of growing older, forever in search of finding the childhood he believed he had lost.

In essence, Elizabeth Taylor and Michael Jackson couldn't be considered a couple at all. Each was too bright and bold to ever really complement the other. No one could ever imagine them as two halves that now completed a whole. Her husbands had often been consorts, all of them there at the service of the queen, bending to her will, absorbed into her world and reflecting her glow and glory as best or powerfully as they could. At times even Richard Burton, despite his power and charisma, knew deep down that partly what had made him Richard Burton, in the eyes of the public, was the fact that she had chosen him. But *that* never seemed the case with Michael, who was always the king of his own universe, never a consort to anyone, never standing in the afterglow of someone else. His brothers—and his onetime manager father, Joseph Jackson—had realized this early on, accepted it, and were as magnetized by his star power as anyone else.

So Taylor and Jackson were always separate entities that somehow clicked without one ever being at the service of the other, even though Michael appeared to love playing the part of the gentleman escort during their public outings. This separateness in a sense made them all the more a compelling pair, all the more a duo that puzzled, intrigued, and ignited the imagination. When they were together, it was admittedly something special, something wondrous to behold. Always he looked at her with adoring eyes and a smile that signaled some secret joy she brought him. Always she glanced at him in a protective, loving way.

How they really came together or why may always be baffling. But Michael Jackson's *devotion*—and devotion is the only word to describe his feelings—to Elizabeth Taylor was different from those past relationships and friendships with Brooke Shields, Tatum O'Neal, and even the woman who had first fascinated him, Diana Ross. He had pursued and courted Elizabeth Taylor, and she had been resistant to his pursuit, perhaps asking herself what on earth this young man wanted. But, gradually, he won her over, and she succumbed to his attention and to his vulnerability. For her, nurturing doomed souls, like actors Montgomery Clift and James Dean, was a part of who she was, at the core of her DNA. Jackson's onetime publicist Bob Jones— clearly surprised by the relationship as it built and took shape—felt that Michael usually didn't want many women around. "There was at least one exception: Elizabeth Taylor," recalled Jones, who was aware of the undeniable fact that "she captured Michael Jackson's imagination."

Something drew them together, bound them, may even have puzzled them as much as every-

one else. Their backgrounds, seemingly so different, made theirs often a seemingly paradoxical union. But those separate backgrounds, those past histories, set the stage for their relationship, provided its exposition and backstory, and established the first and second acts of their individual lives. During what unexpectedly
turned out to be act three of each of their lives, they met and began the friendship. But so much had come before—for each of them.

Chapter 1

ELIZABETH TAYLOR'S CHILDHOOD reads like something of a fairy tale, albeit with its requisite dark side. The second child of a dreamy-looking American couple living abroad, she was born on February 27, 1932, in London. Her mother, Sara Viola Warmbrodt, born in 1896 in Arkansas City, Kansas, was the daughter of an engineer. Ambitious, lively, and outgoing, with large eyes and a friendly smile, Sara met a handsome young dark-haired man with piercing blue eyes named Francis Lenn Taylor, who had been born in 1897 in Springfield, Illinois, and whose family lived in Arkansas City. From the very start, girls were all over Francis, falling into a swoon within minutes after seeing him. One classmate recalled that "he was the first boy I was ever aware of. I could have eaten him like ice cream on a stick."

Not only were there those striking looks, but there was also his background and his breeding. This was no naïve, unpolished local lad unaware of the world. Though his father managed a general-goods store and had a modest income, Francis was the favorite of his wealthy uncle, Howard Young. Living in Saint Louis and married to Francis's aunt Mabel, Howard was a prosperous art dealer with galleries in St. Louis and eventually New York and London, with beautiful homes in those cities as well as in Connecticut, Florida, and Wisconsin. Howard and his wife had no children, and though he was known as a man who did not show his feelings, he doted on Francis and was keenly aware of his nephew's potential. When Francis turned nineteen, Uncle Howard brought him to St. Louis and later to New York and tutored him in the world of high art. Selling paintings was not just knowing the artistic merits of a piece of work. One also had to know the market for it—or how to create a market —and how to mix and mingle with the wealthy, the influential, the powerful. Also important was the image of the dealer. Young Francis—innately elegant and increasingly more and more sophisticated—soon dressed in splendidly tailored suits with the appropriate shirts and ties and shoes. He spoke in an eloquently thoughtful, knowledgeable manner. People took one look at him or heard him speak and instantly assumed he was *somebody*.

Certainly that was how Sara Warmbrodt felt upon meeting him. But it wasn't love at first sight. Too many other things were then going on in her life. Mainly, Sara was hell-bent on building a career for herself. Her ambition? To be an actress; to conquer the world from the stage. Under the name Sara Sothern, she appeared in the stock company of actor Edward Everett Horton, then made her way to Los Angeles, where she debuted playing a lame girl in the drama *The Fool*. She reportedly made a screen test for MGM but nothing came of it. Then, at age twenty-six, Sara appeared in *The Fool* on Broadway. Two years later, she went to London with the drama. Afterward, Sara was back in the States in a small role in another Broadway show: *The Little Spitfire*. But that play closed quickly, no other roles came her way, and Sara, at loose ends, realized she might never have the stage career of her dreams. Then and there, she met up with Francis again. Now an ambitious young man of the world, he was like a knight in shining armor who made her envision another life for herself. About a year later—with permission from Howard Young—they married. Then came their world travels. Uncle Howard paid for their European honeymoon. Then Francis became his uncle's purchasing agent in Europe and traveled the continent, meeting artists and assessing their work. He proved quite adept at his job and prospered. By 1929, Howard had installed thirty-one-year-old Francis as the head of his London gallery at 35 Old Bond Street.

In London, Francis and Sara were a magnetic, young American couple, looking like something out of an F. Scott Fitzgerald novel: boldly attractive and stylish as they shrewdly maneuvered their way through the city's tony social set.

Though Sara was considered a social climber and perhaps too brash, she was balanced by her sedate, rather serious, and cultivated husband. They may not have reached the very top of the British social ladder, but they certainly did all right for themselves. In their circle were Victor Cazalet and his sister, Thelma Cazalet-Keir. Victor was a conservative member of Parliament, lively, aggressive, never at a loss for words, and always impeccably dressed and something of a snob. Thelma Cazalet-Keir became one of the first female members of Parliament. With a sharp sense of the ins and outs of British social decorum, each Cazalet had an array of connections that helped Francis professionally. As for Sara, she loved the luncheons, dinners, receptions, parties, and gala openings that she was now attending.

Sara and Francis's first child, a son named Howard, after Francis's uncle, was born in late 1929. In early 1932, their daughter, Elizabeth Rosemond—named after Sara's mother, Elizabeth, and Howard Young's wife, Mabel, whose middle name was Rosemond—was born. Theirs was a picture-postcard family. Victor Cazalet and his sister, Thelma, became unofficial godparents to young Elizabeth. Francis and Sara moved into a comfortable home called Heathwood in the Hampstead section of London—it had "six bedrooms, three baths, a living room, a sitting room, a large kitchen, and living quarters for a family of servants." Later they also had a small country home outside the city, thanks to Victor. "I remembered seeing the four-room cottage—simple to the point where water had to be heated on the kitchen stove," recalled Hollywood's gossip columnist Hedda Hopper. " 'Little Swallows' was its name, and it sat in the woods of her godfather, Victor Cazelet [sic]; his English estate, Great Swifts, was in Kent." Hopper first met Elizabeth during a trip to England, since she was friends with the Cazelets. The country home didn't remain a simple four-room cottage for long. Francis and Sara completely redid Little Swallows, turning it into a charming showplace. Weekends with the children and friends were often spent there.

Howard and Elizabeth were showered with attention—night and day. A nanny, Gladys, cared for them. A cook prepared meals. A part-time chauffeur drove Sara and the children to their various appointments. Both children were enrolled in private schools.

Elizabeth quickly developed into an angelic-looking girl with dark, almost jet-black hair, flawless skin with a distinct beauty mark, a mole on her cheek—which Sara later emphasized with mascara—and dark blue or violet eyes, as many believed they were, with thick, luxurious brows and lashes. "The doctor told us that she had a mutation," recalled Sara. "Well, that sounded just awful—a *mutation*. But, when he explained that her eyes had double rows of eyelashes, I thought, well, now, that doesn't sound so terrible at all."

Extremely shy, sometimes hiding behind her nanny, she was paradoxically also adventurous and independent. Yet from the day of her birth, she was also delicate. Her health was fragile, with a more serious problem that Sara preferred not to discuss. Elizabeth suffered from a glandular condition known as hypertrichosis, which caused a thin growth of hair all over her body. Doctors assured Sara that the condition was temporary. Indeed, the excess hair soon disappeared. But Elizabeth's condition would reoccur at other times, then quickly vanish again. She was also born with scoliosis—a curvature of the spine—that contributed to endless back problems throughout her life. And she was very soon plagued by accidents. "My earliest memory is of pain," Taylor once recalled. "In the house in London where I was born, there was one of those electric fires that coils and curls. I was still crawling and I remember looking at its marvelous orangey-red color and thinking, Should I or shouldn't I? I did. Thank you very much! Half a finger almost burned off!" At age three, she was stricken with a painful infection of her ear canals; both ears had to be lanced. "For three weeks, she was running a high fever and couldn't lie down," Sara recalled. "She had to sit up in bed. And I was with her all the time, day and night. For about three weeks, I didn't have a night's sleep. She never whimpered and never cried. Her one con-cern was that I wasn't getting to sleep. She was worried that Daddy and I were up all the time. She never cried. It's just something . . . the only way that I know how to describe it is an inner strength." Sara Taylor recalled that as she sat by her daughter's bedside, the girl asked to see Victor. Sitting on the bed, he held Elizabeth and also read to her. Young Elizabeth soon recovered.

One bond between Victor and Sara was their faith. Each was a Christian Scientist. Sara's mother claimed to hold a belief in Christian Science, but others believed that it was Victor who introduced Sara to the complex new religion, which was based on the teachings of the Bible and the writings of Mary Baker Eddy. One aspect of the religion held that health care and healing were possible not through medication or surgery but through a specific form of prayer. Christian Science would be more important to the Taylor household than most realized. On any given opportunity, Sara touted and praised the dogma of her faith. Meetings for Christian Scientists were held in her home. Both Howard and Elizabeth were given lessons in the religion. The Christian Science prayer book was consulted in the Taylor home—for years. If a difficult problem troubled Elizabeth, especially later during her career, Sara sat with her daughter, the prayer book in their hands. Since Sara believed in prayer over medicine, and though her daughter would be treated by an army of physicians throughout her life, Elizabeth learned to live with pain, to seek treatment but also both to fight and to stoically accept physical suffering, especially while going about her various professional and personal obligations, often until the pain became overpowering or unbearable. That ability to cope with pain would, in a sense, enable her to survive. Yet, publicly, she said almost nothing about Christian Science.

Of her early years in England, Taylor said, "I had the most idyllic childhood." "She had a pony there and grew to love animals," recalled Hedda Hopper. Elizabeth herself remembered: "My happiest moments as a child were riding my Newfoundland pony, Betty, in the woods on 3,000 acres of my godfather's estate." The pony—given to her when she was three—was a gift from Victor. "The very first time I got on her back, she threw me into a patch of stinging nettles. But I soon became an accomplished horsewoman. I'd ride bareback for hours all over the property." She also recalled, "My brother and I made pets of all the animals—pet rabbits, pet turtles, pet goats, pet chickens. It was my ideal of bliss." Decades later she would learn that Michael—and just about all of his family—also loved animals.

"You couldn't have wished for a sweeter child," said Hopper. "She would certainly have been happier leading that simple life close to woods and wild things to be tamed, maybe through all her years. But her mother had been bitten by the Broadway bug, and few women recover from that."

From the start, Sara devoted much of her attention to Elizabeth, all the more so when she saw the reaction of others to her daughter. People encountering the impeccably dressed child with the woman's face could not forget her. Not only were there the girl's angelic looks but also her charm and charisma. Howard's handsome looks were also commented on. But although both children were trained to be well mannered and well spoken with the tones and inflections of the English aristocracy, Elizabeth accepted the growing attention in a way that apparently Howard did not. Even as a boy, Howard was his own person. No one would ever tell him what to do or be. Elizabeth was then more malleable. As soon as she could walk, Sara enrolled her in classes at the prestigious Vacani School of Dance. Told that the daughters of the royal family, the princesses Elizabeth and Margaret, studied there, Sara wasted no time. Never did the princesses come to the school itself. Instead, instructors from the school gave them private lessons at their home. Regardless, Sara loved the connection that she boasted of then and in the years to come.

With the other young dancers, Elizabeth performed at a benefit for the school that was attended by the princesses and their mother, the Duchess of York (the future Queen Mother). "I peeked up through the curtain of my hair and began casing the joint," recalled Taylor. "I loved it. I wouldn't leave the stage," she remembered. "It was a marvelous feeling on that stage—the isolation, the hugeness, the feeling of space and no end to space, the lights, the music—and then the applause bringing you back into focus . . ." Because she wouldn't leave the stage, she recalled that the curtain was finally lowered on her. Elizabeth never forgot the experience. Nor did Sara. Much was later made of this benefit by MGM. It became a part of the studio's official biography of her. Already both Elizabeth and her mother had stars in their eyes about the future.

But behind the idyllic facade of life in the Taylor household, a marriage was in trouble. With vastly different perspectives and interests, Sara and Francis often clashed and quarreled. Some believed the marriage became sexless. Francis drank heavily, a fact about which the two apparently argued. Mild-mannered and considered weak, Francis appeared overpowered by Sara's demanding and domineering personality. For a man who, although social, preferred spending some quiet nights reading, he was learning to live with an unending round of social activities—the dinner parties and the nights on the town that Sara seemed to thrive on.

Francis also believed—even then—that he didn't have enough private time with Elizabeth, time when the two of them could do things together and come to know each other better. He must have felt he was being kept away from his own child. With his son, Howard, he appeared to have a good relationship, but Sara seemed unwilling to share Elizabeth.

At the same time, Francis could have a short temper. When the children misbehaved, he struck both Howard and Elizabeth, to the point where, years later, Elizabeth referred to her father as having been abusive.

The arguments and the recriminations between Sara and Francis continued. "Sara and Francis's marriage didn't strike me as a particularly happy one," recalled an art dealer who knew the Taylors in the 1930s. "The couple argued a great deal. Francis had a drinking problem. He drank too much, and his alcoholism became a major source of contention between husband and wife." Their fractious relationship may even have been similar to that of Martha and George in *Who's*

Afraid of Virginia Woolf?, the film that would come to mean so much to Elizabeth. The domestic discord was not lost on Elizabeth. She would always be attracted to strong, independent, tough-minded men who represented what she may have always wanted her father to be. Still, she loved Francis deeply, and in the years to come she understood him better and sympathized with him. She would also always have an affinity for seemingly softer, more sensitive, talented men in need of a special kind of nurturing.

Aside from Sara, Francis had to contend with another demanding personality, his uncle, Howard. Because he and his family had become financially dependent on Howard, Francis had to live by Howard's rules. Rumors also circulated about conflict in the Taylor household because of the close friendships of both Sara and Francis with Victor Cazalet. Not only did Victor influence Sara's dedication to Christian Science, but he was an important engineer of her social world. This shrewd politician brought the likes of Winston Churchill and Sir Anthony Eden into the Taylors' lives, as well as some of England's aristocracy and power brokers. Other than the fact that it was good for the art business, Francis may not have cared that much about the high and mighty. But Sara certainly did. With the witty, clever, and stylish Victor, Sara could laugh, relax, and kick up her heels. Some gossiped that she and Victor had an affair, so much did she appear to relish her time with him.

Yet Victor also relished his time with the sensitive Francis. Over the years, there were whispers and rumblings that Francis Taylor had homosexual leanings, and that Victor, a lifelong bachelor, was one of his lovers. Victor once presented Francis with a sparkling red Buick. The two men were reported to have traveled together and were seen laughing, talking, exchanging private glances, and also drinking together. It was the alcohol that seemed to open Francis up. Sara herself may have wondered about the relationship, but apparently she did not dwell on such thoughts. Nor did she care. Victor was too important to her. Yet Francis also grew close to a young man, Marshall Baldrige, who worked at the gallery. In later years, Marshall would say that he and Francis were merely close friends, like a father and son. But that never stopped the gossip about Francis and Marshall. Or about Francis's friendship with another young man, the Viennese artist Stefan Verkaufen. Another friendship was with the German author Kurt Stempler, who said that he and Francis had a short-lived affair.

The Taylors' lives and their complicated domestic situation changed dramatically as war swept through Europe. In 1936, Italy invaded Ethiopia, Japan threatened China, and a Civil

War began in Spain. In 1938, Hitler's troops occupied and annexed Austria into Nazi Germany. That same year, Germany also annexed Czechoslovakia's northern and western border regions, known as the Sudetenland. In March 1939, Germany occupied the rest of a weakened Czechoslovakia, then Hitler invaded Poland. At any time, England feared an invasion by Germany. Francis and Sara remained at Heathwood as long as they could. Then, according to Sara, a call came from the office of the American ambassador to the Court of Saint James, Joseph Kennedy. Like other Americans in England, Francis was urged to get his family out of the country and back to the States as soon as possible. When asked about the ambassador himself calling the Taylor home, Francis told a friend he never received such a call, that it was simply Sara embellishing on the details of their ultimate departure from England. Regardless, he knew the time had come to return to the States. Plans were immediately made for the departure of Sara and the children. Francis would have to remain behind to close the gallery and tie up other loose ends, then join them later. Francis also urged his young friend Marshall to come to America with him. But Marshall remained in England.

On April 3, 1939, Sara and the children and their nanny boarded the ocean liner SS *Manhattan* and sailed home to the States. For seven-year-old Elizabeth, the trip across the Atlantic seemed a glorious adventure. Part of the Taylor legend has it that while on the SS *Manhattan*, the girl saw Shirley Temple as a Victorian lass in the movie *The Little Princess*. Mesmerized by the action on-screen and by the power of the film's leading lady, pint-size Shirley, Elizabeth was reported to have said: "Mummy! I think I want to be an actress."

Prophetic as the story sounds, Sara later said— once Elizabeth was living in California—that up to that time her seven-year-old daughter "had seen *only* Snow White and one or two Disney films . . . and wasn't the least scrap interested [in making movies]. Neither was I." It's doubtful, however, that Sara herself was not interested.

Elizabeth would later believe she had left her childhood the moment she departed from Heathwood. Though she would be thought of as a quintessentially American star, she never left Great Britain behind. Her very manner of speaking—the sound of a young British aristocrat—would lead to her first important movie role. In the future, whether for films or vacations, she would return frequently to England. Two of her future husbands would hail from the United Kingdom. After her marriage to Richard Burton, she lived there again. In 1963, she would star in the hour-long CBS documentary *Elizabeth Taylor in London*, one of her rare television appearances at the time, in which she provided viewers with a personal tour of the sights and sounds of the London she held so dear. In her later years, she sometimes even had the style of a British matron, which may have led fashion writer Cathy Horyn to observe "that despite the jet-set life, the jewels and the husbands, she retained an Englishness, a hominess, a love of children and animals that was recognizably real." Perhaps most surprisingly, when Taylor turned fifty, she suddenly showed up at her family's old home Heathwood—where she startled the current residents, especially when she asked if their house might be for sale. Obviously, she had thoughts of buying the house back. In Los Angeles during her later years, she told her landscape designer Nicholas Walker: "I've been looking all my life to duplicate an authentic English border." Walker said: "Well, Southern California doesn't have 360 days of rain a year, as England does, but I could create the feeling that she wanted using plants from all over the world." He told her: "If you want delphiniums year-round, I can't do that. But you can have them in short, truncated moments." He recalled: "Dame Elizabeth arched an eyebrow and said, 'That sounds interesting.' " Photographer Bruce Weber remembered: "She took pride in her garden, like most English people." And one of the proudest days in her life would occur in 2000—when she was named a Dame Commander of the British Empire. Somewhere, deep inside, Elizabeth Taylor was profoundly affected by those formative years and the country of her birth. "The happiest days of my childhood were in England," she said years later. But onward Elizabeth went in 1939.

Chapter 2

MICHAEL JACKSON'S LIFE—like Elizabeth's—also had a fairy-tale quality. His was the tale of the rise of a boy prince who overcame adversities to assume his throne but who would forever be haunted by the early years—a childhood he felt he had missed—and who would always be tied to a complicated family he loved greatly yet which he sometimes found himself in conflict with. The complicated feelings would be a part of his identity—and all went back to the time that Joseph Jackson met pert and pretty Katherine Scruse.

Brash, tough-minded, and confident, Joseph Walter Jackson, born in 1928 in Fountain Hill, Arkansas, was the oldest of six children—four boys, two girls—of a strict, emotionally remote, religious schoolteacher named Samuel and his young wife, Crystal, who had once been his student. The marriage of Samuel and Crystal was a troubled one, and by the time Joe was a teen-ager, his parents had split up. "Joseph's mother, Crystal, had had an affair with a soldier," said Joe's son Jermaine Jackson. Afterward, Samuel moved to Oakland and was later joined by thirteen-year-old Joe. Crystal stayed behind with the other children. There was a brief reconciliation, but the marriage collapsed again and was over for good. As affected as he was by his parents' divorce, Joe had suffered another emotional blow that earlier had left him devastated when his favorite sister Verna Mae took ill. "Joseph watched his sister's deterioration from the bedroom door as the adults surrounded her bed," Jermaine recalled his father saying. Following Verna Mae's death, "Joseph sobbed for days." Jermaine believed "that was the last time he shed a tear." Joseph might have been around nine. Hers was the last funeral he attended until Michael's in 2009, recalled Jermaine. "One loss in life sealed our father's emotions."

Perhaps always brooding, and, like his father, Samuel, not someone who could easily show his feelings, Joseph dropped out of high school, became a Golden Gloves boxer, and had big dreams for himself, the kind his other family members didn't. He first met pretty, young Katherine Scruse at a dance in East Chicago, a city in northern Indiana. But intrigued as he may have been, nothing happened between the two. Then, after Joe had a short-lived marriage—one rarely discussed in later years—Joe saw Katherine Scruse again. This time around, his world changed.

A southerner and also a child of a broken home, Katherine had been born in Alabama in 1930, the daughter of Prince Albert Scruse and Martha Upshaw. Her younger sister, Hattie, was born a year later, and in 1934, Prince moved his family to East Chicago. But theirs was another troubled marriage that ended in divorce. Becoming a Pullman porter, Prince often traveled on the road. As a Pullman porter, he was one of a corps of mostly black railroad porters who, from the late 1860s into the twentieth century, were immaculately groomed and uniformed as they tended to passengers in sleeping cars. Such a position attained a certain status because such jobs were not easy to come by. In turn, the Pullman porters, which under the leadership of African American A. Philip Randolph formed the first all-black union in 1925—known as the Brotherhood of Sleeping Car Porters—helped lead to the emergence of a black middle class and was an early sign of a civil rights movement in the black community. Katherine's family was clearly upwardly mobile. Katherine and her sister, Hattie, lived with their mother. Quiet and shy with a sweet temperament, Katherine suffered from polio before she turned two years old. Wearing braces or using crutches until she was sixteen, often teased at school, and walking with a limp for the rest of her life, Katherine's refuge from the taunts of other kids was her love of music, especially the country music that she and Hattie heard over the radio. Katherine also played the piano and the clarinet. When she met Joe, she discovered that he played the guitar and his dream was to be an entertainer.

In 1949, the two married and wasted no time in starting a family that grew almost year by year. In 1950, they had a daughter named Maureen, called Rebbie. The next year Katherine gave birth to a son named Sigmund Esco, called Jackie. Tariano Adaryll, called Tito, arrived in 1953. Then came Jermaine LaJuane, in 1954; La Toya Yvonne, in 1956; twin sons Marlon and Brandon (the latter died in childbirth), in 1957; Michael Joseph, in 1958; Steven Randall, called Randy, in 1961; and a baby girl, Janet Damita Jo, in 1966.

By the early 1950s, Joseph took a job as a crane operator at Inland Steel in East Chicago, earning about sixty-five dollars a week. Joe also worked as a welder to make extra money. No matter what the criticism of Joseph Jackson in later years, the care and welfare of his family came first. "I think it takes a certain type of man to do that kind of job—someone hardened and emotionally strong —and he worked his fingers to the bone to 'earn a life,' as he put it. I think this is where his insistence on 'respect' comes from," Jermaine recalled. Also a hard worker, Katherine, to make ends meet, took a part-time job at Sears, and she learned to stretch a dollar.

Family meals could consist of chitterlings and lots of potatoes. Without much money for games and toys, the kids learned how to keep themselves entertained with such television shows as *Maverick*, reruns of *The Three Stooges*, and old movies with stars like Randolph Scott, and, for Michael, Fred Astaire. In time, Michael developed an intense interest in past child stars, whether it be the kids from the *Our Gang* series or Shirley Temple. During these years, he was aware of Elizabeth as a child star. But his fascination with her had not yet occurred. Early on, Michael also loved animated programs.

The family moved into a small house in Gary, Indiana, their address later becoming almost iconic: 2300 Jackson Street. It was a historical irony—perhaps a fortuitous one—that the family would settle in a home on an otherwise "unknown" block with the same name as its own. In time, they would make Jackson Street famous. The street reportedly had been named after the nation's seventh president, Andrew Jackson. Known for decades as a factory town, Gary, Indiana, had been founded in 1906 by the United States Steel Corporation and named after a founding chairman of the company, Elbert Henry Gary. Its new plant, Gary Works, had opened that year. In 1919, labor unrest resulted in a massive strike that turned violent when striking steel workers had bloody clashes with outsider strikebreakers. At one point,

Indiana's governor James P. Goodrich declared martial law. Some four thousand federal troops were called in. Otherwise, life in Gary was fairly uneventful. Continuing to grow, the city reached a population of one hundred thousand in the 1930s, attracting foreign-born immigrants eager for employment in the steel mills and a chance at a better life. People of color also flocked to the city, African Americans composing 17 percent of its population and Mexicans composing more than 3 percent. For decades, as the steel mills prospered, so did the city's fortunes. But after the Second World War, with competition from abroad, Gary's economic growth slowed, then declined in the 1960s. Unemployment rose. So did the crime rate. So did racial divisions. Later Gary would have one of the nation's earliest black mayors, Richard G. Hatcher. But even before that occurred, Joe must have seen the writing on the wall. For a better life, he'd have to do more than labor in the steel mills. In the meantime, he struggled to stay afloat.

Every single foot of the house in Gary was taken up. "Nine children, two parents, two bedrooms, one bathroom, a kitchen, and a living room were packed tight into a space about thirty feet wide and no more than forty feet deep," Jermaine recalled. "Our home was built in the 1940s, wood-framed, with a tiled pyramid lid that seemed so thin for a roof that we swore it would blow off during the first tornado." Katherine and Joe had one bedroom. The four eldest sons shared the other bedroom with a triple bunk bed: Tito and Jermaine on the top; Marlon and Michael in the middle; Jackie on the bottom. On a pullout sofa bed in the living room, the three girls slept.Randy slept on another sofa. There wasn't much breathing room, and certainly there wasn't much privacy.

The home was "simple and nondescript, but we were comfortable there and never felt that we were poor or in any way deprived," La Toya Jackson remembered. And contrary to the stories later fabricated by Motown, La Toya recalled, the family didn't live in harsh ghetto conditions. Gary itself "boasted clean, comfortable residential neighborhoods like the one we lived in. Our schoolmates' parents were lawyers, teachers, and blue-collar workers." She added: "Even so, Joseph decreed that we were not to socialize with other kids. He and my mother believed that our futures depended on education, hard work, and strict discipline."

The discipline was maintained primarily by Joseph, stern and unyielding. In later years, he said he was hard on the family because of his fears that his children might be exposed to drugs and violence, and both he and Katherine kept a vigilant eye on every move the children made. "He banished the outside world from our home until our home *became* our world. It's easy to understand a parent's desire to protect his youngsters, but Joseph took this to an extreme," La Toya would recall. If any one of the children broke the rules of the house or if they talked back to Joe, he didn't hesitate to forcefully whip them. Just one glance from Joseph was enough to send shivers through the children. Sometimes the kids had no idea what might set him off, when his voice, his eyes, his whole demeanor would turn mean, when his hand or fist would be raised and come down fast and hard on them.

Katherine also disciplined the children—and also had a temper. But unlike Joseph, she showed her emotions and love. Her family was the center of her universe. Her religion served as a guiding force in the children's lives. Raised as a Baptist, and for a long time a Lutheran, she had converted to the Jehovah's Witnesses. Stretching back to the 1870s and founded by Charles Taze Russell, the sect was an outgrowth of the nineteenth-century Bible Student Movement, which taught that the Bible was scientifically and historically accurate. The organization also prided itself on being true to the doctrines of first-century Christianity. Not known formally as Jehovah's Witnesses until 1931, its name was based on Isaiah 43:10: "Ye are my witnesses, saith the Lord, and my servants whom I have chosen." The dictates and doctrines of the Jehovah's Witnesses were strict: birthdays were not celebrated nor were religious holidays such as Christmas and Easter, both considered an outgrowth of pagan rituals. Followers were not to accept military service. Nor were they to salute the flag. Nor could they have blood transfusions. Their tenets were known as "the truth." With the belief that society is corrupt, Jehovah's Witnesses, in many respects, separated themselves from society, its members keeping to themselves. Members also had to abide by all official doctrines. Criticism was neither condoned nor permitted. Those members who broke the rules of the organization or those who left the organization could find themselves "shunned" by other members, even their one-time close friends or family. In time, the Jehovah's Witnesses would grow to have well over seven million followers, with its international headquarters located in Brooklyn.

To spread the word and recruit new members, the Jehovah's Witnesses' publications *The Watchtower* and *Awake!* were sold by members who went from door to door in towns and cities. It was through just such publications that Katherine Jackson first learned of the organization and was converted and baptized in 1963. Raising her family in the religion, Katherine herself and the children at various times would go door-to-door to sell *The Watchtower* and *Awake!* That would include Michael even after he had become famous. On the Sabbath, Katherine and her children also attended Kingdom Hall together. Michael enjoyed the communal atmosphere, the friendship of church members, the guidance of the church elders. His religious beliefs provided him with a foundation of security, and those beliefs were important to the family. That, however, did not include Joseph. He didn't appear to put up a fuss about the religious conversion of his wife, but he never joined the group. The strict rules of the Witnesses apparently appealed to him as a way to help keep the children in line—*and* also separated them from the urban community around them.

In some respects, Katherine Jackson's belief in her nonmainstream religion was not that different from Sara Taylor's belief in the teachings of Christian Science. But with the publication of the newspaper *The Christian Science Monitor*, Christian Science acquired an intellectual cachet that gave it a credibility that possibly lifted it eventually out of the realm of a cult. On the other hand, many frowned upon the Jehovah's Witnesses, mistakenly viewing it as a religion for lower-class, unschooled African Americans. But African Americans would compose about 20 to 30 percent of the group's membership; most Jehovah's Witnesses were white. Still, while others might label the religious organization a cult, Katherine and her children never viewed their faith in this way. Instead, Katherine drew strength from her religion just as Sara drew strength from Christian Science. Though neither would have said it, both had such strong convictions that they no doubt felt the world could be damned for not understanding the power of their respective faiths.

Unlike Sara Taylor, who gave up her own theatrical aspirations rather early and focused on her daughter, Elizabeth, Joe Jackson wasn't as quick to give up his dreams of being a music star. Forming a blues group with his brother Luther and some friends that they called the Falcons, Joe and the others regularly practiced at the Jackson home. According to Jermaine, the group performed "at local parties and venues to put some extra dollars in their pockets." The Falcons eventually disbanded. But unable to leave his music behind, Joe practiced on his guitar, his most prized possession, which he kept locked away in the bedroom closet. "And don't even think about getting out my guitar," he warned the kids.

But it didn't stay locked away for long. Fascinated by the idea of playing the guitar, Tito started to wait for those occasions when Joseph was out of the house and the coast was clear, then took the coveted guitar from the closet and played it while performing with his brothers. At the sound of Joseph returning home in his Buick, Tito would quickly replace the guitar in the closet.

One day, however, he broke a string on the instrument. When Joe saw what had happened, he hit the ceiling and demanded to know who had been messing with his guitar. Tito admitted he was the culprit but he also professed that he knew how to play. Joe was still angry but he calmed down. "Let me see what you can do," he told him. When he heard his son perform, a lightbulb immediately went off in Joe's head. Shortly afterward, he arrived home with a package that was handed over to Tito. Inside was a new guitar for his son. But Joe admonished him that it meant he had to rehearse with his brothers.

Shrewd, ambitious Joseph saw possibilities with his sons. They were not simply *playing* around. They had the potential, in his view, to be a group, to make it to the top. Any number of kids fantasized about music careers or pop stardom. Any number of kids put those dreams aside once they were no longer teenagers. But Joseph Jackson never saw stardom for his boys as a long shot, never as a pipe dream. Stardom was an inevitability. But it would take hard work, discipline, and focus.

The concept of a musical group was a natural because 2300 Jackson Street was a musical home. Not only had Joe performed with his Falcons, but Katherine sang around the house. Among Michael's earliest memories were those of Katherine "holding me and singing songs like

'You Are My Sunshine' and 'Cotton Fields.' She sang to me and to my brothers and sisters often." Growing up hearing the names of famous black performers—Jackie Wilson, James Brown, David Ruffin, and other Motown stars—as a part of everyday life in the home, all the children became steeped in show biz history with a knowledge and respect for black musical giants. They also all liked performing. Though the eldest son, Jackie, was an outstanding athlete with dreams of a career as a baseball star—and was even scouted by the Chicago White Sox—after an injury, or perhaps mainly due to Joseph's insistence, all his energies went into music with his brothers. Jackie was also a terrific dancer and won dance contests with his sister Rebbie in the area. Marlon was a good dancer, too. Tito loved the guitar. And Jermaine not only played bass guitar but also sang lead for a time.

Even before he could talk, Michael's love of music, rhythm, movement, and dramatic pauses and soaring tempos was apparent. "Ever since Michael was very young," Katherine later told *Time*, "he seemed different to me from the rest of the children. I don't believe in reincarnation, but you know how babies move uncoordinated? He never moved that way. When he danced, it was like he was an old person." La Toya also commented that her mother realized Michael was "different" from the time he was born—"quick to walk and talk. . . . She made a point never to boast about any of us, but of Michael, my mother would allow, 'I don't want to say he's gifted but I know there's something special about him.' " He was also a student of music: he carefully watched an entertainer, like James Brown, picked up on his routines, both as an impassioned vocalist and a dancer, and could soon imitate him, adding his own flair and dash. The same was true for Michael of Jackie Wilson, who was his number one idol. In 1963, five-year-old Michael—then a student at Garnett Elementary School—gave his first performance for an audience. He sang "Climb Ev'ry Mountain" in a school pageant. Sitting in the audience were Katherine and her father, Prince Scruse.

That same year, his father at first didn't consider putting Michael in the group. He was too young. But when Michael started singing along, Joe and his sons all saw the boy's talent. Jermaine, who had sung lead, was replaced by Michael. That would be a long-standing point of tension for Jermaine, no matter what he would say in later years.

Daily, the boys were not permitted to stick around school once classes ended to participate in extracurricular activities. Instead, each rushed back home, grabbed his instrument, and practiced. "When the other kids would be out on the street playing games, my boys were in the house working—trying to learn how to be something in life," Joe said. "They got a little upset about the whole thing in the beginning because other kids were out there having a good time." Once Joe returned from work, he watched the boys to see their progress. Rehearsals went from 4:30 to 9:00 p.m. without any letup. A fierce taskmaster, Joe didn't hold back on criticism. Nor did he hold back on raising his hand to keep his sons in line. The boys felt their father could be brutal and that also there was another way to keep them disciplined. But no one could tell the old man that.

La Toya remembered that Jackie received "the most punishment." When she asked her mother why Joseph treated the eldest son so badly, Katherine replied: "I don't know . . . he just never liked him." La Toya always believed that Jackie—basically serious and quiet and a handsome heartthrob for young women—had the potential for major stardom. "But endless psychological and physical battering wore him down." Joseph's favorite? Jermaine, who was, according to La Toya, opinionated, outspoken, stubborn, was also a playful teaser and a family leader. Yet as La Toya perceptively noted, in response to Joe's "volatile nature, all the Jackson kids grew up basically soft-spoken and extremely gentle. We worried about hurting one another's feelings."

Of all the children, Michael was the most sensitive and the most affected by Joseph's corporal punishment—and also the most rebellious, the child who stood up to his father. "Not surprisingly, none of us ever mustered the courage (the foolhardiness?) to defend ourselves against him. Except Michael," recalled La Toya. When still very young, he once ran from his angry father, not ready to be hit. Another time he grabbed a shoe and threw it at his father. Still, he often suffered at the hands of an irate Joseph.

Rehearsals could prove especially difficult. Once Michael was in the group, it was often a battle with Joseph. "If you messed up during rehearsal, you got hit. Sometimes with a belt. Sometimes with a switch," Michael recalled. "But I'd get beaten for things that happened mostly outside of rehearsal," Michael recalled. At home, Michael would talk back when Joe had a tirade, which just incensed Joe all the more.

But early on, Michael, child prodigy that he was—though no one quite thought of him that way at the time—was also the subject of Joe's wrath because musically he insisted on doing things his way. "Now, you do it the way I told you to!" Joe would yell. But Michael would refuse. Sometimes he cried. Joe would continue to demand that Michael do as he was told, to which Michael would say he wouldn't, and in time, he told his father, "Don't you hit me. 'Cause if you *ever* hit me again, it'll be the last time I ever sing. And I mean it."

The beatings weren't the only thing to alienate Michael and his brothers from their father. It was also Joseph's inability to be a part of the emotional life of the family, to express his feelings about anything other than the boys' music. He didn't even want the children to call him Dad or Father. Instead, he was to be called Joseph. They couldn't have a private conversation without fears that Joseph might overhear them. It went on for years, even later when they moved into a larger home in California. Appearing to take joy in frightening his children, he might pound on La Toya's door at night. "Open this door or I'll break it down," he might scream. Later keeping guns in their home, he took a "perverse pleasure in aiming at one of us and squeezing the trigger," recalled La Toya, who said her mother objected to the guns because once on a hunting trip he'd shot out her brother-in-law's eye—by accident. Baffled and bewildered by this man who headed the household, Jermaine believed Joseph was impossible to understand.

Michael, who felt the same way, found his father to be a mystery. "He built a shell around himself over the years, and once he stopped talking about our family business, he found it hard to relate to us. We'd all be together and he'd just leave the room."

The only thing that didn't mystify the children was their father's determination that his sons succeed. Not only were there the endless rehearsals and the isolation from the rest of their Gary community but also there soon were the very early performances. "I rehearsed them about three years before I turned them loose. That's practically every day, for at least two or three hours," said Joe. "I noticed, though, that they were getting better and better. Then I saw that after they became better they enjoyed it more. Then it was time to go out and do talent shows. We won the highest talent show in Indiana and then we went over to Illinois and won there. It got so we could play nightclubs in Chicago like the High Chaparral and the Guys and Gals Club. This was on the weekends. I had a Volkswagen bus and I bought a big luggage rack and put it on top and had everybody on the inside of the bus. One day I noticed when I was coming out of the yard that the instruments on top of the bus were taller than the bus."

Joe wouldn't relinquish his dream for his sons. In this respect, his fierce determination to make the world see his children's talents was not much different from that of Sara Taylor. Both Sara and Joe were fighters to the end, albeit Sara used her charm during such battles. Joe, however, could be openly relentless and ruthless in his drive for his children. Both were propelled by a belief in their children's talents as well as a complicated love for those children.

"Between 1966 and 1968 most weekends were spent on the road building our reputation," Jermaine recalled. Weeknights meant performing locally, mainly at Mister Lucky's in Gary, where they earned their first paycheck. Jermaine recalled, "$11, split between us. Michael spent his on candy, which he shared with other kids in the neighborhood." A cynical Joseph said, "He earns his first wage and spends it on candy to give to other kids."

Otherwise their gigs were at all sorts of places: small clubs, juke joints, dives where the boys were exposed to some of everything, both the upside and dark underside of show business. They met strippers and female impersonators and the sometimes rowdy but always appreciative audiences. Michael remembered the times when he crawled around, looking up the skirts of women in the audience. None of this mattered much to Joe because he kept a very protective eye on the boys. He also understood that boys will be boys. It also didn't matter to Joseph that when his sons performed in the middle of the week, they had school the next day. A performance might not start until eleven thirty, Jermaine recalled. They could sleep on the drive home—where they would arrive in the early hours of the morning. Michael also recalled:

"Sometimes really late at night we'd have to go out. It might be three in the morning—to do a show. My father forced us. He would get us up. I was seven or eight. Some of these were clubs or private parties at people's houses. We'd have to perform." It might be in Chicago or later New York or Philadelphia. "I'd be sleeping and I'd hear my father say, 'Get up! There's a show!' " The feeling was that they could catch up on their studies as best they could. School was secondary for Joseph, not of much consequence. The main thing he wanted—as the time on the road expanded—was a record deal for his sons. But the boys tried to study, especially Michael, who liked to read, to discover new things, places, people through the magic of books and later his travels.

In the midst of what otherwise might have been a storm, with their father always breathing down their necks, with the demands of establishing a professional act, of creating a career, with the need of isolation to build that act and career, Michael and his brothers all found comfort and a haven in their mother. Michael said, "If she found out that one of us had an interest in something, she would encourage it if there was any possible way. If I developed an interest in movie stars, for instance, she'd come home with an armful of books about famous stars. Even with nine children she treated each of us like an only child. There isn't one of us who's ever forgotten what a hard worker and a great provider she was." He remembered always his mother's "gentleness, warmth, and attention."

Chapter 3

AFTER THEIR OCEAN liner docked in New York, Sara, the children, and the nanny traveled by train to the West Coast, arriving not in Los Angeles but in Pasadena, where Sara's father now lived. He had established a chicken farm in the area. Pasadena was also a stop favored by many Hollywood people. There was less hustle and bustle than at the Los Angeles station, and Hollywood personalities could avoid the presence of fans and onlookers. On the West Coast, a whole new world opened up for the Taylor family. Having appeared in Los Angeles in *The Fool*, Sara knew California. But its beauty was all the more striking as she saw it through the eyes of Elizabeth and Howard. The skies were blue and vast. There were the majestic foothills and mountains, the lush flora and fauna, the swaying palm trees, the bougainvillea, the fragrant eucalyptus. Days were warm, sometimes hot but dry. Nights were cool and inviting. Mostly, California offered Sara, as it did for just about everyone else who journeyed there, the idea of limitless promise. Here was a magical place where anything could happen. Of course, Hollywood was there, too.

● ● ●

Upon his arrival in California some months later, Francis had taken over his uncle's gallery, then situated at the Château Élysée hotel in Hollywood. But aware that the gallery should be located in a place where things *happened,* where moneyed people in Los Angeles would take note, he decided to open shop in the Beverly Hills Hotel, the premier hotel in the City of Angels, which had first opened its majestic portals in 1912. Eventually dubbed the Pink Palace because of its pink-painted stucco facade, the Beverly Hills Hotel became famous for its dazzling swimming pool, where everyone scrambled to see and be seen, and its Polo Lounge, where the Hollywood elite—Marlene Dietrich, Loretta Young, John Wayne, or Howard Hughes—as well as ambitious social climbers would pose and posture, dine and make deals. Most sought-after were the hotel's exclusive bungalows, where guests could have great privacy, coming and going as they wanted without being seen but having all the posh amenities that hotel life offered. The bungalows would be the place where Clark Gable and Carole Lombard secretly rendezvoused while Gable was still trying to get out of his marriage; where Marilyn Monroe and Yves Montand would have their sexy, secluded love trysts; where an adult Elizabeth—with her various husbands— would stay on so many occasions; and where later Whitney Houston would meet with music producer Clive Davis to review material for her albums.

Francis's gallery, or rather still Uncle Howard's, would become successful, even more so once his daughter became famous and people sometimes popped in hoping for a sight of the ravishing teenager who might be paying a visit to her father. His serious, knowledgeable style served him well as he dealt—in time—with such clients as Vincent Price, Alan Ladd, Edward G. Robinson, directors Billy Wilder and George Cukor, and one of Hollywood's greatest stars, Greta Garbo, and as he introduced Southern California to such artists as British portraitist Augustus John, known and celebrated for his paintings of Tallulah Bankhead, T. E. Lawrence, George Bernard Shaw, and the future Queen Mother.

In time, the family moved from Pasadena to Pacific Palisades and later to 307 North Elm Drive in exclusive Beverly Hills; they had an additional home in Malibu. As she had done with Little Swallows, Sara transformed her homes into well-decorated, beautifully appointed showcases. In the Pacific Palisades, the family's neighbors included such prominent movie people as actress Norma Shearer, widow of the legendary MGM production chief Irving Thalberg, and Twentieth Century Fox's Darryl F. Zanuck. Elizabeth's playmates were the children of such famous neighbors.

"We all grew up together," recalled producer Richard Zanuck. "She was my sister's closest friend at Pacific Palisades Grammar School. She and my sister were the same age, and I was three years younger. She'd come to our house, and Irving Thalberg Jr. would join us, and we'd have dance classes and things like that. My sister was begging my father, 'Please sign her up!' And he'd say, 'Oh, she's just your friend.'" Darryl F. Zanuck never forgot that he had passed on her and had also previously passed on putting Clark Gable under contract because he thought his ears were too large.

At different times, the Taylor children were also enrolled in the exclusive Willard and Hawthorne schools. As Sara struck up new friendships among the Angelenos, she didn't hesitate to use her London connections. Soon her mind was on the movies. During the filming of *Gone With the Wind*, when there was a search for a child to play Bonnie Blue Butler—the daughter of Clark Gable's Rhett and Vivien Leigh's Scarlett—Sara must have snapped to attention. She had already been told that Elizabeth resembled Vivien Leigh. Her daughter might be perfect for the role. But Francis would not hear of it. He was adamant about the matter. Later Elizabeth herself would say that both parents didn't want her to work at that time.

But Sara's attitude changed. Because Elizabeth was already a dreamy child—a true romantic—

who loved the world of make-believe and who dramatized her experiences, Sara felt the studios had to open their doors to the child and soon went into action. Elizabeth herself now thought of acting in the movies. "When I was a child I was fascinated at the thought of being an actress," Elizabeth recalled. "At first I had wanted to be an aviatrix, a cowgirl, and a doctor. Then I saw a couple of movies, and suddenly I wanted to be an actress. And just as suddenly, I became one." Never lost on Sara were the exquisite looks and the impeccable manner of this darling girl—still always beautifully dressed—with a charming British accent, although Elizabeth also picked up American sounds and could go back and forth between accents.

Ironically, here Francis proved helpful. Stopping by his gallery one day, upon the recommendation of Thelma Cazalet, was Hollywood columnist Hedda Hopper. Hopper relished her visits to England, during which she could socialize with the British upper crust. During those trips, she remained friendly with Thelma and her brother Victor, who had first introduced her to the Taylor family. Chatting with Francis at the gallery, Hopper purchased a sketch by Augustus John.

When Francis told Sara of the columnist's appearance at the gallery, she lost no time in paying a visit to Hopper, who, along with her rival fellow gossip columnist Louella Parsons, was a power broker in town who knew everybody worth knowing and whose columns could help a star on the way up (and damage a star who might soon be on the way down). Gregarious and in love with show business, she had been an actress herself, and not a bad one at all. Born Elda Furry in 1885 in Hollidaysburg, Pennsylvania, and the daughter of a butcher, she ran away from home to New York with hopes of making it in show business. For a spell, she was a chorus girl but got nowhere, then married actor DeWolf Hopper. Because her husband's former wives were named Ella, Ida, Edna, and Nella, she bristled whenever he called her by one of their names. That led her to see a numerologist, which in turn led her to change her name to Hedda. She and DeWolf divorced but had a son named William, who later became known for his role as Paul Drake on the television series *Perry Mason*.

For years, Hopper struggled to stay afloat as an actress, working first in silent features, then in the talkies into the 1930s. On movie sets and at parties, she picked up gossip and was shrewd enough to know when to tell a good story and when to keep something secret, which could give her power as well. Eventually, she left acting and started writing. Because the studios wanted someone to rival Louella Parsons of the Hearst syndicate (who might spill the beans on something that could hurt their stars), they fed stories to Hedda. Then she became so big that the studios saw her potentially as being just as dangerous a power broker as Parsons. No doubt, they felt they had created something of a monster. In 1938, Hopper's career took off with her column "Hedda Hopper's Hollywood," which appeared in the *Los Angeles Times*. She also had her own radio show. In the 1940s, she was so powerful that she made the cover of *Time*. Known for her flamboyant trademark hats, Hopper in time did cameos in such movies as *The Women* and *Sunset Boulevard* and such television shows as *I Love Lucy* and *The Beverly Hillbillies*. A very conservative Republican, later she was a fervent anti-Communist during the rise of McCarthyism. Regardless of the later years, Hedda for decades could be a powerful ally. Or a venomous enemy. Spencer Tracy and Joseph Cotten were among the stars who publicly expressed their disdain for her. Opposed to "race mixing" or interracial relationships, Hopper once became infuriated when African American actress Dorothy Dandridge and actor Anthony Quinn danced together publicly at a benefit, and Dandridge always felt Hopper set out to hurt her career, although later Hedda seemed to accept Dandridge's stardom. Hopper also kept mum about Orson Welles's romance with Lena Horne. (But she let him know she didn't like it.) So angry with Hopper was actress Joan Bennett that she once sent Hopper a skunk for Valentine's Day with a note that read: "I stink and so do you!" Hopper reportedly named the skunk Joan. Most stars, however, simply grinned and bore her jabs and juggled things like crazy to give both Hopper and Parsons scoops to stay on their good sides.

On the day Sara visited Hopper's home, she had decided Elizabeth would "audition" for the columnist. "Now sing for Miss Hopper," she told her daughter. Clearly, the child was not a budding Deanna Durbin or Judy Garland. "It struck me as a terrifying thing to ask a little child to do for a stranger," Hopper remembered. "But in a quivering voice, half swooning with fright, this lovely, shy creature with enormous violet eyes piped her way through her song. It was one of the most painful ordeals I've ever witnessed." It was one of the few times that young Elizabeth lost her composure. But Hopper was enchanted by Elizabeth and wrote about her in her column. "Deanna Durbin's teacher, De Segurola, has a new find—eight-year-old Elizabeth Taylor, whose mother was Sara Sothern, the lame girl in the play 'The Fool,' and whose father, Francis Taylor, has just opened an exhibit of paintings and drawings by Augustus John in the Beverly Hills Hotel." Hedda also joined forces with Sara to help Elizabeth find movie work. But Hopper's enthusiasm did not lead anywhere.

"Nothing her mother and I could do, and we

did plenty—introduced her to studio heads, arranged to have producers listen to her sing—did any good," recalled Hopper.

Eventually, the first real break came through Sara's friendship with the couple J. Cheever Cowdin and his then fiancée Andrea Berens. Upon meeting Elizabeth, Andrea found her captivating. Later Cheever himself felt the same way. "They were not without influence," said Hopper. "Cheever had got some banker friends to put money into Universal Studio. The Cowdins were much attracted to Elizabeth, and because of their influence she was put under contract at Universal." Hopper didn't say it, but Cowdin owned 17 percent of Universal's stock. But before the Universal contract came through, Sara also drummed up interest from MGM executive Benny Thau, and more important, from MGM's chieftain Louis B. Mayer, who apparently wanted to sign Elizabeth. Elizabeth herself preferred MGM. But Sara went with Universal.

From the beginning it was a rocky situation at Universal. A casting director at the studio, Dan Kelly, wasn't impressed, perhaps believing that Cowdin was forcing the girl on them. "This kid has nothing," Kelly wrote in a stinging memo. "Her eyes are too old; she doesn't have the face of a child." He would live to regret those words. Regardless, Elizabeth was signed to a seven-year contract with six-month options. She would be paid $100 a week, with Sara receiving $10 a day for each day she accompanied Elizabeth to the studio. For later generations that might not sound like much, but at the time, it was a good contract for a newcomer. By now, through Sara's push, Elizabeth was represented by one of Hollywood's most powerful agents, Myron Selznick, the brother of film producer David O. Selznick. Like the others, Myron saw something in the girl. Elizabeth appeared in Universal's *There's One Born Every Minute*, opposite Carl "Alfalfa" Switzer of the *Our Gang* movie series. (Not much of a film, *There's One Born Every Minute* would be remembered years later precisely because it marked Elizabeth Taylor's movie debut.) "Elizabeth was there for one year, but studio chieftains always resent anybody who's brought in over their heads through front-office influence. They made sure the girl got nowhere fast," said Hopper. "Her contract was dropped."

Shortly afterward, Benny Thau saw a friend of Sara's at a dinner party. He remembered Elizabeth. When he learned she was no longer at Universal, he soon signed her to a seven-year contract at MGM. But the studio didn't appear to have major plans for her.

Through all of Sara's maneuvers and machinations, Francis professed to wanting little to do with a career for his daughter. Elizabeth was to have a normal childhood.

But now fate intervened in Elizabeth's future *through* Francis. "Her mother tried everything to find her another job, but it was her father who happened to land her at MGM through a chance remark he made to producer Sam Marx," said Hedda Hopper. Actually, it wasn't so much a chance remark as it was part of a concerted effort or strategy on the part of Francis Taylor.

With America's entry in the Second World War following the bombing of Pearl Harbor, on December 7, 1941, Los Angeles was always on alert, fearing a possible attack from Japan. Families stocked up on canned goods in case there was a bombing. Blackouts and air-raid drills were commonplace. During such drills, Francis Taylor, who had become an air-raid warden, found himself lulling away his time in conversation with another air-raid warden, Sam Marx, a producer at MGM.

Francis often spoke to Marx about Elizabeth. Regardless of Universal's decision, he took pride in Elizabeth's accomplishments. After all, she had successfully landed a role and had proven herself capable of appearing before the cameras. That was no easy feat: fear might have overcome other children; an inability to "communicate" with the camera might have occurred with others. But Elizabeth had already shown she had the goods. No doubt he was aware how much his daughter loved make-believe. And he must have also spoken of the family's years in England. (Remember: Elizabeth could still conjure up her British accent.) Marx remembered that he wasn't particularly interested in Francis's talk "about his beautiful daughter, which is not the sort of thing producers fail to hear very often. . . . In fact, you generally hear it quite a lot. So I wasn't paying a lot of attention. . . . I wasn't being very nice to Francis Taylor. Just putting him off." Though Francis's conversation with Marx may have seemed like idle chatter, it proved important.

One afternoon, Francis received an unexpected, urgent call from an exasperated Marx, who talked about his hassles with the casting of MGM's *Lassie Come Home*, which he was producing. Crucial to the film was the role of a little British girl. The young actress Maria Flynn originally hired was not working out. For one thing, according to Marx, she had grown too tall to appear in scenes opposite child star Roddy McDowall. MGM simply had to find a child with the right demeanor, the right look, and also a cultivated British accent that sounded as if she came from Britain's upper class. "MGM had just made a film called *Mrs. Miniver*, and there were six or seven very charming little English girls in that film. And the casting office agreed to get them over to my office around 5 o'clock. And then I remembered Francis Taylor," said Marx.

"Francis Taylor was at his gallery, and he reported that his daughter was over in Pasadena with her mother and possibly would get there but he wasn't sure."

Another version of the story was that Louis B. Mayer, who had not forgotten his meeting with Taylor at MGM previously, had a telegram sent to the Taylor home in Pasadena, requesting that Elizabeth be brought immediately to MGM in Culver City for a test for *Lassie Come Home*. Perhaps Marx had spoken about the child to Mayer, who set the test in motion. But Marx was always adamant about his version of the story.

Hearing the news, an excited Sara knew Elizabeth would have to be prepared and coached—mainly during their drive to MGM in Culver City—for the interview and test. She would have to sit in the right way, speak in the right way, and answer questions about herself in the right way. Essentially, the studio would first like to look her over to see what kind of personality she had. Then they'd have to see if she could do the part. Sara would also devise cues to indicate to Elizabeth when to smile, when to look sad, when to tone down the dramatics, when to pump things up. During the drive, Elizabeth remained cool and calm, listening intently to everything her mother told her. Whatever was going on inside the girl would be hard to say. She knew that the interview was important to her mother, the person to whom she was closest. But she would never succeed if it did not, indeed, also mean something to her.

As Sara drove through the gates of Metro-Goldwyn-Mayer, Elizabeth was entering a special world. Established in 1924, now run by the autocratic yet supremely proficient Louis B. Mayer, MGM was the most powerful of Hollywood studios. A city unto itself, MGM sat on 167 acres in Culver City with thirty sound stages, seven warehouses, thirty-seven acres of outdoor sets as well as acres of outdoor settings with jungles and rivers, plus a police force of fifty officers and four captains, a first-aid department with doctors and nurses, a dentist, a chiropractor, a commissary considered the best in Hollywood, a barbershop and newsstand, a water tower, a power plant, a you-name-it. Some six thousand people were employed by the studio, which could boast of excellent directors, writers, cinematog-raphers, choreographers, set designers, costume designers, hairstylists, publicists, and an astounding music department. Then there were the stars—more than there were in heaven was how the studio described the astounding lineup. At one time or another, MGM would have under contract Greta Garbo, John Gilbert, Jean Harlow, Spencer Tracy, Katharine Hepburn, Greer Garson, Hedy Lamarr, Lena Horne, Ava Gardner, Deborah Kerr, Lana Turner,

Robert Taylor, Angela Lansbury, Dorothy Dandridge, and the king himself—Clark Gable—as well as the great child stars Mickey Rooney, Judy Garland, Jackie Cooper, and Margaret O'Brien. Not only were there stars under contract but also featured players and supporting players, giving employment to a range of excellent character actors and actresses. This sprawling behemoth that could easily intimidate, frighten, even terrify, the strongest of personalities represented the big time, the top of the heap. But the little girl sitting by her mother's side calmly surveyed the place. Young Elizabeth took Metro—as it was often referred to in show business circles—in stride. She understood there was work to be done, that she had to let them know she was right for their movie. As she made her way through MGM, people took notice of her extraordinary looks. Yet no one could really have predicted that she would become the queen of the lot, Metro's most heralded beauty, the greatest movie star certainly of the second half of the twentieth century and, as Katharine Hepburn would say, the last of the great movie stars.

When Sara and Elizabeth arrived at MGM, those other little girls sat outside the producer's office. "At 5 o'clock the casting director and his assistant at MGM ushered in six little girls, all English, with their mothers, with schoolteachers to watch them. And the whole crowd," Sam Marx recalled. "And I started looking them over to see who we would get that would fit this part—when my secretary called in from outside and said there's another little girl just arrived. I said, 'Send her in.' That was Elizabeth with her mother." Sam Marx, *Lassie Come Home*'s director Fred Wilcox, and others were immediately stunned by her appearance. "I still recall she was wearing a kind of blue velvet cape, and to me she seemed in a glow of purple. I don't know whether her eyes, her hair, [were] enhanced by this cape she was wearing but it was truly like an eclipse of the sun. It blotted out everybody that was in the office. You just saw this gorgeous, beautiful darling little girl, which was really what Elizabeth was in those days."

Still, she was a child, and would she be able to perform in front of the camera? "Don't be scared," Sam Marx said. Here Elizabeth's composure came into play. "Oh, thank you, I'm not scared." The other little girls were sent home. She was given her lines and told the basic situation of the scene. After a few minutes, Elizabeth said: "I'm ready now, thank you." Director Wilcox then led her through the audition. "Finishing her lines," said writer Ruth Waterbury, "Elizabeth lifted her head, just as Mr. Wilcox had told her to." "We knew we had a find," said Marx. Marx also said: "We never even tested her in the part. Nothing. She went into the film." That, of course, seems unlikely. MGM would have had to have seen what she looked like on camera. But Marx and no doubt Wilcox knew she really needed no test.

Once MGM signed her for the film, the studio wanted to remake her image. "The studio wanted to pluck my eyebrows and dye my black hair brown," Taylor remembered, "and change my name to Virginia. Certainly not, my father said. Take her as she is, or don't take her."

Lassie Come Home featured child star Roddy McDowall as a Yorkshire lad whose beloved dog, Lassie, has become too expensive for his poor family to maintain. Playing McDowall's parents were veterans Donald Crisp and Elsa Lanchester. The dog is sold to a wealthy squire, played by Nigel Bruce, whose little granddaughter, Priscilla, played by Taylor, loves the dog as much as McDowall's character, Joe. The film follows Lassie's travails as she goes from one master to another, only to be reunited with McDowall's Joe—with Taylor's Priscilla nearby —at the film's conclusion. Having given a lauded performance in John Ford's Academy Award–winning drama about Welsh coal miners, *How Green Was My Valley*, McDowall had already established himself as an important child star. A friendship developed almost immediately between Taylor and McDowall, which endured over the next decades.

Finally, here was a film that let Elizabeth's

natural warmth, her love of animals, and her ability to convincingly play a character shine. Dressed in smartly designed girlhood suits, she looked like the perfect little Englishwoman. Exuding confidence, she proved not only to be a natural in front of the camera but also capable— as had been the case at Universal—of navigating her way through the demands of filming itself. When a cameraman said that she was wearing too much mascara and that it should be removed, Taylor spoke up, saying it wasn't mascara. "That's me." No one who saw the film could fail to notice her. "Elizabeth Taylor, a pretty moppet," wrote *Variety*, "shows up to good advantage as Bruce's granddaughter." Even at the studio, she drew stares. "Elizabeth Taylor was nine years old when I first met her on the MGM lot," recalled the studio's master hairstylist Sydney Guilaroff. "I thought at once she was the most enchanting girl anybody at the studio had ever seen." She was on her way.

During the 1930s and 1940s, an array of talented children were the darlings of the studios, each with his or her own unique immediately identifiable screen persona that lured audiences young and old into movie theaters. In many respects, these were the eras of the great child stars: Mickey Rooney, Freddie Bartholomew, Jackie Cooper, Judy Garland, Roddy McDowall, Margaret

O'Brien, Jane Withers, Peggy Ann Garner, Dickie Moore, Dean Stockwell, and those kids from Hal Roach's *Our Gang* series—George "Spanky" McFarland, Matthew "Stymie" Beard, and Billie "Buckwheat" Thomas—and, of course, the star who was in a league of her own: Shirley Temple. Child stardom didn't come easily. And always it was fraught with hazards. Countless children might do a film or two, then vanish. For children in Hollywood, the situation was as hotly competitive as it was for their adult counterparts. Always there was an awareness among the children, and especially their parents—more often than not their ambitious mothers—that the kids could be dropped by the studios at any time. Looming over them was the prospect that their charms might dim as they grew older, that adolescence could mark the end of all the attention and success. By the time Elizabeth worked at MGM, it was basically already over for Freddie Bartholomew. The supremely talented Peggy Ann Garner would peak in 1945 with her sterling performance in *A Tree Grows in Brooklyn*, which earned her a special Oscar, and though she would appear in television in the 1950s and 1960s, the mighty days of stardom had passed her. Such children as Carl "Alfalfa" Switzer, Allen "Farina" Hoskins, and Billie "Buckwheat" Thomas of the *Our Gang* series had troubled adult lives when the business had lost interest in them and when audiences had forgotten them. Judy Garland and Mickey Rooney would keep working and main-tain their iconic positions, but neither had those *huge* careers as adult *movie stars*. Elizabeth Taylor would prove herself a one-of-a-kind child star who reached the pinnacle of her success asan adult.

Although MGM had signed her to a contract, the studio lent her to Twentieth Century Fox for the role of another British child, this time the doomed Helen in *Jane Eyre*, which starred Joan Fontaine, Orson Welles, and Peggy Ann Garner as the young Jane. Afterward, MGM cast Elizabeth, again opposite Roddy McDowall, again as a ladylike child with a lovely British accent, in 1944's *The White Cliffs of Dover* under the direction of Clarence Brown. Because she worked so well with McDowall, there was talk about teaming them in other films. But the real teaming here was between Taylor and Brown. Like Sam Marx and Fred Wilcox, Brown saw something in those violet eyes and that demure British demeanor of Elizabeth. Within her, there was warmth and perhaps some fire. Clearly, there was drive as well, with both the daughter and, of course, her mother. Brown would not walk away from the film and forget her. Instead, they would soon work together on her most important film of the era.

Chapter 4

IN RETROSPECT, IT was perhaps fitting that the first actual Jackson 5 performance came on Michael's seventh birthday: August 29, 1965. It was the professional birth of an extraordinary career on the day of the birth of the great artist himself. The performance was at a children's fashion show at a local shopping center. By then, the group's name had undergone a change. Some mistakenly believe the group had originally been called Ripples and the Waves Plus Michael. But Jermaine Jackson has said that that was the name of a different group. Instead, they were often known as the Jackson Brothers Musical Group— until, according to Joe Jackson, a family friend, Evelyn Leahy (sometimes spelled Lahaie or LaHaie), suggested something else. Leahy was a model who traveled around the state, and after seeing the boys perform at a shopping mall in Gary, she said that the name the Jackson Brothers sounded too much like something of the past, like the Mills Brothers, who had been successful in the 1940s. When she suggested the name the Jackson 5, Joe snapped it up. There was another version to this story, as well. Katherine said that

Evelyn told *her* about the name change. Perhaps Evelyn had told both parents. Nonetheless, with the new name and Michael in the lead, the group was on its way. Eventually, Johnny Jackson (no relation) became their drummer; Ronny (sometimes spelled Ronnie) Rancifer, their keyboardist. Things moved quickly. Joseph landed the group a contract with the local Steeltown Records, where they recorded the songs "Big Boy" and "We Don't Have to Be Over 21 (to Fall in Love)."

A big break came at Chicago's renowned Regal Theater, where a roster of such legendary African Americans as Ethel Waters, Duke Ellington, Lena Horne, Nat "King" Cole, and Dinah Washington had once performed. On the bill that night with the Jackson brothers was Gladys Knight, who was sitting in her dressing room when she heard them performing onstage. She stepped into the hallway to see who these kids were. "Impressed" was not a strong enough word to describe how Knight felt. She suggested to Joe that he should speak to someone at her record label, Motown. Joe made overtures to the company. But nothing came of that. Knight even did her best to make Motown look at the group. But still nothing.

Then came August 1967, when the boys appeared in the ferociously competitive amateur night contest at New York's famed Apollo Theater —where the audiences were known for being notoriously demanding. Only the best came out on top. Billie Holiday, Ella Fitzgerald, and Sarah Vaughan had all seen their careers get a much-needed jump start when they had won amateur night. But losers might find themselves booed or booted off the stage. "That was the toughest place of all to play," Michael remembered. "If they liked you there, they *really* liked you. And if they hated you, they'd throw things at you, food and stuff. But we weren't scared. We knew we were good." That night, the Jackson 5 took first place. Joseph and his sons were thrilled, even more so when they returned to the Apollo in May 1968 as *paid* performers. Something big *had* to happen now. And it did. Two months earlier—in July 1968—the brothers had been playing at Chicago's High Chaparral when singer Bobby Taylor saw them and, like Gladys Knight, contacted Motown. Finally, Motown paid attention. The company wanted the boys to come to Detroit to audition.

Founded by Berry Gordy Jr., Motown had become a major force in popular music. Contrary to what some have thought, Gordy was hardly some ghetto kid who happened to make good. Gordy had grown up in a staunchly middle-class family. His parents, Berry Gordy Sr. and Bertha Gordy, had migrated from Sandersville, Georgia, to Detroit in search of a better life and more economic opportunities. Gordy Sr. ran several businesses, including a printing shop, to secure a comfortable lifestyle for his family. He instilled in his children a hard-work ethic and a belief in social progress. The seventh of eight children, Berry Jr. was encouraged always to make something of himself. But he seemed at first the least likely of the family to do anything extraordinary. Quitting high school, he became a Golden Glove boxer, then served in the military in Korea. Afterward, he returned to Detroit, where he ran a music store for a time and worked on the assembly line of an auto plant. Through it all, he had a love of music, and he had a great ear for songs that would prove popular.

Just as important, Gordy had drive and a vision. He decided to write music. With his outgoing personality, his gift for gab, his awareness of the importance of visibility (people had to know who you were), he made contacts at Detroit's well-known Flame Show Bar, a top-of-the-line club that headlined famous black entertainers that included Della Reese, B. B. King, and Sarah Vaughan. There he met singer Jackie Wilson, a dynamo of a performer and a sex symbol within the African American community. Michael would always be in awe of Wilson's fancy footwork, his passion and energy, his mesmerizing ability to put a song across.

Working with his sister Gwen Gordy and writer Roquel Billy Davis (known sometimes as Tyran Carlo), Gordy cowrote the hits "Lonely Teardrops" and "To Be Loved" for Wilson, which turned

Gordy's fledgling music career around. Now he had a place in the business. Later, using royalties from various songs he had written, along with an $800 loan from his family, he formed the Motown Record Corporation.

Seeking to change the face of popular music in America (and eventually around the world), Gordy envisioned the day when rhythm and blues–style music would go thoroughly mainstream in a way that even the music of those early and successful masters of rhythm and blues and rock and roll—like Louis Jordan, Chuck Berry, and that whirling dervish Little Richard—had not been able to do. Gordy's idea was to further extend and broaden the appeal of black music (and black musical artists)—and to make black music *something else*. Decades earlier a great singer like Ethel Waters had helped popularize the blues, making it cross over into the cultural mainstream. Eventually, Waters mastered a style and sound that might be called black pop. Though steeped in rhythm and blues, Gordy's vision was music that also acted as a kind of black pop. Michael would be greatly admiring of and influenced by Gordy's concept.

Gordy moved his company into a small building at West Grand Boulevard in Detroit. There, an old photography studio was converted into a recording studio, with offices on the bottom level. Berry lived upstairs. Those who later visited the premises were always surprised that in so small and modest a space came such big sounds, such tremendous hits. The property—eventually known as Hitsville, USA—was open round the clock. Gordy let no record be released without his stamp of approval.

Gordy inspired all those around him. "Loyalty, honesty, and obedience were demanded and often gladly given," recalled Mary Wilson of the Supremes. "Berry was a perceptive judge of character and a quick study of almost anything. He knew how to get people to do his bidding. He knew their talents and weaknesses. After years of observing him I believe he often knew more about us than we knew about ourselves." Women also found him attractive. In time, he had three marriages and three divorces. There were other women in his life as well. Eventually, he would father eight children, including a daughter named Rhonda from his raging love affair with Diana Ross. He would become Ross's Svengali and was determined that she emerge as a star in her own right, not simply as a member of the Supremes.

In 1968, Motown had relocated its corporate offices from West Grand Boulevard to a high-rise in downtown Detroit at 2457 Woodward Avenue, but the company still recorded at its original Hitsville studio. Later the company's headquarters would be in Los Angeles. Regardless of its location, Motown would never be the sprawling behemoth of an MGM that sat on those 167 acres. But the company would be a comparable empire in the way it affected American popular culture. As Michael walked into Motown's office, it was similar to the day Elizabeth Taylor had been driven onto the lot at MGM. This was the top of the line. Motown was not only the greatest record company for black entertainers but also much more. Having made extraordinary inroads into mainstream popular culture, Motown had become one of the great record companies *period*. Some of the greatest musical acts of the twentieth century were on the Motown roster: Smokey Robinson and the Miracles, the Temptations, Martha and the Vandellas, the Four Tops, Marvin Gaye and Tammi Terrell, the Supremes, Junior Walker, Gladys Knight and the Pips, and that much undersung heroine, Motown's first big star, now no longer a part of the roster but whose music remained undiminished, Mary Wells.

And there were all of those huge hits: "My Guy," "My Girl," "Shopping Around," "OOO Baby Baby," "The Tracks of My Tears," "I Heard It Through the Grapevine," "Dancing in the Street," "Heat Wave," "Can't Help Myself," "Please Mr. Postman," "Ain't No Mountain High Enough," "Where Did Our Love Go," "Stop! In the Name of Love," and countless more. But ultimately there would be dissension, discord, and anger among the performers, the composers, and the producers at Motown, mostly directed at Gordy. Though he might never want to see himself as a despot, Gordy could be tough, and in the eyes of some, ruthless. Some Motown performers never forgave him for the way they had been treated. Some complained about unpaid royalties. The writing trio Holland-Dozier-Holland battled Gordy over profit sharing and royalties. By 1968, they left Motown and started their own label. Others complained the company could stifle creativity, especially when it discouraged (some would say even forbade) some artists from writing their own material. Others believed that Motown/ Gordy would drop one act in favor of building another. The Marvelettes, which had been the company's first big girl group, appeared to have been replaced by Martha and the Vandellas. Then came the Supremes, who were given the top writers and arrangers. Marvin Gaye and Mary Wells were among those Motown artists permanently embittered, and sadly, permanently scarred.

Perhaps the most heartbreaking was the case of Florence Ballard of the Supremes. Sensitive and insecure, she may well have created some of her own problems. Still, hers was a story with devastating consequences. Often depressed, she developed a drinking problem. But what ultimately caused an emotional upheaval was her belief that Gordy was pushing both Mary Wilson and her aside to promote Ross. Eventually, Ballard left the group, replaced by Cindy Birdsong. According to Mary Wilson, Ballard received a $160,000 settlement from Motown but she signed away her rights to any royalties from the Supremes' music. After having traveled the world with the group, Ballard ended up back in Detroit, trying for a time for a solo career but without much luck or guidance. The mother of three children, she lost her home to a foreclosure. She ended up on welfare. In 1976, she died of cardiac arrest at the age of thirty-two. It was one of the great tragedies in the music industry, and whether fair or not, Gordy's Motown was held greatly responsible in the minds of the public. Ballard's story would reach legendary heights and serve as the basis for the hit 1981 Broadway musical *Dreamgirls*. And in *Dreamgirls*, the arch villain was a ruthless, cutthroat Berry Gordy–like character.

Nonetheless, this was the world the Jackson kids would soon enter.

One version of the story of the audition was that Berry Gordy was not present that day. Gordy and Jermaine Jackson have said he was present but apparently he had not made his presence known at first. Nonetheless Michael and his brothers were still excited when greeted by

Gordy's top assistant, Suzanne de Passe, along with Ralph Seltzer, the company's attorney and head of its creative division. Joe was informed that the boys were to do an audition tape. Once cameras were set up, Michael went into action, speaking and setting the stage for the group's performance. Those watching sat spellbound as the group—with Michael in the lead— performed James Brown's "I Got the Feelin' " and Smokey Robinson's "Who's Lovin' You." Especially after viewing the black-and-white sixteen-millimeter film—with Michael's complete command of the lyrics and the melody, with his gyrations, with his bold intonations, with his sheer confidence (much like Taylor's when she met with those MGM executives and read for *Lassie Come Home*)—Gordy put the word out to sign the boys.

When presented with the contract in Motown's office, Joe wanted the term of the contract reduced from seven years to one. Gordy agreed to the concession, but he knew it didn't really matter. If they proved unsuccessful, he could drop them after a year. As the boys' guardian, Joe signed the contract but apparently without reading it all the way through. Or perhaps without having read it at all. Nor did he consult an attorney. "Berry did not want outside lawyers looking over any of our contracts," Ralph Seltzer later said. "It was best, Berry decided, that potential contractees read over the agreement in my office and then just sign. If they had a problem with that, they did not become Motown artists. It was that simple."

Unknown to Joe was the fact, as stipulated in the contract, that whatever Motown shelled out to record the boys—money for arrangements, studio time, tour expenses, promotion, you name it— would have to be repaid to the company out of the group's royalties. The royalty rate itself was basically a small one. The brothers would receive 6 percent of 90 percent of the wholesale price, divided equally among all five siblings. It wasn't a lot of money. Nor did Joseph understand that Motown could replace members of the group and that the company would also own the name the Jackson 5, as it owned the names of all its groups. The boys signed that day. Later, Katherine, as a guardian for her sons, signed—also without thoroughly reading the contract. But before the boys could start recording for the company, Motown had to work out a settlement with Steeltown Records, which still had the group under contract. Didn't Joe understand that his sons could not record for one label while still legally bound to another? In the years to come, it would be apparent to the children, especially Michael and his sister Janet, that Joe was not a particularly astute businessman. Eventually, both would steer clear of him when making their own deals.

Michael would become a very shrewd business-man with top advisers, and always in the back of his mind was the realization of what Joseph had failed to do. Yet Michael would also make mistakes and find himself hiring and firing any number of people.

The contract went into effect on March 11, 1969.

The boys' lives changed. During the week, they attended school in Gary and also kept up their gigs at theaters in and out of the Gary area. On weekends, they were back in Detroit, where they recorded some fifteen songs, with singer Bobby Taylor supervising. They also stayed at Taylor's home. Many of the songs they recorded then—and in the future—were not released. Berry Gordy was meticulous in grooming the brothers for major stardom, in making sure that whatever was released would be a winner. He promised them that they would have three successive number one hits.

During the Christmas holiday season, a big event occurred. Though Gordy was now based in California, he arranged for the boys to perform for his guests and himself at his luxurious Detroit mansion, which he still maintained. The boys *and* their father were impressed by the opulent lifestyle stardom could bring. They took it all in: the marble floors, the Olympic-size swimming pool, the paintings, and also the guests. "I'll never forget that night," Michael recalled. "Smokey Robinson was there. That's when I met him for the first time. The Temptations were there, and we were singing some of their songs, so we were real nervous. And I looked out into the audience, and there was Diana Ross. That's when I almost lost it." This marked the start of their friendship and his fascination with her. Motown's publicists soon fabricated the story that was assumed to be good for both the Jackson 5 *and* Diana Ross—namely, that she had discovered the group.

Yet another change came when Gordy wanted the Jackson family to relocate to Los Angeles in order to record at Motown's Hollywood studios. Because Joe did not feel completely secure that everything with Motown would materialize, he had his five sons move west. But Katherine stayed in the Gary home with Janet, La Toya, and Randy. Rebbie had other plans. Having married her fiancé, she settled in the south, which apparently angered Joe. The marriage of any of his children seemed to be an alien idea to him. He still believed that all his children should be together.

Once again Motown constructed its own scenario on the move, saying that Michael actually lived at Diana Ross's Los Angeles home for a time. Even Michael promoted this version. In actuality, Gordy housed the boys first at the Tropicana ("one of the seediest motels in Hollywood," according to biographer Randy Taraborrelli) and then the Hollywood Motel, which "was a dreadful residence for young boys; prostitutes and pimps used it as a place to conduct business." Gordy grew cautious about shelling out too much money on the group. Like Joe, he took safeguards just in case things didn't work out.

At a young age, Michael, though protected by Motown, was still exposed to a far sleazier side of entertainment in America, quite different from the way Elizabeth Taylor was handled by MGM. Yet Taylor would understand how affected Michael was by all he had seen. Gordy also briefly moved the boys into his home, but they "spent many afternoons and evenings at Diana's, walking the winding street between the two," Jermaine recalled. "But it wasn't true that any of us, including Michael, lived with Diana. This was another of those marketing myths—upheld by Michael in his book *Moonwalk* in 1988—for the sake of image." In August 1969, Gordy leased a home for the family at 1601 Queens Road. Michael was enrolled in the Gardner Street elementary school, and for a time, Berry Gordy's son Kerry was his close friend. All the brothers were seduced by Los Angeles as much as the hordes that migrated there annually, seeing it as a sun-filled paradise with endless blue skies, swaying palm trees, stirring sunrises, and stunning sunsets, and the promise of big dreams to be fulfilled with glorious days of sheer pleasure.

"Those were truly wild days for me and my brothers," Michael recalled. California "was like being in another country, another world. To come from our part of Indiana, which is so urban and often bleak, and to land in Southern California was like having the world transformed into a wonderful dream. . . . We were awestruck by California."

The boys received the whole Motown treatment, learning the ropes with top talents: composers, choreographers, and publicists. Gordy had a team of musicians, referred to as the Corporation—which included Freddie Perren, Deke Richards, Fonce Mizell, and himself—work with the group. As "boys," they had to have music that expressed their youthful yearnings and energies, and the idea was to tap into a base with a younger crowd that in time would grow up with the Jackson 5. Eventually, the music evolved from snappy, fast-moving bubblegum soul to the sounds and signs of teen passion and teen angst. But the formula was to keep them young, delaying adulthood as long as possible.

The brothers were prepared—in terms of how they spoke and conducted themselves—to deal with the public and the media. At all times, they were to be gentlemen. Polite, well spoken, well groomed in the style of the late 1960s and early 1970s. Care was taken to correct their grammar. Any rough edges were sanded down. Motown depicted the Jacksons as an ideal American kind of family with a hardworking father and a loving mother. In these days, stories of Joseph's ferocious temper, of his beating of his sons, of his domineering stranglehold on them were rarely, if ever, discussed.

Michael paid close attention. As was often said, he absorbed everything like a sponge. Of all the brothers, he was the most inquisitive and the most observant, preparing himself not only for the immediate future but also the distant one. Early on, he valued collaborating with the best people in their fields. Very quickly, he also realized the importance of publicity and the construction of an image. Much of what he observed during this time he would carry with him for the rest of his life.

Chapter 5

SURPRISINGLY, ELIZABETH HERSELF realized, even before MGM did, that the iconic role that would carry her to the heights of childhood stardom had not yet come. Originally, Paramount Pictures owned the rights to the 1935 novel *National Velvet* by Enid Bagnold. Then MGM acquired the rights. *National Velvet*, at least as a film, was a drama that painted a portrait of a well-ordered, ideal family. An older sister has her first boyfriend. A middle sister is a meddlesome tattletale. A baby brother collects insects in a jar. A father, tough and unyielding on the outside, is really a pushover who likes sneaking food from the dinner table to the nearby family dog. A mother remembers her time as a champion swimmer who swam the English Channel before she settled down to family life. A stable boy, who is an outsider with a troubled past, works for the family and becomes one of its members and eventually reaches manhood through his experiences with them. But at its heart is daughter Velvet, who is sensitive, dreamy, and devoted to a prize horse she has won called the Piebald. Planning at first to enter the Pie in the big steeplechase race but unable to find a jockey, she ends up riding him herself, wins the race, and by doing so, has defied the conventions and the gender roles of her time.

At one point, MGM producer Pandro S. Berman thought of casting Katharine Hepburn as Velvet, making the character older. Hepburn had the right independent temperament to play the girl who dresses as a young man to win the race. But MGM had not put the film into production with Hepburn. Elizabeth was given the Bagnold book to read, and she fell in love with the story and the heroine. When she expressed her desire to do the part, producer Berman listened but believed her too young and much too small to convincingly play a girl whom onlookers believe is a young male jockey.

"Well, it was my favorite book, and I really was a marvelous horsewoman. At the age of three I could jump without a saddle," Taylor recalled. "But when I came down to the producer's office, he saw that though I was eleven, I was only as tall as a six-year-old." Berman measured her, marked her height on his office wall, and told her that she looked like a child. With her love of animals and with her identification with a character who believes her horse must have the chance to prove his worth and defy expectations, Elizabeth told the producer, "Well, I'll grow up."

The story of her strenuous campaign to win the role became the stuff of Hollywood legend. "I was absolutely determined. *National Velvet* was really me," she said. "And there was this place Tip's, where they had a thing called a Farm Breakfast—two hamburger patties, two fried eggs, a great big mound of hashed brown potatoes and after that a whole bunch of dollar pancakes. I used to have two Farm Breakfasts every morning at one sitting. For lunch I'd have steaks and salads, then swim and do exercises to stretch myself." Three months later, she went to see the producer again. Not only had she put on weight, but when Berman measured her again, he discovered she had also grown three inches. Not until decades later when she underwent another transformation to play Martha in *Who's Afraid of Virginia Woolf?* would Elizabeth Taylor be as fiercely committed to a character. Berman would leave those pencil marks indicating her height on his office wall for years to come.

MGM moved forward with Elizabeth as the star of *National Velvet.* The film would costar Mickey Rooney as the hired hand; Anne Revere and Donald Crisp as the parents; Jackie "Butch" Jenkins as the kid brother, Donald; Juanita Quigley as the middle sister, Malvolia; and Angela Lansbury as the older teenage sister, Edwina. The film was to be directed by Clarence Brown, a movie veteran from the days of silents, who had directed some of the studio's greatest stars: Greta Garbo in *Flesh and the Devil* and

Anna Karenina and five other films; Clark Gable and Joan Crawford in *Chained*; Gable and Norma Shearer in *Idiot's Delight*; and later an underrated gem about racism in America, *Intruder in the Dust*. He also succeeded in stripping sound films of some of the melodrama associated with silents. He favored naturalistic dialogue. Most significant, he respected actors, and he was known to let performers go with their instincts. Brown had been especially sensitive to his female stars. Garbo considered him her favorite director. One version of the way Elizabeth was cast is that Brown himself had first suggested her to Berman. Having directed Elizabeth in her previous film *The White Cliffs of Dover*, Brown understood that hers was not an upfront steely kind of drive like Hepburn's or Bette Davis's. Instead, it was cloaked by a surface warmth and an alluring traditional femininity, but underneath was a fierce independent streak, all of which would be the hallmarks of her star persona. Just as important, the drive was there, and Brown sensitively worked with her to let the sweet-tempered drive shine. He also understood perhaps that the way to bring out the best in her was to blur the line between the child's convictions and those of her character. It was star acting where the star's persona was crucial to the development of the character.

"I think *Velvet* is still the most exciting film I've ever done," Elizabeth later said. Filming went smoothly. Yet more now than with her previous films, Taylor experienced the demands, the difficulties, and the adult discipline that were all a part of filmmaking. Movie sets themselves, and everything surrounding them, were adult spheres where the crew and technicians, the makeup artists and wardrobe people might gripe, complain, and curse, where other actors might become impatient if a line was flubbed too often, where action might be halted in order for lighting to be adjusted or makeup to be reapplied, where childhood giggles were not permitted. Some sequences could require endless takes, and the repetition could be deadly. Because scenes were not shot in sequence, Elizabeth had to carry the whole film in her head. The workload was also heavier than those earlier films because, as the lead, she was in so many scenes. Stories also circulated for years that she was thrown by the horse she rode, which caused some of the back problems that later plagued her.

Always there was the knowledge that there was work to be done, and that each moment on a movie set meant money was being spent. She learned to accept the working conditions and the responsi-bilities very quickly, almost amazingly so. Unlike the young Judy Garland, to whom it was said the studio gave pills to pep her up, Taylor managed to keep her energy level high. Through-out, her concentration showed. Years later her costar Paul Newman would comment on his surprise at how quickly she could tap into her emotions.

There would be a classic sequence—both stirring and years later poignant—in which she rode energetically and waved, seemingly to the audience itself. For the young Elizabeth Taylor, with everything still ahead of her, she was optimistically facing—so it appeared—only a sunny future.

Once *National Velvet* was completed, the studio was immediately excited about its prospects and also its new star. Here was a girl now with only four films behind her who could hold her own with seasoned pros. No one, not even that young master of cinema Rooney, could dominate a scene in which she appeared. She had also been easy to work with, disciplined and devoted to the role, living as much as playing the part, which for movies was essential. "She *was* Velvet. And she loved that horse just like Velvet did," said her mother, Sara.

Released in December 1944, *National Velvet* garnered glowing reviews and was selected to play at the prestigious Radio City Music Hall. "Mr. Brown has also drawn some excellent performances from his cast, especially from little Elizabeth Taylor," wrote Bosley Crowther in the *New York Times*. "Her face is alive with youthful spirit, her voice has the softness of sweet song and her whole manner in this picture is one of refreshing grace." Later the *New York Times* named *National Velvet* one of the outstanding movies of the year.

Clearly, critic Crowther was in something of a swoon over Taylor. But he wasn't the only critic to feel that way. "Frankly, I doubt I am qualified to arrive at any sensible assessment of Miss Elizabeth Taylor," James Agee wrote in *The Nation*. "Ever since I first saw the child, two or three years ago, in I forget what minor role in what movie, I have been choked with the peculiar sort of adoration I might have felt if we were both in the same grade of primary school." He added: "She strikes me, however, if I may resort to conservative statement, as being rapturously beautiful. I think she also has a talent, of a sort, in the particular things she can turn on: which are most conspicuously a mock-pastoral kind of simplicity, and two or three speeds of semi-hysterical emotion, such as ecstasy, an odd sort of pre-specific erotic sentience, and the anguish of overstrained hope, imagination, and faith. Since these are precisely the things she needs for her role . . . and since I think the most hopeful business of movies to find the perfect people rather than the perfect artists, I think that she and the picture are wonderful, and I hardly know or care whether she can act or not."

Years later, Pauline Kael called *National Velvet* one of the most likable movies of all time and wrote that "the 12-year-old Elizabeth Taylor rings true on every line she speaks: she gives what is possibly her most dedicated performance as Velvet Brown." She added: "The film is a high-spirited, childish dream; like *The Wizard of Oz*, it makes people smile when they recall it."

At the time of *National Velvet*'s release, America was still firmly in the grip of the Second World War, even though the war in Europe was about to draw to a close. Hollywood had joined in the war effort. Stars like Clark Gable, James Stewart, and Tyrone Power served in the military. On the home front, war bond drives were led by celebrities. At the Hollywood Canteen and the Stage Door Canteen—military clubs of sorts—members of the armed forces on leave could mix with or be entertained by such stars as Jack Benny, Bette Davis, Count Basie, Barbara Stanwyck, Harpo Marx, Joan Crawford, and Ida Lupino. Stars like Betty Grable, Rita Hayworth, and Lena Horne became pinup girls whose pictures were carried by soldiers in faraway places. Aside from these efforts, movies like *Mrs. Miniver* and *Since You Went Away* sought to boost morale by highlighting the effects of the war respectively on "average" British and American families. Films like *Bataan* dramatized the courage of American military forces. A film like

So Proudly We Hail showed the contributions of women to the war. Also released was escapist fare that sought to take audiences' minds off the war: movies like *Cabin in the Sky* and *Meet Me in St. Louis.*

National Velvet showed family warmth and unity, which would benefit not only the individuals but also a community. It clearly challenged attitudes about the power of women and a girl's role in society. Taylor's Velvet believes her horse can be a champion, and when she cannot find a jockey to race him, she steps up to the plate. Never does she fear she cannot do it. Yet though the film shatters gender assumptions, it also reassures its audiences that traditional gender roles will remain in place, and the audience need not fear female revolt. Velvet's hard-edged mother understands her daughter's passion more so than the other characters. Yet the mother, after having been a champion swimmer, had left all that behind when she assumed her "acceptable" roles as wife and mother. She cautions her daughter to leave her champion days behind. Under her mother's guidance, Velvet in essence agrees to go back to "normal" life. But she has made her point, and the movie significantly closes with Velvet back on her horse.

Part of Velvet's appeal, as Taylor plays her, is not just her skill and conviction but also—as director Brown saw—her delicate "traditional" female charms. Audiences were catching sight of what would make Elizabeth Taylor such an international force in the movies to come. She would be, as actress Lee Grant said of Taylor in *Giant*, a "feminist," but she would also have the alluring "feminine" side that would not be associated with more "traditional" feminists. In the years to come, her desirability would make her seem less threatening. But underneath the great beauty, there would always be notes (on-screen and off-) of rebellion and defiance—frequently against the gender roles with which women were saddled.

Following *National Velvet*, it was official: MGM had a major new child star. The studio was so excited that it presented (and publicized) an ecstatic Elizabeth with the horse, King George, she had ridden in the film. Now, Elizabeth Taylor's life changed dramatically. Within the extended Warmbrodt and Taylor households, the family focus shifted to Elizabeth. Uncle Howard beamed with pride, perhaps a bit perplexed but joyous over his grandniece's fame. In England, those who had known the little girl Elizabeth followed her career. Sadly, her godfather, Victor Cazalet, never saw her rise to childhood stardom. In 1943, he was killed in a plane crash.

Everything about Elizabeth's being was soon wrapped up in MGM, which became a third parent, and an overbearing one at that, controlling her activities, her education, her social life, the way she was perceived by the public, and indeed the very way she was to think of herself. She would grow up ever mindful that just about everything she did was being observed, scrutinized, assessed, evaluated, and judged. Every minute of the day was also spent working in one way or another. By the time of the release of *National Velvet*, Elizabeth's work in the movies was dis-cussed so much among her classmates that she became a distraction at the school, and, according to Sara, she was advised to take Elizabeth outof Hawthorne. The other children were actually *staring* at Elizabeth.

In time, Elizabeth was educated exclusively at MGM in what was known as the Little Red Schoolhouse, which at one time or another was the place such other young luminaries as Judy Garland, Margaret O'Brien, Jane Powell, and Debbie Reynolds studied. Until she turned eighteen, daily, between setups, Elizabeth shifted gears and headed to the classroom at the studio—where she was suddenly a child again but expected also to do the required schoolwork. Concentra-tion on the set was one thing. Concentration on her studies was another.

According to writer Ruth Waterbury, Elizabeth was educated in fifteen-minute intervals, which had to add up to at least three hours a day. "This meant that under the law," said Waterbury, "she could be before the camera only another four hours daily. Thus, sometimes a whole group of around one hundred and fifty people would have to sit around idle while she studied arithmetic." With her remarkable powers of concentration, she was able to leave the set, do her studies, return, and immediately get back into character. But her education was spotty. How could it be otherwise? Nevertheless, she was a shrewd pupil. "As she grew older, she showed me what a good student she was. She always had top grades in the subjects that interested her," recalled teacher Dorothy Mullen. Her grades, as Elizabeth herself recalled, were As and Bs.

At MGM, she also had dance and voice lessons. Countless hours were spent posing for studio publicity pictures. There were interviews for the press. "When I'd come home from the studio—I'd get out at twelve, have lunch in the commissary and then have singing lessons," she recalled, "so I'd get home around three—then we'd play." On weekends there might be, especially during her teenage years, get-togethers with other young budding stars—Roddy McDowall, Jane Powell, Marshall Thompson, Richard Long, John Derek— at beach parties, barbecues, sports events. Rarely was there anything spontaneous about those gatherings. Studio photographers might be on the scene, running about to capture the supposedly candid moments. Always she was on display.

"Not being like other children, not belonging to the adult world and not belonging to a children's world, I felt always the outsider. Even the film kids were not really in my mold. Their parents were always giving parties so that the movie magazines like *Photoplay* or *Movie Gems* could come and photograph their children," she remembered. "I'd see that most everybody else—even the kids—were performing almost entirely for the camera. I'd feel absolutely lost."

But there were always the animals that she adored. "Riding a horse gave me a sense of freedom and abandon because I was so controlled by my parents and the studio when I was a child that when I was on a horse we could do whatever we wanted. Riding a horse was my way of getting away from people telling me what to do and when to do it and how to do it." A world away from the studio was also found in the pages of books. "I did a lot of reading, painting, drawing in those days—anything that was escapism, I suppose. I went to the movies all the time." Reading was a constant throughout her life. "Liz is the most voracious reader I know," producer Walter Wanger later recalled. "At least one book every two days. She reads everything: memoirs, historical novels, plays, and the current best-sellers."

At home, she observed her father's lonely discontent. Francis still drank. He also searched for another life, apart from Sara. Rumors circulated that he had met Adrian, MGM's top designer who had created extraordinary clothes for such stars as Greta Garbo, Norma Shearer, Joan Crawford, and the late Jean Harlow—and that Francis and Adrian became lovers. Yet though her parents still argued, Elizabeth, under the circumstances, had a semblance of a relatively balanced home life. No matter what, her parents loved her and doted on her and her brother. Aware of the importance of stability and security away from the studio, Sara and Francis managed to have family dinners and private times at home. During the summers, a teenaged Elizabeth visited her uncle Howard's vast estate in Cedar Gates in Wisconsin.

Elizabeth always loved being with her brother. "I worshiped Howard as a child—and still do," she said. "He's my best friend of all." Of course, they were typical siblings who sometimes poked fun at each other. Because Howard sometimes called her Lizzie the Lizard, she said that jousting led her to detest being called Liz. Otherwise her closest girlfriend during this time was her neighbor Anne Westmore, a child of the famous Westmore family of makeup artists.

Much was done for Elizabeth at the house. She grew up without certain responsibilities that other children had. Throughout her life, she was known for not picking up after herself. At the end of a day, she left her clothes on the floor. Even later, when she might return home after glamorous movie premieres or parties, she dropped her beautiful gowns on the floor without thinking twice. The idea of her ever learning to iron or take care of her own clothes was never entertained by anyone in the Taylor home. Actually, it seemed a rather preposterous notion. Sara did attempt at one point to make her daughter tidier. But she gave up. Ultimately, staff was there to take care of things for Elizabeth. Even with her animals, she rarely house-trained them. Someone else was responsible for that, too. In the years to come, her husbands would find themselves cleaning up dog poop. Still, that family life gave her a secure foundation, the kind an actress like Marilyn Monroe would never have, and though the public and international press might not know it, she always wanted to share the big events of her life, be it marriages or movie openings, with Sara, Francis, and Howard.

The main thing drummed into her head was that discipline had to be maintained at the studio. Elizabeth had to rise early and be prepared for the day ahead, whether it was knowing her lines or being prepped for press interviews. During the drives to the studio, Elizabeth and Sara discussed the day ahead and what was expected of her. At the studio itself, she was to be polite and mannerly, always ladylike. An awareness of being before the public eye and acting accordingly was repeatedly emphasized by Sara and the studio.

Yet despite the pressures at MGM, another part of her enjoyed studio life. "MGM was a very exciting place to be," she confessed. "I've always loved movie stars, loved movies, loved everything about them except doing them. It was so tremendously thrilling to go into the commissary for lunch. They were all there—Judy Garland, Lana Turner, Spencer Tracy, Hedy Lamarr. And there was the lovely, sweet smell of the pancake make-up the women wore—so much more exciting than the grease paint they use now. Every time Clark Gable walked in I just about dropped my fork. He was the epitome of a movie star—so romantic, such bearing, such friendliness."

Surprisingly, following *National Velvet*, two years passed before moviegoers saw her again. She was maturing, and the studio didn't seem sure what kind of role to cast her in next. One of the beneficial aspects of a big studio contract was that MGM's publicity department kept her name before the public with photographs sent to newspapers and with items for the columnists. Hedda Hopper proved important here. Mentioning Taylor whenever possible, Hopper viewed the child as something of a surrogate daughter. Elizabeth kept herself occupied with various projects, one of which was a story about her pet chipmunk, Nibbles, which was published as a book: *Nibbles and Me*. Of course, the studio had done its part to ensure that the manuscript was in publishable shape and indeed that the young authoress found a publisher. But Elizabeth did the drawings that ran throughout the book. *Nibbles and Me* was dedicated to "Mummie, Daddy, and Howard, who love Nibbles almost as much as I do."

At long last, MGM had Elizabeth back on-screen in a movie that marked her return to the world of Lassie, *Courage of Lassie*, again under Fred Wilcox's direction. Here she played a sensitive girl trying to nurse a collie named Bill (but played by Lassie), who has suffered during the war years.

MGM also lent her out to Warner Bros. to appear with Irene Dunne and William Powell in the adaptation of Clarence Day's comedy *Life with Father*, to be directed by Michael Curtiz. MGM charged Warner Bros. $3,500 for Elizabeth's services, which was five times what it paid her. Never did Taylor like the fact that the studio always kept the difference in her salary whenever she was lent out. In the long run, it contributed to some of her later resentment toward MGM. Nonetheless, Sara drove Elizabeth daily to the Warner studio in Burbank, and Elizabeth adapted to the Warner style and culture—less pampered, perhaps less glamorous than MGM's. Having already appeared with Irene Dunne in *The White Cliffs of Dover*, she grew friendly with the older actress. Many of her scenes were with that skilled, idiosyncratic comedienne Zasu Pitts.

She also quickly adjusted to the shooting style of Curtiz—and was well aware of his stature in the industry. Born in Hungary, Curtiz had directed Warner Bros.' biggest stars—Bette Davis, James Cagney, Errol Flynn, Olivia de Havilland—and was on a roll with the direction of such films as *Casablanca*, which won an Oscar for Outstanding Motion Picture; *Yankee Doodle Dandy*, for which Cagney walked off with an Oscar for Best Actor; and *Mildred Pierce*, for which Joan Crawford, having left MGM for Warner Bros., made a stunning comeback that had earned her an Oscar for Best Actress. An experienced tough old bird of a guy, accustomed to being in charge, not taking any flack on- or off-screen, and admired by Warner Bros. for working hard and fast, Curtiz's attitude was that some people worked to live but he lived to work. Because Curtiz was also bipolar, which may have accounted for his mood shifts and temperament, his directing chores helped him ward off his demons.

Life with Father was shot from April 20 to July 21, 1946. It progressed without major problems. But during the filming of *Life*, Sara became openly fascinated by director Curtiz. No doubt

Elizabeth detected her mother's attraction to the director—the intent way she looked at him, the way she spoke to him, the way she hung on his every word. Certainly, those working on the set were aware of the mutual attraction. Before long, the word around Warner was that Sara and Curtiz apparently were having a hot and heavy affair. How Elizabeth felt about that would never be known. It wasn't something she'd ever be eager to discuss. Now a perceptive show biz pro, aware of the peccadilloes, the adventures, intrigues, and vagaries of all the grown-ups around her, Elizabeth's feelings may have been mixed. On the one hand, she may well have felt her father had failed Sara and given her no choice but to seek romance outside the marriage. Or perhaps she believed that Sara had failed the sensitive Francis. Much as she loved her mother, her sympathies for her father never faltered.

MGM no doubt heard about the discord in the Taylor household, which, from its vantage point, could be problematic. Its teenage star had to look as if she came from a typical, ideal American family. Eventually, MGM had to deal publicly with the troubled Taylor marriage when news hit the press that Francis and Sara had formally separated. Sara maintained custody of Elizabeth; there was no way she would give her up. Francis had custody of Howard; there was no way he would give him up. "Francis and Elizabeth's brother, Howard, were residing in bungalow three at the Beverly Hills Hotel, while Elizabeth and her mother continued to live in Beverly Hills," recalled the children's uncle John Taylor. "Most difficult of all for Elizabeth was her parents' separation," recalled hairstylist Sydney Guilaroff, in whom Elizabeth sometimes confided. Born in 1907 in London and raised in Canada, the older Guilaroff had come to New York as a teenager and had first worked at Gimbels. He swept floors, cleaned up, and took care of stock. But ambitious and eager to be a part of New York's glamour, he answered an ad for a beautician's assistant, and thereafter rose to become a well-known and popular hairstylist for New York's wealthy set. After Joan Crawford encouraged him to come to Hollywood, he began working at MGM in 1934, styling hair over the years for the studio's big stars: Crawford, Greta Garbo, Norma Shearer, Ava Gardner, Lena Horne, Lucille Ball, and Dorothy Dandridge. He was the first hairstylist in Hollywood to receive a credit in films. Tall, slender, and almost always dressed in a suit and tie even while working, he had a friendly, relaxed, discreet, and rather avuncular air that made it easy for stars to open up to him. Elizabeth was no exception. "I soon began to serve as a sort of surrogate father in her life," said Guilaroff. "Given Francis Taylor's indifference, my help and concern was both needed and appreciated."

When Sara became ill, an alarmed Francis rushed to her bedside. Or so the couple told the press. Shortly before Elizabeth's fifteenth birthday, in February 1947, the two reunited. The separation had lasted four months. But the real conflicts, divisions, and differences would not go away. Sara and Francis's battles over their children continued until Howard and Elizabeth reached adulthood. Francis absolutely refused to relinquish both his children to his wife. For the children, there must have been the knowledge that Elizabeth's career was embedded in the parental struggles.

Francis, his uncle Howard, and all of the relatives were keenly aware, more so now than ever, that Sara's very existence and her very sense of herself were invested in her daughter's career. Believing that Elizabeth could be one of the greatest film stars of all time, Sara was determined to navigate her daughter through all the professional diffi-culties and all the studio intrigues. No family plans, no social evenings, no other types of gatherings could be considered without looking over Elizabeth's schedule.

Among other actresses at the studio, Elizabeth could appear aloof and distant, which was partly due to her basic shyness. The one young actress she appeared to genuinely like was Judy Garland. She socialized with Jane Powell, but whether that was because of the studio's maneuvers, no one was sure. (All the same, Taylor and Powell were friends for years.) Actress Kathryn Grayson thought Elizabeth could be "highly competitive, rather spoiled, very insecure." Still, Sara was the one who pushed for Elizabeth, always believing that the other teenage actresses could never do, could never represent, what Elizabeth did. Elizabeth was the dream girl, the budding goddess who millions would fantasize over. Of course, Sara was right. Actor Dennis Hopper, who years later would appear in *Giant* with Taylor, remembered that when he was growing up, she was his pillow mate, the girl he went to sleep thinking about. Countless other teenage boys already felt the same way.

A frustrated, stoic Francis repeatedly had to step back—for another reason. When MGM signed Elizabeth to a new contract at $750 a week with a six-month option that would boost her salary to $1,000 a week, Sara was paid $250 a week to watch over Elizabeth. Today's equivalent of $750 a week would be more than $10,000 and Sara's weekly $250 would be almost $3,500. Francis realized that without his daughter's income, the family would have to live in a far more modest way. "I was a child supporting my family," Elizabeth said. "My father took the money. Some of the money was put aside for me, but a lot of the money was put back into the entire family. I was just working the whole time."

Katherine Jackson would also come to realize how important Michael's later career—his income—was to the family's entire way of life. Francis understood that the entire extended family—which included a network of aunts and uncles—was invested in Elizabeth's career in other ways. His uncle Howard still boasted about his grand-niece as did everyone associated with her.

Yet Francis was adamant about not permitting Sara to take control of their son, Howard. The boy himself may have felt just like his father. When a studio arranged to interview him for a film role, he made it clear that he wanted no part of Hollywood. On the day of his appointment, Howard showed up at the studio with his head completely shaved. That was the end of any talk about his working in films. Elizabeth always admired her brother's rebellious streak. Francis began to spend more and more time with his son. Whenever Sara and Elizabeth were otherwise occupied, he'd take Howard off on vacations.

With the end of the war, the studios soon had to contend with changing tastes and attitudes—and the fact that the movie audience had lost some of its innocence. Gradually, Hollywood began to tackle more adult themes with an eventual exploration of social issues that had long festered in American life—and long been ignored by the studios. The Oscar-winning Best Motion Picture of 1946 was *The Best Years of Our Lives*, William Wyler's trenchant drama about troubled war veterans returning home to an America that clearly was a different place. In 1947, Elia Kazan's attack on anti-Semitism, *Gentleman's Agreement*, received the Oscar for Best Motion Picture. Both Wyler and Kazan won Oscars for Best Directing for their respective films. Within the next few years, the list of these adult-themed movies would grow; so would Hollywood's examination of other social and racial issues, as well as female sexuality. Traditional lighter weight fare still predominated. But American movies were becoming more reflective, and a new postwar younger generation was in search of its own stars.

Already the media was turning a postwar focus on Taylor. When she was thirteen, she was asked to perform on a special broadcast from the White House for the March of Dimes. Along with former first lady Eleanor Roosevelt, First Lady Bess Truman, and actress Cornelia Otis Skinner, Taylor addressed a national audience. "The request for Elizabeth came not from Hollywood," said Hedda Hopper, "but from the White House and I know of no one here better fitted for the job." This was a pretty heady experience for a teenager. But Taylor waltzed through—with every eye in the place on her. Not long after the release of *National Velvet*, *Life* magazine photographer Peter Stackpole had visited the Taylor home to take pictures of her. Already the magazine saw her as possibly a budding major figure whose career—and personal life—would be of interest to its readers. Thus began the magazine's splashy pictorial documen-tation of her life on- and off-screen. Naturally, the idea was to present her as a relatively typical American girl with loving parents and a model home life.

In its July 14, 1947 issue, *Life* ran fifteen-year-old Elizabeth Taylor on its cover. Inside, there was no real story, just a full page with pictures and a scant text. But that didn't matter. A *Life* cover remained a great status symbol, almost the ultimate, for a movie star, and MGM considered this a coup. This was the first of her fourteen *Life* covers. MGM also became all the more protective and overbearing. In 1945, when Elizabeth was tempted to stretch her talents and do a play in New York, the studio had put the clamps down on its valuable property and would not let her go east.

MGM decided the time had come to ease her into more grown-up roles and also to use her to reach the youth audience. For a time, the studio toyed with the idea of casting her as Rima in *Green Mansions*, a romantic fable set in South America. But, frankly, Elizabeth, then thirteen when MGM first paid the huge sum of $150,000 for the rights to the novel on which the film was to be based, seemed too young for the role.

Within the next year, MGM still considered starring her in the film. But one delay after another kept the project on the shelf. When it was finally filmed in 1959, a mature Audrey Hepburn would play the role once intended for Taylor. Still viewing her as more British than American, MGM also considered starring her in *Now That April's There*, the story of the daughter of an Oxford don living in America who returns with her family to her homeland after the war.

Then there was the prospect of *Young Bess*, the story of the girlhood years of Queen Elizabeth. MGM owned the rights and was aware that its stars Katharine Hepburn and Greer Garson wanted the part. Deborah Kerr was also a candidate. But the studio held off—keeping the project for Elizabeth. But there must have been concern in the studio's executive offices about her youth—especially after she did a screen test for the part—because the film did not go into production. Talk of it continued for years. Finally, in 1953, *Young Bess* was filmed with Jean Simmons in the role. Likewise, Orson Welles wanted to do *Romeo and Juliet* with Taylor and Roddy McDowall; nothing came of that. Warner Bros. also wanted Taylor for the title role in *That Hagen Girl* with Ronald Reagan, but MGM would not lend her out. (Shirley Temple would go on to play the part.) At Warner Bros., Michael Curtiz wanted to do another film with her. After

Curtiz's reputed affair with Sara, there was no way MGM would have wanted him anywhere near any of the Taylors. Finally, the studio settled on *Cynthia*, in which she played a sickly girl whose parents had to learn to let her live a little. Elizabeth and everyone else knew it was lightweight fare—and weaker than any of the other film projects. But *Cynthia* had its charms, mainly because of Elizabeth, and she received a screen kiss from actor Jimmy Lydon.

While Metro continued its search for the right films, Sara and Elizabeth, again without Francis or Howard, sailed to England—her first real vacation in years. During the crossing of the Atlantic, Elizabeth fell ill. On the ocean liner was socialite and political figure Nancy Astor—the former Nancy Witcher Langhorne of Danville, Virginia, who had become the very famous Lady Astor when she married Waldorf Astor, the second Viscount Astor, who was a member of the House of Lords in Britain's Parliament. In 1919, a rather daring Nancy had become the first female member of the House of Commons in Britain's Parliament. Hearing that Elizabeth was not well, the bewitching Lady, who was also a staunch Christian Scientist and may have known Sara during those earlier years in London, visited Elizabeth and tried to help during her recovery. This was one of the early illnesses—said to be due to food poisoning that also affected her mother—that the press reported on. Whether she was actually distressed by the fact that both her parents were not traveling with her was something no one discussed.

In London, mother and daughter stayed at the posh Dorchester hotel, a favorite of Elizabeth's in the years to come. Suddenly, Elizabeth became ill again with a temperature of 104, this time from a virus infection. Once she recovered, Elizabeth saw her godmother, Thelma Cazalet-Keir, and other family friends. She also visited her godfather Victor's estate and the old family home Heathwood.

Upon her return to Los Angeles, the studio had lined up a series of press events for her. Openings. Interviews. Even a trip to Cambridge, Massachusetts, where she was feted by the students at Harvard, who voted her their most popular actress. Twelve hundred and fifty freshmen gave a party in honor of the fifteen-year-old. Some three thousand people attended a special screening of *Cynthia*.

Soon MGM looked almost frantically impatient to cast her in more mature roles, especially after her appearance in *A Date with Judy* in 1948, which starred perpetual teen favorite Jane Powell. The film was shot in Technicolor, and audiences —seeing those dark locks and those violet eyes—were stunned by her ever-developing beauty. Elizabeth worked opposite Robert Stack, and the two made a glorious couple, looking like a young goddess and god who had descended from Mount Olympus to mix with mere mortals. Something else was apparent now. By the age of sixteen, Elizabeth had a 37-inch bust, a 22-inch waist, and 32-inch hips. With her emerging sensuality, she was ready for full-fledged romance on-screen.

Afterward came *Julia Misbehaves*, in which she was cast as the daughter of a divorced British couple, played by the now "older" stars Greer Garson and Walter Pidgeon, who, of course, by the end of the film, were reunited. Playing a tutor secretly in love with Taylor was Peter Lawford. She developed a heavy crush on Lawford that grew rather intense within the next year or so.

During this time, two incidents occurred that looked as if they'd derail Taylor's career. MGM planned to cast her opposite Peter Lawford again in *Sally in Our Alley*, a story with a London setting about a girl who cannot stop smiling at the boys she sees. Apparently, neither Elizabeth nor her mother felt the story was right. Finally, Sara made an appointment to see studio head Louis B. Mayer. The autocratic and dictatorial Mayer had climbed his way from salesman and movie exhibitor to becoming possibly the most powerful man in Hollywood. He felt he knew what was best for everyone at his studio, and he did not sanction the questioning of his authority. Mayer was also the kind of man—strong and assertive, the complete opposite of Francis—who fascinated Sara.

Perhaps Elizabeth wasn't aware of her mother's attraction to Mayer. Regardless, sitting in Mayer's office, Sara expressed her concerns about the proposed movie *Sally in Our Alley.* According to Taylor, when her mother simply asked if Elizabeth was to sing and dance in the film and when she should start to train, Mayer took them by surprise when he became visibly angry. His attitude was that they had no right to question the studio's decisions for Elizabeth's career. Hadn't the studio already made this girl a star? Then he suddenly blew up. "He used the most obscene language," Elizabeth recalled. He told Sara that she was goddamned stupid and " 'wouldn't even know what day of the week it is. Don't try to meddle into my affairs. Don't try to tell me how to make motion pictures. I took you out of the gutter.' " Finally, an enraged Elizabeth had enough.

"Don't you dare speak to my mother like that," she shouted. "You and your studio can both go to hell." Then she ran out of the room. But Sara stayed behind to try to make amends with Mayer. "I was frightened," Elizabeth admitted. "I didn't know whether I'd get into trouble with my parents, whether he was still being rude to my mother, whether I should go back in. I thought for sure you don't tell Louis B. Mayer to go to hell in his own studio. I felt guilty because his yelling didn't justify my being rude to him." But when MGM executive Benny Thau—the studio official she felt closest to—told her to go back and apologize to Mayer, Elizabeth refused. "My dander went right back up again and I said, 'No, he was wrong,I'm not going to apologize to him.' " She never did. Nor was she fired. Nor did she ever return to Mayer's office. Nor did she do *Sally in Our Alley*. That day marked a turning point for the adolescent. Elizabeth was becoming toughened, although not yet the hard-edged woman she would have to be to survive in the industry as an adult. But her independence was growing as well as her awareness of the way the industry worked. Never did she forget that they didn't fire her; that, in essence, she was of value to the studio.

Yet another incident revealed Elizabeth's dissatis-faction, as well as Sara's, with Metro. After *National Velvet*, Elizabeth had assumed the studio would cast her in lead after lead. But in *A Date with Judy*, Jane Powell played the lead while Elizabeth was relegated to a supporting role. Movies like *Cynthia* and *Julia Misbehaves* cast her as a teenaged ingenue, but the films spent much time dramatizing the plight of the parents. Neither of those later two films offered her much of an opportunity to stretch her dramatic muscles. That may have led to Elizabeth's doubts about continuing to act—and that, in turn, may haveled to a serious disagreement between mother and daughter about Elizabeth's career itself. The pressures of always being *on,* always having a schedule that the studio drew up or approved, always having to fight for some private time, were gnawing away at the teenaged Elizabeth. "All day long, some official was telling her what to do and what not to do. She spent all of her pre-adolescent and adolescent days inside the walls of Metro-Goldwyn-Mayer," said her future director George Stevens. "She had no time to play, no contact with other children."

Fed up, Elizabeth was ready to pack it all in and leave the movies altogether. "In the beginning, when she first started, she just loved it more than anything in the world," Sara Taylor remembered. But there came a time when "she was going to school at the studio, and she didn't have friends like the other girls had, going to parties and things, and I think she felt a little sort of left out. When she'd go to parties, they'd all look at her and think, oh, she was different than they were, she was a movie star, and that sort of hurt her." An exasperated Sara realized that her daughter might be serious about giving it all up, and at one point, she knew it was foolish to fight her, to try to convince her otherwise. Sara said, "We had a talk one day, and I said to her, 'Well, honey, it's just up to you. We didn't want you to be in pictures. And we'd be very happy to have you step out right now, and we could go back to our life.' " Neither parent would force her to do something she did not want. "She thought it over and wrote the most beautiful letter. I've kept the letter," recalled Sara. "And she said, 'Mother, I have, I've thought it over, and I couldn't give it up. It would be like cutting off the roots of a tree. It's my life now, and I'll never grumble again about not going to parties like the other girls and not having dates because I realize now, more than ever, how much I love it and how I couldn't give it up.' And she made her own decision. That's when she was 15. But up until that time, she loved it more than anything because it was just her world of make-believe."

Settling into life at the studio with her new perspective, she formed lasting friendships with hairstylist Sydney Guilaroff as well as designer Helen Rose. A native of Chicago, where she was born in 1904, Rose had studied at Chicago's Academy of Fine Arts. Moving to Los Angeles in 1929, she worked at Twentieth Century Fox in the early 1940s, where she designed for musical numbers in the studio's films. She created lush designs for Lena Horne when the singer was on loan to Fox for the all-black musical *Stormy Weather*. In 1943, Rose went to MGM and eventually became the studio's top designer—creating wardrobes for such stars as Ava Gardner and Lana Turner—and won Oscars for *The Bad and the Beautiful* and *I'll Cry Tomorrow*. Later Grace Kelly chose Rose to design her wedding gown when she married Prince Rainier of Monaco. Kelly also asked Guilaroff to create her hairstyle for the wedding. Like Guilaroff, Rose watched Elizabeth grow up. "There was something about Elizabeth that I could communicate with," recalled Rose. "She was young but she was mature, someone that cared. She cared terribly about people. She was very kind to the wardrobe people. Very kind to the make-up people. You know a lot of stars might be wonderful to L. B. Mayer. . . . But when it came to her wardrobe people or the make-up people or anyone who worked with her, she treated them much better than she did Mr. Mayer. And I think that's a wonderful quality because she was always doing some wonderful little things for people."

Elizabeth also came to the defense of Rose during a difficult period at the studio. MGM was like an armed fortress. Gossip, rivalries, feuds ran rampant. But a battery of publicists ensured that in-house secrets and scandals never became known to the general public. When Judy Garland attempted suicide and was replaced by Jane

Powell in MGM's *Royal Wedding*, Rose was suspected of having leaked the story to Hedda Hopper, a strong supporter of Garland. Louis B. Mayer was furious. Rose was then dumped from designing for the picture. It began to look as if she'd be dropped entirely by MGM. "L. B. Mayer wanted me OUT and PAID OFF," said Rose. "My agent told me to go to the studio as if nothing had happened, which I did, but I was not surprised to find myself without an assignment." Word of "my 'disgrace' got around fast and very few people spoke to me. I ate my lunch alone," recalled Rose. She always remembered that "Elizabeth was the only star that stood by me and went to the front office in my behalf. At the time she was still a youngster, but that was Elizabeth—full of spirit as always." Having spoken with Metro executive Benny Thau, Elizabeth assured Rose that "the incident would soon be forgotten." Had it not been for Elizabeth and MGM producer Joe Pasternak, said Rose, "my life on the lot would have been unbearable."

MGM ended up casting Taylor in its big Technicolor remake of Louisa May Alcott's *Little Women*, directed by Mervyn LeRoy, with a cast that included June Allyson, Janet Leigh, Margaret O'Brien, and Elizabeth as the March sisters and with Mary Astor as their mother. Though it would not be compared favorably with the first 1933 version, which had starred Katharine Hepburn as Jo March under George Cukor's direction, the LeRoy version had its charm, and Elizabeth, cast as Amy and wearing a blond wig, played a character who matured from teenager to a well-traveled, beautifully dressed young woman who walks off with her older sister's onetime beau Laurie, played by Peter Lawford. Most of the film focused on the character's younger years, but Taylor handled the transition beautifully.

Still, Elizabeth and Sara knew something had to be done to ensure better roles, to ensure indeed that her career would not fizzle out, as was the case with other child stars. Shrewdly, mother and daughter took their complaints to Hedda Hopper. They let Hopper know that Elizabeth was threatening to break her contract. As dramatic as any of the actresses she covered, Hedda was up in arms over the studio's treatment of Elizabeth. Hopper sprang into action. "Metro may lose Elizabeth Taylor, one of its greatest potential artists," Hopper announced in her July 22, 1948, column. "She won't play second leads in any more 'B' pictures. Elizabeth proved in *National Velvet* that she can act. The studio has bought story after story for her, then promptly shelved them. One was *Green Mansions*. Elizabeth was rushed through a test for *Young Bess* under Vincente Minnelli's direction as though she were a newcomer. Her manager can take advantage of

California's ruling that a minor has the privilege of disavowing a contract if reasons warrant it. I hope this won't happen."

But Hopper did not stop there. The next month she wrote a column entirely about Elizabeth, titled "Girl Star Shines On in Teens." "When Elizabeth Taylor last visited my home I wrote: 'Hollywood's newest moppet star is a 12-year-old girl who can say more with a flash of her wondrous eyes than most veteran actors can put over with a page of dialogue,' " was the way the article opened. "That was about four and a half years ago, but what a metamorphosis. It is breathtaking. Her eyes still have it, but the fellows in her youthful set today describe her with a whistle that is sweet and low and soft. Her delicate expressiveness, together with the beauty that has matured her into a thoroughly ravishing young lady, makes her—in my mind—a potential young [Ingrid] Bergman. In fact, I will go far enough out on the limb to predict that she one day may likely be the No. 1 lady of the screen." Hopper's comparison of Taylor with Bergman was more prophetic than she could have then imagined. Both would become embroiled in major scandals that many predicted would permanently destroy their careers. Both would prove the naysayers wrong.

In her article, Hopper also reported on the teen star's early dates. MGM's juvenile lead Marshall

Thompson had escorted her out—to the premiere of *The Yearling*. Arthur Loew Jr., son of the powerful movie chain owner, also dated her. Among the public, as Hopper shrewdly understood, there was now a growing curiosity—that would intensify in the years to come—about the young beauty's boyfriends and romantic life. The truth of the matter, however, was that most boys her age were afraid to approach her. How do you talk to so beautiful and famous a girl? In fact, Sara was actually relieved when Thompson had asked for a date.

Taylor herself wanted a boyfriend—badly. She recalled that her first crush was on an extremely handsome dark-haired boy named Derek Harris, later to be known as John Derek. But the great crush was on her costar Peter Lawford. Born in London in 1923, Lawford had an aristocratic background, had spent his childhood in France, and was educated by private tutors. In the late 1930s, he began his Hollywood career. Under contract to MGM, he had already appeared in *The White Cliffs of Dover* with Elizabeth, but they had no scenes together. The dark-haired, gentlemanly Lawford, who was a favorite of the ladies, had had well-publicized romances with Lana Turner, Judy Garland, and later a deeply felt but secret romance with African American actress Dorothy Dandridge. "Peter to me," said Taylor, "was the last word in sophistication, and he was so terribly handsome." "She was incredible," said Lawford. "You just couldn't believe it. . . . The nose was perfect, the eyes, everything. I'd be awfully dumb if I said I wasn't attracted to her sexually." He also recalled: "She was coming on strong, batting those beautiful eyes and saying things like 'You love the beach and I love the beach, so why don't we go together one day?' "

His breeding, his looks, his relaxed manner appealed also to Sara, who thought he was a real catch. But Lawford kept his distance. "He was frightened to death," recalled Lillian Burns, the acting coach at MGM, "because she was sixteen years old, and he was afraid of any involvement. He really cared about Elizabeth as a friend, and he was aware that at that age she was really just in love with the idea of love." Lawford himself said: "The word around the studio was that anybody who touched the girl would be banished forever. They didn't want anything to befoul their investment." But another story also made the rounds—that Lawford was more serious than anyone imagined. Interestingly enough, Lawford was also known as being bisexual, something Elizabeth herself was probably aware of, even at so young an age.

Nevertheless, the truth was Elizabeth had no boyfriend. *That* also bothered the studio, which believed that Elizabeth Taylor's image as a young goddess demanded she should have a proper escort. Now the studio publicists stepped in.

Soon the press reported on the first big Taylor romance with Glenn Davis, a West Point graduate well known throughout the country. For MGM, Davis was ideal for Hollywood's princess. Serving in the military and about to go to battle in Korea, Davis was not only athletic—having excelled at West Point in football (cocaptain of the team), track, baseball, and basketball (captain of the team)—but also good-looking, yet not a pretty boy like John Derek or Lawford, and also admired by the masses as a well-mannered, courtly, all-American type. When Davis was in Los Angeles for a special military game, the two had met on the beach near the Taylors' Malibu home, and that very day Davis asked Sara if Elizabeth could attend the football game in which he was playing the next day. Sara approved. Thus was the start of their courtship. Afterward photographs of the two turned up in the papers. The columnists were falling all over themselves to report that Elizabeth wore Davis's small gold football on a chain around her neck. And though Elizabeth was sixteen years old, there were rumors that she and Davis would become engaged. When Davis went off to Korea, Elizabeth was depicted as the typical American girl back home, waiting anxiously for the return of her sweetheart.

Elizabeth may have liked Davis, but she was hardly swept off her feet by him. "Their romance was largely a studio directive," said Hedda Hopper. Upon learning that Davis was in town, someone at MGM got word to him, asking if he'd like to meet Elizabeth Taylor. He quickly said yes. In turn, Elizabeth was informed that Davis wanted to meet her. Though it appeared as if they were constantly in each other's arms in a romantic swoon, the two could count the number of times they were actually *alone* together without the presence of her parents or studio people or friends always nearby. In truth, MGM "pushed it into an engagement, which Elizabeth never wanted. She liked him. He liked her. And they both knew she was too young to marry," said Hopper.

With the romantic side of Elizabeth's life momentarily taken care of, MGM focused again on the right role for her. What the studio came up with surprised everyone. MGM announced plans to shoot a film called *Conspirator*, which explored post–World War II fears and anxieties about the rise of Communism and its infiltration into the national bloodstream. This was a time—the late 1940s into the 1950s—that saw the rise of blacklisting within the entertainment industry; a time when artists who were thought to be Communists or Communist sympathizers were listed in the publication *Red Channels*; an era when industry members were called before the House Un-American Activities Committee (HUAC) to testify about their political activities or friend-ships and the way Communists had infiltrated their ideology into films, radio, and the new medium of television. This was also the time when a group of Hollywood personalities, led by Humphrey Bogart, Lauren Bacall, and others had gone to Washington, DC, to protest government pressure on the industry and the tactics of the HUAC, which pushed performers "to name names" of fellow entertainment figures with Communist ties or sympathies. Though the rise of McCarthyism had not yet peaked, it had begun. The blacklist itself went into effect on November 25, 1947. Touching on the budding paranoia about Communists, *Conspirator* would tell the story of a recently married couple living in England. The young wife discovers her British husband is indeed a Communist agent and a traitor to his country. The role of the husband was to be played by thirty-five-year-old Robert Taylor, who had been in films since the 1930s. The role of the wife was to be played by Elizabeth, age sixteen when filming began. For MGM, *Conspirator* was probably considered a hard-hitting, provocative film.

Conspirator promised to be her real foray into celluloid adulthood. But concerns were expressed that she was simply too young for the part. For one, Hedda Hopper, still seeing Elizabeth as her darling surrogate daughter, had reservations.

When it was announced that following *Conspirator* Taylor would do a film called *The Tender Hours*, Hopper wrote: "And glory be, she'll play a girl of her own age, 17, at last." (*The Tender Hours* was renamed *Two Weeks with Love*, and Elizabeth's part went to Jane Powell.) The press commented on the age difference between the Taylors. Robert Taylor also felt uneasy about appearing as her husband on-screen. The last thing he wanted was to look as if he were robbing the cradle. But none of that stopped MGM from going ahead with the picture.

With the studio's plans to film *Conspirator* in England with a mostly British cast under the direction of Victor Saville, Elizabeth had the chance to return again to the beloved country of her birth. Preparations were made by Sara for the big trip. She would accompany Elizabeth. Francis would stay behind at the gallery. Howard would remain with his father. Sara and Elizabeth would spend Christmas in London; Francis and Howard, in Galveston, Texas, with friends. Francis was no less frustrated than before. But following their earlier brief separation, he and Sara seemed to have reached a truce. And Francis appeared to have become more decisive about what he would and would not allow Sara to do. No way would he ever have the relationship with Elizabeth that he wanted. At times he might assert himself and put his foot down, but there was too much career momentum now to stop it. He also understood that with Sara's awareness of the politics, intrigues, and machinations at MGM, she was in the best position to make the right decisions for their daughter. Still, the situation with Sara could be unbearable, and quiet as it was kept, other separations followed for the couple.

On the day that Elizabeth boarded the ocean liner to sail for England, she had seventeen trunks of luggage with clothes created for her by MGM's Helen Rose. Along with Sara, Elizabeth was accompanied by a publicist and by Melinda Hudgins of the Los Angeles school system, who was her tutor.

Working on *Conspirator* with Robert Taylor at a studio outside London, Elizabeth felt that indeed her career—now as an adult star—was moving forward. An incident occurred, however—another of those freak accidents to which Elizabeth was prone—that caused alarm for everyone. In a scene in which Robert Taylor's character attempted to kill Elizabeth, he shook her so violently that she suddenly doubled up in pain. Immediately, the startled director, Victor Saville, stopped the cameras. As it turned out, Robert Taylor had thrown out a couple of Elizabeth's vertebrae. For months to come, Elizabeth was under the care of an osteopath. Despite the ongoing pain— and it was serious—she kept working.

Like Elizabeth's previous directors, Saville

learned to contend with Sara, who directed Elizabeth as much as he did. Out of camera range, Sara still had her system of hand maneuvers to signal to Elizabeth how a scene should be played. Sara might put a hand to her mouth to indicate more of a smile or a hand to her eyes to indicate more heartfelt emotion. In the evenings, Sara went over lines with her daughter, and the two discussed interpretations of her character. During filming, there also had to be those daily breaks so Elizabeth could study with her tutor. One minute she was in Robert Taylor's arms. The next minute, she was studying math. So professionally did Elizabeth handle it all that no one ever seemed to consider the psychological effects it might have on her.

In England, Elizabeth celebrated her seventeenth birthday. Mother and daughter also saw old family friends, and just as Sara wanted, they socialized with the British upper crust—luncheons, dinners, parties. Elizabeth even presented to Princess Elizabeth, now wed to Prince Philip and the mother of a baby boy, Charles, a baby silver spoon with a rattle on it. For Americans back home reading about the presentation, it looked as if England had its Princess Elizabeth and America had its Princess Elizabeth, too. Constantly meeting new people, always at the center of attention, Elizabeth was impressed with a sophisticated older actor named Michael Wilding. Before long, she had a schoolgirl crush on him. But there was no time for anything serious to develop.

Upon completion of *Conspirator*, Sara and Elizabeth traveled to Paris, where they shopped, saw the sights, and dined at the city's top restaurants. This was Elizabeth's first trip to the city. Her movies had not been shown there, as far as Sara knew, but she saw the effects and power of her daughter's beauty when the two entered a restaurant. "I saw that everyone had stopped eating and was staring at her. It was so embarrassing. Just at that moment the headwaiter approached us and escorted us into another room. As we came in the new room, the same thing happened. People just looked, speechless, unmoving," Sara recalled. "They sat us at a table against the wall. There was a French couple sitting across from us. The man kept staring and staring. Finally, his wife said in French, 'Stop staring at that girl. It is very rude.' The man retorted, 'My dear, it is no more rude to stare at that beautiful creature than it is to stare at the Mona Lisa. It is like looking at a picture.' "

The same happened when the two went shopping while in Paris. People appeared dumbstruck whenever Elizabeth was in their presence. "They would walk right in front of her and argue among themselves about her eyelashes. They would leave and then return and walk around her once more, still staring." Rattled by the attention, Sara led Elizabeth out of the store without buying anything. "I couldn't stand it," said Sara, who turned to her daughter. "It must have made you nervous having those people staring at you," she said. "Elizabeth, however, didn't take it that way at all. She was absolutely calm. She said, 'No, it's just that they wanted to be friendly.' I've always been so delighted Elizabeth could take her beauty so for granted."

But this was just the beginning of the worldwide attention her daughter's looks would draw. As producer Sam Marx had said: "She's like an eclipse of the sun, blotting out everyone." "In person her beauty was even more breathtaking than on screen. It was not uncustomary to gasp a little when you first saw her," recalled Dominick Dunne. "I didn't want to stop staring at her." Elizabeth herself had already managed to disregard it all, to accept reactions to her beauty and especially her fame itself simply as a part of her being. "I can't remember when I wasn't famous," she once told Dunne. He and so many others believed she wore her fame like a second skin. That would enable her to survive. But her beauty and her fame would be disconcerting to others around her, especially to the men who would soon be in and out of her life.

In the States, Metro's publicity department fed the press stories about *Conspirator* as well as future movies for Elizabeth. Already MGM was touting the epic *Quo Vadis* as her next film, which would costar Gregory Peck and be directed by John Huston in Italy. In this ancient Rome drama about the persecution of early Christians—which would cost the then huge sum of $6 million, the equivalent today would be well over $58 million—she would play Lygia, a woman who is loved by a Roman soldier but will not renounce her Christianity. Afterward, she would film *Father of the Bride* back at Metro. Studio publicists kept the publicity rolling. She was selected honorary queen of the Miss Junior America Pageant. New York's Fashion Academy had named Elizabeth the best-dressed teenager in America. Throughout the 1950s and early 1960s, she was a young style icon who was dazzling in evening wear—the low-cut, full-skirted gowns that emphasized her small waist and ample bosom, showcasing a voluptuousness few could match. Ongoing items appeared in the columns about her romance with Glenn Davis. When Elizabeth had turned seventeen in London, Davis had sent her a set of pearls, and he hired Philip Paval to create a necklace and earring set for her. By now the fan magazines *Photoplay* and *Modern Screen* were covering her every move. Having watched Taylor grow up, the public, much like the studio, was impatient to see her reach adulthood. Elizabeth herself was beginning to feel the same way.

Returning to the States after seven months, Elizabeth and her mother were joined by Francis for a trip to the Miami home of Howard Young. Visiting Elizabeth there was Glenn Davis. As much as Elizabeth, he must have felt himself caught up in a publicized non-romance over which he had no real control. But the attention excited him, and soon there were stories that he would give her an engagement ring. By late March 1949, he accompanied Elizabeth to the Academy Awards ceremony, where photographers had a field day. But by the next month, Elizabeth, apparently weary of the charade, declared her romance with Davis was over. Briefly, the focus shifted to Elizabeth's new escort Lawrence Sheerin. Then talk of that non-relationship fizzled out.

In 1949, *Little Women* was released to mostly good reviews. Though nothing of *Quo Vadis* had been shot, the talk again was about the forthcoming epic. No less than *Time* magazine interviewed Elizabeth with the tantalizing prospect that she'd be put on the cover, apparently in anticipation of *Quo Vadis*. Because of plans for *Quo Vadis*, MGM even announced that Elizabeth would not be in *Father of the Bride*. Instead, the role of the daughter would be played by Jane Powell, and the role of the father by Jack Benny. Elizabeth was set to fly to Rome on June 6 to start filming *Quo Vadis*. Then something happened that the studio had not expected. During another visit to Miami, her uncle Howard introduced her to William Pawley Jr., the son of the wealthy former ambassador to Brazil. Sparks flew. In no time, Elizabeth and Pawley were a couple.

Elizabeth seemed to have really fallen under the sway of the well-bred, tall, darkly handsome, blue-eyed Pawley. In the minds of Uncle Howard, Sara, *and* the press, his family's background and great wealth made Pawley a picture-perfect boyfriend. He had also been a decorated US Army pilot. Photographs ran in one newspaper after another of the two glamorously decked out in swimsuits as they were about to take a dip in the Pawley family pool. Francis may have watched the proceedings with exasperation, keenly aware of a basic fact that everyone else chose to overlook or ignore: Bill Pawley was twenty-eight years old. Elizabeth was seventeen. Still a schoolgirl, she was relieved that she didn't have to take her tutor with her when she visited Pawley in Miami—because school was out for the summer! The romance blossomed all the more when *Quo Vadis* was postponed after Gregory Peck became ill. Word of the film's postponement apparently led *Time* to back off from putting Elizabeth on its cover. Then Hedda Hopper broke the really big news: Elizabeth and William Pawley were formally engaged. The wedding, however, couldn't be planned right away because Elizabeth would not graduate from high school until the next February. In fact, once she had returned from Miami, Elizabeth went back to school for the rest of the summer, making up for time she had lost while in England. If she got in those courses now, she wouldn't have to wait until the following June to finish high school. MGM changed its plans, too, and Elizabeth was put back into *Father of the Bride* with Spencer Tracy and Joan Bennett. The studio shrewdly understood that *Father of the Bride* might benefit from all the possible future coverage of a Taylor-Pawley wedding.

Amid all this media speculation over possible nuptials for the young star, over at Paramount negotiations had begun with MGM to star Elizabeth in director George Stevens's adaptation of Theodore Dreiser's powerful, classic novel *An American Tragedy*, eventually to be called *A Place in the Sun*. The film would dramatize the story of a young man torn between two women: one an alluring wealthy girl, the other a drab working-class young woman. When the latter is tragically drowned, the young man is arrested and then tried for killing her. Stevens was a major filmmaker, whose career stretched back to silents when he had directed Laurel and Hardy shorts and further developed with his direction of such classics as *Alice Adams* with Katharine Hepburn,

Swing Time with Fred Astaire and Ginger Rogers, *The More the Merrier* with Joel McCrea and Jean Arthur, and the moving *I Remember Mama* with Irene Dunne. Stevens—deeply affected by the devastation he saw when he toured war-torn Europe—was in a new phase of his career, moving away from comedies and seemingly lighter fare to films with more adult themes and a darker vision of America. The key role of the tormented young man in this Paramount picture was to be played by the New York–based actor Montgomery Clift, then the hottest young dramatic actor on the scene. Elizabeth's role—that of the wealthy Angela Vickers—would be far more challenging than anything she had ever done, and it might put her in the front ranks of postwar dramatic film actresses.

None of this seemed to matter to Metro, which refused to lend her out for a Paramount film. Because she was now too hot a "commodity" to be left idle—no young star was getting this kind of press coverage—MGM wanted to keep her working almost nonstop in its productions and informed her that while waiting for *Father of the Bride* to go into production, she would film the comedy *The Big Hangover*, to be directed by Norman Krasna and to costar Van Johnson. By anyone's estimation a slight picture, *The Big Hangover* told the story of a man whose allergy to alcohol keeps getting him into "comic" hassles.

Elizabeth was to play his girlfriend. But having read the script for *A Place in the Sun*, Elizabeth—and Sara—had other ideas. The opportunity to work with Stevens and Clift was too important to pass up. While Stevens continued negotiations with Metro, Elizabeth and Sara campaigned for *A Place in the Sun*. Finally, the studio agreed to the loan-out, mainly it was said because MGM wanted Paramount actor John Lund for one of its films. It was also said that there had been confusion as to which role Taylor would play. MGM did not want her to play the poor girl. The part of Angela Vickers was acceptable.

Then the August 22, 1949, issue of *Time* hit the newsstands—with seventeen-year-old Elizabeth gracing its cover—and took the industry by surprise. Magazine covers, of course, were nothing new to Elizabeth. Already she had graced the cover of *Life*, which represented glamour and signaled a star's impact on the public and the industry. A *Life* cover would always be treasured by Hollywood. *Look* magazine, not quite as prestigious as *Life* but just as glamorous, was important also, and it, too, would feature Elizabeth on covers now and in the years to come. But a *Time* cover meant something entirely different. Usually, *Time* cover stories were on political figures or world leaders or great artists, seemingly "serious" personalities. A cover with an entertainer meant that the performer had put an impressive stamp on the culture at a point in history and sometimes that the performer was such a cultural force that even those who had never seen a performance by the star were nonetheless aware of the performer. It was another level of influence and prestige.

Within Henry Luce's Time Life publishing empire, editors maintained close ties with the studios, which were always pitching story ideas, primarily for *Life*. When MGM learned of *Time*'s upcoming story on the new postwar Hollywood stars, certainly the studio pushed for coverage of its stars. What may have helped Elizabeth land on the cover was *Life*'s ongoing interest in her, which indeed was shared with *Time*'s editors. Then, too, MGM clearly saw her as the wave of the future and no doubt conveyed that belief to the magazine.

Focusing on Hollywood's postwar shifts, the *Time* story pointed out that such veteran stars as Clark Gable, Joan Crawford, Spencer Tracy, Bette Davis, Gary Cooper, Marlene Dietrich, James Cagney, Barbara Stanwyck, Humphrey Bogart, and Claudette Colbert, whose careers stretched back to the early 1930s, now faced challenges as they grew older and as audience tastes changed. No longer was the public rushing "by the millions to see a picture merely because one of them [the older stars] is in it," the magazine stated. The same was true for such other seasoned stars as

Errol Flynn, Irene Dunne, Robert Taylor, Greer Garson, Hedy Lamarr, even Mickey Rooney. Such performers as Bing Crosby, Bob Hope, Betty Grable, Tyrone Power, Jimmy Stewart, Olivia de Havilland, and Joan Fontaine were "still-bright." "But the public, according to an experienced Hollywoodsman, is scanning the marquees for new names."

Among the new stars that *Time* pointed out were Ava Gardner, Kirk Douglas, Jane Greer, Shelley Winters, Richard Widmark, Robert Ryan, Ruth Roman, Mel Ferrer, and Audrey Totter, some of whom would live up to *Time*'s star-watch forecast, others who would be forgotten by later generations. Of the bright lights for the future, the magazine felt two stood above the rest and had the goods for huge movie careers. One was Montgomery Clift.

The other bright light—the brightest, in fact—was Elizabeth, whom *Time* believed could develop into one of the greatest movie stars. So much of America already seemed to be in a swoon over her. Midshipmen at Annapolis had voted her "The Girl We'd Abandon Ship For." At Harvard, she was "The Girl We'll Never Lampoon." At MGM, a photographer had told her: "I thought you'd like to know that the boys have voted you the most beautiful woman they have ever photographed." Taylor's response: "Mother! Did you hear what he said? He called me a woman!" Now being paid $1,000 a week, she would earn $1,500 a week the next year. An MGM executive estimated she was a "property" valued at "$50,000,000, maybe even $100,000,000." Today's equivalent would be just about a billion dollars.

"Elizabeth's womanly beauty usually makes strangers forget that she is, after all, only a youngster," *Time* commented, "but her behavior quickly reminds them of it. Beneath her breathtaking face there is scarcely a symptom of sophistication. But Elizabeth, for all her youngish ways, is a purposeful girl in a way that Hollywood admires: she is feverishly ambitious to make a success in pictures." Actually, she was far more sophisticated than the magazine realized. Her *feverish ambition* was tied to a sophistication that even she may have been unaware of. The magazine informed readers that the forthcoming *Conspirator* would spotlight Elizabeth in a more womanly role.

Time's cover story made the entire entertainment industry all the more aware that this teenager was a power player. But despite all this fanfare and the attention, MGM itself seemed to be dropping the ball. To put her in *The Big Hangover*, a routine picture at best, seemed to both waste and exploit her. A great star would need important films. Stevens's *A Place in the Sun* might be one. But it was for Paramount, not

Metro. In the meantime, *Conspirator*, despite the publicity, was hardly causing excitement at the studio, which held up the release of the film. The truth was that she was simply too young for the role.

"Elizabeth was a bit of a worry then to all of us," said MGM producer Pandro S. Berman. "We recognized her beauty, but she didn't have the strength of voice at sixteen or the personality to go with her face." Berman said that later she became "a great technician, a great actress, and a great businesswoman, but at sixteen she was half child, half adult, and she was actually not as good an actress as she had been at the beginning making *Courage of Lassie* or *Life with Father*." Or, of course, *National Velvet*.

The press corps—as breathless about her as a love-struck teenager—continued to follow her engagement to Pawley as the couple commuted between LA and Miami to see each other. When not together, the two wrote letters in which Elizabeth poured out her heart to him. But despite their passion for one another, Pawley never understood Hollywood. And basic questions surfaced. Where would they live? What would he do professionally if in Los Angeles? Then, too, her schedule would keep them apart. As soon as she completed one film, the studio had her set to begin another.

Then, on September 3, an odd item appeared in Hedda Hopper's column. "Bill Pawley Jr. had better return here in a hurry or his Elizabeth Taylor might transfer her romantic interest elsewhere. A local millionaire, who has not been without publicity, is wooing her—but so secretly." Who was Hopper referring to? Sixteen days later, on September 19, Hopper announced that the three-month engagement to Pawley was over. Pawley told Hopper: "I love her very much and I believe she loves me, but due to the distance, her constant work, which all her energy should go into, I feel the only fair thing is to release her from her engagement." Hoping the broken engagement was temporary, Pawley may never have really gotten over the fact that she never came back to him. In fact, on the day of her first marriage, he reportedly arrived at the Taylor home and advised her not to marry. To most of the Taylor family, he must have looked like he was half out of his mind. But Pawley carried a torch for her for years. "He told me he couldn't bring himself to marry anyone until twenty-five years after the split," said a friend of Pawley's. He kept her love letters almost until the end of his life. After Taylor's death, the letters were sold at an auction in 2011. He died a year later, in July 2012.

As the press once again deliriously covered her romantic life, a new media image was being crafted for Taylor. Now she was depicted as spoiled, rather thoughtless, and immature, something of a ruthless, self-centered heartbreaker. No one had forgotten the way she had "broken off" her "romance" with Glenn Davis—the young man who was serving in Korea. Now, no matter what Pawley himself said, everyone felt Elizabeth had duped him, that she had grown bored and moved on to someone else, whoever that might be.

By the next month, the talk was about Elizabeth and her costar in *A Place in the Sun*, Montgomery Clift. Born in 1920 (with a twin sister) and raised by his mother to be something of an aristocrat, Clift and his brother and sister were homeschooled and later had private tutors in the States and in Europe. Once Clift went to actual school, he couldn't completely adjust. At age fifteen, he started acting on the New York stage in such productions as *There Shall Be No Night* with theater legends Alfred Lunt and Lynn Fontanne and later in Thornton Wilder's *The Skin of Our Teeth* with Tallulah Bankhead. Strikingly handsome, with green eyes, chiseled features, and a slight but taut build, Clift would be the most intense actor Elizabeth had ever worked with. Schooled in the Method to use personal experiences to develop his characters and also to question every move and gesture of the characters he played, Clift could become so immersed in his roles that he seemed unable to turn his characters off at the end of a play or a scene for a film. Stars like Spencer Tracy and Anne Revere took their work seriously and had their own techniques for creating a character; of course, those actors no doubt took their characters home with them, but it wasn't as apparent as it was with Clift. Instead, he lived the part twenty-four hours a day. Having already appeared in Fred Zinnemann's *The Search* and Howard Hawks's *Red River*, in which he had held his own with veteran John Wayne, Clift had turned down long-term studio contracts, and in this age *before* Marlon Brando, James Dean, and Paul Newman had made it to the movies, Clift was viewed as a rebel—and a brilliant one ushering in a whole new acting style for the movies.

When Taylor and Clift met, sparks immediately flew. For Elizabeth, the striking good looks were one thing; the burning sensitivity was another. His mastery of his craft impressed her. So did his intellect. Clift responded to her gentleness, her intelligence, her sensitivity, her desire to learn more, and her youthful exuberance. She wanted to enjoy life, not brood over it, to experience it, not to hold back and simply analyze it. Like everyone else, he was stunned by her beauty, yet he wouldn't let that beauty have a power over him. Or so he tried. His nickname for her was Bessie Mae.

Chapter 6

GORDY'S BELIEF IN the boys was soon fulfilled. The very first song of theirs that Gordy released in October 1969, "I Want You Back," became a number one hit. So did the three songs that followed: "ABC," released in February 1970; "The Love You Save," in May 1970; and "I'll Be There," August 1970. Written by Berry Gordy, Hal Davis, Willie Hutch, and Bob West, "I'll Be There" took Michael in a different direction. Rather than an energetic pop tune about puppy love, "I'll Be There" was a soulful ballad, dramatically intense, full of yearning and regret for a love gone wrong yet a love that will never die. "He better be good to you," Michael sang with the promise that no matter what, he'd be ready to rush to the girl's side. While record buyers marveled at his intensity on that song, Michael—aged eleven—was winging it emotionally, singing of emotions he had not yet experienced. Much like sixteen-year-old Elizabeth Taylor when MGM cast her as the wife of Robert Taylor in *Conspirator*, he was being pushed into feelings and relationships (in songs) that he didn't yet understand. Later he admitted he didn't know what he was doing. But somehow intuitively he had dipped into emotions he didn't know he had and temporarily brought them to the forefront to perform a heartfelt rendition. The same happened with their future song "Never Can Say Goodbye."

Now came a whirlwind of appearances. Still promoted as Diana Ross's protégés, the brothers' friendship with Ross, especially Michael's, was used to the benefit of all concerned. The group opened for Ross at Los Angeles's Inglewood Forum, and the Jackson 5's very first national television appearance was as guests when Ross hosted TV's *The Hollywood Palace*, on October 18, 1969. In December 1969, their first album, *Diana Ross Presents the Jackson 5*, was released. But perhaps the appearance—one without Ross— with the greatest impact was on *The Ed Sullivan Show*. Having introduced the Beatles to American television, Sullivan's program could guarantee a huge viewership and also signal a new act's full ascension to stardom. Dressed in vests and bell-bottom pants with hats, and dancing as they sang, the boys—appearing on December 14, 1969—were a sensation. The studio audience and viewers at home went wild. More records hit the top of the charts. Tours followed. Throughout, teenaged girls screamed, shouted, cried, and ran after the brothers with a frenzy not that different from Beatlemania. In fact, the

wild enthusiasm of the group's fans was sometimes referred to as Jacksonmania. At one early
engagement at the Spectrum arena in Philadelphia,
almost en masse, fans jumped from their seats,
rushing down the aisles to the stage. Fearing the
stage might collapse, security quickly got the
boys off it. The concert had to be stopped.

But what neither Motown nor anyone else
could have predicted was that in the midst of all
this, Michael was experiencing one of his first
obsessions, which was indeed Diana Ross. He
observed her closely: the way she lived in high
Hollywood style with a swanky home, the way
she dressed, the way she spoke, the way she
laughed, even the way she made herself up. For
Michael, Ross was larger than life, not a mere
mortal but a real goddess who didn't look, think,
or act like other people.

In Ross he found someone he could learn from,
and not just about show business. Little was said
about Michael's interest in art, but he liked to
paint, not only as a way to express himself
artistically but also to decompress. He may have
thought about those strange, rare occasions in
Gary when his father painted in the living room of
the family home. Jermaine recalled that much as
the very young Michael had yearned to paint,
his father never shared the experience with his
children. With Ross, it was entirely different.
"Diana loved art and encouraged me to appre-

ciate it, too. She took the time to educate me about it," Michael recalled. "We'd go out almost every day, just the two of us, and buy pencils and paint. When we weren't drawing or painting we'd go to museums." Recalling the way she exposed him to "great artists like Michelangelo and Degas," which "was really different from what I was used to doing, which was living and breathing music, rehearsing day in and day out." For Michael, Ross became a kind of everywoman. "She was my mother, my lover, and my sister all combined into one person," he said. "She was the perfect mentor for Michael because he instantly adored her," recalled Jermaine. But the other brothers were also entranced by her.

In time, he even "appropriated Diana Ross' early '70s speaking voice, an uncertain, shy, slightly way of communicating," said Ross's biographer Randy Taraborrelli. There was also an eerie story told by a chauffeur who said that once while driving Michael through Beverly Hills, he addressed him as Michael and Michael insisted, "Please, call me Miss Ross." "So I did," said the chauffeur.

But whatever obsession Michael had with Ross couldn't be so great because, in essence, as a budding star himself, he would mainly have to obsess on himself. No great star can ever reach the pinnacle of stardom without layers of self-absorption. And so it would be with Michael.

Michael also learned much from Berry Gordy. The consummate businessman and a master showman, Gordy understood how to make a deal, how to nurture talent, how to bring that talent before the public eye and to do it with the kind of ease and finesse that Joseph Jackson lacked. Joseph was crude. Gordy was smooth. Joseph had little, if any, interest in what his children thought. Gordy expressed interest in Michael's ideas. Michael wasn't unaware of Gordy's reputation for being callous and calculating and perhaps unethical with his performers, but he chose to focus on Gordy's skills. In a short period of time, Gordy was a father figure, the kind of understanding, patient paternal figure that Joseph could never be. He was willing to relax with the boys and play games like backgammon. Or have chess matches with them. None of this was lost on Joe, who certainly had mixed feelings about the Motown chieftain. For Joe, nothing was ever supposed to come between his children and himself and their mother. But he needed Gordy.

With the hits lighting up the charts, the very late 1960s and early 1970s were heady years for the brothers, as they became teen idols for millions—black and white—across the nation. With the exception only of Diana Ross and the Supremes, they had crossed over in a way that even the most talented and successful of Motown stars had not.

And their huge popularity indicated yet another significant shift in American culture. Their posters were on bedroom walls. Their style—the flashy colorful outfits and hats and especially the big Afros that Jackie, Jermaine, and Michael all took such pride in—became fashion statements not only for adolescents but also for prepubescent kids. Their fans tended to have their own favorites among the brothers. Jackie was the handsome Don Juan. Jermaine was a somewhat serious heartthrob, seemingly not as experienced or yet as confident as his older brother but on his way. Tito seemed to be the most mature and settled. Marlon was the good dancer and backup, sometimes appearing as if he was giving his all to be more than simply someone who looked as if he just might be along for the ride. And Michael, of course, was the all-around favorite because he did what no child his age could do: he was a terrific, passionate singer and splendidly coordinated dancer with the perfect baby face and an impish innocence that endeared him to young and old alike.

In the past, music stars like Little Richard, Chuck Berry, Martha and the Vandellas, Marvin Gaye, Stevie Wonder, and Mary Wells might have been viewed as favorites of rebellious youth, in opposition to their parents' tastes and outlooks. But the Jackson 5, in many respects, were being embedded in both the cultural revolution of the late 1960s *and* the establishment. But no one thought or cared about that. Viewing the brothers as playmates or classmates or buddies for their children, parents didn't seem frightened or intimidated by these wholesome youngsters—the way they would be later with the rise of rap or even with the sexy spirit of disco that would soon appear in the mid-1970s. Family appeal and acceptance was always an important aspect of the Jackson 5's success. The same would be true of Michael himself once he had gone out on his own.

Mainstream media paid attention in a new way, too. Newspapers flocked to interview them. So did the big magazines. *Jet* and *Ebony* ran cover stories that were important in getting the word out to the black community, also in promoting a wholesome, upwardly mobile image of the group. The September 1970 *Ebony* featured the brothers on the cover. Four years later, the December 1974 *Ebony* cover had a photograph of the entire family, all nine children with their parents. It looked like a model family unit. Of course, *Ebony* and *Jet* covers might be expected for a successful black group. But seemingly unattainable was a *Life* cover, which had not had a black entertainer on its cover until Dorothy Dandridge's appearance in November 1954. Afterward, occasionally other black stars would grace the magazine's cover, yet not many. No Motown stars had gone that far until *Life* featured the brothers—with their parents—on the cover on September 24, 1971. A year later the woman publicized as having discovered the kids, Diana Ross, turned up on the cover of the December 8, 1972 issue. When *Rolling Stone* covered the group for its April 29, 1971 issue, it chose to run Michael alone on the cover with the tagline that read: "Why does this eleven-year-old stay up past his bedtime?" An animated television show for kids called *The Jacksons* aired in the summer of 1976, which was a true family affair that also featured Rebbie, La Toya, Randy, and Janet. Originally a four-week show, *The Jacksons* returned for an additional run in the spring of 1977. For a Motown act, theirs had an unprecedented level of success.

They also came face-to-face with racism during a tour that took them to Mobile, Alabama. While being driven to their hotel, they endured the hostile attitude of their white limousine driver, who refused to remove their luggage from the car. Once the brothers opened the trunk to pick up the luggage, there was, said Jermaine, "Ku Klux Klan paraphernalia, clearly intended for our eyes." Inside the hotel, no bellhop helped with the luggage. At the receptionist desk, they were told there were no reservations for them, which, of course, was untrue. Traveling with them and handling their business was Motown's Suzanne de Passe, who put her foot down. In the end, they got rooms but hardly the top-of-the-line accommodations they were now accustomed to.

As the fame and the wealth of the Jacksons expanded, Michael also saw the racism it drew out. He remembered an incident that occurred when his mother was driving a Mercedes from a market in Encino where she had shopped. A white man shouted out to her: "Go back to Africa, you nigger." Michael said, "It hurt me so much that that happened to my mother." Other times, he said, when his brothers would park their Rolls-Royces in a public area, they would return to find "that some guy had taken a key and scratched the car because there is a black man driving it."

Still, throughout all the acclaim and attention, as well as the hassles and humiliations, onstage the brothers were pros. Offstage, they were wide-eyed, energetic, playful, mischievous kids. While on tour, their hotels became their playgrounds. Leading the pack was Michael, a born prankster who loved dropping water balloons outside the hotel windows. All the brothers relished pillow fights, playing jokes on room service, running through the hallways and corridors yelling, yapping, laughing, joking. As Jackie and Jermaine grew older, their hormones raging, they were soon sneaking girls into their hotel rooms, and sometimes Michael hid under beds while Jermaine set out to score with a girl. Often there to super-vise the boys was Suzanne de Passe. On tour also was their tutor Rose Fine, who in her long career had taught such other showbiz kids as Ron Howard, Annette Funicello, and Jodie Foster. Fine somehow managed to sit the boys down for their lessons. Much as it had been with Elizabeth, Michael had to switch gears, maneuvering his way from a world of adult responsibilities to one in which he was a kid again, calm and collected, to study and learn about a world outside show business.

Michael came to love Rose Fine dearly. In fact, all the brothers and the rest of the family, including Janet and La Toya, were fond of her. She was a middle-aged woman who refused to tell anyone her age. The kids knew, though, that she was married and had a daughter and also a grown son, a doctor who had studied at Harvard. He died young, and it devastated Rose and her husband. Warm and friendly, she traveled with the brothers from the time of their first professional tour until Michael was eighteen. Never was she a detached, stern schoolmarm. During all those lonely times on the road—when Michael was away from Katherine, whom he always missed— she gave him motherly comfort. When Rose saw that he was terrified of air travel, she would try to alleviate his fears by holding his hand. After a performance, "I would run to the room," he said. "We'd read and have warm milk and I eeded that so badly. She would always say to me, 'The door's open,' and she would leave her door open."

His education would be spotty. Daily, he had three hours of schoolwork. Rose taught all the basic subjects, such as English and arithmetic. She was a dedicated teacher whom he admired and always credited as the one "who instilled in me a love of books and literature." "I read everything I could get my hands on." La Toya recalled that Michael's room at home would be lined with books on all types of subjects. His favorite topics: philosophy and biography. Interesting him most were the lives of every "great artist, businessman, and inventor that ever was." Puzzling him was why some such remarkable figures self-destructed. Clearly fascinating him, as time moved on, was the decline of Elvis Presley. Nonetheless, he never forgot her, and years later he and his sister Janet took financial care of Rose "until the day she died." Afterward, he and Janet provided for her husband.

Everything grew bigger and grander for the entire family, who moved to a twelve-room house on Bowmont Drive, just north of Beverly Hills. Then in May 1971, there came the really big move to Hayvenhurst in Encino, California. Though their new home was described by Jermaine as "a bland one-story ranch-style property" with typical 1970s decor, the place was far from chopped liver, and it thrilled its new occupants with its flag-stoned patio, where breakfast was served, and its lemon and orange trees. The family could take a swim in its pool. Or play basketball on their own private court. Inside was a sunken living room and a spiral staircase that fascinated the family. There were also six bedrooms. Everyone felt that, unlike the home in Gary, now they could breathe and live with some privacy, although they still shared bedrooms. They were also protected from prying eyes. Jermaine recalled: "Back then, Hayvenhurst sat behind the wrought-iron rails of an electric gate—the start of life lived behind gates."

Despite the money and the public adulation, Joseph and Katherine worked hard to keep the children as normal as possible. Each Jackson child had chores. Each had an allowance of five dollars a week. Money shouldn't be wasted. "Joseph even installed a pay-phone," said Jermaine.

Religion remained an important part of the children's lives. On Sundays, the children and Katherine still attended church together. Michael valued the fellowship and feeling of normalcy when at church, where everyone was treated in the same way.

Michael also continued—now and in the years to come—what was termed the church's "pioneering" missionary work on Sundays. With his mother, he would still go door to door in the California suburbs and in the malls to sell copies of *The Watchtower*. Because of his fame, Michael donned disguises. He sometimes wore fat suits, fake facial hair, wigs. His soft voice might have been a giveaway, though no one seemed to notice except children, who would follow him. Michael enjoyed their attention and said he felt like the Pied Piper of Hamelin, that figure of German folklore and legend who during the Middle Ages had played his pipe and led the rats of the plague-stricken area to follow him out of the city. When the mayor of Hamelin refused to pay him for his services, he played his pipe again and led the children of the area away. For Michael, the Pied Piper was a humane hero to the innocent young. Regardless, he enjoyed such excursions where he believed he saw in the homes where he sold *The Watchtower* another side of life, totally removed from the show business atmosphere that was enveloping him.

Yet attending church services and the "pioneering" work became increasingly more difficult because of the brothers' schedules and their travels. Michael, however, could never leave his religion behind. It was too instilled in him.

By now, Michael was immersed more than ever in the world of entertainment, its history, its transitions, its icons. Sometimes stars have knowledge only of the entertainers they have grown up watching. Sometimes, shockingly, they have no sense or much interest in a long history of entertainment of which they were a part. That was not true of Michael. He couldn't learn enough about movies, music, television, theater. To a certain extent, this was true of all the Jackson children, who, to their credit, were aware of past entertainers, past entertainment milestones, and landmarks. During these years and in those that followed, Michael remained eager to learn as much as he could and to meet those whose talent had dazzled him. At home, he remained a playful, spunky kid, still playing tricks on his siblings, performing magic acts for his mother, fascinated again by the power of illusion.

But for Michael and his brothers, the simple pleasures of home and heart were few and far between. Mostly, it was business as usual: rehearsing (under the unforgiving eyes of Joseph), perfecting new dance steps (often under the choreography of Jackie), mastering new songs, touring, and spending long hours in recording studios. But in the mid-1970s the Jackson 5 faced new career challenges.

Gradually vanishing was that political fervor of the late 1960s, those days of youthful rebellion and student revolt, of a fundamental questioning of America's traditional values and virtues. The protests against the war in Vietnam and the national outrage about the Watergate scandal that led to the resignation of President Richard M. Nixon ultimately gave way to a more relaxed time, a period of both personal examination and escapism. The stormy years of Nixon would be replaced first by the relief and relative calm of the Gerald Ford years, then the short-lived optimism of the Jimmy Carter era. If anything, there appeared, in the mid- and late 1970s, a desire to forget the woes of the world, to withdraw from the demands of social and political issues, to retreat from all those complicated dilemmas—basic inequities and injustices in the system—that had propelled the young of the past decade. Described by Tom Wolfe as the "Me" Decade, the 1970s indeed shaped up as an era when a new generation looked inward rather than outward. Self-analysis. Self-awareness. Staying fit. Eating healthy. Jogging. Exercising. Practicing Transcen-dental Meditation. Taking control of one's body and mind. All seemed to characterize the period.

By the early 1970s, popular music started to change, reflecting the nation's altered mood swings and the more relaxed social atmosphere. Within a few years, a new generation danced and dreamed to the tune of disco that dominated the airways and the music charts. Recording artists like Donna Summer, Alicia Bridges, and Labelle or a group like Chic became favorites of the young. To stay on top meant the Jackson 5 had to musically reinvent themselves. The days of delicious bubblegum soul and that stream of one-hit-right-on-the-heels-of-another was gone. Berry Gordy himself may have believed the group might not have a long shelf life. It had happened with any number of acts at Motown and other music companies. That was the nature of popular culture: music that was direct and immediate to one generation often became dated and then discarded by the next. But Gordy felt differently about Michael, whom he persuaded in 1971 to record a solo record, "Got to Be There," which became a huge hit. Jermaine also recorded a single. In 1972, Michael had another solo hit with the song "Ben," recorded for the movie of that same title. A love ballad of sorts—the tale of a dying boy who felt his pet rat, Ben, was his only friend—"Ben" was a precursor to some of Michael's future romantic songs. So successful was he—in communicating youthful angst in matters of the heart—that "Ben" was nominated for an Oscar for Best Original Song for the picture. Jackson performed it at the Academy Awards ceremony, held in 1973.

Michael had four solo albums—*Got to Be There* and *Ben*, in 1972; *Music & Me*, in 1973; and *Forever, Michael,* in 1975. The latter two were commercial disappointments. Jackson, however, held off from a solo career, part of his reluctance growing out of concern about his family's reaction. Joe Jackson was determined that Michael succeed *with* his brothers. So the Jackson 5 *had* to survive in this new era. Working hard to come up with a new sound, the group was successful, in late 1973, with the thumping and rousingly sexy disco hit "Dancing Machine." Two years later, they had another disco hit "Forever Came Today." But these hits seemed like exceptions in the drift of their career. Joe Jackson and his sons saw a wall standing in front of them. That wall was Motown. No longer was Motown able to consistently come up with songs for them that marched to the beat of the times. The Jackson 5 had to create another beat, another rhythm that would mark a new maturity or outlook to match that of their evolving fan base. The group had to perform music that could lead the brothers into young adulthood—with their fans right by their side. Of all the brothers, Michael was most vocal about their professional dilemma.

But compounding Michael's professional frustrations were personal ones. By 1974, his brothers Tito, Jackie, and Jermaine had all married. Marlon would wed in 1975. No longer was there that daily brotherly camaraderie that had meant so much. "An understandable change occurred as each of them became closest to his wife and *they* became a family unit unto themselves. A part of me wanted us to stay as we were—brothers who were also best friends—but change is inevitable and always good in one sense or another," Michael said. Especially hard for him was the situation with Jermaine, who had married Berry Gordy's daughter Hazel in 1973 and thus was bound, in some way or another, to side with his father-in-law once there was any showdown with Motown.

In the mid-1970s something else ate at and depressed Michael as he experienced the pangs and torments of adolescence. Uppermost on his mind was his appearance, which he felt was marred by a terrible case of acne. "I got very shy and became embarrassed to meet people because my complexion was so bad," he said. "The effect on me was so bad that it messed up my whole personality. I couldn't look at people when I talked to them. I'd look down, or away." It became hard to go out because he would have to face people. He drastically changed his diet, eliminating greasy foods. "That was the key," he said. For someone who grew up enjoying fast food, it wasn't easy. Later he stopped eating meat altogether.

Michael also agonized over his features. Jermaine recalled that Michael hated his nose. "It widened noticeably," Jermaine commented. Not helping matters were family taunts about his looks. Michael was dubbed "Big Nose" by his brothers *and* his father. "Hey, Big Nose, come over here," said Joseph. All of this led to Michael's later plastic surgery. (In fact, the first thing he would have done would be rhinoplasty, which was performed by the physician Steven Hoefflin.)

In time, the other Jacksons also changed their looks.

By 1974, everyone knew that as the youngest member of the group, Michael was also artistically the strongest and, surprisingly, perhaps *personally* the strongest. Realizing that the rest of the family was denying the inevitable—that it was time to leave Motown—he decided to take control of the situation. "I know most people don't think of me as tough or strong-willed, but that's just because they don't know me," Michael later said in his book *Moonwalk*. Few entertainers understood image as shrewdly as Michael, who was well aware that the public perception of him was being soft and malleable. He created that impression perhaps as a defense mechanism, a way of protecting himself by seeming harmless and nonthreatening, even later perfecting that soft breathy voice that was used in public but not in private. His strength became boldly apparent when—because no one else made the slightest move to alter the situation with Motown—Michael took action.

"I went over to see him, face to face, and it

was one of the most difficult things I've ever done," he said of his confrontation with Berry Gordy. "If I had been the only one of us who was unhappy, I might have kept my mouth shut, but there had been so much talk at home about how unhappy we *all* were that I went in and talked to him." In very definite terms, he explained that the group didn't have any real control over its material, to select, to write, to produce their songs. Defensive and annoyed, Gordy, like Louis B. Mayer, believed he knew what was best for his performers. No one was going to tell him how to handle his business. But Michael stood his ground, and the exchange with Gordy became heated.

But not once did he back down. He was then sixteen, and his confrontation with Gordy was similar to Elizabeth Taylor's confrontation (at just about the same age) with Louis B. Mayer at MGM. Michael, however, had more leverage that he may not have been fully aware of. At that point, he was a major Motown star. But at the time of her protest at MGM, a teenaged Elizabeth had not yet reached major stardom. Most significant, though, Elizabeth hadn't been afraid to walk out of MGM. After her confrontation, she had a new confidence in herself. So now did Michael. Though his feelings were complicated and con-flicted, he knew the time had come to leave Motown. Part of Michael would always look up to, admire, and basically love Berry Gordy, the surrogate father who helped put the Jackson 5 on the map. Part of Michael was also affected by a conversation with Diana Ross, who believed Gordy had the group's future in control. She felt that the brothers should stay at Motown. By then, Ross and Gordy were lovers, and Gordy clearly had been her Svengali, pushing in every way possible to showcase her great talent. But despite Diana Ross's advice, Michael had made up his mind. "We could have stayed with Motown," he said, "but if we had we'd probably be an oldies act." Ironically, later even Ross would leave Motown.

Joe Jackson now stepped into action. After negotiations with Ron Alexenburg, who headed Epic Records, a division of CBS Records, Joe decided the Jackson 5 would sign with that company. He didn't much care what anyone else thought, including his sons. In most respects, Joe Jackson's decision was wise. Reportedly, the group still had a mere pittance of a 2.7 percent royalty rate at Gordy's company. Subtract from that the expenses that Motown still deducted, and it wasn't a lucrative deal, to put it mildly. At Epic, the royalty rate would reportedly be 27 percent of the wholesale price of a record. A healthy $750,000 advance also sweetened the deal. One snag was that the president of CBS Records, Walter Yetnikoff, reportedly balked at the idea of letting the Jacksons write their material, but Alexenburg was said to have fought for the group and worked out concessions. Presented with the new deal, Michael, according to Jermaine, was hesitant about signing. Aware of his son's admiration for Fred Astaire, Joseph—in a calculated move—promised him a dinner with Fred Astaire if he signed, which Michael soon did. But Joe didn't know Astaire. The dinner never came. It appeared he was simply talking off the top of his head. "You have no idea how angry I was," Michael later told Jermaine. "I didn't believe another word Joseph said after that."

Perhaps the most emotional indication of the career shift about to take place occurred when the brothers, including Jermaine, were set to perform at New York's Westbury Music Fair in Long Island in 1976. The entire family was upset when Jermaine did not join his brothers onstage. One version of the story was that Motown had called and told him not to walk onto the stage. Jermaine said, however, that though he had flown into New York to be with his brothers, he had no intention of performing and informed them before show time. His father was furious. The rest of the family was also enraged. Not only would the performance that night have to be drastically altered, but Joseph also had lost his son—his favorite—to Berry Gordy. The brothers didn't speak to Jermaine for the next six months. Aside from

Joseph's reaction, Jermaine's absence at Westbury most affected Michael. Always Jermaine had stood at Michael's left during performances. "I *depended* on being next to Jermaine," he said. "And when I did that first show without him there, with no one next to me, I felt totally naked onstage for the first time in my life." In the future, conflicts between Michael and Jermaine would grow to the point where the brother to whom Michael had once felt so close was someone by whom he felt betrayed and appeared to detest. Much the same thing would happen for him with his sister La Toya. It all contributed to a family dilemma that troubled him in the years to come.

Moving forward with Epic, Joe filed a lawsuit to break the group's contract with Motown. When the case reached the courts, it was then revealed that Joe, as the boys' manager and guardian, had never really read the Motown contract. Nor had Katherine. After protracted arguments, Joseph got his sons out of the contract—but at a cost. Motown retained legal trademark ownership of the name the Jackson 5. An adamant Gordy would not give it up. The brothers' professional identity had been snatched away from them. Henceforth the group was known as the Jacksons. As Michael expected, Jermaine stayed with Motown. He was replaced by Randy.

At Epic, the group worked with the prize-winning, successful team of Kenny Gamble and

Leon Huff. Based in Philadelphia, Gamble and Huff were already legends in the making. Working with such artists as Harold Melvin and the Blue Notes, the O'Jays, Jerry Butler, and Archie Bell and the Drells on their Philadelphia International Records label, Gamble and Huff turned out huge hits: "If You Don't Know Me By Now," "Love Train," "Only the Strong Survive," and "I Can't Stop Dancing." For the Jacksons, Gamble and Huff produced the albums *The Jacksons* and *Goin' Places*. But despite such hit songs as "Enjoy Yourself" and "Show You the Way to Go" and despite the fact that Michael wrote such songs as "Blues Away" and "Different Kind of Lady," mostly the sales were not like the old days. In the end, much as Michael respected Gamble and Huff, he felt their musical tastes were not right for the group.

Acting to protect his sons from a professional disaster, Joe arranged a meeting with CBS president Walter Yetnikoff. To the family's surprise, he asked Michael to accompany him. No doubt Joe was honest with himself, that without Michael the group had no clout, no credibility, no professional *presence* in the minds of the music executives. In the end, the meeting helped keep the group alive. The brothers began work on a third album, *Destiny*, that later proved successful and had the hit "Shake Your Body (Down to the Ground)," written by Michael and Randy. Now that Jermaine was no longer in the group—and discovered that his solo career at Motown was not going very far—Michael appeared to bond protectively with his baby brother, Randy. That protective bond stretched back to the years when the family had lived in Gary. Daily, Michael would pick up Randy after school, and the two walked home together. In the years to come, Michael appeared to feel that Randy was not given enough credit for his talents, that Randy was considered an afterthought rather than an important member of the group and as a musician as well. In later years, however, the brothers would have a terrible rift.

But even before the completion of *Destiny*, Michael veered in a different career direction. By then having met Sammy Davis Jr., he marveled at Davis's talents: a richly versatile artist who sang, danced, did impressions, and acted. In turn, Sammy, who playfully called Michael the midget, saw something of himself in this fiercely gifted kid. Closely observing Davis, Michael learned something about career management. Having begun his career in the act known as the Will Mastin Trio with his father and "uncle" Will Mastin (despite the press releases, Mastin was actually not a relative but a family friend), Davis had been a child prodigy who became the group's spark plug, its dynamo, its main attraction. Eventually, Davis left the group to go out on his own, stretched himself artistically, and became an even bigger star. At this point, Michael, impressed by Davis and still transfixed by Diana Ross, also witnessed Ross, having left the Supremes, triumph not only as a solo recording artist but also as an Oscar-nominated actress for her performance in *Lady Sings the Blues*. From Davis and Ross, Michael understood the power of striking out on one's own, even when everyone else was dead opposed to it.

Joe and Katherine, however, had a simple credo: family came first. Still itching to stretch his creative wings, Michael let the family know of his intention to appear as the Scarecrow in the movie musical extravaganza *The Wiz*. Based on the Broadway musical that had been a reworking of *The Wizard of Oz* for a black cast, the movie was to star Diana Ross, to be directed by Sidney Lumet, and, among the other stars, was to include the legendary Lena Horne. Supervising the music was maestro Quincy Jones. The family, however, balked at the idea of him doing the film, especially since Motown was producing it. How could he deal with a company that had robbed them blind? But Michael wouldn't back down. Eventually, the family accepted his decision, perhaps assuming it was just a temporary kind of experimentation for him.

La Toya accompanied him to New York for the filming. Staying in an apartment in the city's exclusive Sutton Place, it marked their first time of living on their own. Occasionally, Katherine visited. On one visit to *The Wiz* set, Katherine became alarmed by a scene in which Michael as the Scarecrow lay on a table with a buzz saw about to slice him apart. "Get my son off that table!" she exclaimed. "You're not going to do this to my son!" When the director called "Cut," La Toya remembered that Michael had to assure his mother that it was only a movie. Once he completed *The Wiz*, and following the release of *Destiny*, Michael moved full steam ahead—*on his own*. Now he decided to do an album without his brothers. Already he had performed on those four solo Motown albums—while still with the group —but this time around he would call all the shots, select material, decide on musicians, be totally in charge.

Chapter 7

ONCE WORK BEGAN on *A Place in the Sun*, director George Stevens took the production to Lake Tahoe for exterior sequences. Clift arrived on location with his drama coach Mira Rostova. Actress Shelley Winters—cast as the dowdy Alice in love with Clift's character George Eastman—brought her sister, Blanche, along. Always by the side of the underage Elizabeth was, of course, Sara. Elizabeth recalled that she completed work on *The Big Hangover* "at 5 one evening, and by 8:30, Mother and I were on the train to Lake Tahoe for scenes in *A Place in the Sun*." The protective Sara, concerned about Elizabeth's fragile health, repeatedly complained because the weather was often cold and damp and the water in the lake was often freezing. Yet the actors had to pretend it was summer and warm.

Before working with Clift, Elizabeth was already developing into a strong actress. *National Velvet* had proven that, and so had *Little Women*. Critic Mel Gussow would later say of Elizabeth that although she had a "lack of professional training, the range of her acting was surprisingly wide." The truth was that although she had not studied at an acting school and was not a student of the Method, Elizabeth by now had excellent training within Hollywood's system. Over the years, working with directors like Clarence Brown, Michael Curtiz, Mervyn LeRoy, George Stevens, and soon Vincente Minnelli—and appearing opposite such seasoned pros as Spencer Tracy, Irene Dunne, William Powell, Mary Astor, Donald Crisp, Anne Revere, Greer Garson, Mickey Rooney, Walter Pidgeon, and Nigel Bruce—she learned to listen as an actress, and to understand that on-screen her emotions had to match theirs. Or she would have to take the lead and create the emotional foundation for a scene, which in turn they would have to match in order to build the scene. She also understood lighting and the camera itself, being able to *be* the person while the camera recorded her feelings. "I noticed on the set, even in costume tests," said designer Irene Sharaff, "that she has an instinctive rapport with the camera and seems completely at ease, a gift which may partly account for that elusive quality which makes a few stars shine more brilliant than others." She was doing the very thing that James Agee wrote was crucial for the movies: being the right person for the role.

What she needed, however, were challenging characters, not the standard fare that MGM wasted her on. The same had been true of other great stars at MGM and other studios. Everyone from Garbo to Davis to Cagney to Gable to Bogart to Crawford to de Havilland had a lineup of movie duds. That was both par for the course as well as the downside of studio life. For stars like Davis, Crawford, and de Havilland, it was a constant battle for better roles and more challenging films. In her own way, Taylor fought MGM, whether it be through that earlier threat of breaking her contract or by repeatedly trying to get into better pictures. But she was still a teenager, and her rebellious fires were growing; the full-fledged rebel had not fully matured. Acting with Montgomery Clift, though, was a true awakening that made her more aware of technique and another type of concentration.

She would always say Clift made her take acting—and the whole thought process associated with it—more seriously, that it wasn't simply play and make-believe. In time, she would work with the most discussed New York actors of the postwar era: James Dean, Paul Newman, Marlon Brando. Though she never considered herself a Method actress, she clearly had, as did such performers as Tracy and Revere, her own method of getting inside a character, and it wasn't just instinctual, although instincts were important to understanding the characters she played. She *lived* her characters, too. But partly because she was studio-trained, she had developed her process and powers of concentration to the point where she carried the character inside herself but didn't let the characters come forth until the cameras rolled. Because the acting schools themselves were stage-oriented, teaching students how to perform in theater with its particular demands—not for cinema, which had a whole other set of rules—the lack of continuity could prove difficult and devastating for stage actors when they first worked in films. Such stage-trained actors as Clift, Newman, and Richard Burton would be surprised, as Newman once said, how quickly she could tap into her emotions, and each would learn about film acting from her. Director Mike Nichols recalled that she had a talent only the rare few possessed: "That secret, where they do something while you're shooting and you think it's *okay,* and then you see it on screen and it's five times better than when you shot it. That's what a great movie actor does. They don't know how they do it, and I don't know they do it, but the difference is unimaginable, shocking. This feeling that they have such a connection with the camera that they can do what they want because they own the audience. Elizabeth had it."

In Lake Tahoe—and later when the production moved back to Paramount—George Stevens saw the way his two young stars were attracted to each other—the way they gazed into one another's eyes, the way they spoke or laughed together—which he understood was important to the picture.

They were playing characters who fell intensely in love, crossing social barriers, as their relationship developed and blossomed. Despite the presence of Clift's coach Mira Rostova, who most people on the set thought was a pretentious pain, the actor wouldn't let her inhibit his interactions with Taylor. In *A Place in the Sun*, the teenage Taylor often would have to be the pursuer. During the key scene in which they actually meet, Clift would be alone at a party, in the den playing pool. Though his character George Eastman was the nephew of a powerful businessman, George has grown up poor and is eager to make his profes-sional mark in life. But he's a social misfit around his uncle's wealthy and privileged friends. Out of loneliness, he has become involved with the working-class young woman played by Shelley Winters. But once he has seen Taylor's Angela Vickers, he's captivated. In that scene, as he plays pool, Angela catches a glimpse of him, then enters the room, impressed by his one-man game. Wondering why he's alone, she asks, "Being exclusive? Being dramatic? Being blue?" She's decided she wants to know him better. The sequence ends with her taking
him off to dance. "Come on, I'll take you dancing—on your birthday, blue boy," she says.

Another key scene—when the two profess their love for each other—occurs as they dance during another party. Suddenly, Taylor's Angela feels everyone is staring at them. It's simply the self-consciousness of youthful love. She leads him out of the large room into a smaller adjoining one. Here, in a series of dramatic close-ups, were some of the most intense scenes in the history of American movies, sensitively conveying the power of physical desire. As Clift buries his head on Taylor's shoulder, she tells him, "Tell Mama. Tell Mama all." It's an odd line for a teenage girl to say to the boy she loves; Taylor herself questioned it. But director Stevens was insistent that she say the words as written. In so many ways, the vulnerable, tormented George Eastman looks in need of a nurturing mother, and Taylor here becomes mother/lover and, in a strange way, earth mother, as well.

Still relatively new to Hollywood, Shelley Winters had appeared in such films as *The Great Gatsby*, in 1949, and *A Double Life*. In *A Place in the Sun*, Stevens deglamorized her and let her wear little makeup. She had to ultimately represent every-thing the character Eastman hoped to escape. Though Winters had no scenes with Taylor, the two saw a lot of each other and became friendly. Winters witnessed not only Clift's attraction to Taylor but also the response of the crew to her. No one seemed able to take their eyes off her—"with that beautiful black, curly hair, enormous violet eyes, tiny waist and gorgeous bosom."

She also saw the way Elizabeth had been isolated, growing up in a cocoon under control of the studio system and her mother, who, said Winters, "kept running around, complaining that because George Stevens had made Elizabeth go in that cold lake in a bathing suit, she would never be able to have children; to my knowledge, for the next twenty years Elizabeth never stopped having children."

Winters observed that, in many respects, Elizabeth seemed unaware of the way the real world worked. Except when in front of the camera, she was accustomed to having everything taken care of for her. "One day I was sitting in the one warm dressing room with Elizabeth," recalled Winters, who was then writing a letter and asked Elizabeth for the date. "She answered that she didn't know. I noticed the *Hollywood Reporter* on a chair next to her and asked her to look. She did and said, 'It's no good, it's yesterday's *Reporter!*' So much for MGM's Little Red Schoolhouse! I guess Elizabeth went to the Richard Burton University because when I met her again in later years she had acquired a very good British public school education and was much wiser, if sadder."

Of Elizabeth, Stevens said: "She had an artificial patriarchy imposed on her—the studio. It took the place of her retiring father. The studio, like a domineering parent, was alternately stern and adoring." Aware always that though she was a professional, Elizabeth still was very young, Stevens took time to guide her through the release of emotions so crucial to her character. He also was respectful of Sara—and didn't intervene with her coaching Elizabeth from the sidelines. For Winters, George Stevens was "the finest director and kindest man I was ever privileged to work with."

"Both Elizabeth Taylor and I fell madly in love with him. When we would see the rushes at night in the projection tent, we would each sit on opposite sides of him," said Winters. "The whole experience was a joy."

For Elizabeth, working on *A Place in the Sun* under Stevens's direction as much as with Clift as her costar would change her artistically. Earlier in his career, Stevens had mastered comedies, sometimes with significant social implications— such films as *Alice Adams* and *Woman of the Year*—in which American attitudes on class and gender would be questioned and criticized. He understood comic timing and comic reversals. But in this postwar period, as he made fewer films and freed himself from the constraints of the studio system, he turned away from comedies to dramatize a sometimes cruel or insensitive culture in such films as *A Place in the Sun, Shane,* and *Giant.* In total, Elizabeth would appear in three films directed by Stevens. It was *A Place in the Sun* that most influenced her as an actress. Though it would take her time following the film to find other compelling characters, she nonetheless would give some of her most complicated performances playing deeply troubled heroines in conflict with themselves and at odds with the attitudes of society, in such films as *Raintree County, Cat on a Hot Tin Roof, Suddenly, Last Summer, BUtterfield 8, Who's Afraid of Virginia Woolf?*, and even her underrated Katharina in *The Taming of the Shrew.*

During filming, Winters believed that "Monty was developing a terrific crush on Elizabeth. She loved being with him; he was fun and intelligent, and she had great respect for his talent. But she had been a working, sheltered child. Even then she was longing for the bright lights and the glamorous figures of the celebrity world."

Said Winters: "Sometimes he would drive me around the mountains in the little Ford jalopy that we used in the picture, and he would talk about other things. But he would make a special hesitant sound in his throat and had a dark look in his beautiful black eyes when he spoke about Elizabeth. It was a dead giveaway to the depths of his feelings for her. She would tease him and flirt with any attractive man within range of those violet eyes, but I think she was too young to realize how much she was hurting him."

But there were other aspects of Clift's personality Winters either did not see at that time or that later she was not willing to discuss publicly. Clift had an ongoing relationship with an older woman, the singer Libby Holman, who had been embroiled in a scandal in which it was believed she had murdered her millionaire husband. Later he developed a close relationship with older actress Myrna Loy. No one could quite figure out what these relationships were all about, just as many were not sure what kind of relationship he had with his coach Mira. Clift, however, made it clear that Mira was his coach, not his lover. He also had same-sex relationships. During these years and those to come, he had various male lovers and often a series of one-night stands. For a time, women interested him as much as men. "If Monty liked you—man or woman you ultimately went to bed with him," his good friend actor Jack Larson said. "If he liked you, he couldn't keep his hands off you—touching—caressing—hugging—he was very physical and very, very affectionate." But Clift was elusive, restless, and, sexually, hard to pin down. Still, to those who saw Elizabeth with Clift—including Sara—it was apparent that she was drawn to him and might even be in love with him.

"Watched Elizabeth Taylor and Montgomery Clift do a sizzling love scene in 'A Place in the Sun,' " Hedda Hopper reported after visiting the set when interiors were shot at Paramount in Hollywood. "Not a carpenter, electrician, prop man or laborer left the set. Some even sat on top of ladders to get a better look. That Liz gets them all—from 15 to 50. What a dish!" Hopper added: "I tried to watch Monty's girl friend, Mira Rosovakaya [*sic*]. . . . She never leaves the set."

Regardless, the Taylor-Clift relationship grew more complicated than either was prepared for. In later years, there were stories that at some point in their lives they were briefly lovers. Still, the romantic Elizabeth had to accept the fact, as filming drew to a close, that if she were to have a relationship with Monty, it would be a friendship. Once she accepted that fact—and it took time—she never looked back. He became her closest friend outside of her family, more so than her childhood friend Roddy McDowall. When she visited New York, she often stayed at Clift's place just as he often stayed at hers during trips to Los Angeles. The two shared secrets and opened the doors to look into each other's soul. When together, they were in their own world, one which others were not privy to. Seeing his emotional bruises and scars, she loved mothering him and was devoted to him for the rest of his life. With Monty, she indeed had one of the greatest, most enduring relationships of her life.

Once *A Place in the Sun* wrapped, life for Elizabeth was back to normal, meeting the demands of MGM. Even while completing the film, "I spent my free time and Sundays having my wardrobe fitted for *Father of the Bride*," she said. There were also the usual makeup tests, hairstyle tests, costume tests that were photographed or sometimes filmed and which took up hours of her day. Never was there any letup. The MGM publicists kept her occupied with a steady stream of premieres and photo ops. Even casual dates with singer Vic Damone and baseball star Ralph Kiner were covered full blast by the press.

In late January 1950, Elizabeth completed her high school requirements with an overall B average. Her favorite course had been civics, in which her final grade was a ninety-eight. No longer would she have to attend school on the MGM lot. Once she turned eighteen the following month, she would not be required to have a guardian—meaning Sara—at the studio. "I don't have to have my mother with me on the set, but I certainly intend to," Elizabeth told the press. "Now that I'm an alumna, mother and I will have more time together. We can share all our plans and confidences." Naturally, Sara was relieved that nothing had changed between the two of them. The studio kept her on salary. But what Elizabeth really wanted now was her independence and freedom.

Arranging for her to "graduate" with a class from LA's University High School, MGM had no intention of missing this kind of photo op. The day before the actual ceremony, Elizabeth was outfitted in a cap and gown for MGM photographers. They did the same the next day at the actual graduation.

Work also began on *Father of the Bride*, the comic tale of the trials and tribulations of a beleaguered father, played by Spencer Tracy, as he gives the hand of his daughter (played by Elizabeth) in marriage. There was irony in the casting of the mother character in the film. When Sara had appeared in the play *The Fool*, she had worked with prominent actor Richard Bennett. Sometimes his young daughter visited him backstage and spent time playing in Sara's dressing room. That little girl had been Joan Bennett, now cast as Elizabeth's mother. Taylor and Tracy got along well and remained friends. Under the direction of Vincente Minnelli, their scenes together had a warmth and intimacy that was genuine, not manufactured. So pleased was MGM with the rushes for the film that already there were plans for a sequel, *Father's Little Dividend*.

Life seemed to go on as before—or so it

appeared. But for Elizabeth, something momentous had occurred. She had fallen in love—this time for real, she believed. Perhaps it was partly a way of compensating for her then possibly unconsummated relationship with Montgomery Clift. Perhaps it was partly a desire to break free from the studio. No doubt, like many young women of her generation, it was also the belief that love, followed by marriage, was part of her manifest destiny. But Elizabeth also wanted to get away from home. Earlier she had received a marriage proposal that left her cold. Multimillionaire Howard Hughes, who had dated a lineup of Hollywood stars, from Katharine Hepburn to Ava Gardner, set his sights on Elizabeth, offering a million dollars if she became his bride. Impressed with Hughes's offer, Sara had the Hollywood lawyer Greg Bautzer draw up an agreement. But Elizabeth flatly refused. She was not going to be sold off to the highest bidder. Later she expressed her feelings bluntly: "I married to get away from my parents," she said.

Now thoughts of marriage and a white picket fence around a dream house in which she'd reside with a dream prince were on her mind night and day. During the previous November, she had been a bridesmaid at Jane Powell's wedding, and certainly she must have asked herself when her day would come. By then, she had already met the young man of her dreams, Nicky Hilton, or rather Conrad Nicholson "Nicky" Hilton Jr., the son of the enormously wealthy Hilton Hotels magnate. Good-looking, social, pampered, accustomed to a life of luxury, and the oldest of three sons, young Hilton, born in Texas in 1926, was said to be his father's favorite. Though Nicky had experienced his father's ups and downs—during the Depression, when Conrad Hilton Sr. saw his hotel empire just about collapse and went broke—that was a distant memory. By 1940, the senior Hilton was back in the millions, with homes in Malibu and Bel Air, and he socialized with the rich and famous. By then, he and his wife Mary, though devout Catholics, had also divorced. Then Hilton Sr. married actress Zsa Zsa Gabor. Nicky dropped out of Loyola College, joined the navy, and then returned to Los Angeles, where he was a well-suited, highly social young man about town. The girls were crazy for him, and he was crazy for them.

Having observed Elizabeth from afar, not only on the screen but also at social events whenever and wherever he could, he was mesmerized. He had even gone to the bridal party of Jane Powell at Los Angeles's glamorous nightclub the Mocambo —mainly in hopes of seeing Elizabeth. To say that Hilton was rather obsessed with her would not be an exaggeration. But he still hadn't been intro-duced to her. Finally, he met her at the

Paramount studios. The day after their meeting, she arrived home to find three dozen long-stemmed yellow roses waiting for her. There followed an overflow of gifts, phone calls, dazzling nights on the town, and nonstop attention, adulation, and adoration from the ardent young Hilton. Conrad Hilton Sr. liked her immensely; so did Nicky's mother, Mary. For the Taylors, there was, as perhaps expected, a mixed response. Costume designer Helen Rose recalled that "there was no happier person than Sara Taylor. Francis was not so sure. Elizabeth was still in her teens and very unsophisticated, and though Nick was in his early twenties, he had been reared by a wealthy indulgent father and was considerably spoiled. Yet, theirs seemed like a storybook romance." For Sara, Nicky could give Elizabeth a life of comfort, privilege, and social standing. The two also looked terrific together. One issue of concern was religion. Because the Hiltons were Catholics, Elizabeth agreed to study Catholicism, with plans to convert to the religion. Nothing was said, at least not publicly, about Sara's Christian Science.

Finally, on February 21, 1950—just six days before Elizabeth's eighteenth birthday—Hedda Hopper broke the news that Elizabeth would wed Hilton on May 6. Her maid of honor would be her childhood friend Anne Westmore. One of the bridesmaids would be Jane Powell. Another would be Mara Reagan, then the girlfriend of Elizabeth's brother, Howard, and later his wife. Howard Taylor would be one of the ushers. Nicky's brother would be best man. MGM's costume designer Helen Rose would create Elizabeth's wedding gown as well as those of the bridesmaids. MGM would foot the bill. "They can afford it after the price Paramount paid them for Liz's services in *A Place in the Sun*," said Hopper. Another great designer, Paramount's Edith Head, who had designed Elizabeth's stunning gowns in *A Place in the Sun*, would create her going-away suit. The rest of Elizabeth's trousseau would be done by Ceil Chapman in New York.

Word of the upcoming nuptials surprisingly had not come from the Taylor family. Instead, Conrad Hilton Sr., so excited "to have Elizabeth Taylor a member of his family that he couldn't keep his secret," broke the news to Hopper. Shrewdly, Hilton Sr. understood that Hedda was the columnist he should talk to.

Afterward came a whirlwind of activities. Elizabeth, Nicky, and Sara flew to Chicago, then on to New York, where Elizabeth's trousseau was fitted. In New York, Elizabeth made radio appearances. There was a stampede to give the bride-to-be all sorts of perks and gifts. After she appeared in an ad for Gorham's fine silver, the company presented her with a solid silver dinner service for thirty-six people. After she had posed for another company in a sumptuous mink coat, she was given the coat. Still another company presented her with expensive carpets that were shipped to the West Coast. Her uncle Howard sent her pearls valued at $65,000. So many wedding gifts had arrived at the Taylor home that furniture had to be moved out to make room for everything.

Requests, pleas, and inquiries for Elizabeth's services poured into MGM. Producer Stanley Kramer wanted to borrow her for his film *Cyrano de Bergerac*, but Metro refused to loan her out. Later William Wyler wanted her for the lead in *Carrie* opposite Laurence Olivier. Elizabeth was eager to work with the director and the actor, but MGM didn't let it happen. Instead, there was renewed talk about her appearance in *Quo Vadis*. The studio also let the press know that the Fashion Academy had selected Elizabeth in the Best All-American field on the list of Best Dressed Women of 1950. The California Florists Association named her the Flower of Womanhood. Some coverage must have seemed silly to Elizabeth. But it was all a part of the way Hollywood operated, a way that MGM kept her name out there. *The Big Hangover* would be released shortly after the wedding, and *Father of the Bride* would hit theaters a few months later.

The real wedding would be a perfect tie-in for the celluloid one.

Finally, Hedda Hopper made the pronouncement that everyone in the industry knew—and which the *Time* cover story had confirmed: "Not many girls in society, on the screen or stage or in any walk of life have had the acclaim and publicity that have been given Elizabeth Taylor."

Everything had moved so quickly that Elizabeth barely had time to think. Or, more important, she barely had time to get to know her future husband. Taylor herself may have questioned what was happening in her life and if her decision was the best one. Two days before the wedding, she took ill with a cold and a fever and was pumped up with penicillin, then spent much of the day in bed, though she rose in the afternoon the next day for the wedding rehearsal. Afterward, she returned home and went to bed again.

Finally, on May 6, the big event went as scheduled at the Church of the Good Shepherd in Beverly Hills. Thousands of spectators— standing four feet deep—lined up across the street from the church to catch a glimpse of the bride. Traffic was directed by MGM's police chief Whitey Hendrey, who stationed Beverly Hills cops and studio officers outside the church to handle the cars and the crowd.

Among the guests inside: Spencer Tracy; Fred

Astaire; Rosalind Russell and husband, Freddie Brisson; Ginger Rogers; Van Johnson and his wife, Evie; William Powell and his wife, Diana; June Allyson and her husband, Dick Powell; Gene Kelly and his wife, actress Betsy Blair; Peter Lawford; Bunny Waters; actresses Janet Leigh, Terry Moore, and Amanda Blake; Alice Faye and her husband, Phil Harris; former child stars Mickey Rooney, Roddy McDowall, and Margaret O'Brien; Joan Bennett and her husband, the producer Walter Wanger; actor George Murphy and his wife, Julie.

Not present that day was Montgomery Clift, who, like William Pawley Jr., was opposed to the marriage. Pawley had heard stories of Hilton's excessive drinking and violence—and perhaps that was why he had pleaded with Elizabeth not to marry Hilton. For Monty, the wedding represented the possible loss of his soul mate. Throughout the Taylor-Hilton courtship, she was in communica-tion with him, sometimes calling him, sometimes writing letters, revealing her fears and mixed emotions, asking his advice. She no doubt wanted Clift to tell her to break it off. He never did. Both knew that she really wanted Clift to ask her to marry him. No matter what Clift's sexual preferences were, she would have dropped Hilton in a minute to run off to the altar with Clift. At one point, she reportedly asked if he'd come see her after the marriage to

Hilton. His response was that Hilton was not his kind of guy. Nicky was too brash and frat boyish for Clift. In the end, her marriage to Hilton was painful for Clift. Thus he stayed away from the ceremony.

As Elizabeth glided down the church's candle-lit center aisle on the arm of her father, Helen Rose observed: "Francis was tall and handsome and carried himself with assurance and poise. When he and Elizabeth walked down the long aisle to stand before the altar, young girls the world over vicariously lived this fairy tale event." Still, Elizabeth's nervousness showed. So did the effects of the cold and fever. However, once she and Nicky had exchanged vows, the couple was jubilant and radiant. As they left the church, the fans outside screamed and shouted for them. The two entered a limousine and were driven off as photographers continued to snap pictures. Then the crowd stormed inside the church to see the carpeted aisle and the flower arrangements still adorning the church and the altar. The actual ceremony had taken about fifteen minutes. But in the end, it was, like Grace Kelly's marriage to Prince Rainier a few years later, one of the great weddings of the twentieth century, to be discussed for years to come.

Afterward, at the reception held at the Bel-Air Country Club, Elizabeth and Nicky stood with their parents to receive their guests in the reception line; this took about five hours. Once many guests had started drinking champagne and dining, others still stood in line to extend best wishes to the newlyweds. Finally, Elizabeth and Nicky slipped away by plane to a deluxe lodge at Pebble Beach. Later they flew to Chicago and then on to New York, and on May 24, they sailed on the *Queen Mary* to Europe for a three-month honeymoon. It all looked glorious. At the reception, while Sara beamed, Conrad Hilton Sr. turned to his former wife, Nicky's mother, Mary, and reportedly said: "They've got everything, haven't they, our boy and his wife? Youth, looks, position, no need to worry about where their next meal is coming from." "Maybe they have too much," the former Mrs. Hilton responded. "I don't think it's going to be easy for them." "Nonsense," said Hilton Sr.

"I am sure Sara and Francis Taylor breathed a sigh of relief," recalled Helen Rose. "Their beautiful daughter was safely married to a rich, handsome socialite husband—what could possibly go wrong? Apparently everything, and very quickly."

By the time the couple arrived in Cherbourg, France, on the *Queen Mary*, tension was building. Though Nicky knew he had married a famous young woman, he clearly hadn't anticipated the extent and breadth of her fame. Everywhere, people clamored to see her. And not just the fans. The famous, the celebrated, the privileged in Europe yearned to meet her. Photographers were always around. At each arrival on their honeymoon, the press asked the couple questions, but few were interested in what Hilton had to say. Though no one called him Mr. Taylor, that was how he was received. He may have shrugged it off and given a smile, but the whole thing eventually gnawed at him. "He was completely spoiled, completely charming," said writer Ruth Waterbury, "and he had grown up in an atmosphere as colorful as Elizabeth's without one trace of the discipline of hers." Very quickly, his temper became foul, his language abusive.

In Deauville, France, Elizabeth, because of her age, was not permitted to gamble at the casino. But that did not stop Nicky, who loved gambling, drinking, and carousing, all of which seemed to excite him more than spending private time with his bride. From Deauville, he motored with Elizabeth to Paris in a sky-blue Cadillac that "they picked up in Chicago on their way from Hollywood to New York." The car had also been brought over on the *Queen Mary*. In Paris, they were pursued right and left and attended a wedding anniversary party for the Duke and Duchess of Windsor. Sophisticated, worldly, and wickedly witty, the Europeans were a whole different breed from America's nouveau riche.

Nicky was bored by them. But they piqued Elizabeth's curiosity. Already, on those trips abroad with Sara, she had been exposed to the manners and mores, even the fabulous foibles and follies, of the Continent's high and mighty, and she wanted to see more, learn more, experience more. In Paris, Nicky hit the casinos again, often leaving Elizabeth alone in their hotel room. She wanted more time with him. He wanted more time having fun on his own. He also wanted the attention back on himself. The role of consort clearly did not appeal to him. "Mr. Hilton spent most of the time away from her when they were in France on their honeymoon," Taylor's attorney William Berger later said. "He spent night after night at the casino and remained away until 5 or 6 in the morning and forced her to take a cab back alone. This also was true after they returned to Los Angeles."

Soon the international press asked if she would have children and give up her career. Elizabeth said that time had not come yet. But Nicky stressed that when she was a mother, she would stop acting. In truth, she had no real intention of giving up her career. She amused herself by thinking she might, but the career, and her own ambition to see how much farther she could go, were a part of her core, the essence of her identity.

From Paris, the couple traveled to London, then to Florence, Venice, and Rome. Rumblings of deep troubles in the marriage spread through Europe and then in the States. Their arguments became public. As he hit the dice and roulette tables, Hilton didn't seem to care what anyone said. Elizabeth frequently called her parents, who were becoming alarmed about their daughter's situation. True, she had said that she had married to get away from her parents, but part of her was also lost without them.

In Rome, they had an audience with the pope. Elizabeth paid a visit to the set of *Quo Vadis*, which was finally being filmed, with Deborah Kerr in the role of Lygia. As a lark, the film's director, Mervyn LeRoy, cast Taylor as an extra. Something was very clear to Elizabeth on that set. Though she might have been weary of the control the studio had over her, at least on a movie set she was valued, appreciated, and never ignored. There she talked with her friend Sydney Guilaroff, who was working on the film, and who was shocked by how thin and pale Elizabeth looked. While everyone there knew Elizabeth, Guilaroff realized no one knew exactly who Nicky was. "Elizabeth looked so unhappy that I drew her aside and asked what was wrong," Guilaroff recalled. "She poured out her heart to me. Her marriage was a farce, nothing like the romantic parts she had played on the screen. Real life for her was filled with disappointment and bitterness. She was married to a man who treated her like a child and spent little time with her, preferring to busy himself with his friends and the frivolous pursuits of the idle rich."

By July, *Father of the Bride* became a huge hit, then the most successful comedy in MGM's history and eventually an Academy Award nominee for Best Motion Picture. For the millions who had not seen her walking on her father's arm down the aisle of the Church of the Good Shepherd, they could now watch her walk the aisle with movie dad Spencer Tracy. The on-screen wedding gown, designed by Helen Rose, drew raves—and copies sold in huge numbers in department stores around the country. MGM moved ahead with plans for the sequel *Father's Little Dividend* and then *Love Is Better Than Ever* to costar her with Larry Parks.

By September, Elizabeth returned to Hollywood, reportedly without Hilton, then took off again. Reaching her in Chicago, Hedda Hopper asked point-blank if she and Hilton had separated. Denying rumors of a split, she said that Hilton was with her, which indeed he then was, in an attempt at a reconciliation. But she didn't tell Hopper that. The couple planned to drive to her uncle Howard's home in Wisconsin, then would visit Nicky's mother in El Paso. "Hedda, believe me. I am happy," said Elizabeth. "When I am not, I will tell you."

Soon filming began on *Father's Little Dividend*. By November 1, the film was completed. For the time being, Elizabeth's marriage seemed back on track. But Hilton's irrational flare-ups continued. At one point, when the couple arrived at a hotel in Los Angeles, she was unpacking while being visited by her mother and Barbara Thompson, the wife of actor Marshall Thompson. "What the hell is going on here?" Hilton asked. It appeared he was annoyed because she was with her mother and a friend. But who could say what set him off? Taylor tried to calm him down. But he was in a foul mood. It was only one of many such incidents.

Early the next month, Elizabeth and Hilton separated. She moved back into her parents' home. Nicky went on a hunting trip in Mexico with his father. There was hope they might reconcile, and there were attempts on Hilton's part. But for Elizabeth, it was over. "They have everything—money, position, jobs, families," Hedda Hopper said. "A more striking couple can't be found. And what have they got to quarrel about? He wants her to give up her job, have babies and make a home. She won't give up her job, and won't have babies until she's ready. She wants her career and Nicky too."

That was part of the official line. But a disturbing darker truth had already been hinted at in some of the stories about their arguments abroad. Hilton's temper could turn violent, and when he drank, he was an ugly drunk. In time, there would be drugs. He wasn't ready for marriage. He wasn't ready for responsibilities. He wasn't ready to have a woman who drew more attention than he did. Elizabeth wasn't ready, either. She was indeed too young. "A month after the wedding I knew we'd made a mistake," she later said. But she had made the attempt to salvage the union; her romanticism wouldn't permit herto do anything less. Though there were stories that he had struck her, she never publicly confirmed such stories until years later. Once the couple returned to the States, and during the time Elizabeth filmed *Father's Little Dividend*, a loud and nasty argument broke out. Hilton hit her and kicked her hard in the stomach. "He was drunk and I didn't know I was pregnant," she later said. "So it wasn't malicious. But God did not put me here to have a baby kicked out of my stomach." She lost the child she was carrying.

Shortly before Christmas, Taylor filed for divorce. Through her lawyers Jules Goldstone and William Berger, she charged mental cruelty. The marriage had lasted seven months, seven days, seventeen hours.

Back at work on *Love Is Better Than Ever*, she became close to the film's director Stanley Donen. Having started his career as a dancer on

Broadway and then as Gene Kelly's dance assistant, the dark-haired, good-looking Donen had gone on to direct Fred Astaire and Jane Powell in *Royal Wedding* and would later strike gold when he codirected the classic *Singin' in the Rain* and made such other films as *Funny Face* and *Two for the Road*. Sensitive to Taylor, Donen was seen around town with her, dancing at nightclubs, having quiet dinners at restaurants. In all likelihood, Sara believed it was too soon for Elizabeth to become involved in another romance. Nor did Sara like the fact that Donen was married, even though his wife of three years was divorcing him. The fact that Donen was Jewish may have been of concern, too. She also may have hoped her daughter and Hilton would reconcile, but when Hilton made headlines after a nasty public fight with an air force officer at the Mocambo, everyone in the Taylor household knew he was as reckless, headstrong, and immature as ever.

Still, because of Sara's insistence that Elizabeth stop seeing Donen, mother and daughter had a major fallout. Clearly, there were "difficulties between Miss Taylor and her family," commented writer Louis Berg. "She gave the appearance of being extremely docile—she fooled her own parents—when she was in a state of rebellion." Elizabeth decided to move out of her parents' home and, for the first time, get a place of her own. A young woman named Peggy Rutledge, who was hired as a personal assistant, found the perfect apartment for Taylor. Rutledge also stayed there herself. As Sara and others knew, Elizabeth's emotional state was fragile, and it was best that she not live alone. MGM felt the same way. Still, once living under her own roof, Elizabeth had her first real taste of freedom, and it was an exhilarating experience.

"My mother was my best girl friend, my mentor, my constant companion," Elizabeth later said. "I told her every kind of inside fear I had." But now that Elizabeth was making her own decisions, perhaps for the first time Sara felt she could not reason with her daughter. The balance of power had shifted. Never again would she have the control over her daughter that she had once exerted.

Finally, Elizabeth was breaking away from childhood, saying good-bye to adolescence, to youth itself, as much as she could. Long remembered would be *Time*'s account of her response when she was told that photographers had voted her "the most beautiful woman they have ever photographed"—Taylor had been ecstatic to be called a woman. Within a few years, she would be called the most beautiful woman in the world. Yet she understood that she still had a distance to go, which led her to make another of her famous comments: "I have the emotions of a child in the body of a woman." She had always wanted to look and be older, which led her at times to almost over–make up her fabulous face. But her body had developed quickly. By her teens, she had filled out, not really voluptuous but certainly on her way. The men who eyed and flirted with her were surprised that she was still a girl. She herself understood she had not yet matured, that her decisions were not fully thought out, that they could be rash. She wasn't yet seeing the world as an adult.

Francis stood on the sidelines, perhaps happy to see Elizabeth on her own but concerned about her. Now, though, Elizabeth became estranged from both her parents. Her newfound independence—coupled with an emerging defiance—grew, per-haps a delayed rebellion that should have begun during adolescence.

In April, Elizabeth was escorted by Donen to *Father's Little Dividend*'s Los Angeles premiere. Opening to good reviews, the film became another box office success. Still, Elizabeth was aware that while her name on a marquee brought in patrons, especially younger ones, big roles were not coming her way. MGM itself was in the midst of change. After decades as Hollywood's most powerful movie mogul, Louis B. Mayer now struggled to hold on to his position and empire. All the studios had been dealt a serious blow in 1948 when the Supreme Court decreed that they had to divest themselves of the block of theaters which each studio owned and which proved crucial in the distribution and exhibition of their movies. Television was also making inroads in American life, on its way to becoming a potent cultural force that would eat away at the movie audience. In time, many studios released their long-standing contract players. The studios needed fresh blood, not only stars who could lure in audiences but executives who could package new films that met audience needs. In 1951, Louis B. Mayer lost his throne. His long-standing nemesis Nicholas Schenck, the top man at MGM's parent company, Loew's, fired him and put writer/director/producer and socially conscious Dore Schary in his place. In time, those wholesome family pictures with their idealized view of American life and culture would go by the wayside. Yet with all the shifts in Hollywood and at the studio, and while other stars would come and go, MGM had no intention of letting that happen with Taylor. But MGM wasted her. It failed to put her in challenging roles.

Two years had passed since *Time* had predicted she'd be the star of the future. Very soon, such actresses as Grace Kelly, Audrey Hepburn, Marilyn Monroe, and Kim Novak would begin their rise to great careers. Ava Gardner also came to greater prominence. Taylor's performances in such films as *Little Women, Father of the Bride*, and *Father's Little Dividend* had been entertaining and engaging; commanding the screen was second nature to her. But such lackluster films as *The Big Hangover*, *Conspirator*, and *Love Is Better Than Ever* did nothing to advance her career. *Love Is Better| Than Ever* was even shelved for a time because of the political problems of her costar Larry Parks, who was soon blacklisted because of his political beliefs. MGM also had her do a cameo appearance, along with Clark Gable, June Allyson, and Esther Williams, in the forgettable *Callaway Went Thataway*.

At the time of *Father's Little Dividend*, she had renewed her MGM contract, but at every turn, she felt constricted and stifled. William Wyler had wanted her not only for *Carrie* but now also for *Roman Holiday* to costar her with Cary Grant (the roles eventually went to Audrey Hepburn and Gregory Peck). George Stevens hoped to cast Elizabeth and Montgomery Clift in *The Dipper*. But as in the past, when Orson Welles, Michael Curtiz, and others sought her services, the studio would not budge. Now discussions sprang up about putting her in the adaptation of Sir Walter Scott's classic adventure tale *Ivanhoe*, to be filmed in England and starring Robert Taylor and Joan Fontaine, with Elizabeth in a supporting role, that of Rebecca. Elizabeth balked at doing the picture and argued with producer Pandro S. Berman. Writer Ruth Waterbury said Elizabeth also believed the studio was trying to separate her from Stanley Donen and that when Taylor told Berman she wouldn't go to London, he informed her that she'd be taken off her salary. "He knew she needed the money," said Waterbury. Elizabeth was concerned about finances, mainly because now that she was on her own, she had to think about money for the first time in her life. Though Elizabeth worked steadily, she was not at the top tier of salaried stars such as Gable. She also spent lavishly, not only on herself but others as well. She also bought cars for her father and reportedly had given her mother a Cadillac. Of course, she also did not deny herself anything. Much was spent on clothes, on entertaining, on anything that struck her fancy. There were also medical bills. "I've got to work," she told Hedda Hopper in May 1951. "You don't need the money?" Hopper asked. Elizabeth replied: "That's what you think. I've had weeks of hospital doctor bills. During my last picture I had to keep a nurse on the set. And those things cost money." So finances were important to her now and would be more so in the years to come. Berman understood her financial needs. Thus he made the salary threat. But Elizabeth was adamant. "Then she said she'd just walk through the role," said Waterbury.

She ended up in the hospital again. Because no

one said what the problem was, there was talk that she'd had a breakdown. One thing was clear, though: the only person permitted to see her at the hospital was Donen.

Otherwise much of the focus in the media was on her private life. Taylor may not have seriously questioned the attention on her love life, at least not now. This kind of coverage simply went with stardom's territory and stretched back to the days of such iconic stars as Chaplin, Swanson, Garbo, Gable, Davis, Tracy, and Hepburn. Unlike celebrity figures of a later age, the classic stars' personal lives drew interest mainly because they were so compelling on-screen. But now, Elizabeth, the actress, ran the risk of being overshadowed by Elizabeth, the celebrity.

Nonetheless, Elizabeth would have to do *Ivanhoe*. Accompanying her to England were her assistant, Peggy Rutledge, as well as an MGM publicist Malvinia Pumphrey and her husband.

When *A Place in the Sun* hit theaters in August, it received rave reviews. So did Elizabeth. "The real surprise of *A Place in the Sun*," wrote *Look* magazine, "is the lyrical performance of Elizabeth Taylor. Always beautiful, Miss Taylor here reveals an understanding of passion and suffering that is electrifying." Writing in the *Los Angeles Times*, Edwin Schallert agreed: "What has given the picture special illumination is the role of Angela Vickers allotted to Miss Taylor. Here is a heroine as beautifully created as any seen in recent days on the screen. What Miss Taylor brings to the picture as a young actress is sheer magic. There is no question to my mind but that she will be a top contender for Academy honors." He added: "But little less effective is Clift in this, his finest screen effort. He, too, should be an award contender. He hits just the right note in a role that requires the most delicate shading." The *New York Times* called the film "a work of beauty, tenderness, power, and insight. . . . Elizabeth Taylor's delineation of the rich and beauteous Angela also is the top effort of her career. It is a shaded, tender performance." Ultimately, *A Place in the Sun* received nine Academy Award nominations, including Best Actor for Clift and Best Actress for Winters. Though also nominated for Best Motion Picture, it lost to *An American in Paris*. Of the six awards the film did win, Stevens won Best Directing and Edith Head won for Best Costume Design (Black-and-White). Elizabeth, however, did not win the Best Actress nomination that many felt she deserved.

Despite the critical success of *A Place in the Sun*, Elizabeth found herself making *Ivanhoe*. Angry with MGM, feeling trapped in useless roles, and also not feeling well physically—suffering from blinding migraines and painful ulcers that kept her on a diet of baby food—she still hadn't fully recovered from the disillusioning marriage to Nicky. *Ivanhoe* director Richard Thorpe complained to Pandro S. Berman that she was sleepwalking through the movie. Despite her threat to just coast through the picture, "I knew she wouldn't," said Berman. "I knew even at nineteen she was actually too much of an artist to deliberately ruin a part."

Berman was frank with director Thorpe. "I told him to get what he could out of her, then do every damn line over again when they got back to Hollywood," recalled Berman. "The lady was always good at improving a performance in the dubbing stages. She'd do it professionally, even if she disdained what she was doing." In the completed *Ivanhoe*, as the Jewess (which was how the character was then described) Rebecca, she would appear subdued, rather passive, and melancholic. Her character would not win the hero's heart. Instead, Robert Taylor's Ivanhoe would end up with the blond Joan Fontaine. Taylor's seeming distance from her character, however, made her Rebecca all the more moving and affecting, a portrait of a young woman with her emotions on hold, a woman hurt in love who emerges as the film's romantic/emotional focal point. Here, too, her beauty would prove intriguing and powerful. How could someone so magnificent-looking lose or even fear losing in love? Of course, Elizabeth now knew what it meant to lose at love and also (because of her relationship with Clift) what it meant to yearn for someone she would not have. Sensitively, she would convey her character's vulnerability, bringing her personal experiences to a character who otherwise might have been flat and uninvolving.

While filming in England, Elizabeth was ready to meet even more of the sophisticated and the worldly, both within Hollywood and outside it. Shelley Winters had understood that the teenage Elizabeth was eager to take on the world. Unlike some performers who talked only about show business and who mixed almost exclusively with other movie folk, Taylor was already casting an eye to politicians, to heads of state, to royalty. Nor was she content simply to socialize with people her age. When she had arrived in London to film *Ivanhoe*, Lord and Lady Mountbatten had invited her to a lavish party, which she happily attended and where she even struck up a friend-ship with Princess Margaret. The curiosity about her was still growing as much within the European aristocracy as within the mass audience. "Elizabeth Taylor is worshiped," British actress Joan Collins would say within a few years. "The girls simply adore her. Their great ambition is to look like her; you can see 1000 imitation Elizabeth Taylors any day in London."

Interestingly enough, once Collins was working in Hollywood, she was dubbed "the poor man's Elizabeth Taylor" and, for a time, dated Nicky Hilton.

But with all that attention, something else was on Elizabeth's mind. She was once again ready for a love that could lead to marriage and full adulthood.

Born in 1912 in Leigh-on-Sea, Essex, Michael Wilding originally planned to become a painter but stumbled into acting. Elegant and urbane with an aristocratic bearing, he was one of British cinema's most popular actors in the late 1940s and early 1950s, appearing in such films as *Three, In Which We Serve*, and Hitchcock's *Stage Fright*, opposite Marlene Dietrich and Jane Wyman. Having met Elizabeth during her earlier trip to England to film *Conspirator*, he and Taylor had flirted, but Wilding, like Peter Lawford, knew he was playing with fire. She was still a teenager.

But Wilding hadn't stopped thinking about her. Once she arrived in London for *Ivanhoe*, he called, took both Elizabeth and Peggy Rutledge to dinner, then invited Elizabeth to dinner alone the next evening. Before Elizabeth knew what was happening, she was in love with him. He was honest about his life and situation. Though married, he planned to divorce his wife, Kay

Young. He also wanted Elizabeth to know that basically he was broke. Though he had made money, he couldn't somehow hold on to it. Regardless of his financial state or hers, and regardless that he was twenty years her senior, her decision to marry him didn't take long at all.

Many would be hard-pressed to figure out why Elizabeth fell for him. Perhaps after the catastrophe of Hilton, she sought a mature, more experienced and worldly man. Wilding certainly was that. Perhaps it was his easygoing gentleness that may have called to mind her father. Perhaps it was his balance, his sanity, his awareness of who he was.

Shortly before leaving London, she cabled her mother, saying she was thinking of her and couldn't wait to see her in Beverly Hills. Her name *and* Michael Wilding's were signed to the cable.

The families and friends of Elizabeth and Nicky, as well as the public at large, had no choice but to accept the fact that the Hilton marriage would never be patched up. The reason why? Elizabeth announced plans to marry Michael Wilding. What delayed the nuptials was Elizabeth's divorce, which would not be final until the end of the year. Nor was Wilding's divorce finalized. For the moviegoing public, Elizabeth Taylor no longer looked like that innocent girl it had loved for so many years. As for Elizabeth, she didn't seem to care what the public thought.

For Taylor's parents, such a forthcoming marriage was much too soon. But Sara understood that there was no use trying to talk to Elizabeth. MGM didn't like the possible fallout from the publicity. This was still a nineteen-year-old girl embarking on a second marriage to a man who—though in the process of divorcing his wife—was technically still married. And he was an older man, at that. Interestingly, at one point press accounts listed Wilding's age as forty-two. Other times it was forty-one. Then it became thirty-nine. Meanwhile, Wilding was "a mere child at heart," Elizabeth told the press.

At MGM, some questions must have been asked as to whether Taylor might run off to live in England. Rushing to star her in *The Girl Who Had Everything*—a remake of Metro's big 1931 hit *A Free Soul*, which had starred Norma Shearer and Clark Gable—the studio felt that the title alone was perfect for Elizabeth. Perhaps more important, the film might take Elizabeth's mind off Wilding. But the script was in terrible shape. While MGM scrambled to get it into shape, once her divorce was finalized, Elizabeth hopped on a plane and flew to England—with the intent of marrying Wilding. Seeing her off at the Los Angeles airport were a resigned Sara and Francis.

"The sight of the week," said Hopper, "was Elizabeth Taylor's parents waving her off on a plane that carried her 6000 miles to marry Michael Wilding, a man old enough to be her father."

Michael Wilding may not have known what was hitting him. He certainly loved this teenager, but marriage so soon? Regardless, he met Elizabeth at the London airport. Ready as she was to tie the knot, in her haste in leaving Los Angeles, she had forgotten to bring her divorce papers. The marriage was momentarily post-poned, but not for long. The divorce papers were "radio-photo-ed" to England.

Thus, on February 21, 1952, Liz and Mike, as the press now called them, separately entered London's Caxton Hall, where, during a fifteen-minute ceremony, they were married. British producer Herbert Wilcox and his wife, British actress Anna Neagle, were their witnesses. As they left Caxton Hall, Taylor looked "dainty and dewy-eyed," but Wilding "was looking apprehensive." No wonder. Outside, more than a thousand people lined the street, all the while shouting and screaming, while waiting for a glimpse of the newlyweds, or to be more precise, to see Elizabeth. The couple "was pushed and squeezed as they struggled to their car." In many respects, it was a replay of the day she had married Hilton. "Elizabeth Taylor Wedding Turns

Into Minor Riot" was the front-page headline in the *Los Angeles Times*. The bride was now nineteen. The groom's age was listed as thirty-nine. Afterward, the couple honeymooned in Europe and then moved into an apartment in Mayfair.

"Michael is a sweet, charming person," said his former wife Kay Young, "but I don't think he's the right type for marriage. He's afraid of responsibility." Young may have been right. Perhaps he also was not right for marriage because there were whispers he might be gay. Or bisexual. But perhaps reluctantly Wilding soon had to develop a sense of responsibility. Or at least try. He also had to start to think about finances.

While she remained in London, MGM rushed to get a Taylor picture into production. No matter what its reservations about her marriage, the studio knew all too well that Elizabeth was the one young star about whom there was an intense public fascination, the kind that had been reserved for great movie legends. MGM talked of a film *Saadia* to be shot in Morocco with Taylor and Italian star Vittorio Gassman. But nothing came of that. Though she was set to return to the States to do *The Girl Who Had Everything* in April, delays piled up because the script still needed work, according to MGM. This turned out to be true, but what was really holding things up was Taylor's demand for more money.

MGM had to renew her contract. Though the studio system was in the waning days of its great power, these were still the years when movie companies had ironclad contracts that gave little breathing space for its actors and actresses. Taylor felt comfortable at MGM, where she still had friendships with Helen Rose and Sydney Guilaroff, as well as executive Benny Thau and with producer Pandro S. Berman, despite their battles. She had no desire to leave the studio. A new deal was negotiated, but it was a tough one. Top representatives of teenaged Elizabeth pressured the studio into terms that provided her better money. Yet she still was not really free to select her films or her directors. But what made the new deal sweeter to Taylor was MGM's agreement to put Wilding under contract, too. That was the kind of power she now had. When Wilding had visited her in Los Angeles before the marriage, she had made sure he got out and met people. Understanding industry politics and policies, she was teaching Wilding the rules of the game of the town. And from her vantage point, the rules of the game also meant that if the studio wanted her, it would have to take him, too. Her deal would be in effect in June.

Meanwhile, Elizabeth enjoyed lying low in their deluxe Mayfair apartment—just being Mrs. Wilding. At one point when there was a fire in the apartment building, Taylor and husband simply refused to leave. It soon was extinguished. Apparently, even the fire was willing to defer to Elizabeth Taylor.

In June 1952, Taylor returned to Los Angeles. At the airport, she carried a stray kitten that a waiter had given her—a picture-perfect image for her arrival. Still in England, Wilding would join her later. In the meantime, she had to find a new home. "I may just turn that chore over to Mike," she said. She had other things on her mind. So did MGM. She let studio officials know that she'd have to start *The Girl Who Had Everything* immediately. "I hit them with the news that I was going to have a baby and that they had better not delay things if they wanted me in the picture. What a rush and a scramble to put the picture before the cameras in two weeks with a fast polishing job."

Elizabeth had turned twenty that past February, and she was now calling as many of the shots as she could. *The Girl Who Had Everything*—the story of a beautiful spoiled daughter of an unscrupulous attorney who falls for one of his gangster clients—was quickly assembled with Latin heartthrob Fernando Lamas as her gangster boyfriend, Gig Young as her devoted other boyfriend, and veteran William Powell as her attorney father. It was directed by Richard Thorpe, who had directed *Ivanhoe*, which had not yet opened. MGM wanted to keep her happy: Helen Rose did the costumes; Sydney Guilaroff was the hairstylist. Once Wilding arrived in Los Angeles, the house hunting was put in his hands. "The only thing is that house hunting has been a problem," he said. "Everything we have looked at appears to cost some fantastic price like $60,000 to $100,000. We had no thought of such an investment." Finally, they moved into a home on Summit Ridge Drive, north of Beverly Hills, that sat on a high flat knoll on three and a half acres.

With Michael yet to establish himself in Hollywood, Elizabeth became the breadwinner in the Wilding household. Within a few months, she acquired control over the US bonds, now valued at $47,000, that had been kept in trust for her and represented some of the savings she had accumulated during her years as a minor at MGM. The court had required that 10 percent of her earnings be put in a savings account and 15 percent be invested in the bonds.

Of her impending motherhood, she said, "I hope it will mean a new growth in my work. But even that isn't important compared with the meaning of the event itself."

Clearly, her work as an actress meant much to her. The advance buzz on *Ivanhoe* was strong. "In it Elizabeth is credited with giving one of her finest portrayals," said Hedda Hopper, "as the tragically menaced Rebecca, who is eventually saved in fierce combat by Robert Taylor."

Opening that October, *Ivanhoe* received some glowing reviews. The *Los Angeles Times* called it "rich in dramatic happenings on the grand scale" and commented that "Miss Taylor, [George] Sanders, and the British actors fare perhaps the best in attaining the requisite conviction for their portrayals." In the *New York Times*, critic Bosley Crowther wrote that "a remarkable forcefulness is achieved and the picture brings off a serious lesson in fairness and tolerance not customary in spectacle films. Credit for this may be given to Elizabeth Taylor, in the role of Rebecca, and Felix Aylmer, as Isaac, as well as the men who made the film. For both of these able performers handle with grace and eloquence the frank and faceted characters of the rejected Jews." Crowther also named *Ivanhoe* one of the top ten pictures of the year. Not only did *Ivanhoe* become a box office champion, but it also won an Oscar nomination as Best Motion Picture. Excited by the two Taylors' appearances in *Ivanhoe*, which was far sexier and more compelling than the coupling of Robert Taylor and Joan Fontaine, MGM was now making plans to team the two Taylors again in the period pictures *Knights of the Round Table* and *All the Brothers Were Valiant*, with Richard Thorpe directing and Berman producing. Elizabeth Taylor, however, ended up doing neither film.

Socially, Elizabeth still saw some of the old crowd, those young studio people who Nicky Hilton had thought were bores. When Jane Powell gave birth to her second child, a daughter, Elizabeth and Michael were among the first to visit her in the hospital. She was also still friendly with actor Marshall Thompson and his wife, Barbara, and in touch with Anne Westmore. But her social life moved in another direction. During the early years of his career, Wilding's closest friend was another struggling actor named James Stewart who eventually changed his name —obviously, because Hollywood already had *its* James Stewart—and became a swashbuckling matinee idol known as Stewart Granger. Hedda Hopper would always be "suspicious" of the relationship between the two men and would find herself with a lawsuit when she wrote that they were homosexuals, which both men vehemently denied. During these years, the Wildings spent time—dinners and parties—with Stewart Granger and his young wife, British actress Jean Simmons, who, with her dark hair and striking eyes, bore a resemblance to Elizabeth. Montgomery Clift and Wilding also got along. More of the newly emerging hot young stars in Hollywood, such as Rock Hudson and Carroll Baker, would eventually be guests at the Wilding home.

Constantly adding to her menagerie, Elizabeth now had a retriever given to her by Uncle Howard to go along with her toy poodle, as well as three baby poodles, a wire-hair dachshund, four cats, and one bird. Constantly cleaning up after them were the household housekeeper *and* Wilding. But, as always, none of that fazed Elizabeth. Nor did she pick up after herself. Again that was still left up to the housekeeper. Nor did she know much about cooking or maintaining a house, other than instructing a staff on how she wanted things done. She also remained constantly late for appointments and engagements. Her mother once said that Elizabeth's tardiness had been the only thing that had ever made her impatient with her daughter. Elizabeth didn't even bat an eyelash about that. If she was late, she was late. It was *their* problem, not hers.

On January 7, 1953, twenty-year-old Elizabeth gave birth via cesarean to a seven-pound three-ounce son, Michael Howard Wilding, named after her husband and her brother. Or, as her uncle Howard might have liked to think, after him as well. Pictures of mother and son and of mother, father, and son ran in newspapers around the country. In May, Elizabeth was named Mother of the Year by the Society of American Florists. She really looked like the "girl" who had everything.

But MGM was impatient to put its prized commodity back to work. There was talk of teaming her with Robert Taylor in yet another historical film based on Sir Walter Scott's *Quentin Durward*. The film would later be produced, but without Elizabeth. Sometimes it appeared as if the studio considered her for just about any of the big-budgeted pictures, but, from her vantage point, not for the dramatically challenging ones. Elizabeth knew she had to get back to work. She needed the money. Though Wilding went into the film *Torch Song* opposite Joan Crawford, no one was pounding on the door to give him a role.

Then came a request for Elizabeth from Paramount. The studio had been filming *Elephant Walk*, a romantic drama set against a backdrop of a tea plantation in British Ceylon. Starring in it were Vivien Leigh, Peter Finch, and Dana Andrews under the direction of William Dieterle. Emotionally fragile and bipolar—although her condition at the time was undiagnosed—Vivien Leigh had preferred, after her Oscar-winning triumph in *Gone With the Wind*, to act on the stage in England and only occasionally did movies, which was unfortunate. Film captured perfectly the moods and tones of this subtle, sensitive actress, born for the power of the close-up. In 1951, she had won a second Oscar for her performance as Blanche DuBois in *A Streetcar Named Desire*. She, of course, was the actress to whom the girl Elizabeth had been compared. She was also reported to be Elizabeth's favorite actress.

Now the talk in Hollywood was about what had happened during Leigh's work on *Elephant Walk*. Married to Laurence Olivier, Leigh had a disastrous love affair with her costar Finch. In the midst of filming, she suffered a nervous breakdown so severe that the production lurched to a halt. Paramount was in a panic. Finding a replacement for Vivien Leigh was not going to be easy. Some long shots of her already filmed would be kept in the movie. Now the studio wanted Elizabeth, who was rushed into the picture without much time to prepare.

Moviegoers would always remember the action sequence that marked the climax of *Elephant Walk*. The tea planter and his lonely wife, played by Finch and Taylor, live in a luxurious mansion that sits on the migration path of the region's elephants. Throughout the film, those elephants struggle to return to their grounds and finally do so in a spectacular sequence during which they bulldoze the walls surrounding the home, then enter, almost by the front door, and stomp away, trapping Taylor. As she runs up a staircase, the elephants demolish the staircase itself. The sequence would be pure delirious movie fun, more so than the critics would be willing to acknowledge, and though Elizabeth was not a damsel-in-distress kind of actress, she—with the help of a stunt double—handled the sequence beautifully as audiences jumped and screamed along with her.

But as Taylor noted, "It was about this time in my life that I began my really ludicrous series of accidents—and there have been too many to be believed." Surprisingly, an accident occurred while Taylor was posing for stills in a jeep with costars Andrews and Finch. Because it had to look as if their hair was blowing in the wind, "an airplane propeller was trained on us," said Taylor. A tiny piece of metal had flown in her eye. "Every time I blinked, there would be the most awful scratching sensation." Later a doctor told her, "My dear, you have a foreign object in your eye." "Anybody I know?" asked Taylor. But it was a far more serious accident than anyone realized at first. There was soon a fear she might lose that eye. Not only was the metal deeply lodged, it had also rusted. Surgery was performed. "They can't knock you out because you have to keep your eye open and stare at a certain spot on the wall. They have a needle with a tiny knife at the end and you can hear them cutting your eye." Later an ulcer formed on the eye, and there was another operation. Fortunately, the surgery was success-fully performed. But there were weeks of recuperation, during which both of her eyes were bandaged.

●●●

Afterward, MGM immediately put Elizabeth into *Rhapsody*, another romantic-triangle film in which she played a spoiled wealthy young woman torn between two classical musicians, played by Vittorio Gassman and newcomer John Ericson, under the direction of Charles Vidor. On the day after completing *Rhapsody*, Elizabeth took off with her husband and son for a much-needed two-month vacation abroad.

Their first stop was London. "We want little Michael to meet his grandparents," said Elizabeth. "He'll stay with them when we go on to the Continent." Then Elizabeth and Wilding traveled to Stockholm. But suddenly Elizabeth took ill with influenza, or so the press was informed. Bed rest was ordered, but she flew to Copenhagen, despite the fact that she now suffered from a blinding migraine. Plagued by migraines for years, the debilitating headaches came more frequently than the public knew. But that was not her only ailment. Also suffering from back problems, she was in excruciating pain. Once at her hotel in Copenhagen, she collapsed. The story broke that the twenty-one-year-old star had heart problems and that she had also suffered a nervous breakdown. Though reports of the heart problems were dismissed, the breakdown stories continued. Wilding himself said it was a "nervous collapse" but "nothing serious." But how could someone have a nervous collapse that in some way was not serious? And what would bring on a "nervous collapse"? Was it the heavy movie schedule? Was it the fact that she, as the principal money earner in the marriage, was worried about her finances? Was it postpartum depression? No one was saying. A statement was issued that her influenza had "worsened her condition."

With lingering questions about what precisely ailed her, the couple ignored the press and left Copenhagen by car to go to the countryside in search of peace and quiet. But in less than a half hour, they rushed back to their hotel. Elizabeth was ill again. A doctor was called in. A few days later their son, Michael, was brought from London to join his parents. Surprisingly, a relatively composed-looking Elizabeth greeted her son at the airport. But for those who looked more closely, it was apparent that she was troubled and tense. Leaving the airport, the family returned to their Copenhagen hotel. Elizabeth and young Michael each immediately went to bed.

"Reports of her illness have all been wildly exaggerated," Wilding said when the couple returned to London in October. "She has a nervous heart but it is nothing very serious. She has been overdoing it." Clearly, she was strained and restless. But about what was anybody's guess. Was her life not playing out the way she had been programmed—by Hollywood—to believe it should? A happy perfect marriage. An adorable son. A successful career. These were early signs of discontent and discord in the marriage. Tending to Elizabeth's particular crises—and her mood swings and her need for attention—was Wilding, who may have now fully realized that his child bride was precisely that—a child bride. The studio's official line was that she suffered from "nervous exhaustion." Nonetheless, MGM's remedy for such exhaustion was simply to put her to work in a period drama being shot in London, *Beau Brummell*, opposite Wilding's longtime friend Stewart Granger.

At the end of the year, when asked her New Year's resolution, Elizabeth stated simply: "It would be a wonderful new year for me if when next Christmas season came around I had succeeded in overcoming many of my faults. My wish is to develop the qualities I admire so much in my husband. I love his patience, calmness, and his wonderful live-and-let-live philosophy."

Not long afterward, stories circulated that there were serious problems in the Wilding household.

Chapter 8

PUTTING OUT FEELERS about producers to work with on a solo album, Michael spoke to Quincy Jones, who, during the making of *The Wiz*, observed Michael's still untapped powerful potential. "I saw his sensitivity," said Jones. "He didn't miss a thing." This kid could one day own the business. To Michael's surprise, Jones suggested himself as producer for the proposed album. Therein the two began their extraordinary collaboration.

By then, Jones had smashed through barriers and established himself as one of the most accomplished and respected creative artists in the music industry. Having started his career while still in his teens, the Seattle-born Jones had studied at Schillinger House (later the Berklee College of Music), was a talented trumpeter, had toured around the world, and had served as an arranger or producer or musical director with some of the most talented, original music stars of the twentieth century: Dinah Washington, Frank Sinatra, Ray Charles, Lionel Hampton, Count Basie, Sarah Vaughan, Billy Eckstine, and the contemporary funk team the Brothers Johnson.

He also became an executive at Mercury Records, emerging as one of the first African Americans to hold such a position at a white-owned company, no small feat during the years of his rise. But he had achieved even more. One of the first African Americans to write scores for Hollywood films, including *In the Heat of the Night* and *The Pawnbroker*, he was also one of the first to be Oscar nominated for his scores on such films as *In Cold Blood* and *Banning*. Jones clearly knew the music business inside and out, yet the bigwigs at Epic Records balked at bringing Jones in to produce Michael's album, saying he was too associated with jazz. Aware of what he wanted, Michael, however, saw something the Epic executives didn't and was insistent. Jones came on board.

Working on the album that became *Off the Wall*, Jones and Michael recorded music by England's Rod Temperton, who composed the title song "Off the Wall" as well as "Rock with You"; Carole Bayer Sager and David Foster's "It's the Falling in Love"; Paul McCartney's "Girlfriend"; Tom Bahler's "She's Out of My Life"; and Stevie Wonder and Susaye Greene-Brown's "I Can't Help It." Also included were songs by Michael: "Don't Stop 'Til You Get Enough," "Workin' Day and Night," and—with cowriter Louis Johnson—"Get on the Floor." On all but two songs—"She's Out of My Life" and "I Can't Help It"—Michael not only performed the leads but also the background vocals. And at times, it was partly a family affair. The openings—musical intros of sorts—for the songs "Don't Stop 'Til You Get Enough" and "Workin' Day and Night" were the syncopating sounds of Michael, Janet, and Randy on "a casaba, cowbell, and glass bottle" that were originally done for a demo tape but used in the final production. Who could ever forget that, following the opening of "Don't Stop 'Til You Get Enough," there is suddenly another sound: "Jackson screams and the orchestra explodes," said music critic Tom Fusilli. "Sweeping strings, punch horns, bass, drums and handclaps form the foundation under Jackson's vocals." Michael also went to town on "Burn This Disco Out."

Making the album *Off the Wall* was a demanding but exhilarating experience. Jones pushed Jackson to explore new emotional aspects within himself to expand his vocal range. "I wanted him to sing down low," said Jones. "A lot of his habits came from Motown. They wanted him to sing high, but by then we had a relationship of trust, an honesty with each other." Quincy Jones recalled that after recording the ballad "She's Out of My Life," Michael was so emotionally drained by this tale of lost love that he broke down. Originally, Jones thought the song would be good for Sinatra, which of course it might have been. But Michael's version was perfection. The same was true of his other ballads on this classic album. On those earlier songs with his brothers—"Got to Be There," "Never Can Say Goodbye," and "I Wanna Be Where You Are," he had set the stage for these new ballads. Yet he believed his brothers had never been enthusiastic about performing the material. Michael himself said: "The ballads were what made *Off the Wall* a Michael Jackson album."

Released in 1979, *Off the Wall* not only carried Michael musically in a new direction but also brought the Jackson image forward. He was no longer a precocious kid possibly one step removed from the deeper emotions in some of his music but was now right in its grip. One could imagine him smoothly dancing in the clubs or maturely talking about matters of the heart—and heartache. Michael Jackson became Michael the young man who appeared to have experienced the music he sang. Whether he actually had was still open to question. But who cared—at this point, the music was so good.

Publicity photos for the album also displayed a more mature Michael. Dressed in a dark suit and bow tie, he looked like a dapper yet sensitive and sweet-tempered young man ready to go out on the town. He appeared different from the Motown kid in other ways. By this point, he had undergone cosmetic surgery to slenderize the "big nose" that had tormented him when he looked in the mirror—and especially when taunted by his father. His nose job became an open secret not only in the industry but within the general public. Some criticism within the African American community started—and grew within the next few years—that he was trying to escape being black, but the criticism at this point was nothing drastic. Most were too excited by the music and the emergence of the new Michael Jackson.

The critics praised the album. *"Off the Wall* presents Michael Jackson as the Stevie Wonder of the Eighties,"* wrote Stephen Holden in *Rolling Stone*. "Jackson's vocal syncopation is reminiscent of the master's breathless, dreamy stutter. Throughout, Jackson's feathery-timbered tenor is extraordinarily beautiful. It slides smoothly into a startling falsetto that's used very daringly. The singer's ultradramatic phrasing, which rakes huge emotional risks and wins every time, wrings the last drop of pathos from Tom Bahler's 'She's Out of My Life.' " Holden concluded: "A triumph for producer Quincy Jones as well as for Michael Jackson, *Off the Wall* represents discofied post-Motown glamour at its classiest." It earned three American Music Awards for Michael's solo efforts, but Michael was disappointed that only one song on the album garnered two Grammy nominations.

Though "Don't Stop 'Til You Get Enough" was nominated as Best Disco Recording, it lost. The song won, however, for Best R&B Vocal Performance, Male. Years later, in 2008, *Off the Wall* was inducted into the Grammy Hall of Fame. For Epic, the best news was that it was a huge commercial success. It was the first album by a solo artist to have three US top ten hits: "Don't Stop 'Til You Get Enough," "Rock with You," and the title track.

Following the success of *Off the Wall*, Michael was even more pursued, discussed, and sought after as he not only further captured the imagination of the fans but also of other celebrities. In many respects, he was always starstruck, no matter how famous he himself became. But now in what turned out to be a very outgoing period for him, he seemed eager to meet even more of the famous, the powerful, the much-discussed. During this time, he was to meet an array of such stars as Gregory Peck, Gene Kelly, Yul Brynner, and Cary Grant.

He formed special friendships with established female stars, women who seemed to offer him a motherly comfort and perhaps a motherly wisdom. He struck up friendships with such stars as Liza Minnelli and Jane Fonda, both adult children of stars of the Old Hollywood that fascinated Michael, both accomplished in their own right, each an Oscar-winning actress, Minnelli for *Cabaret*, Fonda for *Klute* and *Coming Home*. His interest in Liza Minnelli, daughter of Judy Garland, was not a surprise. He was thrilled when she took him to meet her father, director Vincente Minnelli.

But no doubt many observers were indeed surprised by his friendship with the controversial, highly political Fonda, who had shocked and alienated some Americans during the war in Vietnam when she was an antiwar activist and was sometimes called "Hanoi Jane." Michael was hardly a political firebrand; if anything, he seemed apolitical. And Fonda seemed too serious about politics and social causes to take an interest in anyone who didn't have such interests, although later Fonda would make some twenty-two exercise videos that became hugely successful and altered her public image. But Michael was different for Fonda. That immense talent and that boyish innocence were obviously appealing. Michael also was now more intrigued than ever by the prospect of an acting career in films. He could learn from Fonda.

At one point, she invited him to visit her in New Hampshire, where she was shooting the film *On Golden Pond* with her father, Henry, and Katharine Hepburn. Before his arrival, Jane Fonda spoke to Hepburn, known for her feisty temperament, seeking her permission to have him on the set. Hepburn was not happy, Fonda recalled. "Then the crew said, 'You don't understand. It's Michael Jackson!' "

In the beginning, Hepburn didn't seem to have any idea who he was, but she liked him, even seemed captivated by him. "He wanted to be a movie star," said Fonda. "And he had a tape recorder with him, and every day I would bring him to the set, and in between scenes she would sit down in a chair and pull over a chair for him and tell him stories. I wish I knew where those tapes were.

"And every story embedded a lesson. For example, she talked about Laurette Taylor—and anyone who was alive to see Laurette Taylor in [The] Glass Menagerie [on Broadway] has seen as great a moment of acting as [there is]. So she described to Michael seeing this transcendent piece of acting [and how]." Hepburn stressed that an artist has to stay hungry. New challenges always had to be taken. Said Fonda: "What a great thing to say to a young, rising star like Michael. 'You gotta stay hungry.' "

Michael, of course, was eating it all up. He was coming face-to-face with history told to him by an eyewitness. He also talked to Henry Fonda and, afterward, remained in touch with Hepburn.

Relaxed on his visit to the On Golden Pond shoot, he stayed with Fonda in her cabin for ten days. Fonda recalled that the two even went skinny-dipping together. And they spent time talking into the night "about acting, life, everything. Africa. Issues. We talked and talked and talked." By then Michael had read more and was eager to learn more about the world. Fonda believed his intelligence was "instinctual and emotional, like a child's. If any artist loses that childlikeness, you lose a lot of creative juice." From her perspective, Michael created a world around himself to protect his creativity.

Maybe some of these women brought to Michael's mind his gentle tutor, Rose Fine, who had opened the door to a world of knowledge.

It was also as if meeting some of these women was a prelude to Elizabeth.

Three years after *Off the Wall*, Michael and Quincy Jones worked together again on the album *Thriller*.

From the beginning, Michael wanted *Thriller* to be a big album, bigger than *Off the Wall*. Already trying to top his own record, he also remained resentful that *Off the Wall* had not won him the major awards that he knew he deserved. With focus and a rush of energy, plus some adrenaline-fed nervous tension, he embarked on his collaboration with Jones. Recording began on April 14, 1982, at noon at the Westlake Recording Studios in Los Angeles. The budget for the album was $750,000. Once again Michael and Jones gathered an expert creative team of writers and musicians. Originally, thirty songs were recorded. But only nine would meet the rigorous standards of both Jackson and Jones and thus be included on the album.

Four of the songs on the final album were written by Michael: "Beat It," "Wanna Be Startin' Somethin'," "Billie Jean," and "The Girl Is Mine." Rumors would long persist that "Billie Jean" grew out of Michael's experiences with a crazed fan who believed he was the father of her child. But that was denied by Michael. "There was never a real 'Billie Jean,' " he said. "The girl in the song is a composite of people we've been plagued by over the years. This kind of thing has happened to some of my brothers and I used to be really amazed by it." For Michael, these obsessed women were deadly serious, and "Billie Jean" was a way of coping with such situations and also releasing himself of certain tensions. "Wanna Be Startin' Somethin' " expressed his feelings about the contentious wife—ever ready to create a scene —of one of his brothers.

As was his fundamental technique for creating his music, Michael—who could neither read nor write music—would first work out a song in his head, then after it had taken shape sing it into a tape recorder, working it over until the number was right. He also enlisted the help of other family members to do demos of the songs. On "Beat It," Janet performed backup. He used the demos to fine-tune his work and make important changes and additions to the sound. He once described his process "as a gestation, almost like a pregnancy or something. It's an explosion of something so beautiful, you go, Wow!" He also said: "The lyrics, the strings, the chords, everything comes at the moment like a gift that is put right into your head and that's how I hear it." Afterward, during the actual recording, he performed from memory.

The first track to be recorded was Michael's duet with Paul McCartney on "The Girl Is Mine." For Michael, it was always exciting to work with McCartney.

Again there was music by Rod Temperton—not only the title song (which he originally called "Starlight" or "Midnight Man") but also "Baby Be Mine" and "The Lady in My Life." Some might view "Thriller" as something of a novelty song, a spooky, scary and maybe even sometimes corny number that opens with the sounds of a creaking door and floorboards, with thunder and wind sounds, and a howling dog. It also had a voice-over by Vincent Price, the star of sweet, dopey B-horror movies. Rod Temperton recalled that during his cab ride to the studio to do the actual recording of "Thriller," he wrote Price's spoken introduction to the song. Whether corny or scary or not, all the elements came together perfectly.

What would make "Thriller" a monumental song would be the video for it.

The other two songs were "P.Y.T. (Pretty Young Thing)," written by James Ingram and Quincy Jones, and "Human Nature," written by Steve Porcaro and John Bettis. Among the musicians were jazz saxophonist Tom Scott, who played the lyricon on "Wanna Be Startin' Somethin'," bassist Louis Johnson on "Billie Jean," and on "Beat It," master guitarist Eddie Van Halen performing the guitar solo.

Creative differences surfaced between Michael and Jones. The two reportedly disagreed on the introduction to "Billie Jean," which Jones thought was too long. But Michael wanted it in because he said it made him want to dance. At one point the song was to be called "Not My Lover" because Jones thought the Billie Jean title might make people think of tennis star Billie Jean King. Obviously Jones decided to stick with the original title. But a story that Jones initially did not want "Billie Jean" on the album was emphatically denied by Jones. "And this whole fallacy of me not liking 'Billie Jean' is a lie," he said. "It is some lie that started somewhere. Anybody can hear that record's a smash. And also I know where it came from."

Jones, however, felt that a song by Michael and Greg Phillinganes called "P.Y.T." didn't work. But he liked the title. In the end, the song itself was dumped but the title was used for the song that James Ingram and Jones wrote. When the final nine songs were completed, neither Jones nor Michael was satisfied. The music wasn't jelling the way they wanted. A week each was spent remixing each of the nine songs. After almost seven months, *Thriller* was completed on November 8, 1982. Epic Records released it on November 30, 1982. Ultimately, *Thriller* presented yet another portrait of a mature, romantic Michael Jackson. It would also delve into "darker," sometimes disturbing themes of paranoia, fear, and violence.

The accolades poured in. Some perceptive critics now saw Michael's impact on American culture tied in with attitudes on race. "*Thriller* is a wonderful pop record, the latest statement by one of the great singers in popular music today. But it is more than that. It is as hopeful a sign as we have had yet that the destructive barriers that spring up regularly between white and black music—and between whites and blacks—in this culture may be breached once again," wrote John Rockwell in the *New York Times*. Rockwell also wrote of Jackson's "ethereal tenor"—and its historical significance. "His deployment of that voice, which he mixes subtly with all manner of falsetto effects, is the greatest example of this sort of erotic keening since the heyday of Smokey Robinson. Ever since the craze for the castrato in the 17th century, high male voices, with their paradoxical blend of asexuality and sensuousness, ecstasy and pain, have been the most prized of all vocal types, and Mr. Jackson epitomizes such singing for our time better than anyone, in any musical genre."

But Rockwell also saw the broader cultural significance of the album—and Michael. "Black music lurks at the heart of nearly all American pop, but it is an old, old story that blacks tend to be slighted by white audiences, a few established older superstars partly excepted. Black performers' mass success waxes and wanes, and in recent years it has been waning. The dangers of isolation —more particularly, of whites being cut off from the roots of what they perceive as their own music—have only been reinforced by radio, with its 'demographics' playlists that reinforce a musically insensitive and morally indefensible segregation."

Rockwell also addressed those critics who professed that Michael was not black—and those who would have preferred that he not be. At the same time, there was the idea that Michael really neither could nor should be classified as a black artist. He had supposedly "transcended" race. Of course, no white artist was ever required to "transcend" his or her race. Rockwell took note of this fallacy. "Mr. Jackson's appeal is so wide, however, that white publications and radio stations that normally avoid 'black music' seem willing to pretend he isn't black after all. On one level, that's admirable, in that color distinctions are often best avoided altogether. But Mr. Jackson is black . . . he still works honorably within the context of contemporary black popular music at its fervent, eclectic best. If this album is anywhere near as successful as *Off the Wall*, it may remind white audiences of what they are missing elsewhere."

History would be made, of course. *Thriller* was a smash hit, rapidly selling at that time some twenty-seven million copies and proving to be the biggest-grossing album of all time. But what added to the album's appeal and boosted sales were the videos made from the singles "Beat It" and "Billie Jean." Here Michael's brilliance as a dancer was put on dazzling display, under the guiding light of choreographer Michael Peters. Michael also enjoyed making the videos because here was his chance at another stab at a movie career. Steven Spielberg had talked of starring him in a movie version of *Peter Pan*. But nothing would come of that. For Michael, the idea was that maybe his performances in his videos might make Hollywood see his potential as a leading man.

But ironically what added to the album's status as a classic was the video that followed of its title song. No video before or after had the force or power of the video for "Thriller." It was a sign of Michael's artistic and marketing skills that he got it made. Initially, there had been no plans to even release it as a single. Nor did CBS Records president Walter Yetnikoff, as well as Michael's close adviser and lawyer John Branca envision a video of the song, according to writer Nancy Griffin. But Michael believed a new video would help maintain the album's sales. At one point, Epic's head of promotions, Frank DiLeo, liked the idea of a third video from the album, and a video of "Thriller" seemed the right choice.

Michael then moved forward with plans. Having seen director John Landis's film *An American Werewolf in London*, Michael invited Landis to Hayvenhurst to discuss a video of the song. Landis wanted to do it as a short thirty-five-millimeter film. After a concept had been worked out, the budget would be $900,000. CBS's Yetnikoff was not excited about a new video. Michael decided to put up his own money. Eventually, Yetnikoff forked over $100,000.

Landis's script for "Thriller" was about a guy on a date with his girl at a movie theater. They watch a horror film, then things really turn scary as he is transformed before his terrified date's eyes into a ghoul with a werewolf face with a beard, fangs, and monstrous bulging eyes. Part of the video was filmed at Los Angeles's Palace

Theatre. Part was filmed on the streets of downtown LA. A group of top-notch talents was enlisted for the production. Oscar-winning makeup wizard Rick Baker created the astonishing transformation for Michael. Robert Paynter was hired as the cinematographer. Michael Peters worked again with Michael on the choreography. Landis's wife, designer Deborah Nadoolman Landis, did the costumes. Cast as Jackson's girlfriend was pixieish Ola Ray, a twenty-three-year-old former *Playboy* Playmate, who was clearly fascinated by him. "Michael is very special," she said at the time. "Since we've been working together we've been getting closer. He was a very shy person, but he's opened up. I think he's lived a sheltered life. He knows a lot of entertainers, but he needs friends that he can go out and relax and enjoy himself with."

Ray proved to be the right "girl" for the video. Hers was a "kittenish" sexuality. The girl in the video couldn't come on too strong. She had to seem as innocent as Michael. Yet she was sensual, to the point where audiences would be waiting for the two to hook up. Because of his Jehovah's Witness background, which forbade premarital sex, Michael shied away from conversations about sex. As much as he could, he probably also shied away from thoughts about sex. But such thoughts were definitely there. When shooting the sequence at the Palace Theatre where Michael and Ray walk outside the movie house, Landis wanted another take. Something had not jelled between Michael and Ray, namely Michael's ardor for the girl. "Make it sexy this time," Landis recalled telling Michael, who then asked: "How?" Landis told him: "You know, as if you want to fuck her." Michael clearly did not feel comfortable hearing that! According to Nancy Griffin, Landis also said that at one point Michael confessed he was a virgin. But when Landis reshot the sequence, there was a sexy Michael! Ray herself was so captivated by him that indeed the two on-screen were a couple as they glanced into each other's eyes and endearingly smiled to one another. A big moment in the *Thriller* video—before Michael's transformation—occurred when he tells Ray: "I'm not like other guys." Here the lines between Michael on-screen and off- were clearly blurred, much to the enjoyment of his audience. Will there be a big confession or announcement? Of course, it turns out he's not like other guys because he's a ghoul, a zombie.

The most memorable sequence is the dance of the zombies that concludes the video. Accompanied by some twenty dancers, all in ghoulish makeup and costumes, Michael himself was made-up to look gaunt and ghostly. Dressed in that red jacket, he moves to the beat of the music—and to the beat of his own dancing style: smooth, precise with unexpected stylized twists and turns. Indeed he seems splendidly other-worldly.

During filming, guests showed up to witness Michael in action, according to Griffin. Eyes were glued to the white limousine that pulled up with its passenger, Jacqueline Kennedy Onassis. Having flown in from New York, she was then an editor at Doubleday and Company and had come to discuss publishing Michael's memoirs—which would become *Moonwalk*. Arriving at other times were Michael's parents, Katherine and Joe; Rock Hudson; Quincy Jones; and Fred Astaire. Marlon Brando also appeared on set. Everyone had the feeling they were witnessing something extraordinary in the making. Yet no one could have predicted just how extraordinary.

Interestingly enough, MTV, then a station devoted to airing videos, had not shown interest in the work of African American artists. In fact, MTV was considered downright hostile to black music. Finally, Yetnikoff at CBS had to threaten to pull all of CBS's other videos if MTV did not air Michael's. As it turned out, Michael's were among the most popular on the station. Also filmed was the documentary *Making Michael Jackson's Thriller*, which was shown on MTV. Videocassettes of the documentary then sold on the new home video market.

The video for "Thriller," however, caused problems for Michael with the Jehovah's Witnesses. According to Jermaine, the group viewed the video as "evil and satanic," because it was thought to celebrate the "occult and the unseen world." Two Jehovah's Witnesses had been on the set during the filming. At one point, Michael wanted to have the negative of the video destroyed because of his concern about the Witnesses' reaction. Thus there was a disclaimer by Michael at the start of the video: "Due to my strong personal convictions, I wish to stress that this film in no way endorses a belief in the occult." Director John Landis had written it.

This became a difficult time for Michael with the group. When his schedule permitted, he still attended Kingdom Hall about four times a week with his mother. He also donned disguises as he went door to door selling Jehovah's Witnesses publications. While on tour, a male and female Witness were sometimes by his side. No one could say he wasn't a dedicated Witness. But in time—around 1987—he would leave the organization because it inhibited him artistically. It was not an easy decision—for him or Katherine. But Katherine supported him.

Although record buyers were ready to fall at Michael's feet following the release of both *Off the Wall* and *Thriller*, perhaps the precise moment that his megastardom was cemented and certified in the mind of the vast public at large came with his appearance on the television special *Motown 25: Yesterday, Today, Forever*. It was an appearance that almost didn't happen and ultimately revealed his tough-minded refusal to give up on his convictions pertaining to all things related to his career and image.

A television special that celebrated Motown Records' quarter-century anniversary, *Motown 25* gathered the company's great stars to perform their big hits: Mary Wells, the Marvelettes, Martha and the Vandellas, the Temptations, the Four Tops, Smokey Robinson and the Miracles, Junior Walker, and Diana Ross and the Supremes. For Motown, this was a tricky situation because of the resentment that many of its performers still harbored about their treatment by the company, specifically by Gordy. Motown had already been faced with lawsuits from performers, including, of course, the Jackson 5. Embittered performers struggled with the decision as to whether they would appear. Especially wounded was Marvin Gaye. He had a bitter divorce from Gordy's sister Anna Gordy, and he accused Motown of having remixed his personal 1981 album *In Our Lifetime* without his consent and rush-releasing it. But he eventually signed on for the show. Gladys Knight and the Pips, however, chose not to participate. Clearly, Motown wanted the Jackson 5, con-sidered by many to be the company's last great act.

While the brothers agreed to perform, along with Jermaine, Michael held off. There was much discussion and debate among Michael and his managers Ron Weisner and Freddy DeMann. Michael's position was that he didn't want to do television. Perhaps true. But everyone knew that Motown wanted only Motown hits. Michael, however, wanted to perform one of his recent big hits released by Epic. He wasn't going to budge in what would amount to another confrontation with Gordy, the man he, in other respects, still idolized. No one could persuade him to do otherwise. Everyone knew Michael was currently the biggest name in popular music. With plans for the show to be taped in April but still without Michael on board, Gordy met with Michael—ironically—at a Motown studio where Michael was editing the mix for "Billie Jean." The two talked at length. By the end of their impromptu meeting, Gordy agreed to let Michael perform "Billie Jean." His Motown compatriots must have delighted at his demands—and his standoff. Michael would perform first with his brothers and then—on his own—do "Billie Jean." It became one of the most memorable moments in television history of the twentieth century, as Michael, once his brothers had left the stage, told the audience how much he liked the old songs. But he liked the new ones, too. A black fedora was passed to him, and wearing a spangly black jacket (that was actually his mother's) and one sequined white glove, designed by Bill Whitten and destined to become a signature piece, he gave a mesmerizing perfor-mance of "Billie Jean." It wasn't just Michael in song that magnetized the audience; it was Michael performing his soon-to-be-signature dance, the moonwalk, giving the illusion that he was walking without doing so at all, a both eerie and hauntingly beautiful, magical series of move-ments. Earlier, with the Jacksons' hit "Dancing Machine" in 1974, Michael had perfected a dance called the robot—stiff rhythmically robotic movements—that became a craze. Now having studied the gliding style and intricate routines of street dancers, he had taken all he had seen to a new artistic height, a new state of grace. Perfectionist that he was, he had choreographed the number. The night before the show, he rehearsed, meticulously reworking his move-ments, in the kitchen of the home at Hayvenhurst. During the show itself, he made it work splen-didly for the space of the stage. He also had decided on the camera work and the lighting.

In the midst of all those Motown stars—all stars for whom Joe and the rest of the family had the utmost respect—Michael had outshone everyone. "He just stole the show," Joe Jackson was said to have exclaimed to Katherine as they sat in the audience. At that precise time—when the program aired on May 16, 1983—audiences around the country saw him in an altogether different light. It was a splendidly coordinated, glowingly hypnotic performance in which he had stretched his own artistic boundaries. Even viewers who knew nothing about dance or current popular music or were not necessarily diehard Jackson fans could not turn away from the greatness they witnessed on those boxes with images that sat in their homes. The child entertainer had become as great as, if not greater than, Elvis, Sinatra, the Beatles, James Brown, Jackie Wilson, Diana Ross, Sammy Davis Jr., and that forgotten great entertainer of the early twentieth century who could do it all—sing, dance, and act—Ethel Waters. For Michael, the greatest compliment was given the morning after the broadcast. A call came from Fred Astaire who told him, "I watched it last night, and I taped it, and I watched it again this morning. You're a helluva mover."

But not everyone was captivated by Michael's performance. Jehovah's Witness officials criticized and disapproved of his moonwalking, so he said, accusing him of "doing burlesque dancing and it was dirty." He was told never to dance like that again.

Chapter 9

IN EARLY 1954, Sara wrote a series of articles on her daughter for *Ladies' Home Journal*. Titled "Elizabeth, My Daughter," these were no shocking exposes about a spoiled child. Some details of Elizabeth's early years were embellished. Some details were glossed over. Certainly, Sara would never reveal the deep friction between Francis and herself, nor comment on a period of estrangement from her daughter. But they were a mother's heartfelt feelings for her child. Sara was crafting a mythology about Elizabeth that ironically enough was based in some ways on a fundamental truth. Elizabeth benefited greatly from a relatively secure childhood with a sound family support system.

No matter what, Sara still and always would love her daughter deeply. Though Sara might not approve of certain aspects of Elizabeth's life, her daughter still basically could do no wrong. Francis felt the same. So did Howard. In turn, Elizabeth's deepest emotional connections and commitments were still to her parents, her brother, and now her child. Howard also had become a father himself, and Elizabeth would always have affection for his wife and his family. As for Michael Wilding, she loved him, too, but that love was never as powerful as her feelings for the others. A great love—outside that family unit—was still something she yearned for even if she might not have yet admitted it to herself. In her films, she had been bred on the idea of great loves, and for her, real life should conform to what the movies had led her to believe.

Whether at the studio or at her home, she spoke her mind and had a temper that flared easily. Sometimes growing impatient with Wilding, she also seemed to enjoy, even thrive on, a good domestic quarrel. But Michael wasn't someone to argue with, since his temper could never match hers. Instead, he had that calm detachment that in her New Year's resolution she said she hoped to find. Asked about Elizabeth, Wilding said: "What is it like being married to a glamour girl? Well, it's like visiting the circus: the lions seem something quite terrible to us, but to the trainers who work with them it's something quite different. Except that Liz isn't like a lion—a bad simile!" He had said more than he intended. Years later Elizabeth's personal assistant Tim Mendelson would say with affection that "she had a genius for creating chaos around her."

Both she and Wilding were also aware that his career had stalled in a terrible way and perhaps permanently. "MGM signed me, brought me over to do *The Law and the Lady* with Greer Garson and sent me back," he said. "They suspended me because I wouldn't do one story [*Latin Lovers*] and then after that there were no stories and Liz was having the baby and we were finding a house and all that. Then came *Torch Song* and two in Europe and then they loaned me to Fox for *The Egyptian*." Though he had a poetic quality, put to good use in the films *Torch Song* and *The Glass Slipper*, with Leslie Caron, he wasn't star material by Hollywood's standards. Neither he nor Elizabeth wanted to admit it, but he was always overshadowed by his young wife. Like Hilton, a frustrated Wilding was becoming *Mr.* Taylor. In some respects, a frustrated Elizabeth felt she was taking care of him.

Once Elizabeth had returned from Europe— from her would-be vacation and from her work on *Beau Brummell*—MGM was quick to star her in a film based on F. Scott Fitzgerald's post–World War I story "Babylon Revisited," which was updated and retitled *The Last Time I Saw Paris*. Now set in post–World War II Paris, it told the story of an American writer who falls in love with a young American woman whose family has lived in France through the war. She's spoiled, uninhibited, and rather reckless—and also in delicate health. He's struggling to hold on to himself and to see his talent flourish.

Ultimately, both are derailed by too much money and without the realization, as Fitzgerald believed, that in American lives there are no second acts.

Serious and perceptive with a tough masculine edge, the film's director Richard Brooks had begun his career as a newspaper writer, then became a novelist, and then with director John Huston cowrote the script for *Key Largo*. Later he would direct *Blackboard Jungle*, a story of rebellious high school students that would be important in the career of the young Sidney Poitier; *Elmer Gantry*, which would bring Burt Lancaster an Oscar; *Sweet Bird of Youth*; *In Cold Blood*; and *Looking for Mr. Goodbar*. He would also direct Elizabeth again in *Cat on a Hot Tin Roof*. Though Brooks originally wanted Montgomery Clift for the role of the writer in *The Last Time I Saw Paris*, the part went to MGM's Van Johnson. Exteriors were shot in Paris with Johnson. But most of the movie was filmed at MGM, starting in April 1954. Working hard to please its star, MGM redecorated Elizabeth's dressing room and added a nursery. Again Helen Rose designed a glamorous wardrobe for Elizabeth, and Sydney Guilaroff created simple yet lush hair-styles, including a short poodle cut that became popular. With a script by Julius Epstein, Philip Epstein, and Richard Brooks, *The Last Time I Saw Paris* was part romantic drama and part ill-conceived attempt to look at a lost generation. Though the film failed to capture Fitzgerald's world of glittering, doomed young souls, glimmers of Fitzgerald's tale were there nonetheless, and Elizabeth identified with its immensely desirable but lost, fragile heroine. The film would mark a turning point in her career. Though it would have none of the power or tragic grandeur of *A Place in the Sun*, *The Last Time I Saw Paris* would wake Elizabeth from a slumber and make her think again about *acting*.

One of her most affecting scenes occurred late in the film. After a night on the town, she arrives home in the midst of a heavy snowfall. Dressed in a vivid red gown, designed so dramatically by Helen Rose, she steps out of a cab that then goes off. Delicately, she walks up the steps that lead to the door of her home. When she tries to open the door, the chain inside is still on. From the outside, she can see her husband who, having had too much to drink, has fallen asleep on the staircase. She calls to him but there is no response. Thinking he doesn't want to see her, she leaves and walks down the driveway of her home as the snow continues to fall heavily. The visual contrast between the fragile beauty in red and the heavy snowfall is sweeping Hollywood romanticism, yet under Brooks's direction and Taylor's performance, it works and is moving. "When we were shooting the scene in which she wanders ill through the streets of Paris, I told her I wanted her to look like a drop of red blood against the dirty snow of the streets, and her whole body conveyed just that feeling. She was a natural actress who could use all the elements of her life like a memory bank to call on for the emotions of the role. She didn't talk about her secrets, but she used them," recalled Brooks. "Elizabeth felt the story more deeply than anyone else, and she had marvelous imagination."

"I did enjoy doing *The Last Time I Saw Paris*, even though it wasn't supposed to be a good film," she said.

In March, *Rhapsody* opened to mixed reviews but rhapsodic ones for Elizabeth. "The fact that they found quite a bit of nonsense in *Rhapsody* did not prevent the New York film critics from enjoying it," Richard Griffith wrote in the *Los Angeles Times*. "Elizabeth Taylor was showered with their very best prose, and one gave up the attempt to do justice to her and contented himself with the simple statement that she 'looked sublime.' "

Reviews that focused on Elizabeth's beauty were nothing new. Reviewers of *Elephant Walk* and *The Girl Who Had Everything* often commented on her fabulous face. All the focus on her beauty was often frustrating for Taylor. And in the years to come, she could appear resentful of the fuss about the looks. Yet those discussions of her beauty overlooked and refused to acknowledge the simple fact that beauty on-screen is never *just beauty*. Any number of sensational looking models, who had glistened and glittered in the pages of glossy fashion magazines, discovered it was an entirely different ball game in movies. It was never the idea of standing still and looking pretty. Beauty on-screen came only when there was a spark, a luminous quality that sprang from inside the actress, revealing or suggesting innermost feelings or her fundamental connection to the role she was playing, the emotion she was conveying. At those times when a movie goddess really had no character to play because of an inadequate script, she had to draw from those innermost feelings or her view of life. It was what a star persona was all about. Garbo languished in her metaphysical despair; Harlow exulted in her jaunty high spirits, her sexy ability to banter with the boys, to tell them off if necessary.

Though Elizabeth often dismissed her movies of this period, they were in many respects gorgeous photoplays that afforded audiences the opportunity of being in the presence of Luscious Liz for a couple of hours, of seeing that spark within her start to sizzle or erupt. Dazzlingly costumed by Helen Rose, she was like a painting or lush piece of sculpture, an image—as George Stevens understood—of unattainable beauty and glamour, of idealized perfection. "When I had someone as beautiful as Elizabeth, and there are very few women that beautiful," said Rose, "I had to be very careful not to overdress her, to keep everything I did very simplified because it's like a beautiful jewel. You don't put it in a very ordinary setting. You're very careful of the setting, and I had to be very careful because naturally I want to set a fashion trend. But being a costume for a motion picture, I couldn't set a fashion trend. My job was to keep Elizabeth Taylor looking like Elizabeth Taylor." But it was never a flat image without blood or warmth, passion or sensitivity, as again Stevens knew

Out of all of cinema's great goddesses, she appeared the most understanding of the dilemmas of mere mortals, perhaps the warmest and most down-to-earth.

But at this point, she considered her career as "only a way of making money. It was very hard to take any great interest in a career of playing the perennial ingénue."

Especially distasteful was *Beau Brummell*, one of the few films in which she seemed unable to connect to what's going on around her. Movies such as *The Big Hangover* and *Love Is Better Than Ever* were forgettable throwaways. Still, she brought to other films an intense romanticism, even a dreamy suggestive melancholia. Also important were the signs of rebellion in these characters—the fire within Elizabeth herself—who were in search of something to give meaning to their lives, and who in such films as *Rhapsody* and *The Girl Who Had Everything* were clearly and ironically in conflict with their fathers, which represented the conflict of their own identity.

Emanating from her were a vulnerability, a gentle sensitivity, and sometimes, as in *Ivanhoe*, an inexplicable melancholia that drew audiences to her. In these films, she was also a troubled beauty. Her young wife or girlfriend characters also displayed flashes of anger, resentment, frustration, and drive that the films did not fully explain. In her opening scene with her aristocratic, social-climbing father (Louis Calhern) in *Rhapsody*, she announces, just before one of his society luncheons, that she's leaving his household, that, in essence, she's tired of living a useless life. At a conservatory where young musicians study and rehearse around the clock to perfect their art, she yearns for the love of a brilliant young violinist played by Vittorio Gassman, who sees her love as clinging, suffocating, and destructive, so much so that he walks out on her. She tells herself that in the future she will not be the one who loves but who is loved. Ultimately, she has a destructive relationship with another brilliant but insecure musician, the pianist played by John Ericson. Then to prove her worth to her former lover, she helps the pianist to rehabilitate himself, learning to stand on his own two feet, but most significant, to respect himself and his talent. In turn, she comes to love the pianist more deeply than she realized.

Upon completing *The Last Time I Saw Paris*, Taylor, Wilding, and their son went on another vacation to London, where again they visited his parents.

Once back home, she endured a round of social/professional activities and obligations. Money was very much on her mind. She appeared in advertisements for various products such as LUX soap. She also gave tips for beauty columns. The couple sold their home on Summit Ridge Drive and bought a new eight-room modern showplace at 1375 Beverly Estate Drive in Benedict Canyon. To purchase the new home, Taylor had to go to MGM for a $150,000 loan. She felt humiliated by the way MGM treated her when she asked for the loan, but she also needed money because of something else she had kept secret: she was pregnant again. MGM put her on suspension as it did other female stars during their pregnancies. Still, there were health concerns within the Wilding household. Wilding was plagued by back problems and was briefly hospitalized. In December, the Wildings returned to England: his mother had died; his father was ill, and they eventually brought him to California to stay with them.

In late February, Elizabeth entered the hospital in Santa Monica where she had—by another cesarean section—her second son, Christopher Edward Wilding, born on her birthday, the twenty-seventh. In newspapers around the country, photographs showed a radiant twenty-three-year-old mother holding her baby. During her first pregnancy, she believed she had gained too much weight. Afterward, it was torture to lose it. She was a tad fuller in her films now, her figure all the more voluptuous and womanly. Watching her weight more carefully during the second preg-nancy, she went on a strenuous diet following Christopher's birth. This was the start, however, of the weight problems that would dog her throughout her life. As she admitted, she also enjoyed a good meal.

Something else important was happening in her life that she immediately saw as a great professional challenge and opportunity. Months earlier she had learned that director George Stevens was set to film—for Warner Bros.—an adaptation of Edna Ferber's novel *Giant*, a sprawling generational epic set in Texas. Its heroine, Leslie Benedict, was an independent woman who ages from an eighteen-year-old bride to a matriarch in her fifties. It would star up-and-coming handsome leading man Rock Hudson and a young New York actor about whom there was a buzz in Hollywood—James Dean, who had already completed *East of Eden* and *Rebel Without a Cause.* Elizabeth yearned to play the female lead. But Stevens was set on Grace Kelly.

By now, Kelly had appeared in the critically lauded *High Noon* and a trio of films directed by Alfred Hitchcock: *Dial M for Murder, Rear Window,* and *To Catch a Thief.* Having won the Academy Award for her performance in 1954's *The Country Girl,* Kelly was possibly now the leading young actress in Hollywood. Audrey Hepburn also had quite a rise in films, appearing in the role William Wyler originally wanted Elizabeth for in the 1953 *Roman Holiday,* which won Hepburn an Oscar. What had become of *Time*'s forecast that she would be the actress of the new era? Taylor became friends with Kelly and Hepburn, each of whom she liked. But she was aware of the irony that despite the success of Kelly and Hepburn and the rise of Marilyn Monroe, she was still America's most famous young film actress, the one people across the country were interested in reading about. That irony may also have grated on her.

"I did *A Place in the Sun* at Paramount, and tried hard in it," she said. "I felt I had done well and now maybe MGM would give me a break. It gave me a bit of heart, which was soon lost again—lost under a morass of mediocrity. Not just the scripts. I was mediocre, too." MGM and the other studios, she knew, wasted the careers of any number of stars. It took grit and fight to survive in Hollywood—really a man-governed world. Women such as Bette Davis and Olivia de Havilland had battled with their studio, Warner Bros. Marilyn Monroe would eventually fight like mad with her studio, Twentieth Century Fox. But a studio could turn vicious. In the 1930s, the dark-haired Kay Francis—once the highest paid actress in Hollywood and for a time the queen of the lot at Warner Bros.—sought better roles from her studio. In the end, a vindictive Warner Bros. put her in even worse films or used her rarely until finally her contract ended. By then, she was just about finished in films. She ended her film career in B movies. But she returned to the stage.

Rarely was Elizabeth thought of as a fighter for professional issues. Producers like Pandro S. Berman, however, knew she was quick to speak her mind about the films she was assigned. MGM's Benny Thau knew that, too. Now, though, Taylor's professional rebellion and drive were growing, especially when she heard that Grace Kelly, who announced her plans to marry Prince Rainier of Monaco, would not be able to do *Giant* at Warner Bros. Instead, MGM, which had Kelly under contract, was rushing Kelly through *The Swan* and *High Society*. At this point, director George Stevens "settled on me," Taylor said. But MGM wouldn't agree to the loan-out to Warner Bros.

Elizabeth would not back down. "I had to go almost on a sit-down strike," she said. By now, her language was no longer that of a polite young American princess. It could be salty, and the expletives could fly. In the years to come, the language would become saltier, to put it mildly. This was all a part of her maturing process and also a still evolving toughness that proved essential for survival in the industry. Finally, MGM consented to let her do the film but on its terms. Warner Bros. agreed to pay MGM $175,000 for Taylor's services and also agreed to possibly lend James Dean, then under contract to Warner Bros., to MGM for a picture. "I got no extra money for it. MGM got the money," she said. "It was just a chance to do a part that was an opportunity and with a director like George." At the same time, MGM planned to star Taylor and dark-haired Italian actress Pier Angeli in "Oriental roles"—each a young woman of a different caste—in a film called *Bride of India*. Other films considered for her were *Maryanne* and then *Raquel*. For Elizabeth, these were other nothing films. In the end, she didn't do any of them. But she had won the battle to star in *Giant*.

• • •

But while Elizabeth prepared for *Giant*, Wilding's career continued to spiral downward. Though it was reported that he asked to be released from his MGM contract, that announcement was made to save him face. For a man facing career problems and who was married to a big female star, Hollywood could be a brutal territory. To most in the industry, including MGM, he was superfluous, someone who might be used to make a request to his wife, even to answer the phone and take a message; in many respects he was a replay of the doomed husband in *A Star Is Born*.

Their marriage was in deeper trouble now. Those rumors of marital difficulties were not just rumors. Though she always found Wilding fundamentally charming and never spoke ill of the father of her children, he simply was not strong or forceful enough for her. She said they were better suited to be brother and sister. In truth, the marriage didn't excite her.

Work started on *Giant* with additional cast members: Academy Award–winner Mercedes McCambridge as Hudson's tough sister, Luz; Dennis Hopper, Fran Bennett, and Carroll Baker as the adult children of the Benedicts; former child star Jane Withers; newcomer Australian actor Rod Taylor; and stage actress Judith Evelyn as Taylor's aristocratic mother. Scenes were filmed first in Virginia. Then Stevens moved the production to Marfa, Texas, for a long location shoot. Daily, an estimated six hundred automobiles—filled with onlookers—descended on the outdoor set, which Stevens basically kept open. Before Elizabeth joined the cast, Stevens had asked Hudson whom he preferred as the leading lady, Grace Kelly or Elizabeth Taylor. Without blinking, he said Taylor. The two became lifelong friends. At night, they would sit, talk, and drink cocktails. There was some chatter that she and Hudson might be having an affair. The rumors must have reached Wilding, who showed up in Texas. Though Hudson was gay, which Taylor apparently knew at this time, even Hudson's future wife Phyllis Gates—theirs would be a studio-arranged marriage—wondered about the relationship when she visited the *Giant* set in Texas. "He devoted much attention to Elizabeth," Gates said. "It wouldn't have surprised me if Rock made a play for Elizabeth hoping to maintain his balance of power in the *Giant* company."

A lot of talk centered on the moody, sometimes difficult actor James Dean. He and Hudson often clashed. At first, Dean kept his distance from Taylor, was even rude to her on set, and hung out often with Carroll Baker, the other newcomer. But as Dean and Taylor worked together more closely, he fell under her spell, unable to resist her, and became utterly captivated. A famous picture was taken of Dean on a sofa reading a magazine with Taylor, who's fallen asleep, by his side. The magazine was *Look*, which ironically had Taylor on its cover. When Wilding visited his wife, Dean reportedly said to him: "You better know right away, Mike, I've fallen in love with your wife." Though said in jest, there was some truth to his statement. At the same time, he, like Hudson, confided in her and revealed something seldom shared with others; stories of his bisexual relationships.

When Dean stopped hanging out with Carroll Baker to spend his downtime with Taylor, Baker admitted she felt left out. But she too was mesmerized by the actress. "I never got tired of looking at her or listening to her talk. For one thing, she had the most fascinating point of view. She never spoke of people, things, or situations as any other person might have. She had a reality of her own, an MGM reality. Her judgments and dialogue came straight out of MGM movies, but she actually meant them. It was fascinating!" Baker recalled. "My feelings about Liz probably seem extreme, but to me, at that time in my impressionable young life, she was truly the pinnacle of what being a star meant. I loved her—I adored her—I worshipped her. She was truly regal." Once the cast and crew were back in Los Angeles to film at Warner Bros., Baker's fascination grew. At the end of a day's work, Baker noted that everyone else was anxious to get away, except for Elizabeth "who was always the last person to leave the lot." Baker began joining Taylor in the star's dressing room. "It was like watching the preening of a magnificent bird! Before the wardrobe woman left for the day, she would assist Elizabeth out of her costume and into a starched, immaculately white surgical-type gown." Baker would put on records. She'd also fix Elizabeth a drink. "I carefully rehearsed the ingredients," said Baker.

"2 jiggers of Beefeater's gin
"A small tonic water
"Serve in a tall glass over 4 ice cubes
"Garnish with a lime wedge."

Those days with Nicky Hilton when Elizabeth barely touched the booze were now long gone. During the filming of *Giant*, she and Hudson also had their special concoction, something referred to as a "chocolate martini," a mixture of vodka and a chocolate liqueur. Though her drinking still did not seem to be a problem, her reliance on alcohol was growing.

Baker couldn't forget the "uniquely terrifying experience" of being a passenger as Elizabeth drove her white Cadillac. Never did she seem aware of other drivers on the road—who just "might have the right-of-way." En route to a restaurant, Baker was startled as Elizabeth hit a parked car and then drove right into another one. "The driver was so dumbstruck at the sight of Elizabeth Taylor that he forgot to complain, and when he stepped out of his car, she glared daggers at him for having dared to be in her path in the first place," said Baker.

Once Taylor entered the restaurant, "The diners dropped their forks and stared in openmouthed wonder at Elizabeth's every movement and gesture, and the poor girl couldn't relax for a second during lunch. With all her fame and beauty, she was so sincere and sweet and charming and had at times such a helpless, little-girl quality." Baker grew to feel protective of her.

Throughout the filming of *Giant*, Elizabeth was often ill and in physical pain. Some days it might be her leg. Other times it could be her back. At one point, a crippling pain in her right leg forced her to enter St. John's Hospital in Santa Monica. A blood clot had to heal before she was permitted to return to work. In excruciating pain with sciatica, she ended up walking on crutches. The diagnosis: she had a pinched nerve in her spine. Yet because *Giant* had several months more before its completion, she'd have to live with the pain. Stevens tended to dismiss her illnesses as being psychosomatic. In time, her husbands would note that she could exaggerate the slightest ailment, and while her illnesses afforded her the chance to back out of engagements or professional obligations, indeed to just withdraw from the whirl of activities around her, sciatica problems were very real. So were most of her other ailments. Future husband Mike Todd once wanted to send George Stevens X-rays of Elizabeth's spine as a Christmas card. Nonetheless, there was no telling Stevens that her ailments were not psychosomatic.

Other problems with Stevens flared up. "Shooting the film turned out to be murderous," Elizabeth remembered. During her earlier time on *A Place in the Sun*, she recalled that she had been a minor. "George couldn't have treated me more wonderfully. I found out on *Giant*, that he tends to like having a patsy or two on a film. Jimmy Dean was one and I was another, but I'll say this for George—he usually picks people who can answer back."

Later, Taylor, who rarely discussed the pressures or tensions of moviemaking, recalled in detail an occasion when Stevens exploded with her in front of cast and crew. The scene to be filmed was of Taylor's Leslie, having temporarily separated from her husband, Bick, back in Virginia for her younger sister's wedding. Waiting for an exceptionally long time to be called to the set, Taylor sat in her dressing room with her makeup man and hairdresser. After an hour, she left her dressing room to see what the problem was. The set was quiet. Stevens sat in his director's chair, looking annoyed and down to his last shred of patience. Standing by were the extras and the crew.

When she asked what had happened, Stevens lashed out at her for holding up production for over an hour. "Just who the hell do you think you are to keep these people waiting?"

When she explained that she'd never been called, he asked: "Just how much do you think you can get away with? What did you do when you came back from lunch?"

She had worked on her makeup, she told Stevens, had her dress ironed, and waited in the dressing room. He then exploded that all she cared about was her makeup, which, he said, she assumed was more important than the people waiting for her. "Well, I have news for you," he said. "It isn't."

"That wasn't what I meant. I've been waiting in there. No one called me."

She remembered that Stevens just stared her down and that he had said "something suitable like 'Go to hell' or something unprintable."

She found an assistant director who realized indeed that no one had called her to the set. Stevens, however, didn't seem to care. "Of course," said Taylor, "Stevens never said a word to me. Then I had to go out and act before all the extras that he'd done his tirade in front of. I was quivering—and in the scene I was supposed to cry." She wondered if Stevens had behaved like this and spoken to her in such a way in order to get the emotion he wanted for the scene.

She also remembered the day that she sat watching dailies—footage that had recently been shot—with Stevens and others. Having already completed his work on the film, James Dean had left the company. As she sat in the projection room, the phone rang. Stevens answered and was shaken. There had been an accident. Twenty-four-year-old Dean, who had been driving his Porsche en route to road races in Salinas, had collided with another car. Throughout filming, the studio had forbidden Dean to enter car races. Now the worst had occurred. "I've just been given the news that Jimmy Dean has been killed," Stevens told everyone in the room.

Like everyone else, Taylor was stunned. Because the news had not yet really broken, they called newspapers and hospitals, trying to get it verified or denied. She recalled that later that night, as she walked to her car, she saw Stevens and cried that she couldn't believe it. "I believe it," Stevens said. "He had it coming to him. The way he drove, he had it coming." But Elizabeth knew that Stevens had admired Dean's work. She had observed him watching Dean as the actor shot a scene. "George would smile, but he didn't ever let Jimmy know that he was fond of him."

Chapter 10

OFF THE WALL. Thriller. Motown 25. The Jackson family was thrilled with Michael's success. But there was also the feeling that now was the time for him to perform again with his brothers, who, career-wise, seemed at loose ends. Jermaine's marriage to Berry Gordy's daughter Hazel had ended and he was back at the family compound. Other brothers had marital troubles, too, along with other woes. Accustomed to fabulous homes, cars, clothes, and women, Jackie, Tito, Jermaine, and Marlon had families now with mounting expenses for their lavish lifestyles. None would ever be able to go back to the way of life in Gary, Indiana. They also thrived on performing. What else could they really do? But without Michael onstage with the brothers, concert promoters and the record executives didn't have much interest in the group. Both Joseph and Katherine wanted to see their sons together onstage again in a reunion tour. The brothers felt the same way.

Talk began of a new album and a new tour for the Jacksons that would bring money into the coffers. "Michael has had very big success and sometimes the success of the Jacksons got undermined a bit," said Tito. "I think the tour is a chance for us to show our success, too."

No family member had more influence over Michael than his mother, and it is safe to say that Katherine's advice, more than anyone else's, persuaded Michael to agree to both an album and a tour. But it was not easy going, primarily because stage-managing the reunion plans was Joseph. Long dubious about his father's business skills, a twenty-one-year-old Michael, in 1979, had refused to renew the management contract with Joseph. In essence, he had fired him. "All I wanted was control over my own life," he said. "And I took it. I had to do it." His brothers also knew letting Joe handle things could lead to disaster. They, too, were cutting business ties with him.

But also greatly distressing Michael and the rest of the family was their father's philandering. All sorts of stories circulated about his affairs, reckless encounters, and his mistresses. In 1980, Katherine grew suspicious of Joe's relationship with a young woman who worked in his office. Convinced that Joe was having an affair, Katherine apparently reached the breaking point. With her children Randy and Janet by her side, she arrived at the office, confronted the woman, and even physically assaulted her, according to a police report filed. She was warned to stay away from Joseph, but she maintained that there had never been anything romantic between Joe and herself. When Michael heard of the physical confrontation, he reportedly went into denial. His mother could never do such a thing. Nonetheless, word of the incident alienated him even more from his father.

There had been other more serious incidents in the past. Recalling that his mother had been "devastated, livid, confused" by Joe's behavior on one occasion—when Joseph had an affair with a woman who previously chased after Jackie—Jermaine remembered that Janet and Rebbie "pleaded with Mother to 'leave him, divorce him' and couldn't stand the sight of 'the dirty down dog.' Janet yelled and screamed in his face for the hurt he had caused." Jermaine also recalled: "Michael wept with hurt anger, also advising Mother—quietly—to kick out our father." For a few days, Katherine Jackson just up and walked out of their home. Bewildered and saddened, Michael wanted to go with his mother but he had no idea where she was. Katherine returned. However, in 1974, Joe's womanizing led to a permanent breach in the marriage when he fathered a daughter named Joh'Vonnie by a young woman named Cheryl Terrell. In 1982, Katherine filed for divorce. Perhaps because of her religious convictions and perhaps because she still loved Joe, Katherine did not go through with it. But things between Joe and Katherine were never the same. Michael had seen all this and carried the hurt inside. His mother, Katherine, was more complicated than she appeared.

For Michael, however, there was no avoiding Joseph, who in November 1983 arranged a meeting with his six sons, including Randy, at New York City's elegant Tavern on the Green. Joe then laid a bombshell that may have taken the brothers by surprise: Joseph announced that he had hired Don King to produce the huge Jackson reunion tour.

Known for promoting high-powered boxing bouts, King was considered a master at fastidious promotion that, in some way or another, seemed to spotlight him as much as the events being publicized. Flashy and outspoken, a wheeler and dealer in and out of the boxing arena, with many big-named friends—and a national reputation— he was immediately identifiable by his big smile, his high spirits, and his hair that seemed to stand on end. Born in Cleveland in 1931, he had a checkered past. He had attended Kent State College but dropped out. Then through grit and shrewd deal making, some of which was considered nefarious, he had handled major boxing events with a true showman's flair, notably "the Rumble in the Jungle," the 1974 bout

280

between Muhammad Ali and George Foreman, and "the Thrilla in Manila," the 1975 third bout between Muhammad Ali and Joe Frazier. Among the boxers he would promote over the years were some of the sport's biggest names: not only Ali, Frazier, and Foreman but also later Mike Tyson, Evander Holyfield, and Salvador Sanchez. King was considered—in some circles—to be unscrupulous and devious, someone never to be trusted. Many boxers ended up suing him for defrauding them.

King also had a shocking criminal past. In two separate cases spanning thirteen years, he was charged with killing two men. In the first, he had been tried for shooting a man in the back, but it was judged justifiable homicide. The man had attempted to rob King's employee. In the second case, however, he was found guilty of second-degree murder for stomping an employee to death. His conviction was later declared "non-negligent manslaughter," for which he served almost four years in prison but was pardoned by Ohio's governor Jim Rhodes in 1983. Now King had come onboard to promote the tour called *Victory*.

Getting the *Victory* tour into motion was an unabashed mess. Negotiations became involved and intense, with a slew of lawyers and advisers. Local promoters had to deal with one Jackson family representative after another. No one seemed to know what was going on. Hundreds of calls by any particular local promoter were the norm. Perhaps because of prompting by Katherine and also perhaps because of a kind of guilt he felt about having left his brothers behind, Michael finally agreed to the tour and worked on the *Victory* album, which they completed in early February 1984. But he steered clear of Don King.

Michael saw himself as a gentleman and a class act, which indeed he was; from Michael's vantage point, King was neither. It was said he came to detest the loud, bigmouth King "whose boisterous obsession with self-promotion does not hide the fact that he has no experience in music promotion," *People* magazine commented. "Michael reportedly sent King a letter stating in no uncertain terms that King could not speak or deal for Michael." Said King: "We have been voted into silence."

Still clearly trying to break free of professional ties with his brothers, Michael had signed a $300,000 deal with the publisher Doubleday and Company to write his autobiography, which, at age twenty-four, seemed premature. What sweetened the deal was the fact that his editor would be Jacqueline Kennedy Onassis, whose children, Caroline and John, were Jackson fans. Michael also hoped plans would materialize for him to star in *Peter Pan*, to be directed by

Steven Spielberg. Of course, these were major players that Michael was thrilled to be associated with. But he no doubt felt his family simply would not let go.

In connection with the tour, a lucrative deal had been struck for two Pepsi-Cola commercials, featuring the brothers. But because of his health food diet, Michael was hardly excited about endorsing Pepsi-Cola. Most grating was the simple fact that he would be at the center of commercials. Eventually, a resentful but resigned Michael acquiesced. He could, perhaps, enjoy the financial benefits that he'd reap. His brothers got about a million apiece. Michael, however, would earn $5 million. He made demands on how the commercial was to be shot, how he could be used. Notably, the Pepsi commercials were the brain-child of Don King. That commercial would ultimately have devastating, lifelong effects on Michael.

On January 27, 1984, under the direction of Bob Giraldi—a wizard of helming music videos—filming of one of the Pepsi commercials began at Los Angeles's Shrine Auditorium before a live audience of thousands. During the fourth day of what was becoming a long shoot, Michael—dressed in a sparkly jacket and wearing his now signature sequined single glove and with his hair glistening with the gel that was always so carefully and fully applied—descended a staircase while dancing and singing special lyrics set to the tune of "Billie Jean." At the bottom of the stairway, his brothers would join him in song. Throughout the set, there were hot lights and flashes, all part of the elaborate paraphernalia that would add to the excitement of the commercial. But suddenly, one of the lights popped, causing sparks to fly, which caught onto Michael's hair. People in the audience gasped as they saw something that Michael at first was unaware of. His hair was on fire. Then Michael felt an intense pain and cried out. His aide and friend Miko Brando, the son of Marlon Brando, rushed to his side. "I tore out, hugged him, tackled him and ran my hands through his hair," Miko told *People* magazine, which reported that Brando's hands were also burned. Technicians, grips, and others ran to Michael. The fire was extinguished.

Paramedics soon arrived, and Michael was rushed off to Cedars-Sinai Medical Center. Through it all, he refused to remove his glove. Even in the midst of excruciating pain, he held on to his professional identity, perhaps the *only* identity he was certain of. At first, he declined any medication to bring relief from the pain, partly because of his Jehovah's Witness indoctrination. Medicine was viewed by him as a drug. His own personal health regime—the vegetarianism, the refusal to go anywhere near the greasy fast foods he once loved which had caused the terrible acne, his belief that his body was his temple and had to be kept clean and pure—led him no doubt to view drugs as bodily pollutants. His own belief in himself also led him to feel he could withstand the pain until it ran its course and subsided. But eventually he took a pain analgesic.

Later *People* reported: "The fire had scorched a palm-sized second-degree burn on his crown, which surrounded a third-degree burn about the size of the hole in a 45-rpm record." His physician Steven Hoefflin as well as Katherine, Joseph, and Randy Jackson accompanied Michael as he was transferred from Cedars to the burn center at the Brotman Medical Center in Culver City. Ironi-cally, only a few weeks earlier, Michael had visited patients at the center. That evening, calls came from Diana Ross and Liza Minnelli. After a day, he was released from the center, but he visited patients before returning home. Later, in lieu of a lawsuit, he persuaded Pepsi to donate $1.5 million to the Michael Jackson Burn Center at Brotman.

Everyone involved downplayed his injuries, making it appear as if this injury was nothing serious and without long-lasting effects. But that was far from the truth. Part of his scalp was forever damaged. Surgery would be performed to "laser the scar tissue and stretch part of his scalp over the burned area." He would live with pain from those burns for the rest of his life. It was then also that the drug Demerol came into his life, prescribed to numb some of the pain, to make his life bearable. In the years to come, he would wear wigs to hide his scars and his partially bald scalp. Sadly, too, for the young man who had grown up refusing to take drugs, he would eventually find himself addicted to painkillers, something that Elizabeth Taylor would well understand.

Early stardom as children working —with full responsibilities— in professional adult worlds: Elizabeth Taylor in her breakthrough role in *National Velvet*.

Michael Jackson with Ed Sullivan at the time of his historic performance with the Jackson 5 on *The Ed Sullivan Show*.

Family ties, family complications: Elizabeth with her reserved art dealer father, Francis, and her assertive mother, Sara, who managed her career.

Michael (far right) with the entire Jackson family, (first row, left to right) his siblings Marlon, Randy, Tito, and La Toya; (top row) Jackie, mother Katherine—warmhearted and always determined to keep her family united—ambitious father Joseph, Janet, and Jermaine.

Influences and lifelong friendships: Elizabeth with
Montgomery Clift—one of the great loves of
her life—in *A Place in the Sun.*

Michael with one of his idols Diana Ross and maestro
Quincy Jones, who produced the groundbreaking
albums *Off the Wall* and *Thriller.*

Emerging as major adult icons: Elizabeth with James Dean and Rock Hudson on the set of *Giant*.

Michael in performance at one of his concerts.

Love in the ruins: Elizabeth, at the height of her legendary beauty, and husband, producer Mike Todd, tragically killed in a plane crash.

Michael and wife Lisa Marie Presley during their short-lived, highly publicized marriage.

At the peak of their international fame: Elizabeth with her children—son Michael (in her arms), daughter Liza (back to the camera), and son Christopher—on the set of *Cleopatra* when her "scandalous" love affair with actor Richard Burton (above) drew worldwide attention and outrage.

An optimistic, confident, and jubilant Michael at the time of *Thriller*, an artistic triumph, and the bestselling album of all time.

Discovering a
new world
together:
Elizabeth
and Michael,
hand in hand
and all smiles,
spending a day
at the racetrack.

Elizabeth and
Michael at
the American
Music Awards
where Michael
was a big
winner.

Michael and Elizabeth and an elite gathering
of stars that included Whitney Houston and
Liza Minnelli as Michael was honored by the
United Negro College Fund.

Putting on a
brave face
though each
was battling
debilitating and
painful physical
ailments:
Michael and
Elizabeth at
Michael's 30th
anniversary
concert in
New York.

Chapter 11

IN EARLY OCTOBER 1955, Elizabeth entered UCLA Medical Center. The week before, she had suffered through a bout of the flu. Now she underwent tests to determine her latest illness, which was believed to be a gastrointestinal ailment. Later in the month, she was home again. Though Elizabeth had been advised by doctors to rest, such advice was ignored. In November, she journeyed to Morocco, where Wilding was filming *Zarak* with actor Victor Mature. Rumors were rampant that Taylor had a dalliance with Mature, something she would never discuss publicly but which made the pages of the scandal-driven magazine of the 1950s, *Confidential*.

Before she even knew it, she also had an affair with Frank Sinatra, a notorious womanizer, in Los Angeles. For years, there were stories that she became pregnant and that apparently she thought they might marry. And it was rumored that she aborted the child.

Then she met Kevin McClory, a good-looking, dashing, dark-haired Irish screenwriter who was a descendant of the great literary Brontë family. After serving in the military during World

War II, he worked as an assistant to director John Huston on the films *The African Queen* and *Moulin Rouge*. Social, sophisticated, charming, and intelligent, McClory smoothly swept her off her feet. Spending secluded weekends with him at a borrowed Malibu beach house, she was excited by the secrecy of their affair. Again she thought about marriage. Apparently, McClory did, too.

Her career was now veering in a new direction. She was about to enter a high artistic phase, capturing roles that challenged her and drew critical attention. Next up for her was an adaptation of Ross Lockridge's towering Civil War novel *Raintree County*, in which she would play the troubled Southern belle Susanna Drake who believes she has "Negra blood"—that her father's Negro mistress, who is her beloved caregiver, is actually her mother. Married to Susanna is a schoolteacher John Shawnessy in Indiana—to be played by Montgomery Clift— who is opposed to slavery and ultimately joins the Union army. He finds himself torn between his bewitching, despairing wife and his former sweetheart, played by Eva Marie Saint.

Believing *Raintree County* could be an epic on the scale of *Gone With the Wind*, MGM's Dore Schary poured the studio's resources into this big-budgeted drama that would cost $5,000,000, a then huge sum, and would be filmed in the new sixty-five-millimeter process under the direction of Edward Dmytryk. Part of the film would be shot on MGM's back lot. But the company would also travel to Danville, Kentucky, for location scenes. Not lost on Elizabeth was the fact that her stock at MGM had risen because of the advance buzz on *Giant*, the very film MGM had not been willing at first to let her do. Yet MGM still talked of casting her in lightweight fare like *Sultana*. In early 1956, her MGM contract had little more than two years to go. Already her thoughts were on the future, with or without MGM. But most important now was that she'd work with Clift again.

Though Clift's career remained in high gear with the 1953 hit *From Here to Eternity*, which won him another Academy Award nomination, he had dropped out for about three years, appearing in no films. Part of the reason for the absence was due to his search for the right roles. Known to brood while considering a role, he turned down such films as *Sunset Boulevard*, *Desiree*, *Friendly Persuasion*, *Bus Stop*, *Prince of Players* (in which Richard Burton eventually appeared). Nothing seemed to pique his interest. When he did work, there could be problems on the set. He had battled with director Vittorio De Sica on the film *Indiscretions of an American Housewife* and with Alfred Hitchcock on *I Confess*. Though he was drinking and clearly in need of a rest, he wanted to return to the theater and began rehearsals for a new production of *The Seagull*. At one point, he had taken a break from rehearsals and had flown to Los Angeles for meetings about possible films. He stayed at Elizabeth's. Wilding was away. But because of his drinking, even she found him hard to handle and made frantic calls to his friends, asking for advice. Ultimately, she helped him weather his way through the storm of his demons. But once back in New York, he was again at emotional loose ends. He saw friends, including Libby Holman, remained in contact with his psychiatrist, and also broke off a relationship with a young actor. There were again reckless one-night stands with various new lovers. Finally, he realized he should work, focus on something other than himself. Elizabeth persuaded him to do *Raintree County*. They'd spend time together again. Now he had signed a three-picture deal with MGM.

Spending time with Clift while filming *Raintree County* helped take Elizabeth's mind off the sad state of her marriage. Having returned from Morocco, Wilding still suffered from the back problems that had put him in the hospital a few months earlier. He also had a lot of time on his hands while Elizabeth continued to carry the financial weight of maintaining the family and the home and living up to Hollywood's standards.

Godfather to both of Taylor and Wilding's sons, Clift often spent time at the couple's home in Benedict Canyon. In turn, Wilding visited Clift often to discuss the troubled state of his marriage. Elizabeth and Clift's relationship remained com-plicated as they confided in each other about their problems, their fears, the drift of their lives. There remained, however, a sexual current that could drive Clift crazy. "He wanted her badly—he got very cut up after she married Nick Hilton—and they tried to start up their affair again after she got divorced," actress Diana Lynn told Clift biographer Patricia Bosworth. "They kept trying until she married Michael Wilding." For years, she had known that her childhood friend Roddy McDowall was gay, and at one point, she had introduced Clift to McDowall in hopes the two would hook up. But Monty remained troubled and no happier than she was—and his attraction to her was no less intense. "Elizabeth invited me to a dinner party at her house," Debbie Reynolds recalled of an incident that happened around this time. "After dinner, Elizabeth and Montgomery Clift went for a swim. They laughed and giggled while making out in the water in front of us all. They were having a great time. Even though Monty had boyfriends as well as girlfriends, it was obvious that he and Elizabeth had been intimate. Elizabeth could seduce any man, gay or straight."

Often Taylor and Wilding were at their best when entertaining with others around, when they didn't have to face each other alone. To the amusement of some guests, Elizabeth frequently talked about her money problems. Carroll Baker remembered some of those evenings when Elizabeth always served a cold buffet. Though she had a live-in nanny for the children and daytime help, "I can't afford servants who stay after five o'clock," she said. "God, how I hate being poor!"

By most Hollywood standards, Elizabeth and Wilding lived well. "Each time I see the Wildings they have found a higher hilltop," Hedda Hopper said. "Their present home commands the most widely ballyhooed view in the world, the mansion-studded canyons of Beverly Hills, polka-dotted with swimming pools and a sweep of flat land beyond to the ocean." Carroll Baker recalled that Taylor and Wilding's ultramodern, four-bedroom home was splendid, "a luxury model fit for the pages of a glossy designer's magazine." But Elizabeth didn't see it that way. "By Hollywood standards" for her, said Carroll Baker, "it was apparently a medium-income compromise. Liz spoke of that dream house as if it were a hovel, and Michael was in complete sympathy with her." Wilding told Baker: "I do believe MGM might give Elizabeth a bonus soon, and if they do, we simply must get a better house." "Yes," said Elizabeth. "I'm fed up with working so hard and having to live like this!"

The evening of May 12, 1956, at the home—or rather its aftermath—would always be remembered as a horror from which there was no escape. Things had started well. Elizabeth and Monty were taking a break on *Raintree County*, which proved as grueling a shoot as *Giant*. Location scenes had already been shot in Tennessee and Kentucky. Now they were working on the MGM lot. Evenings like this one were used to unwind, gripe about things that had occurred on the set, and to talk movie talk in general. Lots of gossip. Pretty good food. A time when industry friends could shoot the breeze. Among the guests were Rock Hudson and Phyllis Gates, with whom Hudson would later have one of those "arranged" Hollywood marriages that served as a cover or a beard to brush aside the stories of Hudson's homosexuality. No one talked about that, but everyone was aware of it, and among the group at Taylor's home, no one cared one hoot. Along with Monty at the house was his buddy from New York, actor Kevin McCarthy. There was some drinking but no one had a lot, especially Monty. Wilding, whose back pains were driving him to distraction, lay sedated on the couch much of the evening.

As the gathering drew to a close, Clift left in

his car. McCarthy left in another. The road from Taylor's home was long and treacherous with unexpected curves and twists. Carroll Baker recalled that on those occasions whenever she left the house, she always drove slowly and often almost missed one of the curves. On this particular evening, Clift in fact missed a curve, and his car whirled out of control and smashed into a telephone pole. Driving ahead of Monty, McCarthy looked back and could not believe what he saw. He jumped out of his car and rushed to help Clift. The windshield of Clift's car was shattered, and he lay trapped inside the car. "The motor was still running like hell. I could smell gas. I managed to reach in the window and turn off the ignition, but it was so dark I couldn't see inside the car," said McCarthy. "Then I saw him curled under the dashboard." Immediately, he rushed back to Taylor and Wilding's home and cried that something terrible had happened to Monty.

The police and an ambulance were called. Then the others ran down the hill from the house. When McCarthy and Wilding had tried to stop Elizabeth from going, she had cried, "No! No! I'm going to Monty!" Once at the car, McCarthy said, "She was like Mother Courage. Monty's car was so crushed you couldn't open the front door." Elizabeth screamed for help and then somehow did what no one else could. She crawled inside the car. Half unconscious, Clift moaned in pain. His teeth were half knocked out. Two were caught in his throat, said McCarthy. "She stuck her fingers down his throat and she pulled those teeth. Otherwise he would have choked to death." Blood was everywhere. His nose and jaw were broken. Clift's physician Rex Kennamer arrived at the scene. "He was barely conscious," Kennamer recalled. "As I peered in at him through the shattered door window, something quiet astonishing took place. Monty regained not only his senses but also his good humor. He opened his eyes and recognized me. 'Doctor,' he gasped, 'I'd like you to meet Elizabeth Taylor. Elizabeth, this is Dr. Kennamer.' " It took about a half hour before an ambulance arrived. But the press—hearing of the accident—got to the scene and snapped pictures.

"Get those goddamn cameras out of here," she shouted. "Get the hell away or I'll make certain none of you ever works in Hollywood again."

Then she rode in the ambulance with him to Cedars of Lebanon Hospital. When he was finally taken into the hospital's operating room, she broke down.

Hospitalized for weeks and in excruciating pain, Clift had to have his jaw wired, and extensive dental work had to be performed. Later, he had cosmetic surgery. But he never looked the same. And his life itself was never the same. A nerve on the left side of his face had been severed, making that part of his face immobile. Afterward, he found himself often taking painkillers. In a show biz world, where friendships came and went, Elizabeth, however, was a constant for him. Visiting him every day, Elizabeth nursed and encouraged him. "He was the kindest, gentlest, most understanding man I have ever known," she said. "He was like my brother; he was my dearest, most devoted friend." Tennessee Williams, Truman Capote, and others, who knew Clift in New York, never forgot Taylor's devotion to him. In many respects, she helped save him to continue with his career, and his life itself. But the accident had robbed him of the joy of living.

Elizabeth's own life was about to undergo a dramatic, rather radical transformation: she met producer Mike Todd. Her lover Kevin McClory was then working on producer Todd's star-studded film *Around the World in 80 Days*. Enterprising, energetic, and one of the great showmen in twentieth-century entertainment, Todd had been born Avrom Hirsch Goldbogen in Minneapolis around 1908. (Todd never liked telling the truth about his age.) The dirt-poor Goldbogen family moved to Chicago, a teeming metropolis well suited to the grit and aggressiveness of young streetwise Avrom. At seventeen, he was a pitchman putting on shows for Chicago's Great Fair. He had also audaciously renamed himself Mike Todd. Then he moved on to New York. Through drive and unabashed chutzpah, he launched such hugely successful Broadway productions as *The Hot Mikado* with the legendary Bill "Bojangles" Robinson; *Star and Garter* with another show biz legend, Gypsy Rose Lee; and *Up in Central Park*. With his hit production of *Hamlet*, he boasted, "I made more money out of *Hamlet* than Shakespeare did."

Always living high on the hog, Todd went through millions and was known sometimes as a hustler, even at times a con man. He always seemed like a man on the make, eager not only to mount one show-stopping production after another but also to be a part of the upper echelons of society. Self-educated, he became conversant on any number of subjects, including art, poetry, and other cultural matters. Though he didn't have a depth of knowledge, he had a true appreciation for art, which he shared as he joyously mingled with the rich and the famous, the movers and shakers of New York.

Todd also had two failed marriages. His first was to Bertha Freshman, a young love whom he soon outgrew. His wandering eye was always falling on one show biz beauty or another. He had a steamy affair with Gypsy Rose Lee and was also involved with Marlene Dietrich, to name only a couple of the women he fascinated. But when he tried to divorce Bertha, she flatly refused. Then she died of a collapsed lung while being operated on for a damaged tendon in her finger. In 1947, he married actress Joan Blondell. They divorced three years later. Afterward, Blondell didn't even want to hear his name. She said he had spent all her money.

Now Todd set out to conquer Hollywood with *Around the World in 80 Days*. His primary stars were David Niven, newcomer Shirley MacLaine, and Mexican actor Cantinflas. To ensure a large audience for the film, Todd persuaded a gallery of stars—Marlene Dietrich, Frank Sinatra, Buster Keaton, Red Skelton, Jose Greco, and John Gielgud —to accept small roles, or cameos. Because he couldn't pay them, he offered instead perhaps a painting by Picasso or a Rolls-Royce. He was such a salesman that they accepted. He also developed Todd-AO, which was a new wide-screen process. Everything about *Around the World in 80 Days* would be lavish and spectacular.

While working on the film, Todd became involved with actress Evelyn Keyes, best known for playing one of Scarlett O'Hara's sisters in *Gone With the Wind*. Sophisticated and highly intelligent, Keyes had been married to director John Huston. She knew her way around Hollywood and intellectual circles. But she had no idea what Todd was soon up to. Hearing rumors of McClory's affair with Taylor—the two had been spotted around town and even attended the opening of *Moby Dick* together—Todd requested that McClory introduce him. McClory assumed it was perhaps to get her involved in a project. But Todd had other things on his mind.

The Wildings were invited for an afternoon on Todd's rented yacht along with Evelyn Keyes, Elizabeth's agent Kurt Frings, and his wife, playwright Ketti Frings, Kevin McClory and others. A few weeks later Todd invited the Wildings, along with about two hundred additional people, including Evelyn Keyes, to a dinner he gave for the prominent broadcast journalist Edward R. Murrow at a rented Hollywood mansion. On that evening, like so many others, every eye in the room was on Elizabeth, who, said Ruth Waterbury, arrived "in white satin, very décolleté, her dark hair, her dark tan very much in contrast. She wore diamonds about her throat, and the skirt of her gown was so full that when she sank down on the green-carpeted floor, the white satin made a perfect circle around her." Taylor and Todd exchanged greetings but said little more— although Waterbury said their eyes met more than once. Wilding left the gathering early. Kevin McClory escorted Elizabeth home around 2:00 a.m. Perhaps without realizing it, Wilding had opened the door to the final dissolution of his marriage. On July 19, 1956, Hedda Hopper announced the separation of the Wildings.

Following a six-week delay because of Clift's accident, Elizabeth prepared to depart for more location work on *Raintree County* in Danville, Kentucky. For the time being, Wilding moved into the home of Stewart Granger. Later he flew to Sweden to shoot a film.

Hearing news of the separation, Mike Todd—a man who knew what he wanted and was determined to get it—didn't waste any time. He arranged a meeting with Elizabeth at MGM, where he had set up an office. Once Todd was alone with her, he told her, "I love you. I am going to marry you." As startled as she was by his blunt declaration, she was as attracted to him as he was to her. Thereafter began his great courtship of the most beautiful woman in the world.

Once she was in Danville, Todd called nightly. Flowers were sent. Gifts arrived. Upon her completion of *Raintree County*, Todd sent a private plane to pick her up and bring her to New York just to spend time with him. She loved the gifts, the attention, the forceful personality, the sexual magnetism. The press loved it all, too. Once word was out that they were seeing each other, Taylor and Todd were a far more interesting media couple than Taylor and Wilding. Would Todd tame this Hollywood wild child? Would their extravagant romance lead to marriage or frizzle out? What about another age difference? She was twenty-four. Like Wilding, Todd, who some believed was fifty-one, was old enough to be her father and had a grown son by his first wife. With a second divorce coming so early in her life, did she understand what she was doing? What about her young children? Was her life careening out of control?

By now, Wilding was reading the same stories about his wife that everyone else in the country read. Seen publicly with Todd, she was obviously in love with him. In late September, Wilding returned to Los Angeles from Sweden to see Elizabeth and also to visit his ailing father, who was still living at Taylor's home. Met at the airport by Elizabeth's agent Kurt Frings and her assistant Peggy Rutledge, Wilding realized that Elizabeth was nowhere in sight.

Once Kevin McClory became aware that Todd and Taylor were in love, he was said to be infuriated. Todd had lifted the woman he loved right out of his arms without his even being aware of what was happening. He stopped speaking to Todd, and he carried both a torch and a grudge against Elizabeth for years to come. McClory later reconciled with Todd, and he stayed in the movie business and later wrote the screenplay for the James Bond film *Thunderball*.

At MGM, Pandro S. Berman, as always, was mainly interested in getting Elizabeth back to work—as the star of the movie version of Tennessee Williams's controversial Broadway hit *Cat on a Hot Tin Roof*, with Joshua Logan directing. But there was one possible obstacle, and that was Mike Todd. Though he thought the role as Williams's frustrated, sexy Maggie the Cat was perfect for her, Todd had gotten it into his head that Elizabeth should retire from the screen and just be Mrs. Todd. That was, of course, once she divorced Wilding and married him. Elizabeth herself was in agreement—seemingly. "What nonsense!" Hedda Hopper exclaimed. Now that she was finally getting the dramatic roles she fought for, how could she suddenly give it all up? Amid much media speculation, she flew to New York in the fall of 1956 not only for the premiere of *Giant* but also for Todd's *Around the World in 80 Days*.

Giant opened mostly to glowing reviews, with praise for Taylor, Hudson, and Dean. In the *Los Angeles Times*, Philip K. Scheuer wrote: "*Giant* is at once, paradoxically like life and bigger than life—most realistic when it is most theatrical, and larger than life whenever it slows the tempo to reality." He noted that "a preview audience reacted with something so close to accumulated awe." When the Oscar nominations were announced, *Giant* had nominations for Best Motion Picture, Best Directing, two Best Actor citations—one for Rock Hudson, the other for James Dean. Also nominated was Mercedes McCambridge for Best Actress in a Supporting Role. But as with *A Place in the Sun*, Elizabeth was overlooked. Still, her performance would not be forgotten.

In a prefeminist age, audiences watching *Giant* saw Taylor's fire and rebelliousness in key scenes in which her character, Leslie Benedict, defied her husband Bick's standards as well as his Texas male-centric racist culture. In one sequence that would resonate with audiences for decades to come, when the men lounge around in the evening to discuss politics and the women are relegated to sit among themselves in another section of the huge Benedict living room, presumably to have some mindless female chatter, Taylor's Leslie joins the men's group to hear their conversation and possibly contribute her own opinions. But an embarrassed Bick, who believes she has stepped out of her socially designated gender role as a passive wife, tells her that they're talking business. Then he soon adds, "We're talking about politics." Taylor's Leslie responds, "You married me in Washington, remember. I lived next door to politics." She adds that she was brought up on politics. When one of the men says: "Don't you go worrying your pretty little head about politics," she responds angrily: "You mean my pretty empty head, don't you?" Finally, after other exchanges, she tells the men: "If I may say before retiring, you gentlemen date back one hundred thousand years. You ought to be wearing leopard skins and carrying clubs. Politics. Business. What is so masculine about a conversation that a woman can't enter into?" But throughout as she spoke her mind in this scene and others, she maintained a traditional femininity. Her allure was contrasted with the independent, rather butch style of Bick's possibly lesbian sister, Luz, who clashes with Leslie and soon after dies. In opposition to her husband Bick's bigotry toward Mexican Ameri-cans, Taylor's Leslie also defies racial lines. She challenges class lines as well—through her friendship with the ranch hand Jett Rink, played by Dean. In its own way, *Giant* was forecasting a new day for postwar women in America as well as for minority groups.

Off-screen, most were quick to judge Elizabeth by the era's standards: with one divorce and another on the way, she had not fully accepted society's designated roles of acquiescent wife and mother. Yet the young and some of the old were fascinated by her quest for love, by her determination to go against the precepts laid out by society for women. Unlike the gorgeous, ladylike Grace Kelly or Audrey Hepburn, or the perky all-American Debbie Reynolds and Doris Day, each an important icon in her own right, Taylor and Marilyn Monroe were boldly sexual, flaunting society's rules on a woman's place and challenging the very idea of female submission in the realm of sexual politics. In the fledging *Playboy* magazine, Monroe's nude calendar shocked the era, but it did represent a woman's freedom regarding her body. Taylor's marriages and divorces, played out on the front pages of newspapers in the States and abroad, also represented a liberation from society's proscribed roles for women. Always upfront with Elizabeth were her self-assertion and independence. None of this had fully come to the fore, but it would soon, and the public was watching her with rapt attention.

In early October, Hedda Hopper reported that Elizabeth would go to Lake Tahoe to begin divorce proceedings. Taylor was coy as to whether she would marry Todd. "We haven't got that far yet," she said. Later there was talk about a Mexican divorce—and more talk about Taylor retiring from the screen. "What's this bilge about you retiring?" Hedda Hopper asked her. "Well, if I got the Mary Martin role in *South Pacific*, nothing could keep me away from it," she told Hopper. "But I've never been crazy about a career.

I never wanted to be an actress." Here Taylor was rewriting her own history, and Hopper knew it. She also understood that Elizabeth would never be able to give up her career, never be able to move away from the public eye.

Again, Hopper, ever Elizabeth's mother hen, expressed other concerns. "I'm sorry about this divorce. Liz is so young, only 24. Rather impulsive and excitable. Mike Todd is excitable, too, and he knows how to woo a girl," Hopper said. "I hope and pray that after her divorce she will take some time to consider her next move. But knowing her as well as I do, I doubt if she will." Out of the picture now were Taylor's parents, who surely felt like Hopper but again could say little to deter their daughter from doing exactly as she pleased. Both Francis and Sara were also concerned about their daughter's health and her emotional state. None of that mattered. In late October, she made it clear: "I will marry Michael Todd as soon as I obtain my divorce." In November, Taylor filed for divorce in Santa Monica before taking off for New York with Todd.

The next month she was admitted to New York's Harkness Pavilion at Presbyterian Columbia University Medical Center, where, on December 8, she underwent surgery for a herniated disc and spinal fusion. Her Christian Scientist beliefs again helped her cope with the pain. It was a matter of believing that pain could be endured—and conquered—through prayer and focus. But pain also had to be accepted. In the *Los Angeles Times*, Louis Berg said that "amateur psychia-trists" believed her illnesses and health problems were not real, just "hysterical." One day she might appear crippled by pain. The next day she might hop on a plane and take off for who knew where. "But it was the nature of injury, as anyone with a crushed disc could tell you, that she should suffer excruciating pain one instant, and immediate relief the next. The pressure on the nerve is touch and go." Todd would later say he had the X-rays to prove hers was a medical condition, not a psychological one. Once out of the hospital, she was soon indeed back on the go and determined to marry Todd right away. But there was still the ticklish problem of her divorce from Wilding.

Todd and Taylor flew to Mexico, where they hoped to marry. The plan was that she'd get a quickie divorce there. But in order for the divorce to be immediately granted, Michael Wilding had to appear in Mexico. In the end, Wilding—still charming, still gracious, still understanding, still calm, and still bittersweetly enchanted by his young wife—came to the rescue and arrived in Mexico. For him a strained but magical part of his life was ending. There was only one Elizabeth. Newspapers ran photographs of Taylor with her soon-to-be former husband Michael Wilding and soon-to-be new husband Mike Todd. Once the decree was granted, Wilding boarded a plane that night for Los Angeles. "Well, that's it," he said.

Debbie Reynolds said that "in order to settle her divorce quickly," Elizabeth "sold a very expensive painting and gave the proceeds and all her savings to Wilding." But stories also spread that Todd had paid Wilding a handsome sum to come to Mexico —and then get out of the picture.

Rumors also spread that Taylor and Todd pushed for that quickie divorce because she was pregnant by Todd.

On February 2, 1957, Elizabeth Taylor and Mike Todd were married in Acapulco at the estate of Mexican political figure Melchor Perusquia. Of all her weddings, including the spectacular first to Hilton, Elizabeth—wearing a Helen Rose–designed mauve dress with a dramatic hood—looked most beautiful at this one. In her hand, she carried a bouquet of white and butterfly orchids and lilies of the valley. Taylor's long dark hair coupled with her tan brought out the brilliance of those violet eyes. In attendance were her parents, Sara and Francis; her brother, Howard, and his wife, Mara; and Mike Todd Jr., who at twenty-six was a year older than his new stepmother. Singer Eddie Fisher was Todd's best man, and his wife, Debbie Reynolds, was

Elizabeth's matron of honor. The couple honeymooned at the seaside estate of a former president of Mexico.

It was far from a perfect honeymoon. Though photographs show a magnificent-looking Taylor, about to reach the height of her beauty, she also looked tense at times and not completely at ease. Later it was revealed that she remained in pain from her back problems. Not having fully recuperated from her surgery, she planned to do so in Mexico—*during her honeymoon*. Though attentive to her, Todd himself was pepped up, eager to make new deals, eager to promote *Around the World in 80 Days* for its international release. When the couple flew by private plane from Acapulco to Mexico City for a party, he saw that she was in unbearable pain. But onward they went nonetheless, fulfilling social obligations, meeting people, smiling, laughing, and schmoozing. During the Todd years, her drinking increased, partly because of an unending round of social engagements, partly to keep up with Todd, and perhaps partly to dull some of her physical agonies. In the end, there were too many activities, too many gatherings, too many people, for her to get much rest.

When the couple arrived back in Los Angeles, yet another party was thrown to welcome them home, this time by Sydney Guilaroff and Helen Rose at Guilaroff's home. "We started with twenty-five of their best friends and ended with eighty-five," said Rose. "Everyone seemed to be 'The Todds' best friends.' " That night, Rose remembered, "Elizabeth sparkled with the diamonds Mike had given her as wedding gift. Elizabeth had never been more beautiful." Nor had Rose "ever seen her happier—before or since."

The parties went on until finally Taylor and Todd *had* to face the music—the facts of her health. On February 10, when Todd flew Taylor back to New York for further treatment, their plane was met at the airport by an ambulance—and the press—which sped her to Presbyterian Columbia University Medical Center in Manhattan. During these health crises, photographs, which captured her tension and her discomfort, were compelling and oddly enough contributed to the public conception of her as a still larger-than-life goddess—even in her chronic illnesses. Often enough wearing a mink with her makeup dramati-cally applied, she remained beautiful and imperious, an unearthly figure not to be defeated by pain, able to rise above it somehow, never letting her glamour be diminished by it.

Following her New York hospital stay, she was back in action again, much too soon, flying with Todd to a home they had leased in Palm Springs, where she would recuperate while the couple would continue their honeymoon. But after she attended a banquet with Todd at Los Angeles's Ambassador Hotel, the pain shot up again, and she was flown back to New York to Harkness Pavilion for treatment.

Then she returned to Los Angeles for the Academy Awards ceremony. Resplendent in what looked like a Grecian gown and wearing a diamond tiara that Todd had presented her with, she stole the show even before the awards were announced. That evening George Stevens won another Best Directing Oscar. But *Giant* lost the Best Motion Picture award to Todd's *Around the World in 80 Days*. Of course, *Giant* was the better picture, but Todd had done such a brilliant showman's job of schmoozing with everyone in Hollywood—making friends, smiling, chatting, telling funny stories, and showing up always with his dazzling wife by his side—that he had won the industry over. George Stevens must have winced that *his* star had so blatantly promoted someone else's movie, even if that someone else was her husband.

Before anyone knew it, Taylor and Todd were off to Paris, then London, where again she took ill, now bedridden with an aching back. But there was an additional concern. Now it was announced that she was pregnant. Oblivious to any questions about the pregnancy and her health, she was soon on her feet again, and the couple set out to leave London's Heathrow Airport for Nice. Here an incident occurred that made news around the world. Arriving late at the airport, they missed their flight. A very dramatic public row ensued—with each blaming the other for the missed flight —as photographers snapped pictures like mad. Years later Taylor would say that the public quarrel was a joke. For once being late for a flight "was his fault and not mine. I was teasing him unmercifully and all these photographers and reporters were standing around. It was a kidding fight, but we were both using 'Olde English' language and 'Old Italian' gestures that are even better than language. Some photographer got a picture, and it was maybe Mike's favorite picture of us. I call it the only talking still picture in the world. I mean, there's no doubt about what we are saying to each other." Todd chartered a plane to fly them to Nice, but there would be a two-hour layover in Paris. "I don't want to go to Paris," said Liz. "It bores me." They flew *directly* to Nice.

In Nice, the couple attended the Cannes film festival, where *Around the World in 80 Days* was shown. "We had rented a villa, La Fiorentina, just outside Monte Carlo near St.-Jean-Cap-Ferrat, about three months into our marriage. The most beautiful house you've ever seen," Taylor recalled. "I was in the pool, swimming laps at our home, and Mike came outside to keep me company. I got out of the pool and put my arms around him, and he said, 'Wait a minute, don't joggle your tiara.' Because I was wearing my tiara in the pool! He was holding a red leather box, and inside was a ruby necklace, which glittered in the warm light. It was like the sun, lit up and made of red fire. First, Mike put it around my neck and smiled." Then he presented her with matching earrings and a bracelet. "Since there was no mirror around, I had to look into the water. The jewelry was so glorious, rippling red on blue like a painting. I just shrieked with joy, put my arms around Mike's neck, and pulled him into the pool after me. It was a perfect summer day and a day of perfect love."

Quarrels and fights, some public, some private, continued, all becoming a part of their image as a tempestuous couple. Socializing often with the Todds were Eddie Fisher, who considered Todd his best friend, and his wife, Debbie Reynolds. Reynolds recalled that at dinner one evening, the Todds had a fierce argument: "Elizabeth said something to Mike that caused him to haul off and hit her, knocking her to the floor," said Reynolds, startled and upset as the couple screamed and shouted at each other. "I went after Mike, jumping on his back and pummeling him so he would stop fighting with Elizabeth. Suddenly everyone turned on me. Eddie accused me of being naïve. Mike told me that Elizabeth could 'take it.' I honestly thought he was hurting her, but Elizabeth told me to stop being a Girl Scout. How did this turn into something *I* did wrong?"

Neither the press nor the public could get enough of their extravagant lifestyle, especially as Todd lavished gift after gift upon her. She wore sable and mink. The couple traveled in their private plane—dubbed the Liz by Todd—equipped with a double bed and a boudoir. They had a $25,000 white Rolls-Royce, equipped with a bar and telephone, and residences in Los Angeles; Palm Springs; New York on Park Avenue; and Westport, Connecticut. There were also three toy poodles. Usually, Todd shopped with her and indulged her at every opportunity. She also indulged herself at every opportunity, occasionally with complaints from Todd. The owner of a shop remembered that Taylor strode in alone one day and bought a sapphire mink coat from stock. "Next day," said the store owner, "Mike brought it back . . . without comment." But that kind of thing was the exception to the Todds' rules.

Staying at exclusive hotels and dining at elegant restaurants, they also enjoyed the company of the high and mighty. Todd loved her passionately but shrewdly; he understood how she could help promote his career. With her access to powerful people and with a worldwide fame he would never match, she opened doors, which he could then brashly walk through and make an impression. Nicky had been resentful of her fame. Todd luxuriated in it.

He knew, too, that the stories of their opulence would delight and inspire wonder. Every Saturday night was a gift night for Liz. And mainly the gifts were jewels—fantastic one-of-a-kind jewels, necklaces, bracelets, earrings of the most precious gemstones: diamonds, emeralds, sapphires. The necklace, bracelet, and earrings he presented her with in Nice were only a few among so many more. When Todd had given her a 29.5-carat diamond engagement ring, he boasted: "One day's receipt from *Around the World in 80 Days*." But sometimes Elizabeth could be so casual about the ring that it seemed like a trifle to her—in the eyes of the public. One day while shopping in Beverly Hills, she let the owner of the shop try on her ring. As she was leaving the store, the owner said: "Don't you want it back?" She had "forgotten" about it—or had she?

She loved every piece of jewelry Todd or anyone else gave her. Marilyn Monroe may have sung "Diamonds Are a Girl's Best Friend," but Elizabeth Taylor lived that way. Lovely jewels had been given to her by the likes of Bill Pawley, Nicky Hilton, and Wilding, and from Uncle Howard—nothing for her that was out of this world but *sweet,* she might say. Holding on to those jewels with an awareness that more would come, she would have one of the greatest private jewelry collections in the world.

But there was also a backlash that would continue in the years to come, from people offended by her extravagance. "Elizabeth Taylor will be 25 Wednesday, and a lot of people, shocked by her apparent frivolousness as she approaches the momentous date, are asking: 'When will she grow up?' " commented Louis Berg of the *Los Angeles Times.* If there were any misconceptions about her, said Berg, they "are Elizabeth's own fault. She flaunts her reckless and defiant feelings, and deliberately—out of defiance —tries to fool people into thinking she is more flip and foolish than she actually is." Yet Berg seemed sympathetic to her. "Miss Taylor is trying to recapture the foolish years she never had . . . when did Elizabeth ever have a chance to be a teenager?" Oddly enough, Berg touched on the very mixed, conflicting feelings that many in the nation had about her.

Suffering from premature labor pains, Taylor's health reached a crisis point in late July. When she was admitted to New York's Harkness Pavilion at Presbyterian Columbia University Medical Center, Todd said: "She's in terrible pain but unless it's a sheer outstanding emergency they don't want to take the baby for two and a half weeks." Todd remained by her bedside. "She's been crying all the time." He added: "She had a bad night last night. The night before they gave her an anesthetic or something and she slept pretty well."

Even with this latest news about her health, no one would have been surprised if she suddenly surfaced and was off to a party. But with fears for the baby's life, as well as her own, she stayed put. On August 7, 1957, she gave birth—again by cesarean section—to a four-pound four-ounce premature baby girl named Elizabeth "Liza" Frances Todd, named after her father and herself. Remaining in the hospital for thirteen days, Elizabeth was told by her doctors in no uncertain terms that now with three cesarean births, she could not give birth to other children. *Life* magazine ran a picture of mother and daughter on its cover. *Esquire* magazine would also later run a picture of the two. As Liza grew older, she was often seen with her brothers as the three traveled with their mother around the world. It would always be a juggling act for Elizabeth to have quality time for the children. Her career would have its demands. But the children never expressed any anger with their famous mother.

In late September, *Raintree County* premiered in Louisville, Kentucky, and then in Beverly Hills.

Though the film received mixed reviews, Taylor won fine notices. "Whereas most of the characters in the picture are flat and two-dimensional," wrote the *Los Angeles Times*, "Miss Taylor's possesses exceptional depth." Some critics named *Raintree County* one of the year's best films.

She was back on the road with Todd for *Around the World in 80 Days*—with trips to Honolulu, Sydney, and Hong Kong, all part of a world tour and all ongoing international promotion for the film. But Elizabeth took ill again, this time with an attack of appendicitis. In December, she and Todd returned to Los Angeles, where she had her appendix removed. After spending Christmas in Palm Springs, they resumed their travels in January 1958, flying to London, later to Prague, then to their main destination, Russia. Naturally, Todd hoped to exhibit *Around the World in 80 Days* there. In Moscow, citizens did not seem to know much about Taylor, much less Todd. Throughout the trip, Todd snapped pictures of his wife, one of which, rather grainy and out of focus, ended up nonetheless on the cover of *Look*.

"Living with Mike Todd," said Elizabeth, "was like living with a circus."

"You know I've chased lots of things in my life, including happiness," said Todd, "and I finally caught it when I caught that dame."

• • •

"I'm Saying Good-by to the Movies" was the title of the article "by Mrs. Michael Todd" that ran in the March 16, 1958, issue of the *Los Angeles Times*. "I won't really be leaving show business; I'm just thinking of retiring the commodity known as Elizabeth Taylor, movie star," she wrote. "I don't think in all the years I was an actress I was ever truly happy. I don't think I've ever really been happy before."

This time the retirement talk sounded real, although it came at a surprising time. After the disappointments of not being nominated for the Academy Award for her performances in *A Place in the Sun* and *Giant*, she had finally won a Best Actress nomination for *Raintree County*. Still, she planned two films before calling it quits. One would be in Todd's ambitious plans to film Cervantes's *Don Quixote*. The other would be for MGM.

MGM balked at her idea of retirement and also a film with Todd. Still under contract to the studio, Taylor was *its* star, not *his*. Instead, she finally began work on the already-scheduled adaptation of Tennessee Williams's *Cat on a Hot Tin Roof*. Because of the production code in Hollywood, the drama's more controversial and explosive themes, those dealing with homosexuality and a loveless marriage, would have to be watered down or perhaps edited out altogether.

Now signed to write and direct was Richard Brooks—the director of *The Last Time I Saw Paris*—who worked hard with fellow screenwriter James Poe to create a film acceptable to the code yet true to Williams's themes. For those watching the completed movie, some of those "shocking" themes, though somewhat buried, nonetheless would still be apparent. Taylor's costar was Broadway actor Paul Newman, not yet a bona fide movie star but certainly on his way. Originally, MGM wanted the production shot in black and white as a sign that it was a "serious" dramatic film, but Brooks said that with Taylor's violet eyes and Newman's blue ones, it *had* to be shot in color, which would create a hotter, sexier image. In the end, *Cat on a Hot Tin Roof* was filmed in glorious Technicolor, and Brooks had one of Hollywood's hottest couples on-screen.

Todd thought the role of Maggie was perfect for her. Helen Rose recalled, "He would see the 'dailies' and he talked to anyone who would listen about Elizabeth's brilliant performance and what a job Richard Brooks was doing." Todd was convinced it would be her finest film.

With her marriage, her travels, and now this challenging role, Elizabeth was undergoing one of the great transformations of her life. Before marrying Todd, she had lived in a cocoon. MGM shielded her, covered up for her, promoted her, and defined who she was in the public imagination and sometimes in her own. As Carroll Baker had recalled a few years earlier, "Her judgments and dialogue came straight out of MGM movies." Now even more pampered than ever before—she loved the jewels, the furs, the first-class hotels and restaurants, the snapping to attention of all who saw her when she entered a room—she was moving, however, out of the realm of Hollywood into a broader, more complicated world. Todd's life itself was a major step in altering her perspective; his poverty-ridden childhood; his hustler's view of life; his experiences in topsy-turvy vaudeville—and then in the superchic sophistication of New York theater; his drive, energy, and confidence; his language; his refusal to take no for an answer; his comprehension of living on one's own terms—all helped her move forward. The travels with Todd around the world exposed her more to politics and diverse cultures. It would be a mistake to say that Todd endowed her with all these new perspectives. On her own, she had been moving toward a broader worldview. That had already started with her trips abroad as well as those visits to cities like Chicago and New York. Todd simply introduced her to more and varied experiences, and rather than fearing what she was seeing and hearing, she embraced it all. She also was seeing even more ways to assert herself and to use her own powers, to make demands, also to keep exploring and examining and not to live by Hollywood's rules. Many actors and actresses let the culture of Hollywood define them, which could be deadly. Hollywood could drop you in a minute—and then who were you?

Perhaps in this desire to fully break out of the cocoon and to live her view of a "normal" life as wife and mother, she appeared as if she might indeed give up her career. She would do the same at other points in her life. But her career and her work as an actress meant more to her than she appeared willing to admit—to herself. That, of course, had been true even during the marriage to Nicky Hilton. She would for a time make one movie a year. But she would not forsake that career, no matter what she said publicly.

But then suddenly, in the midst of her personal transformation, something happened that shocked everyone, something that shook her to the core, something that became a part of the tragic legendary life of Elizabeth Taylor.

In March 1958, Todd was set to fly to New York with Elizabeth to accept an award from the Friars Club as Showman of the Year. While working on *Cat on a Hot Tin Roof*, Elizabeth had taken ill again, this time running a 102°F fever from a virus. Nonetheless, Todd still planned on her accompanying him to New York.

He also tried to persuade *Cat on a Hot Tin Roof* director Richard Brooks to join Elizabeth and him on the flight east. "We'll fly in and come right back and be ready to shoot Monday," Todd said to Brooks. But Brooks told him bluntly: "You're insane. If she has a cold and can't work for two days, how inthe hell is she going to get on a plane and be back and healthy enough to work on Monday? She shouldn't go."

Finally, her physician Rex Kennamer insisted that she not travel. Having first met Kennamer the night of Monty's accident, she had liked and trusted him. Soon after, he became her personal physician. On this occasion, she was so ill that she had no choice but to stay in Los Angeles. Before leaving home for the airport, Todd—in retrospect —seemed jittery and even strangely apprehensive, kissing his wife good-bye several times. Todd told the butler, "All right now. Make sure and look after everyone for me."

Just before his private plane, the Liz, took off from Lockheed Air Terminal in Burbank at 10:41 p.m., Todd called Elizabeth, saying he would call again when the twin-engine plane stopped to be refueled. The weather was foul. It was raining heavily. Yet Todd appeared to brush aside any concerns. With Todd were writer Art Cohn, then working on the story of Todd's life, and two pilots, Bill Verner and Tom Barclay. Always the confident optimist, Todd most likely assumed all would be well. But during the flight, the plane ran into treacherous weather. Ice formed on the wings. The plane did a nosedive and crashed in Grants, New Mexico.

In the early morning hours, Elizabeth was in bed at the twelve-room villa that she and Todd had rented. Unexpectedly, Todd's executive secretary Dick Hanley, her physician Rex Kennamer, and columnist Jim Bacon arrived at the house. Todd had enjoyed Bacon's company and had invited him to take the flight to New York. But the columnist backed out because of the weather. In the early hours of the morning, an Associated Press reporter had called Bacon from New Mexico with chilling news of a plane crash. In turn, Bacon spoke to Todd's secretary Hanley—and thus went to the house. "The minute we walked in that bedroom door," Dr. Kennamer recalled, "Liz knew why we were there." Todd and the three others on the fligh had all been killed in the crash, their bodies almost burned beyond recognition. "Her first impulse was to run away from the news," recalled Hanley. "Although she had been in bed with a fever of 102, she jumped out of bed in her bare feet and darted through every room in the house, tried to get outside. She screamed so loud that even the neighbors heard her, and went completely hysterical. As she dashed for the front door and the open street, Dr. Kennamer grabbed her and we took her up to bed. She submitted to the sedative that eventually quieted her." The news quickly spread through Hollywood. Later Elizabeth granted Bacon an interview, which turned out to be the scoop of his career.

Friends and associates arrived at the Taylor-Todd residence. Among them were Sydney Guilaroff, Helen Rose, Taylor's agent Kurt Frings, and her secretary Peggy Rutledge. Todd's close friend, singer Eddie Fisher, was then in New York. Elizabeth's three children were in the home. But Elizabeth was not in shape to care for them. Fisher's wife, Debbie Reynolds, took Taylor's three children to stay at her house. Also at the Taylor-Todd house were MGM executives Eddie Mannix and Benny Thau. Even they had been moved by the tragedy that now enveloped this young actress. Also arriving at the home in Coldwater Canyon was Hollywood's great recluse, Greta Garbo. The Taylor family came. Photographs captured a grim-faced Francis driving a distraught Howard and his wife, Mara, as they left Elizabeth's home. The death of Todd and the young widow he had left behind drew the attention and sympathy of all of Hollywood, as well as the nation itself.

"I have never seen anyone so grief-stricken," said Helen Rose, who remembered that Elizabeth stayed in bed for several days—and could not stop crying.

A memorial for Todd drew a huge turnout of some nine hundred members of the movie colony, at Temple Israel on Hollywood Boulevard. Among those in attendance was, rather touchingly, Michael Wilding. No matter what, Elizabeth was still in his thoughts.

Not attending the Hollywood tribute was Elizabeth, who headed to Chicago for the funeral. Escorting Elizabeth through a throng of reporters, photographers, and newsreel cameramen at the Los Angeles airport were Dick Hanley and MGM's publicity chief, Bill Lyons. Also by Taylor's side was Sydney Guilaroff, who had considered traveling with her to Chicago. But Elizabeth told Guilaroff she wanted Helen Rose to go, which he said he well understood. On the flight were her brother, Howard; Dr. Rex Kennamer; and Todd's friends, columnist Jim Bacon and Eddie Fisher. At the airport, there were also curiosity seekers, said Rose. Crowds were also at the Chicago airport—and outside Elizabeth's hotel, the Drake, "to see Elizabeth in her misery." "It was during this trip I realized what it meant to be a glamorous film star and the pressures involved," said Rose.

In Chicago, Elizabeth was escorted by her brother, Howard, and Dr. Kennamer to Waldheim Cemetery. A tent had been pitched for Todd's family and friends. Inside were seats and the casket with Todd's remains. For Elizabeth—still suffering a fever—the day was all the more painful because of the circus-like atmosphere. "When we arrived on this windy, wintry day," said Helen Rose, "the cemetery was packed with people—mostly women and children. We were told some of them had been there since early morning and had brought their lunches in paper bags." Rose also recalled: "We had to squeeze into the enclosure where the services were to be held. Howard and Rex held Elizabeth by the arms. She was still very ill and weak." Everyone was aware that Todd's ninety-two-year-old mother was too ill and infirm to attend the services. A band of twelve Gypsies showed up with violins and offered to play music for the rites. Their offer was declined. On a nearby road, cars were double-parked, causing a minor traffic jam. Onlookers called out to Taylor.

Standing over the casket, Mike Todd Jr. called his father "the greatest human being I've ever known." Twice Elizabeth cried out, "No, no." As the casket was about to be lowered into the ground, Elizabeth gently touched it, sobbing, "I love you, Mike."

"Reporters later wrote that Elizabeth hurled herself hysterically over Mike's grave," said Eddie Fisher. "It wasn't true. After the service, she asked us all to leave the tent and then spent a few moments there alone. When she emerged, the crowd surged through the barricades, surrounding her, shouting and snatching at her clothes."

Afterward, Elizabeth sat in the limousine with her head resting on her brother's shoulder. But the vehicle had problems getting through a crowd of some three hundred people, still hoping for a glimpse of Liz. "People swarmed all over the car, rocking it back and forth and pounding on the windows," recalled Fisher. "Please, for God's sake, get the car moving," Elizabeth cried.

Todd's death affected her in profound, unexpected ways, again dramatically altering her life *and* her evolving view of life. Having lived before the public eye, she later appeared resentful of the public's demands on her. Her defiance against prevailing social attitudes grew and intensified. So did a suspiciousness of the motives of people she encountered, especially at the studio. For a time, she was emotionally adrift, not sure what to do with her life. Yet, ironically, more than ever, she seemed determined to live her life completely on her terms. Her stoic Christian Science beliefs helped sustain her. "Half of life is dealing with fate, with the unforeseen," she said. "The night I said goodbye to Mike Todd and went to bed while he went to the airport, I had no idea that the next day my whole life would be changed and that nothing would ever change it back again. Sometimes you just have to wait until the blow hits you, and then do the best you can."

Surprisingly, acting also sustained her. It enabled her to distance herself from her own life by living out the emotions of a character. Some of her most exciting performances would soon come. There would be a newfound fire and toughness in those performances. For Elizabeth, there would also be a problem in terms of her acting career, and that problem once again would be her studio, as far as she was concerned. But now she would be ready to fight head-on. "I believe you have to put up your dukes and fight, even if you don't know what you're fighting against."

A few days after Todd's funeral, the Academy Awards were held. The Best Actress award, for which Elizabeth had been nominated for *Raintree County*, went to actress Joanne Woodward for *The Three Faces of Eve*. By coincidence, Woodward was married to Elizabeth's *Cat on a Hot Tin Roof* costar Paul Newman.

At MGM, director Richard Brooks continued filming *Cat on a Hot Tin Roof*, shooting scenes that did not involve Elizabeth. Word was that the production would have to shut down, pending her return, which MGM hoped might be in another week or two. But as far as Elizabeth was concerned, the studio didn't care about her grief. She questioned the motives of studio executives

Benny Thau and Eddie Mannix when they had visited her home after Todd's death. Had they come merely because MGM was concerned about her returning to work on their damn picture? Yet Helen Rose recalled, "The studio asked us not to pressure Elizabeth into going back and finishing *Cat on a Hot Tin Roof*. They were considering either recasting it or shelving it entirely. Despite the rumors of the studio's 'cruelty to the stars,' it was Benny Thau himself who told me that Elizabeth's health was more important than the film." But not every executive looked at the situation the way Benny Thau did. Recalling the studio's insensitivity, Richard Brooks remembered the day he received a call from Todd's secretary Dick Hanley.

"I think you ought to get up here because this girl is hysterical. She's about to go off the deep end." Arriving at her home, Brooks was led to her bedroom, where Elizabeth "took one look at me and started screaming."

"You son of a bitch!" Brooks remembered her yelling. "I guess you're here like all the rest of these bastards who have been here all day long! 'When am I going to go back to work?' And she named them all, all the executive staff from the studio, including the producers of the movie," said Brooks. "They had gone there with flowers and doleful voices and all that crap, but what they finally got around to asking each time was, 'So, how soon do you think you'll be back, honey?' Well, she saw me and figured it was the same deal."

"Elizabeth, if you don't want to come back to the movie," Brooks told her, "don't come back. It's a movie—that's all it is. If you don't do it, they'll start over and find somebody else to do it. If you never want to come back, that's fine."

"I'm never coming back," she told Brooks. "Fuck you and the movie and everybody else."

Yet she couldn't deny the connection she felt to her character Maggie, in part because of Todd's enthusiasm about her performance.

Quietly, Elizabeth contacted Guilaroff, who was styling her hair for the film. Did he think she should return to work? He gently told her, "Yes, I do. For Mike's sake. He said it was a wonderful part for you." She resumed work on the film. "Never missed a day and was never late," said Brooks.

"Fortunately, she was able to quickly put herself back into the part of Maggie," said Guilaroff. "With the emotional resonance she brought to the role from her recent tragedy, it was a triumphant performance for Elizabeth, one of the finest of her career." With *Cat* completed, she still had a deal with MGM to make one additional film within the next three years. But there would be no love lost between the studio and her.

Between $3 and $5 million was left by Todd to Elizabeth and his son, Mike Todd Jr.

Completing *Cat on a Hot Tin Roof*, Elizabeth made plans to rent a new home, to flee memories of Todd at their old residence. Later there were reports that if she appeared in John Huston's *he Unforgiven*, she would be paid "the highest price any woman to date has ever received for a motion picture." At this point, before she had even peaked in acclaim or popularity, she was considered Hollywood's most important star.

With her brother, Howard, and his wife, Mara, Elizabeth flew to New York in June. On the flight was Hedda Hopper, who shortly before had visited her and told her readers, "I've known and loved Elizabeth Taylor since she was 10. My admiration for her today is unbounded." During the flight, the two talked until the early hours of the morning. Elizabeth still wore the engagement ring and bracelet Todd had given her, a gold chain with diamonds running through it. On the third finger of her right hand, she wore the wedding ring she had given Todd, which had been the only thing salvaged from the plane crash and fire.

In August, *Cat on a Hot Tin Roof* opened to solid reviews. "It was a powerful stage drama and it is a powerful screen drama, and Brooks has exacted—and extracted—stunningly real and varied performances," wrote the *Los Angeles Times*. "Miss Taylor is astonishingly good." Later the paper wrote that here she had surpassed all her previous portrayals. In the *New York Times*, Bosley Crowther wrote of Elizabeth: "She is terrific." *Variety* called it "an intense, important motion picture." "Elizabeth has a major credit with her portrayal of Maggie. The frustrations and desires both as a person and a woman, the warmth and understanding she molds, the loveliness that is more than a well-turned nose—all these are part of a full-scented perceptive interpretation. That she performed in this manner under the stress of recent tragedy makes her performance certain to provoke conversation."

Early on, there was Oscar buzz. But then the Taylor life took another surprising turn that ultimately ruined her chances for that Oscar and forever changed the nation's view of her.

Consoling her over Todd's death was Eddie Fisher, who spent hours with her as they reminisced about Todd. Philadelphia-born, the fourth of seven children of Russian-born Jewish immigrants, Fisher had dropped out of high school in his senior year to pursue a singing career. Having appeared on the radio show *Arthur Godfrey's Talent Scouts*, he soon performed with bands. His career took a turn upward following his performances on Eddie Cantor's radio show.

After a stint in the army, Fisher appeared on TV variety shows, had hit records like "Oh! My Papa" and "I Need You Now" and his own TV show *Coke Time With Eddie Fisher* from 1953 to 1957, then *The Eddie Fisher Show.*

Before long, rumors were afloat throughout Hollywood and then New York that perhaps Elizabeth and Eddie were spending *too* much time together, that perhaps their friendship was more than a friendship. By September 1958, when Fisher flew to New York to perform at Grossinger's in upstate New York, Elizabeth joined him. Her children remained in Los Angeles. Their time at the resort did not go unnoticed. It seemed to make it official in the eyes of the press and public. Mike Todd had not yet been dead six months. But already the Widow Todd and her late husband's best friend were having a hot and heavy love affair. What made their romance all the more a sensation was that Fisher was still married to America's girl next door, Reynolds, who as everyone knew, had been matron of honor at Taylor's wedding to Todd— and who also had cared for Elizabeth's children at her home when the tragedy first struck. Could there be a more shocking or juicier scandal? Apparently not. The media descended on them.

As Taylor boarded a plane in New York to return to Los Angeles, she said talk about a romance with Fisher was "garbage." But no one was buying that, either. When asked why she was going to Los Angeles, the Taylor temper flared. "Because I've got three children there!" For the public, there was the question of what type of mother she was.

Once she arrived in Los Angeles, she was met by her agent Kurt Frings—and the press. In her arms, she demurely carried a Yorkshire terrier—and acted as if she didn't see all the reporters and photographers and ignored their questions. A TWA wagon carried Taylor and Frings about one hundred yards, from the plane to a Cadillac that was waiting for her. When one reporter pleaded for a comment, Taylor simply said, "Hello." Asked if she planned to see Fisher and Reynolds while in Los Angeles, she replied, "I don't know. I just got here." Asked to make *some* statement, she told the press corps, "But I have nothing to say." Afterward, she checked into the Beverly Hills Hotel. But the media followed her luggage, which was taken to a private residence in Beverly Hills.

A phalanx of publicists, agents, managers, and studio people—all were consulted at some point by the three players in the drama. A lid had to be kept on this scandal. And everything had to be done to salvage the careers of Taylor and Fisher —and of Reynolds, whose image might somehow be tarnished if personal stories about her domestic situation hit the press. Later generations might be hard-pressed to understand all the discussion, all the outrage, all the curiosity of the media and public. But this was the tail end of the staid 1950s, a conformist age when the nation seemed afraid of its own shadow, when its citizens were expected to adhere to traditional gender and marital roles, something Elizabeth had already challenged in her films and her off-screen life. But this scandal could wreck her career. For Americans of the Eisenhower Age, her behavior was considered an affront to public decency and morality.

"I am not in love with Liz and Liz is not in love with me," Fisher announced before he flew back to Los Angeles. Once there, he stayed for several hours at the residence of his friend Joey Forman before returning to his home with Reynolds. But when the two were alone, all hell broke loose. In no time, the couple "engaged in a heated argument over his conduct and the fact that he had failed to let her know he was staying in the East an extra week," the *Los Angeles Times* reported. "The couple seemed to be on the way to reconciling late in the afternoon when, together, they vaulted a rear wall to escape newsmen and Eddie escorted his wife to a nearby doctor's office." But the coverage did not stop there. Once Debbie and Eddie returned home, Fisher wasn't around long. He "again deserted the house, evaded newsmen by walking in one door of a hotel and out another and didn't return until after 1 a.m. He was reported to have again left early yesterday to spend the night with Forman." Every move and maneuver of the three principals was being monitored, scrutinized, analyzed, and discussed.

Taylor received a phone call from Hedda Hopper. Exactly what was going on? Hopper wanted to know. Elizabeth and Hopper then had what turned out to be an explosive conversation. Elizabeth wasn't answering Hopper's questions. Then Taylor—in essence—told Hopper to back the hell off. It was *her* life—and, if anything, Mike Todd would have wanted her to go on living. Later an outraged Hopper reported that Elizabeth, upon being asked how she could embark on such an affair, especially so soon after Todd's death, had said: "Mike's dead and I'm alive. . . . What do you expect me to do? Sleep alone?" Across America newspaper readers were outraged. So was Taylor, who said she had been misquoted. "What happened was this," Taylor recalled. "The columnist asked if I was aware how much Mike was in love with me, and I said 'Oh, God, you know how much I loved Mike. I loved him more than my life. But Mike is dead now, and I'm alive, and the one person who would want me to try and live and be happy is Mike!' " Interestingly, in *Cat on a Hot Tin Roof*, Taylor's Maggie, in response to the animosity of her husband, Brick, over the death of his friend

Skipper, which he held her responsible for, had cried out: "Skipper is dead. And I'm alive! Maggie the Cat is alive." Taylor always believed that Hopper had lifted the "false" quote about Todd from the film. But Hopper was adamant—and angry—and turned with a vengeance against the actress she had praised from the time Taylor was a little girl.

As recounted by the press, it was a gorgeous, scandal-ridden adulterous drama of devotion and betrayal with a trio of characters, each living out public perceptions or misconceptions about them. There was the naïve, gullible but passionate young husband, suddenly transfixed and falling head over heels in love. There was the sweet, seemingly adoring girlish wife, mother of two, completely unsuspecting and caught off guard by the shift in her husband's affections. And at the center of this stormy tale, there stood the dark-haired, violet-eyed temptress, aware of her powers of seduction, aware of a home she was wrecking but seemingly heartless and hell-bent on her own gratification. Of course, the situation was far more complicated and complex, but the press and public went with it, and the headlines in newspapers around the country told the story in daily feeds.

"Marriage Breaks Up Amid Rumors Singer Courted Miss Taylor," reported the *Los Angeles*

Times on September 11, 1958. Then followed one juicy headline after another.

"Eddie Fisher Talks; Says He's Sick Man"
"Debbie Will Seek Divorce from Eddie"
"Debbie Divorces Fisher;
Wins Million Settlement"
"Debbie Not Bitter,
Just Wants Her Happiness."

So pervasive was the coverage that the September 12, 1958, edition of the *Los Angeles Times* ran an editorial under the banner:

"Three Cheers for Love!"

While crisis piles on crisis elsewhere in the universe, it is comforting and reassuring to be reminded that something is stable in a restless world. Good old Hollywood goes along in its accustomed groove, stirred not by events in far-off Formosa or the Middle East but engrossed at present in the romantic affairs of Eddie Fisher, Debbie Reynolds and Elizabeth Taylor. "I am still in love with my husband," says Debbie. "I'm not taking anything away from Debbie Reynolds because she really never had it," says Liz.

There must be some hope for sanity when such homey touches as these compete for front-page space with Quemoy and Lebanon and Sherman Adams.

Of course, some might now ask who Sherman Adams was, unaware that he was once President Dwight David Eisenhower's beleaguered White House chief of staff who was forced to resign after a political scandal in 1958.

In the years to come, the public would become accustomed to stories about stars who had adulterous affairs or who lived together or had children without the benefit of marriage. Such stories would be fun to read. But rarely would such tales engender huge public disapproval. If anything, Elizabeth Taylor had altered this aspect of the culture. It would become yet another sign of female independence and assertion.

Though Fisher and Reynolds were clearly established stars, accustomed to dealing with the press, neither had ever experienced this kind of nonstop scrutiny. Fisher's career suffered. And it was hard for him to accept the public scorn and ridicule. Sitting in front of his television set one evening, he was pleased to hear entertainer Steve Allen announce that Fisher would appear on his program the following week. But then Fisher was shaken when he heard loud boos coming from the studio audience. Later, his own television program, *The Eddie Fisher Show*, ran into problems. On one occasion, when Taylor was backstage viewing the live broadcast, network officials were said to be irate because "she defied an NBC edict to Fisher to keep her away." The network denied the story. But nobody believed that. In early 1959, Fisher lost his TV show, presumably because of low ratings. Fisher was in the early stages of a decline also fueled by alcohol and drugs. Later it was revealed that Fisher was bipolar.

But Fisher fell deeply in love with Taylor. Everything revolved around her. "I loved buying things for Elizabeth. She was always so delighted and surprised, no matter what it was. The most expensive presents were jewels. An emerald wedding ring, the first gift I ever gave her, a diamond bracelet, an evening bag with 'Liz' spelled out in twenty-seven diamonds for her twenty-seventh birthday. I bought black pearls, rubies—whatever caught my eye—and little charms for a bracelet she had. The NBC peacock in gold and different colored stones. A platinum Michelob bottle, her favorite beer. A Dom Pérignon bottle of platinum and emeralds. Eventually that bracelet weighed about forty pounds. It was ridiculous but she wore it."

Because of public sympathy, Reynolds received good press. Earlier she had appeared in the classic musical *Singin' in the Rain*. Now she starred in one movie after another: *The Mating Game* and *The Rat Race* and later the very successful *The Unsinkable Molly Brown*, which won her an Oscar nomination. Yet as much as the public liked her, her career did not reach the heights of Taylor's.

For Elizabeth, the scrutiny itself was nothing new. But never before had she been depicted as a scarlet woman, even when she had divorced Wilding to marry Todd. Now there were repercussions. The Theater Owners of America dropped plans to give her their Star of the Year award, which went instead to actress Deborah Kerr. "Miss Taylor's selection for her role as Maggie the Cat in Tennessee Williams's *Cat on a Hot Tin Roof* appeared to be a cinch until headlines blazed the so-called affair between her and singer Eddie Fisher. Sympathy for Debbie Reynolds as Fisher's wronged wife spread like fire," the executive editor of the organization explained in rather bluntly honest terms. "The movie industry is at the mercy of public opinion and to award Miss Taylor the honor at a time like this was out of the question."

In Hollywood, she was socially ostracized. "Until Debbie filed for divorce we didn't dare go out in public," said Taylor. "Friends, at least people I thought were friends, didn't seem to want to have anything to do with us."

"Liz Taylor's Year of Disaster" was the title of columnist Joe Hyams's article at the start of 1959.

"Elizabeth seemed to feel bewildered by the fact that the public had turned against her," said Hyams. "The same public which had cheered and envied and asked for autographs jeered her the few times she went out of the house. Mail poured in to her studio from people who said they would never go to see her in another picture.

"The tide of sentiment against her, let loose by the break-up of the Eddie Fisher–Debbie Reynolds marriage, is reminiscent of the flood of ill will once directed at Ingrid Bergman," Hyams added, recalling the international criticism and headlines that actress Ingrid Bergman drew when, while married to a physician in Los Angeles, she had a "notorious" affair with Italian director Roberto Rossellini that led to a child born out of wedlock in Italy. Bergman had also felt the brunt of an enraged Hedda Hopper. When stories first surfaced that Bergman might be pregnant, Hopper had flown to Rome to interview her. Bergman admitted she planned to divorce her husband. But said little else. Just before the interview ended, Hopper asked: "What's all this I hear about a pregnancy?" to which Bergman responded: "Good heavens, Hedda. Do I look like it?" Returning to Los Angeles, Hopper wrote that there was no truth to such pregnancy rumors. Of course, when that was proven wrong, Hopper turned on Bergman. In Hollywood itself, movie folk gossiped like mad, enjoying nothing more than a lively scandal. But most didn't make moral judgments. It was only when scandals went public through the media—and might affect box office receipts because of the public's outrage—that industry leaders became "high-minded." For a time, the scandal wrecked Ingrid Bergman's Hollywood career. She was considered a scarlet woman, an outright whore. On March 4, 1950, she was even denounced on the floor of the United States Senate by a representative from the state of Colorado who referred to her as a woman of "mental abnormality" and asked if she was suffering from "the dreaded mental disease schizophrenia." The representative also stated: "Under our law no alien guilty of turpitude can set foot on American soil again. Mrs. Petter Lindstrom [Bergman's married name] has deliberately exiled herself from a country which was so good to her." In essence, it was being said that Bergman, born in Sweden, should not be permitted to return to the United States. Later she made an extraordinary comeback. But it took years. Now a similar outcry was directed at Taylor. Her mental health would also be questioned, and later, amid *another* scandal, she would find herself denounced on the floor of the House of Representatives.

But with all the hue and cry and the public censure, something else happened with the Taylor image. It was always said that America wanted its own brand of royalty, not designated by birth but by a combination of style, accomplishment, and most significant, a larger-than-life persona. The Kennedy family, especially John and Jackie, would be precisely that. Some of the great movie stars had been that, too. In many respects, Elizabeth was still the great American princess who had lived an extraordinarily charmed life. But now she was becoming something else that Americans might have had mixed emotions about yet still respected and held in awe: she was described as the nation's Scarlett O'Hara, a seemingly vain, spoiled, thoughtless, reckless, even ruthless, calculating, and manipulative heartbreaker who walked all over others to get what she wanted—and who ultimately, was somehow triumphant and always compelling to observe. This would be part of the Taylor image for years to come, and most observers lost sight of the real woman.

Such an altered image may have depressed her or pressured her or turned her skeptical and cynical about people, about friendships, about the industry she was so much a part of, and it surely contributed to the intake of pills and booze that she consumed then (and in the years to come) and added to her health problems. "Elizabeth said she didn't give a damn what anybody said, but I knew she was hurt," Eddie Fisher recalled, "particularly by newspaper remarks like the one from Maxine Reynolds, who called her 'the biggest slut in town.' I cared very much, because I loved Elizabeth and because she had done nothing more sinful than fall in love with a married man." Fisher also recalled that the most stinging comments had come from Hedda Hopper and others who charged that neither he nor Elizabeth had loved Mike Todd.

Regardless, Elizabeth maintained her self-control in a way that Fisher was unable to do. In some respects, Taylor dealt with the scrutiny and the public judgments as something to be expected, as part of the game of fame. And that Christian Science upbringing again fortified her with a belief, conscious or not, that anything could be endured or overcome with prayer or concentration.

On the night that Taylor and Fisher appeared at the Oscar ceremonies in Los Angeles, she felt the greatest blow from the scandal. Nominated as Best Actress for *Cat on a Hot Tin Roof*, she lost the award to Susan Hayward for *I Want to Live!* Many believed the scandal had killed her chances. Afterward, she was back in Vegas with Fisher, then back in Los Angeles, where she entered Cedars of Lebanon Hospital—this time to have her tonsils removed.

But an Oscar winner or not, Taylor's career soared. *Cat on a Hot Tin Roof* was a huge hit. Audiences may have expressed anger with her, but they were fascinated, and once they sat in theaters, Taylor delivered a performance that made the price of admission worth it. And despite the decision of the Theater Owners of

America not to give her its top award, *Film Daily* —in its poll of more than two thousand movie, television, and radio reviewers—selected her as the favorite film star of 1958. A professor at UCLA, who invited her to give a talk to students in the motion picture department, told the press in no uncertain terms: "Miss Taylor has been invited because we consider her to be one of the great actresses of the day." Getting lost in all the press coverage and public outrage was indeed the fact that she was a remarkable actress and a more serious one than most realized. Of course, the still-angered Hedda Hopper, not about to pass on any opportunity to get a dig in at her once-favorite actress, added her two cents. "When they say Elizabeth Taylor is a dramatic actress it makes me laugh."

Offers poured in. The September 27, 1958 edition of the *Los Angeles Times* reported that she was signed for the then astronomical sum of $500,000, to play the lead in *Two for the Seesaw.* Producer Jerry Wald rushed to star her as Sheilah Graham in his film about Graham's love affair with F. Scott Fitzgerald in *Beloved Infidel.* Ultimately, she appeared in neither film. But that didn't stop other producers and directors from pounding on her door. Finally, she agreed to star in another controversial Tennessee Williams drama, a tale of incest, corruption, cannibalism, and homosexuality, *Suddenly, Last Summer,* which would costar her with Montgomery Clift and Katharine Hepburn under the direction of Joseph L. Mankiewicz.

The media covered the scandal into the next year. There was much to-do when Taylor, in March 1959, converted to Judaism in a ceremony performed by noted Rabbi Max Nussbaum at Temple Israel. While married to Todd, Taylor considered adopting Judaism but Todd "refused to let her do it," said Fisher. "Why? What difference will it make?" Todd had asked. Fisher also discouraged her. But Elizabeth had made up her mind and began studying the religion. Hers was one of the big star "conversions" of the era. Marilyn Monroe and Sammy Davis Jr. also converted to Judaism. Still, most were baffled by Taylor's decision. "What the hell does she see in all these Jewish guys?" asked her befuddled uncle Howard. During the conversion ceremony, "Elizabeth's mother and father were there, too, in what appeared to be a state of shock," said Fisher, who also recalled that there followed "an avalanche of hate mail. It didn't bother Elizabeth. She sincerely believed in what she had done, and then forgot all about it." For Fisher, the criticism of Elizabeth had "an anti-Semitic tinge." But Taylor "was incensed by a newspaper story claiming in banner headlines that she had converted because she had gone insane and was now confined to the Menninger Clinic," said Fisher. "We were going to sue, but then decided to go to dinner at Chasen's, where everyone in Hollywood would see us. The newspaper eventually printed an apology in headlines of the same size." Ironically, the night of that dinner at Chasen's, she looked heavier and haphazardly made up and coiffed. For one of the rare times in her public appearances, the tension and pressure showed in her face; so, too, did her vulnerability.

When Fisher appeared at the Tropicana hotel in Las Vegas, Taylor took up residence at a luxurious ranch in the city with her three children, a nurse, and a valet. "In Las Vegas, I got my first real taste of what it would be like to live with her," recalled Fisher. "Children, pets, servants, minor problems transformed into major tragedies, confusion, chaos, everything at fever pitch," recalled Fisher. "In Las Vegas a chronic sore throat suddenly became seriously infected, and I remember looking in her mouth and seeing large white abscesses." She was rushed to the hospital. "Living with her was like living with a hurricane; each storm built in intensity, then subsided into an eerie calm as the eye passed, only to begin all over again."

Without any letup, the public fascination continued, sometimes reaching a frenzy. Years earlier, when Sara had noticed the way the

French had stared at her daughter even before she was world-famous, she witnessed a phenomenon that now intensified. Just to see Elizabeth Taylor in all her beauteous glory became almost legendary, even at this point in her life. On Eddie's opening night, she was accompanied by her parents and her *Cat on a Hot Tin Roof* costar Burl Ives and his wife. Outside the nightclub, Fisher was "shocked to see pickets parading in front of the hotel carrying signs that read 'Liz Go Home' and 'Keep the Marriage Vows, Eddie.' " At Taylor's entrance, the flashbulbs went off, and patrons in the nightclub gawked and nearly fell over themselves to get a closer look at her. "The Fisher opus was more sideshow than show with the audience seemingly more interested in Elizabeth Taylor's nightly entrances (ah, the great craning of necks, the undertone of 'there she comes now . . .') than in Fisher's singing." Said Fisher: "The only word to describe it is pandemonium. Elizabeth created a commotion wherever she went. And whether or not she liked it in public, she seemed to thrive on it privately."

Finally, the couple wed in a Jewish ceremony in Las Vegas on May 12, 1959. That very morning the Fisher divorce suit was filed in Nevada. Among the guests were Taylor's parents as well as Fisher's parents, who had flown in from

Philadelphia; Elizabeth's brother, Howard, and his wife, Mara, who was Elizabeth's matron of honor; MGM executive Benny Thau; Sydney Guilaroff; Kurt and Ketti Frings; and Dr. Rex Kennamer. It was good Kennamer was there. Just as she'd taken ill before her marriage to Hilton, Taylor was ill on this wedding day—suffering from a sinus condition. Was she having second thoughts? Following the ceremony, the couple flew to Los Angeles. Then it was on to New York, and from there to Barcelona for a honeymoon on the yacht of producer Sam Spiegel and then to begin work on her next film, *Suddenly, Last Summer.*

As she had done on other occasions when love had entered her life, she let it be known that her movie career would soon end. "My personal life has always been more important to me than anything else," she said. "I want to devote my full time to being a wife and mother." Of course, everyone had heard *that* before.

During this time, and most notably on August 29, 1958, as Elizabeth Taylor, come hell or high water, was embracing life, refusing to shy away from her thirst for more to come, an integral part of her later life was just beginning. On that day, in Gary, Indiana, the couple Joseph and Katherine Jackson welcomed into their lives their seventh of nine children, a boy named Michael.

Chapter 12

SOON BACK ON a demanding schedule, Michael traveled to New York for a tribute at the American Museum of Natural History. Then came the major awards shows, first the American Music Awards on January 16, 1984, where he won multiple awards, including Favorite Pop/Rock Male Artist, Favorite Pop/Rock Album for *Thriller*, Favorite Pop/Rock Single for "Billie Jean," and Favorite Pop/Rock Video for "Beat It." He also was the youngest person ever to win the Award of Merit that night. Accepting the award and thanking his parents as well as Diana Ross, who was there that night, he was dressed in a dazzling military-style red jacket with gold trim—and dark glasses. The latter was for a time part of his signature look. He would even wear them during a visit to the White House when he met President and Mrs. Reagan. It was partly a stylish statement: the glasses added to his glamour and enhanced his mystery, the idea of a not wholly accessible star who was keeping something back and hidden. But the glasses also helped him shield himself from the stares, from the people who wanted to get too close. The eyes are the window to the soul, and the soul was something he had to preserve for himself.

Accompanying him was model and actress Brooke Shields. Then came the Grammy Awards on February 28. Again Michael's date was Brooke Shields. A young beauty with a full mane of brown hair and magnificent brown eyes with thick, luxurious brows, Shields had grown up in the public eye. With her assertive mother, Teri Shields, as her manager, Brooke had been a model since 1966—at the age of eleven months—in an Ivory soap ad. Her mother had kept her working. French director Louis Malle had starred a twelve-year-old Shields as a girl growing up in a brothel in the controversial 1978 film *Pretty Baby*. By age fourteen, she was the youngest model ever to land on the cover of *Vogue*. She also appeared in a controversial commercial for Calvin Klein designer jeans in which she was seductively sprawled out as she said, "You want to know what comes between me and my Calvins? Nothing." By the time Michael met Shields, she had also starred in such films as *The Blue Lagoon* and *Endless Love*. Some comparisons at the time were made between Shields and the young Elizabeth Taylor. Yet lovely as Shields was, she did not have Taylor's fires of defiance nor her Old Hollywood beauty. Shields, however, was a stunner. She exuded a sweetness that may have undercut her seductive-ness. Though Michael clearly liked Shields and enjoyed her company, their relationship went but so far.

It's been questioned as to whether Michael really wanted Shields on his arm the night of the Grammys.

The story has been told by biographer Randy Taraborrelli that on the day of the Grammys, Shields unexpectedly showed up at the Jackson home in Encino, asking to see Michael. Could she attend the Grammys with him? she reportedly asked. Apparently, Michael was caught completely off guard and quickly consulted his sisters Janet and La Toya, who were in the house that day. "I don't want to take her. I really, *really* don't," Michael said. La Toya reportedly responded: "Well, then *tell* her. Tell her no if you don't want to take her."

"But I can't," Michael said.

"Why not?" Janet reportedly asked.

"Because I don't want to hurt her feelings."

In the end, he took Shields to the awards ceremony, along with his sister La Toya.

When a Jackson employee asked what Shields was like, Jackson responded, "She's okay." Referring to the Grammy night, he told the employee, "I only took her to help her out. There was no romance. Not at all. We're friends. All of this was strictly for her, for the sake of publicity.

She's nice. I like to help her out when I can. It was good P.R. for her to be seen with me." So much for a hot and heavy romance. For those observing Michael and Brooke, she seemed a safe date, hardly about to jump in the sack with him, hardly possessing the sexual assertiveness that Michael might not be able to handle. At another time, he said that he and Shields had been "romantically serious for a while." But Shields maintained theirs was mainly a friendship.

Perhaps the most telling comment on the Jackson-Shields relationship occurred at the Grammys—when Michael seemed more interested in someone else. Waiting for Michael at the theater was child actor Emmanuel Lewis, with whom Michael had developed a friendship. The star of the TV series *Webster*, Lewis, who was about to turn thirteen, stood about three feet six inches; afterward, he would grow another six inches, but no taller. He also had the air of a young child. Seemingly enchanted by the actor, Michael was often seen carrying Lewis in his arms. The two were also featured on a cover of *Jet* magazine. But the question on everyone's mind was a simple one: Why was Michael, then almost twenty-six, hanging out with Emmanuel Lewis?

Nonetheless, the Grammys was a triumphant night for Michael. He broke records at the awards ceremony. He won Best Vocal Performance, Male in three categories: in Pop for "Thriller," in Rock for "Beat It," and in R&B for "Billie Jean." "Billie Jean" also won Best Rhythm & Blues Song, and Michael and Quincy Jones won as Producer of the Year (Non-classical). "Beat It" won Record of the Year. *Thriller* also won the grand prize as Album of the Year. In addition, Michael walked off with the award for Best Children's Album for his recording of *E.T. the Extra-Terrestrial*. In all, he took home eight awards. The night was all the more important for him because he paid tribute to his idol Jackie Wilson, then ill and incapacitated.

Career-wise, Michael Jackson was sitting on top of the world.

Yet if there is a precise time when Michael Jackson began to unravel, when indeed the tragic torment set in, it was probably *after* the release of *Thriller*. Ecstatic with the album's success, Jackson had attained a goal he long dreamed of. But it may also have been his undoing. A range of problems enveloped him. He aspired to top himself, which would not be easy, and the standards by which he measured himself would be impossible to meet. He would also continue to suffer the effects of the accident. Ongoing tensions within his family would continue. And there would be the heightened coverage by both mainstream media and the tabloids that would throw off his equilibrium. Aware that legions of international fans were curious about him, the media excitedly chronicled his every move with cover stories in *People, Rolling Stone, Newsweek, Time,* and later *Vibe*. Few stars received this kind of coverage, which bordered on the hysterical. At first, the coverage centered primarily on his music, but in time he discovered the burden of the scrutiny of his private life. That intense scrutiny would jar and jolt him, and as Carrie Fisher, the daughter of Debbie Reynolds and Eddie Fisher, who was a friend to both Michael and Elizabeth, understood, possibly only one other celebrity would understand the harsh, unrelenting glare of the spotlight, having endured it herself: that would be Elizabeth.

No doubt there were now far too many questions about whom he dated, whom he had romantic feelings about, and even when—now in his early twenties—he might marry. In interviews with his soft, high voice, he was hardly the sexual magnet of the man on records and in videos. Now the media asked questions that would never have been publicly posed in the past. Much of the coverage of Elizabeth and Michael marked major shifts and a transition in the press—and in worldwide media. The first sign of that shift had occurred in the 1950s with the publication of the magazine *Confidential*, which had specialized in going behind the facade of star images. Those days of studio portraits of beautifully made-up, lit, posed, and costumed stars had given way to tabloid images of stars in disarray, sometimes looking disoriented or drunk or doped. Photographs aside, the stories in *Confidential* could prove destructive to careers. Sometimes the new tabloid publications—that followed the success of *Confidential*—took real incidents and sensationalized them. Other times they concocted stories that weren't accurate or true. Some stars fought *Confidential*. But it wasn't until Dorothy Dandridge and Maureen O'Hara sued and testified in court that the maga-zine ultimately collapsed.

However, the ground that was broken by *Confidential* led the way to such publications as the *National Enquirer*, *The Globe*, and then the *Star*, as well as such television programs as *Hard Copy* and *Inside Edition*. Whereas *Confidential* might have suggested aspects of a star's sexuality that might have proved shocking to an earlier generation, the new tabloid media were upfront. Mainstream media now asked franker questions. In his music, Jackson had established himself as an adult star, as a sexually potent yet sexually ambiguous matinee idol. Having ascended the ranks of stardom few attain, he was both legendary at this young age and also mythic. Now the audience wanted to know about the real Michael Jackson, the young adult. But he appeared unwilling to share *that person* with the public.

In the 1980s, a dramatic change had come about

in his personality, in his outlook on his life. He had grown increasingly reclusive and withdrawn. At an earlier time, he seemed to jump into interviews with relish. Now he appeared to avoid the press whenever possible, to retreat from public appearances and statements *unless* it was for promotion. On the one hand, he understood that a star has to be *seen*. Invisibility could kill a career. On the other hand, he maintained whatever privacy he could by *controlling* what the public actually saw—or read.

Whenever he agreed to interviews, he did so "with a cordon of managers, other Jackson brothers, and, in one case, his younger sister Janet parroting a reporter's questions before Michael would answer them," commented music writer Gerri Hirshey. When she conducted an interview with him for a cover story in *Rolling Stone*, Hirshey noted: "The small body of existing literature paints him as excruciatingly shy. He ducks, he hides, he talks to his shoe tops. Or he just doesn't show up. He is known to conduct his private life with almost obsessive caution, 'just like a hemophiliac who can't afford to be scratched in any way.' The analogy is his." But whether he agreed to interviews or not, the press coverage continued unabated. Comments were made on his every move, much as was the case with Elizabeth in the past and in the present. But Elizabeth always handled the media skillfully and refused to let it influence her behavior.

For a time, he admitted that most of his "friends" were the animals in his menagerie at the family compound at Hayvenhurst, where he kept a llama, two fawns, and a ram. A favorite was his snake, Muscles. In fact, the entire Jackson family, including Joseph, said La Toya, loved animals. In addition to those other animals, Joe Jackson told *Time* magazine: "Michael has three parrots, two pairs of swans, one's a black pair, one's white. Sometimes those swans get to fighting out there, plopping around in the water out there, and it wakes you up. He has some peacocks. I like animals, but I can be tired of them after a while. Michael never gets tired of an animal. He is like a child."

Michael also developed a strange affinity for mannequins. "I guess I want to bring them to life. I like to imagine talking to them. You know what I think it is?" he once said. "I think I'll say it. I think I'm accompanying myself with friends I never had. I probably have two friends." He added: "That's what it is. I surround myself with people I want to be my friends. And I can do that with mannequins. I'll talk to them." There would also be Bubbles, the chimp, that he carried with him—and who the rest of the family also enjoyed.

But Michael also confessed to loneliness, commenting that he was "one of the loneliest people in the world." He also said he wouldn't wish his loneliness on anyone.

Such talk about mannequins and his obsession with his pets appeared to be a way of derailing the persistent curiosity about his love life. His fascination with Diana Ross was still well known and well publicized. In 1982, he wrote her hit song "Muscles." Together they had graced the covers of *Ebony* and *Jet*. But no one thought of the two as a romantic couple. They looked endearingly like a very close brother and sister. Questions openly arose about Michael's sexuality. Was he gay? Looking as if to avoid such questions, a nineteen-year-old Michael had let it be known in 1977 that he had a crush on young actress Tatum O'Neal. Though the two dated, no one seemed to think it was a romance. O'Neal herself didn't see it that way, either.

In the late 1970s, rumors had circulated—on the grapevine, in the years before the blogosphere—that he had had a relationship with a handsome African American actor generally known as a womanizer. Somehow the actor had taken a liking to Michael, perhaps attracted as much by Michael's fame and talent as by his personal appeal, and as the stories had it, Michael was in a swoon. But the actor's interest soon waned, and he had ditched Michael, leaving him heartbroken apparently from his first significant romance. Whether there was any truth to the story remains undetermined. The most preposterous part of the rumor was that Michael planned to get a sex change to be able to marry the actor. The entire family, including Katherine, seemed thrown off-balance by such comments and quickly came to Michael's "defense," pointing to his "girl friends," such as Tatum and Brooke. Trying to dispel various rumors about her son, Katherine publicly said, "There have been a lot of rumors about Michael, that he has had operations to have his eyes widened and his cheeks changed and everything. Those things are simply not true. He had only one operation, on his nose." But she appeared most emphatic about denying the stories about his sexuality. "They also say Michael is gay. Michael isn't gay. It's against his religion. It's against God. The Bible speaks against it." Joe Jackson also publicly announced: "Michael isn't gay."

Michael himself felt compelled to comment on his sexuality, stating simply that his dates and relationships with girls just hadn't worked out. His fame was partly to blame. Most young women had preconceived notions of who he was. Others were trying to figure him out. He also believed some girls wanted to know what made him tick. Or they hoped to "rescue" him from his loneli-ness.

But he was as emphatic as other family members about letting it be known that he was not gay. When a vocal coach mentioned the rumors, Michael told him: "I know. The other day a big, tall, blond, nice-looking fellow came up to me and said, 'Gee, Michael, I think you're wonderful. I sure would like to go to bed with you.' I looked at him and said, 'When's the last time you read the Bible? You know you really should read it because there is some real information in there about homosexuality.' The guy says, 'I guess if I'd been a girl, it would have been different.' And I said, 'No, there are some very direct words on that in the Bible too.' " In many respects, the subject of sex itself was taboo.

Yet at the same time, when singing and dancing, he projected a strong sexuality—when dancing in some videos or onstage he might grab his crotch and kick a leg up. Yet his was also an androgynous sexuality. That was all part of his appeal. The androgyny, the inherent gentleness, the soft voice, the delicate features (thanks to the surgery and makeup), the lithe body frame all made him seem less threatening and all the more vulnerable. It was part of what also drew very young fans to him and also made children around the world adore him.

But beneath that exterior, there was a tougher person, both on- and offstage. Audiences detected the steely determination to ascend to new heights in his career, the determination to make shrewd business connections that would ensure his autonomy and his power. It was all a part of the subtext of the Jackson performances and persona that made him more complicated and intriguing—to observe, enjoy, and hopefully understand.

Though he moved professionally in one direction, accepting the responsibilities of adulthood, privately and emotionally he moved in another direction, withdrawing from the adult world. He identified with Peter Pan of J. M. Barrie's play *Peter Pan, or the Boy Who Would Not Grow Up.* In his 1904 play and, later, his 1911 novelization of the story, Barrie created a whimsical adventurous boy who can fly. His name was partly inspired by Pan, the Greek god of the woodlands, and it was always said that the inspiration for the story itself followed in the wake of the death of Barrie's older brother David in a skating accident at age fourteen. Barrie's grieving mother seemed to find solace in the fact that her departed son would always remain a boy. In Barrie's story, Peter Pan—on an excursion to Bloomsbury—meets a lovely girl named Wendy Darling and her two brothers, John and Michael. Enchanted by them as they are by him, Peter flies them off tothe island of Neverland. There they encounter the Lost Boys and also the wicked Captain Hook as well as Tinker Bell and Tiger Lily. Always there are adventures and magical moments. At one point, Wendy expresses to Peter her romantic feelings for him. But he tells her that he will always think of her as a mother to him. In time, Wendy returns to her home with her brothers and the Lost Boys. They will eventually grow up. Peter Pan, however, will never grow up and will always reside in his Neverland, yet he promises to visit Wendy every spring. For Michael and so many others, Peter Pan preferred the innocence and purity of childhood to the grinding and deadening responsibilities of adulthood. The character was a potent symbol for Michael, who now cherished the idea of holding on to or recapturing his childhood.

Still living in Hayvenhurst in Encino without any apparent desire to ever leave, he did seek more privacy, more personal space where he could create and even entertain, and, of course, remove himself from Joseph's presence. In 1982, he had decided to do a complete overhaul of the family home. A year later, the renovation was completed. His new studio at the house became his sanctuary, the place where he could be alone, sometimes working on dance steps or music, other times indulging himself in his passions and obsessions. Covering the walls were pictures of his favorite stars. But he no doubt now had visions of another place, all his own, one that would be both an adventure and fantasyland where he might recapture the magic of a childhood he had lacked and where he could escape from the pressures of his career. Yet that was still in the distance. For the time being, he still lived at home, still enjoyed the security of family life and time spent with his sisters La Toya and Janet (to whom he said he was closest), and still followed the tenets of the Jehovah's Witnesses.

But even in the remodeled Hayvenhurst, he sought to live in the cocoon of an idealized childhood he believed he never had, a marked difference from Elizabeth. She often struggled, whether through her marriages or her open defiance of conventions, to break free of the cocoon. Painfully aware now that he had missed a lot, he appeared fascinated by other children in the business, past and present. Part of the appeal of Brooke and Tatum as well as actress Kristy McNichol was they also had been child stars, growing up in a tough adult business without time for play, games, and childhood passions. A former child star from the past who intrigued Michael was George "Spanky" McFarland, best known as the spunky, chubby character Spanky in Hal Roach's *Our Gang* series, later called *The Little Rascals*. Once he was no longer a cute little kid, McFarland's career basically was over. As a young adult, he had left show business, joined the Air Force and later became a salesman. He also moved back to Texas, where he was born. His was a very settled life. Later Michael went out of his way to meet McFarland, first at the 1984 Oscar ceremony when McFarland and Jackie Cooper (another former child star) presented an Honorary Oscar to *Our Gang* creator Hal Roach. Afterward, he also tracked down McFarland that night at the Governors Ball. McFarland appeared surprised by the attention Michael lavished on him, saying that as a kid he had watched the *Our Gang* series on television and that McFarland had inspired him. The *Star-Telegram* in Dallas later reported that during a three-night stopover of the Jacksons on tour at Texas Stadium in 1984, Michael again saw McFarland. By one account, he even stayed at the entertainer's home. McFarland's wife, Doris, recalled: "He asked us to turn off the air conditioner because he was cold. He sat in a rocking chair and watched television with us, covered in an afghan." Just being in McFarland's presence seemed to bring him comfort.

Michael was also fascinated by the greatest of child stars, Shirley Temple. Finally, he got to meet her through his childhood friend David Gest, who had become a producer and knew many stars from Hollywood's past. When Michael visited her home in Woodside, California, she came to the door wearing an apron. She had been in the kitchen preparing a meal for them. Like Spanky McFarland, Temple may have been totally surprised by the attention and praise paid to her by the most famous music star in the world. At first, the two didn't seem to know what to say to each other. But his visit pleased her, and the atmosphere at Temple's home was warm and friendly as they dined together. Temple showed him photographs from her movies. She still had the dresses she had worn in her films. Frequently, she rubbed his hand, a way of letting him know she understood him. He recalled that when he asked if she had enjoyed her career, she said simply that she had loved it. After her career in the movies, she had veered in another direction and become the United States Ambassador to Ghana and later Czechoslovakia and the Chief of Protocol of the United States. She also had a settled life as a wife to the businessman Charles Alden Black and as the mother of three children. By the time Michael met Temple, he also knew Elizabeth. That day, Temple frequently asked Michael about Taylor and told him to be sure to tell her hello. Both Temple and McFarland had survived many storms to arrive at mature, satisfying lives. Michael seemed to be searching for their secrets of adjustment to adulthood.

Of then current child performers, he had become friendly not only with Emmanuel Lewis but also with Corey Feldman and later Macaulay Culkin, the star of the hugely successful film *Home Alone*. Perhaps for Michael those were the

Lost Boys of the Peter Pan story, trying to find their path in life. With ever increasing feelings of isolation and alienation from grownup life, he saw those former child stars as his true compatriots. Only they could understand what he experienced and what he believed he had lost.

"I used to think that I was unique in feeling that I was without a childhood. I believed there was only a handful with whom I could share those feelings," he later said. He recalled that upon meeting Shirley Temple, they cried together, "for she could share a pain with me that only others like my close friends Elizabeth Taylor and Macaulay Culkin know."

On July 6, 1984, the *Victory* reunion tour finally opened in Kansas, then was to work its way to such other cities as Dallas, Philadelphia, Chicago, Denver, New York, and finally, Los Angeles on December 9, 1984. The brothers' *Victory* album was also released. Yet the tour—dogged by one problem after another—proved to be a breaking point for Michael. Jackie Jackson suffered a serious leg injury, which prevented him from performing in the first half of the tour. Controversy sprang up because of ticket prices. Though each ticket cost $30, fans were required to buy four tickets, which prohibited some fans from attending. (That idea had been cooked up by Joe and Don King. Michael had opposed it from the beginning.) There were other complications in purchasing tickets. Throughout, a contentious Michael found himself in opposition to Joseph and King. Throughout, he used his clout to ensure he would not let them run the show. No songs from the album were performed in the show because it was said Michael had refused to rehearse with his siblings. Michael also nixed plans for a movie company to film one of the concerts, and he vetoed a European leg of the tour.

He simply wanted to be done with the tour, and so it seemed, with family obligations as well. It was all a mess that led to at least six lawsuits for damages that could add up to $182 million. But Michael felt he had done his part for the family. At that time, the *Victory* tour proved to be the biggest in rock history, playing in twenty-three cities and selling some 2.3 million tickets. From the tour, each of his brothers was said to have earned from $5 to $7 million. Michael donated his earnings to three charities, including the United Negro College Fund. At the end of the last show, Michael made a surprise announcement: this marked the last time the brothers would perform together. It shocked the family—and King.

Despite any feelings of loneliness, Michael gleefully hobnobbed with the famous—and the legends. In turn, the famous and the legends were eager to hobnob with him. Writer/biographer A. Scott Berg recalled a dinner at Katharine Hepburn's New York town house at 244 East Forty-Ninth Street. There was much excitement because Michael would be a guest. When British playwright Tom Stoppard, who was having dinner at the nearby home of Stephen Sondheim, heard the news, he sent over a request for Michael's autograph for his children. "Out of the question," said Hepburn. Broadway producer Irene Mayer Selznick, the daughter of Louis B. Mayer and former wife of David O. Selznick, requested that Berg relay to her every detail of the evening. Had he known about Irene Selznick's request, Michael would have been pleased. David O. Selznick was a hero of his. With the idea of surpassing the success of *Thriller* still looming large in his career goals, he had an anxiety similar to Selznick's. After producing *Gone With the Wind*, Selznick was said to have been haunted by the fear he might not ever be able to top himself.

The moment of Jackson's arrival was etched in Berg's memory: "He was wearing sunglasses and a satiny blue uniform trimmed in gold braid. Onstage, it would probably look dazzling. Up close it looked flimsy and gaudy, like something Professor Harold Hill might have sold to some boys in Iowa along with some tin trombones." But Berg confessed: "I found it difficult to take my eyes off him—not because he was a star, but because he looked so unusual. His body was even slighter than pictures suggested; his skin was taut and a beautiful tawny shade; his nose, with its tiny bridge, bore little resemblance to any other nose I had ever seen. At twenty-five, he had the demeanor of an extremely polite ten-year-old. He spoke in a gentle voice, full of sweetness and wonder."

Among the guests were Hepburn's niece Katharine Houghton (who had costarred as Sidney Poitier's love interest in *Guess Who's Coming to Dinner*) and journalist Cynthia McFadden. Some seemed surprised, however, by his level of conversation. Though Michael professed that Hepburn was his favorite movie star, he appeared to draw a blank about which of her films he liked. In fact, he didn't appear to know much about any of her movies. No doubt he was drawn to her public persona, the older Hepburn who turned up on television interviews.

"He fascinated me," Hepburn told Berg. "He's an absolutely extraordinary creature. He's worked his entire life, entertaining professionally since he was three, and he's never lived a single moment, I mean not a moment, in the real world. He doesn't know how to do anything but write his songs and thrill an audience. He's this strange, artistic creature, living in a bubble, barely touched by anything in the outside world."

Still, there was a moment that surprised even Hepburn—when she discovered that no matter how thrilled he might be by the pleasure of her company, Michael was climbing the star ladder to the rung on which the most elusive and potent megastars resided. Having met such idols as Fred Astaire, Gene Kelly, Liza Minnelli, Jane Fonda, and Hepburn herself—and of course those magnetic entertainers he appeared to love most, Diana Ross, James Brown, and Jackie Wilson—he was eager to meet even more, especially two considered the ultimate movie stars of the twentieth century. The first was Hollywood's most mysterious and aloof goddess who shunned the public eye. According to Berg, Michael asked Hepburn, "Do you know Greta Garbo?" Then came a second question: "Do you think you could introduce me to her?" Hepburn was neither pleased nor amused. "Absolutely not, Michael."

Aside from Garbo, the other star who Michael yearned to meet but apparently had not mentioned that evening was Elizabeth. Having grown up observing her from afar, he had always been aware of her. He probably could not remember a time when he didn't know of her. Yet there were other stars who also fascinated him. His brother Jermaine once recalled that in Michael's rooms—at the remodeled Hayvenhurst in 1983—there were photographs of Ava Gardner because he "loved her grace and beauty." Later there would be photographs of Shirley Temple. But by this point in his life, Michael was clearly captivated by Elizabeth as the ultimate star. He witnessed the glories and the star spectacle of her life and career in a way he had not with Astaire, Gene Kelly, and Hepburn, whose careers stretched back to the now very Old Hollywood. In a way, Elizabeth's career did, too. But Elizabeth Taylor had become a midcentury star who cast a glow over the rest of the century. Michael was dazzled and captivated by the career highs and lows, by the endurance, by the power of her unending fame, and perhaps by her refusal to live her life on anyone's terms but her own. Just as important was the fact that she had been a famous child star who, having survived it all, had not retreated from the public eye just as he knew he never could. What was the secret of her endurance and her survival?

Much had happened in Elizabeth's life since Michael's birth—and much of that he had grown up actually witnessing.

Chapter 13

IF ELIZABETH TAYLOR'S life had ended on that August day in 1958 when Michael was born, she would still have been a legendary figure. But her life had taken astounding twists and turns since that day, of which Michael was aware. Possibly no movie star was as constantly written about or even debated over.

Her marriage to Eddie Fisher kept her in the headlines in the late 1950s and early 1960s. Taylor's career continued to soar. Her performance as the troubled Cathy in the international hit *Suddenly, Last Summer* earned her a third Oscar nomination and also won her the Maschera d'Argento—the Silver Mask—the Italian equivalent of the Oscar. Said Fisher: "Elizabeth had an off-screen image as a wicked woman and a reputation for being a very difficult actress to handle, but with a track record like hers, she was in enormous demand. There weren't enough hours in the day to read all the scripts and film projects submitted to her." Then came the big career event. One morning while Elizabeth was bathing, Fisher took a phone call from producer Walter Wanger, then planning an epic on Egypt's Queen Cleopatra. He wanted no one but Elizabeth to play the role. But she had balked. On the phone that day, Fisher called out to Elizabeth, "Wanger still wants you to do *Cleopatra*." Almost as a joke, she shouted, "Tell him only if he pays me a million dollars." Fisher relayed her words. To Taylor's surprise, Wanger worked out a deal to do precisely that. Today that salary would come to more than $8 million.

The million-dollar salary became the most talked-about movie deal of the era, which, as film historians later noted, marked a major shift in Hollywood—and the power of a movie star. It was indeed the movie that changed Hollywood. In this case, though it was not acknowledged as fully as it should have been, a woman had led the way to the emerging new Hollywood. In the decades to come, at one time or another, such male stars as Sylvester Stallone, Tom Cruise, Will Smith, and Denzel Washington would rule the roost in the movie industry, and as big as such female stars as Jane Fonda, Julia Roberts, Angelina Jolie, and Jennifer Lawrence would be, for far too long none would outearn most of the important men in the business. That had not been the case with Taylor.

But while Taylor was ready to move forward to a new phase of her career, MGM had another idea. Still under contract to the studio, she had to do another film for MGM before she would be free to star in *Cleopatra*. Taylor did everything she could to persuade the studio to release her. But MGM, seeing the publicity and the box office returns from her films, ironically two of which, *Giant* and *Suddenly, Last Summer*, were done on loan-outs to other studios, refused to let her just walk away. She would have to film *BUtterfield 8*, based on the John O'Hara novel about a high-class call girl who has a tragic end. Despising the script, she asked such writer friends as Tennessee Williams, Joseph L. Mankiewicz, and Paddy Chayefsky for suggestions to whip the screenplay into shape. MGM rejected all the suggestions.

Producing *BUtterfield 8* was Pandro S. Berman, who had lost all love for the woman he believed he had led to stardom with *National Velvet*. Berman always thought the real problem—which blinded "her sure dramatic instincts" for the role offered her—was money. MGM was paying her only $100,000. She said, however, that the role disgusted her. Finally accepting the fact that there was no way out of her MGM contract *or* the role, she decided to make life hell for MGM and Berman. "She demanded everything, and on some of the things I gave in to her. She insisted upon the picture being shot in New York. She insisted on Helen Rose's coming to New York to do her clothes," recalled Berman. "She demanded that some of her regular crew be sent to her. I agreed to all that." Much to the consternation of the movie industry, MGM also agreed to cast Eddie Fisher in an important supporting role. Having appeared on-screen only once before, opposite Debbie Reynolds in *Bundle of Joy*, Fisher had been pleasant and agreeable, but he was not a movie star. But "she was making every effort to piece together a marriage, which from the beginning, had little chance of survival," Helen Rose remembered, believing that Elizabeth was also making "an effort to give Eddie stature." The perceptive Rose showed sympathy for Fisher when she commented: "This was a mistake as he was not good in the film and it only added to his insecurity."

Also causing problems on the film were Elizabeth's ongoing health issues, now a part of her movie star legend. As in the past, when she traveled with husband Mike Todd despite excruciating back pain, she still appeared to disregard advice of family, friends, and physicians to take better care of herself. A simple cold could become serious overnight, which was just about what happened shortly before production began on *BUtterfield 8*.

Stricken with double pneumonia, Taylor was rushed to the Harkness Pavilion in New York. "Elizabeth was so heavily medicated that she was out cold in the ambulance," Fisher recalled. "Lights were flashing and sirens screaming as we turned in to the hospital. And at that moment Elizabeth sat up on the stretcher, took a compact out of her bag, and started fixing her face. 'Get me my lip gloss,' she said, handing me the bag." With the decline of his singing career, Fisher found himself often being nursemaid to Elizabeth, and in time, the studio depended on him to keep things in control. Other times she appeared to dramatize health issues that were not serious. But for Fisher that was simply life with Elizabeth.

Still, the problems on *BUtterfield 8* mounted. "The wardrobe for the film was in New York and ready to be fitted, but Elizabeth was in bed with the flu. The studio hoped I could complete the fittings so the film could be started," recalled Helen Rose. But once Rose arrived in New York, she was informed that Elizabeth was ill and could neither see nor speak to her on the phone.

Cast members Laurence Harvey, Dina Merrill, Mildred Dunnock, Betty Field, and Susan Oliver were all aware of her displeasure with any number of things. "She didn't like the director we hired, Daniel Mann," said Pandro S. Berman. She may have had reason for not liking Mann, known as a Method director. When she was to film a scene in which her character showered, Mann instructed her to play the scene as if the faucet were a penis. Taylor stormed off the set. "Elizabeth said we couldn't make her act and she would do a bad job, because she hated the character of Gloria," recalled Berman. "I was sure that her desire to be a pro and co-operate with other actors, and her sense of obligation to her public would protect me from her doing any such thing." Berman was right.

Mann himself noted that, despite her protestations, she took her work more seriously than she wanted to admit. At times, she asked to redo a take, feeling she hadn't given her best. In the end, her performance would be riveting. The opening sequence—when her character Gloria Wandrous awakens alone in the apartment of a socially prominent man who picked her up the night before—was a marvel that was close to the purely visual performances of stars in the silent era. With a minimum of dialogue, she had to communicate Gloria's curiosity about the apartment in which she found herself, also her maneuvers to put herself together to leave the apartment, and then her defiance when she finds an envelope in which the man has left her money for the night—a sign that he regarded her as little more than a prostitute, the very thing her character Gloria prides herself on not being. Throughout the opening sequence, she was primarily dressed in a formfitting slip, her figure now lush and perhaps almost overripe, her sensuality at its height. Like Dorothy Dandridge in *Carmen Jones*, hers was a natural sensuality (essential for her character) that was unmatched by most other actresses on-screen. The rest of the movie was, as she had known, disjointed with a script without focus or finesse. Critic Pauline Kael summed up the film's faults best: "The John O'Hara novel that seemed perfect for the movies, plus the role that seemed perfect for Elizabeth Taylor—and this is the garish mess it became. Daniel Mann's direction is maybe even worse than the Charles Schnee–John Michael Hayes script." Nonetheless, in the tradition of the great stars, Elizabeth Taylor's performance made the film worth seeing.

With *BUtterfield 8* completed, she was finally free to make *Cleopatra*.

From beginning to end, few other films in movie history drew the attention of *Cleopatra*, its only rival for that distinction being *Gone With the Wind*. The production of *Cleopatra* made Elizabeth Taylor the most famous woman in the world. Yet absolutely no other film was plagued by so many delays, mishaps, miscalculations, and plain screw-ups. Originally, Twentieth Century Fox had envisioned *Cleopatra* as something of a low-budget quickie, possibly with Joan Collins as Cleo. But once Taylor was signed, producer Walter Wanger turned it into a first-class, big-budgeted spectacle with a top-flight director, Rouben Mamoulian, and costars Peter Finch and

Stephen Boyd. Taylor wanted the film shot abroad —and in Todd-AO, the widescreen process developed by her late husband, Mike Todd. Fox decided to shoot the film outside London at Pinewood Studios. With the weather conditions— often chilly and damp—there were countless delays in filming exteriors. This proved to be the first significant miscalculation.

Then one disaster after another struck the production, making headlines around the world. Always new health crises dogged Elizabeth. At one point, she was in such pain that after specialists attempted to treat her, she was hospitalized, believed to be suffering from meningitis. As it turned out, the cause was a dental problem. The remedy: several teeth were removed.

Afterward came *the* major crisis. At the Dorchester in London, Elizabeth struggled with yet another cold, but this time with near-deadly results. Suddenly, Elizabeth was struggling to breathe and soon fell unconscious. A physician —"one of the greatest anesthesiologists and resuscitationists," recalled Elizabeth—was attending a party at the Dorchester and was asked to come to her suite. He determined that her condition was so grave that she was rushed by ambulance to the London Clinic. Nine other specialists were called in, including the queen's physician. "They got me to the hospital, slit open my throat, and stuck a pump down to take this stuff out of my lungs—which if you molded it into a ball and threw it on the floor would bounce." A tracheotomy had been performed. Once again she had contracted double pneumonia, but now there were fears she might not survive.

Every day seemed to bring some new medical complication. Because she had taken antibiotics for past pneumonia bouts, those antibiotics were now of no use. Because the veins in her arms had broken down from so much medication from so many injections, they injected the veins in her legs. But phlebitis set in in one of her legs. Then a doctor flew in from the States with a different, much needed antibiotic. Alerts and bulletins were issued as international publications and wire services covered her condition. Outside the London Clinic, hundreds prayed for her. At one point, there were stories that she had died. Her parents flew to London. Eddie Fisher looked near half out of his mind. Fox considered replacing
her with another actress.

Somehow, she pulled through and recovered. "Out of every hundred who have Miss Taylor's type of pneumonia, rarely do two survive," said one of her physicians, Dr. Carl Goldman. "She lived. She lived because she simply would not die," said Ruth Waterbury.

"What made her become ill again, then?"

Waterbury asked. "Was it nerves? Was it her need for drama, and if it was, why did she need drama? Was she actually bored, without being aware of it?"

Nonetheless, her survival was a kind of miracle that transformed her in the eyes of the public. Not only had the scarlet woman been forgiven for her wicked sins, but now the Taylor legend took on mythic proportions. Here was a star who had confronted death and conquered it.

Photographers, reporters, and camera crews recorded her return to the States for rest, recuperation, and sunshine. Carried from her plane in a wheelchair, wearing mink and mascara, she was gorgeous Liz.

In the meantime, she had won her fourth Academy Award nomination, this time for the film she hated, *BUtterfield 8*. On the bleachers outside the Santa Monica Civic Auditorium on April 17, 1961, some twenty-five hundred fans had waited for the arrival of the stars, primarily Elizabeth, for the Oscar ceremony. Rarely in Oscar history had an audience sat so breathlessly waiting to hear the Best Actress winner. Inside when Yul Brynner called out her name, the applause was thunderous as Elizabeth Taylor slowly—by then she was recovering from a blood clot that had developed in her leg and healed— walked onstage to accept. "I really don't know how to express my gratitude for this and every thing. All I can say is thank you. Thank you with all my heart." Afterward, she went to the ladies' room—where she fainted. But she soon appeared in the pressroom with fellow Oscar winners, where she almost fainted again—until actor Burt Lancaster caught her. Yet true to her determination to ignore health issues, she attended the post-Oscar party, where Oscar host Bob Hope observed: "Everybody wondered whether she'd be able to make it up the aisle. But . . . she was still at the party dancing and drinking. That Oscar must have gotten the old adrenaline flowing." She didn't seem to think twice about the effect alcohol might have on her recovery or her health down the road. Following the party, she and Fisher returned to the Beverly Hills Hotel bungalow where they were staying—for a nightcap with her friends Audrey Hepburn, Mel Ferrer, and Yul Brynner. The next week a photo of Elizabeth, holding her statuette, graced the cover of *Life* with the banner that read: "An Oscar at Last." Many, including Elizabeth herself, would say her illness had won her the award. Early on, Shirley MacLaine had been a favorite for her performance in *The Apartment*. But in all truthfulness, her performance in *BUtterfield 8* had been tough, biting, and vulnerable. Fisher's former wife Debbie Reynolds said: "Hell, even I voted for her."

• • •

During Taylor's recuperation, Spyros Skouras and other executives at Twentieth Century Fox decided to dump London and instead shoot *Cleopatra* at Cinecittà Studios in Rome. There were new principal players: Rex Harrison as Julius Caesar and Richard Burton as Marc Antony. Elizabeth's childhood friend Roddy McDowall was set to play Octavian. Its cinematographer would be Leon Shamroy, one of the industry's finest. Oscar-winning costume designer Irene Sharaff would create Taylor's costumes. With his own list of complaints about the production, director Rouben Mamoulian had also made the mistake of giving an ultimatum: unless his demands were met, he threatened to leave the picture. In her contract, Elizabeth had director approval, and she reportedly informed the studio: to let him go. Few stars in Hollywood history, especially women, had the kind of power that Taylor now exerted. Having finally freed herself from studio control, she basically never again would let anyone tell her what to do professionally.

Elizabeth's near-death battle had changed her. "I think it was my subconscious which let me become so seriously ill. I just let the disease take me. I had been hoping to be happy, pretending to be happy. But there was something deeply desperate inside me and I was consumed by self-pity. I had stopped thinking. I had stopped reading. I had stopped discussing anything—just numbly agreed with everything Eddie said," she said. "I really believe that whole lives can have turning points. Mine came with that pneumonia."

Mamoulian exited from *Cleopatra* and never made another film. Now Taylor gave Fox her two choices for director: George Stevens or Joseph Mankiewicz. Having filmed the biblical epic, *The Greatest Story Ever Told*, Stevens didn't want to become involved with another spectacle. After much pressure and cajoling, Mankiewicz accepted.

A Hollywood veteran whose career stretched back to the 1930s when he was a producer at MGM, Joseph L. Mankiewicz was a highly sophisticated, well-educated, exceptionally literate writer/ director who was a member of a celebrated family. His brother Herman J. Mankiewicz had cowritten with Orson Welles the Oscar-winning screenplay for *Citizen Kane*. Joseph himself had won back-to-back director/ writer Oscars for his classic films *A Letter to Three Wives* and *All About Eve*. Having worked with such stars as Bette Davis, Katharine Hepburn, Spencer Tracy, Kirk Douglas, Ava Gardner, Linda Darnell, Rex Harrison, Gene Tierney, and a young Marilyn Monroe, he understood star temperament and proved himself especially adept at creating fascinating and multi-dimensional female characters—and drawing complex performances from actresses, as he had done with Elizabeth on *Suddenly, Last Summer*.

Doing all it could to make its star happy, Fox provided a luxurious villa for Elizabeth, Fisher, and her children, who she kept with her as much as possible, for the duration of filming. She also adopted a little German girl named Maria. Suffering from a terrible hip deformity, the child would successfully endure several operations. Elizabeth's every command or whim was tended to. Stories spread that because she loved the chili at Chasen's in Los Angeles, such chili would be specially prepared for her, carefully packed, then taken to the airport and flown to Rome, where, upon arrival, someone would be there to pick it up and carry it to Liz.

Filming on *Cleopatra* the second time around proved even more difficult than the first with new delays, new production hassles, and new health crises for Taylor, all reported on by an international press corps. A major problem was that there was really no complete script once production began. Director/writer Mankiewicz was literally writing the movie as he went along. After long workdays, he wrote during the night.

Producer Walter Wanger constantly struggled to stay on top of everything and also to deal with the Fox executives in the States. The day before the first scene was to be shot, on September 24, 1961—with Elizabeth praying to the Egyptian goddess Isis—Wanger discovered that the statue of Isis looked "comic rather than imposing." A crew was assigned to work through the night to alter the statue. A planned procession sequence hit a snag when the elephants could not be controlled. Wanger had to contact England in order to have a new crew of animals sent over. In his notes, Wanger commented that on the night before filming began, "We are waiting for the costumes to be completed and fitted. Of the sixty sets needed only one is ready. Every day that we are not before the cameras costs us $67,000 in overhead."

During production, an endless stream of politicians and dignitaries visited the set, just about all of whom wanted to meet Taylor. For the high and mighty in Rome, an audience with the pope wasn't as high on their list as was a jaunt to the *Cleopatra* set, said Wanger.

In December, Taylor developed phlebitis in one of her legs again. Doctors feared a blood clot might set in, but she pulled through it.

However, the production reached a new level of coverage with new headaches for everyone concerned when rumors sprang up that Mrs. Eddie Fisher was falling in love with her costar Mr. Richard Burton—a "happily" married man.

At this point in his career, Richard Burton was a celebrated stage actor. Born Richard Walter Jenkins in 1925, in Pontrhydyfen, Wales, the son of a coal miner, and the twelfth of thirteen children, he showed dramatic promise as a teenager and was taken under the wing of his schoolmaster and Shakespearean scholar Philip Burton, whose last name the young Richard ultimately took. Athletic and handsome with a rich baritone voice, he studied briefly at Oxford and later served in the Royal Air Force as a navigator. Working in British theater in the late 1940s and 1950s, he scored with critics and audiences in such classical productions as *Hamlet, Coriolanus*, and *Othello*. Many believed him to be the heir to Laurence Olivier's theatrical throne. Though Burton had worked in such Hollywood films as *My Cousin Rachel, Alexander the Great*, and the hit epic *The Robe*, movie stardom had eluded him. But when seen by Joseph Mankiewicz on Broadway in the Lerner and Loewe musical *Camelot* about King Arthur and Queen Guinevere, Burton was hired for the film. Interestingly, President John F. Kennedy and his wife, Jacqueline, were reported to have loved the music from Camelot—and Burton's rendition of the song "Camelot." (Of course, following her husband's assassination, Jacqueline Kennedy dubbed the short period of Kennedy's presidency *Camelot*.)

Married to his early love Sybil, with whom he had two children, Kate and Jessica, Burton had a reputation as a raconteur, as a heavy drinker, and as a notorious womanizer with a legion of affairs, often with leading ladies: among them, Claire Bloom, Jean Simmons, Susan Strasberg, and others. Yet it was always said he would never leave his wife. When the stories first broke that he and Elizabeth were having an affair, show biz insiders probably didn't take it seriously. Nor probably did Burton himself. It was just Richard Burton being Richard Burton. He was both casual and crude about his exploits. After the first occasion that he and Taylor made love, he boasted ungraciously to a few actors and crew members on the set of *Cleopatra* that he had "nailed" her in the back seat of his Cadillac the previous night.

Elizabeth Taylor was possibly the most famous woman alive, more so than even Jacqueline Kennedy. Her marriages, her divorces, her widowhood, her scandalous affair with Eddie Fisher, her health crises, and her career milestones had been chronicled for two decades. Now, just when the public had "forgiven" her scandalous, adulterous affair with Eddie Fisher, here she was again involved with a married man. She didn't seem to care that she might be "wrecking" another home. That was how she was perceived by the worldwide public, which now looked on, both outraged and fascinated by her affair with Burton.

Photographers and reporters trailed Taylor, Burton, and Fisher. Pictures of Taylor and Burton out on the town. Pictures of Taylor and Burton sunbathing on the deck of a yacht. Pictures of Elizabeth—on the boulevards of Rome still wearing her Cleo makeup—with Francis and Sara Taylor, who flew to Italy at their daughter's request. Pictures of a distressed Fisher in Rome, then when he flew home to the States, aware that his marriage to the love of his life was effectively over. The wire services couldn't get enough pictures and stories. A new term, drawn from a pesky reporter named Paparazzo in Fellini's film *La Dolce Vita*, now came into the international lexicon: the paparazzi. Hordes of photographers followed her day and night. "Every time I run around there are grinning, leering, shouting photographers," said Wanger. "They are everything and everywhere. They are like the cats of Rome, hiding on rafters, hiding under beds, always screaming for a morsel. They were like birds, too, with nests in the most unlikely places. The lovely trees surrounding Elizabeth's swimming pool were alive with photographers with long-lens cameras fighting to get pictures."

In the States, a Congresswoman from Georgia

censured Taylor, saying the actress "had lowered the prestige of American women abroad and damaged goodwill in foreign countries, particularly in Italy. It is my hope that the attorney general in the name of American womanhood will take the measures necessary to determine whether or not Miss Taylor and Mr. Burton are ineligible for re-entry into the United States on the grounds of undesirability." Perhaps most shocking was the Vatican's weekly newspaper *L'Osservatore della Domenica*, which criticized Taylor for "erotic vagrancy." Even Sara and Francis Taylor, while in Rome, had become upset by their daughter's behavior. "I heard that Elizabeth had an argument with her parents," Wanger recalled. "Her father apparently spoke harshly to her, and Liz, who adores her mother and father, was so upset she spent the night crying."

Though Burton handled all the fanfare well— he seemed to relish it—he was, in a sense, in way over his head. Fisher had been, too. The casual affair did, indeed, become the great love of Burton's life, and he couldn't break away from her.

Said Wanger: "I have been told by responsible journalists that there was more world interest in *Cleopatra*, which I produced, and in its stars— Elizabeth Taylor, Richard Burton, and Rex Harrison—than in any event of 1962." Wanger was diplomatic in including Harrison, who was merely an afterthought during the production, though his performance would later be lauded. The real interest was in Taylor and Burton.

Amid all of this, the budget for *Cleopatra* soared to the then astronomical sum of $40 million, making it the most expensive movie ever made at that time. Today its cost would come to more than $300 million. A re-creation of a twelve-acre Roman Forum—actually larger than the *real* Forum—had been built. A harbor had been created. A royal barge was constructed. One Taylor costume was made of pure gold at the cost of $6,500. All in all, as has been documented, the film used "26,000 gallons of paint, 6,000 tons of cement, 150,000 arrows, 8,000 pairs of shoes, and 26,000 costumes."

Though *Cleopatra*'s production problems and delays were blamed on Taylor, who still suffered blinding migraines and back ailments, Wanger knew to target her was unfair. "She takes her responsibility seriously, and being a perfectionist, she will be under tremendous strain," he said. She was in pain "some of the days we have worked, but she has said nothing about it and refused to have the doctor." Then her emotions—and her distress about her relationship with Burton and the international scrutiny—took a toll no one could have anticipated. As quiet as the studio tried to keep it, she took an overdose of

Seconal and was rushed to the hospital. Wanger said it had been a case of food poisoning. But no one was buying that. "It wasn't a suicide attempt," Elizabeth said at another time. "I'm not that kind of person, and Richard despised weakness. It was more hysteria. I needed the rest. I was hysterical, and I needed to get away." She recovered. But the film was further behind in its schedule.

Ultimately, heads started to roll. At Twentieth Century Fox, Spyros Skouras had to answer to his stockholders and the moneymen. Eventually, he was out of a job, replaced by Darryl F. Zanuck, who, having left Fox, returned once again as its head of production. Fox also had another troubled production, *Something's Got to Give*, starring another troubled leading lady, Marilyn Monroe, whose absences caused delays and an escalating budget. "No company can afford Monroe and Taylor," a Fox spokesman said. In too deep to replace Taylor, the studio did fire Monroe from what would be her last film. She would die not long afterward from an overdose of pills. Wanger was also unceremoniously fired. Taylor "was so angry she wanted to quit," said Wanger. But both Wanger and Mankiewicz persuaded her to stayon the picture.

Darryl F. Zanuck assumed control of the film—and its editing. Mankiewicz's conception was a literate drama with lots of spectacle but also a telling examination of love and politics for a woman who understood power and was determined to use it—in a man's world. In many respects, his *Cleopatra* was also a telling examination of the star power of Elizabeth Taylor. Because of its length and also its characters' definitions, Mankiewicz considered dividing *Cleopatra* into two movies, but Fox rejected the idea.

Supervising the editing of *Cleopatra*, Zanuck saw it as an old-style epic. The second half of the film would have far too many uninspiring battle scenes. Everything Mankiewicz had built—the psychology of his characters—would fall apart. Having had high hopes for the film, Taylor would ultimately be despairing of the finished product. *Cleopatra* also became a bitter disappointment. Still, *Cleopatra* would have dazzling sequences. Her entrance into Rome—with its elephants, dancers, and giant Sphinx that carried the queen and her son—was brilliantly conceived and shot by Leon Shamroy. So was the sequence of Cleopatra's barge coming to Rome. In the first half of the film, Taylor would be vibrant, shrewd, ironic, commanding, and spellbindingly gorgeous.

Burton had not anticipated it, but he had fallen so deeply under Taylor's spell that his marriage to Sybil ended, amid much emotional torment for

404

everyone concerned. Once Sybil left Rome, she reportedly never saw Burton again, which surely caused him pain. Both he and Taylor went to England, where he socialized with his old theater group, some of whom were loyal to Sybil and unaccepting of Elizabeth. But in time, most found her hard to resist. Philip Burton recalled that he didn't know what to do. He loved Sybil. But then he came to love Elizabeth. Burton's siblings felt the same way.

While in England, the two starred in *The V.I.P.s* with an international cast that included Orson Welles, Louis Jourdan, Margaret Rutherford, Maggie Smith, and Rod Taylor, which became a huge international hit.

After all the publicity and public outrage, *Cleopatra* opened in 1963—and promptly received a drubbing by many critics. But audiences flocked to see it. Some delighted, however, in saying the movie never recouped its cost, though Twentieth Century Fox's David Brown said that was not true. It may have taken *Cleopatra* time, but indeed, said Brown, it was in "the black" and turned a profit, helped later by a huge sale to television. The film won four Oscars: for Leon Shamroy's color cinematography; for the costumes of Irene Sharaff, Vittorio Nino Novarese, and Renie; for set decoration; and for special visual effects.

The Sturm und Drang of the Taylor and Burton

saga didn't end there. The two married in Montreal on March 15, 1964, then traveled to the States, stopping first in Boston, where Burton performed in *Hamlet*. At their Boston hotel, the couple were besieged by frenzied fans and onlookers. Some actually pulled hair from Taylor's head. Pictures showed a distressed Taylor, perhaps one of the rare occasions when even she was stunned by the impact she had. Once Burton performed *Hamlet* on Broadway, nightly Elizabeth arrived at the theater after his performances. Huge crowds lined the streets of New York to see *her*. Often now she seemed more focused on his career than hers. Burton appeared with success in such films as *Beckett, The Spy Who Came in from the Cold*, and *The Night of the Iguana*. Often, too, she seemed to prefer to work only with him. Another hit followed for the couple, *The Sandpiper*, directed by Vincente Minnelli. She also wrote *Elizabeth Taylor: An Informal Memoir*, published in 1965. It seemed to be an attempt to explain herself and clear up certain misconceptions about her.

During the years with Burton (as well as those earlier with Eddie Fisher), she continued to have her children with her. Photographs might turn up of Elizabeth's sons on the set of *Cleopatra*. Photographs might turn up of Elizabeth and her daughter Liza in Puerto Vallarta when Elizabeth joined Burton during the filming of

The Night of the Iguana. Photographs might turn up of Burton and Taylor at an airport with her four children by her side. Burton also adopted Elizabeth's adopted daughter, Maria, who took his last name. Liza Todd and Burton's daughter Kate became close friends. Even during the adolescence of Elizabeth's sons and daughters, whatever normal youthful rebelliousness they might have had remained relatively private. With all the public outcry about the Taylor-Burton love affair before and even after their marriage, never was there great criticism of her as a mother. And Burton was known to have been a good father to all the children. Her children appeared to deal with her fame much as young Elizabeth had: it was just a fact of life that one had to work around. There were no public scandals involving the kids. And as they grew older, they joined her at the big events in her life.

The film careers of Elizabeth and Richard veered in a new direction when the two signed to star in the screen adaptation of Edward Albee's *Who's Afraid of Virginia Woolf?* Originally, screenwriter Ernest Lehman had wanted only Taylor, but Burton became part of the deal.

Who's Afraid of Virginia Woolf? was a triumph for both Taylor and Burton. Uncharacteristically cast as a seemingly weak man dominated by his wife, Burton was forcefully understated. For the role as the fiftyish character Martha, the thirty-four-year-old Taylor gained weight and deglamorized herself. Irene Sharaff, who designed the film's costumes, said: "For Elizabeth, it was the first part that did not depend on her looks."

All four principal actors—Taylor, Burton, George Segal, and Sandy Dennis—earned Oscar nominations, as did writer Lehman, first-time film director Mike Nichols, and cinematographer Haskell Wexler. The movie was also up for Best Picture. But it lost to *A Man for All Seasons.* In the end, Elizabeth and Sandy Dennis walked off with awards, as did Wexler, Sharaff, and Richard Sylbert and George James Hopkins for Art Direction and Set Decoration. But Burton and Segal were left in the cold. Losing the Oscar damaged Burton and perhaps added to marital conflicts. He was well aware that Elizabeth was now a two-time Academy Award winner. Designer Vicky Tiel, who watched the awards abroad with Taylor and Burton, recalled: "The look on Richard's face—he was furious! Years and years of teasing Elizabeth about her acting, her grammar, her voice. And she beat him at what he did best. Even though they stayed married for years, something changed that night. Elizabeth was upset for Richard." Tiel added: "Richard never got over that loss, nor his childish jealousy toward Elizabeth."

Taylor and Burton went on to film Shakespeare's

The Taming of the Shrew, directed by Franco Zeffirelli. Here she tackled a classical role—and pulled it off. But the films that followed, almost to the letter, were disappointments (to say the least): *Doctor Faustus*; *The Comedians*; *Hammersmith Is Out*, an oddball comedy directed by Peter Ustinov that ironically won Taylor and Burton Italy's David Di Donatello Award; and the Tennessee Williams drama *Boom*.

When Burton earned another Oscar nomination for a critical success as Henry VIII in *Anne of the Thousand Days* in 1969, Taylor campaigned for him. Perhaps this would be the charm that finally won him the Academy Award. The couple returned to the States for the Oscar ceremony, at which they stole the show as they entered the theater. Taylor was lush and sensual in a lavender gown designed by Edith Head with Elizabeth's input. In many respects the dress had been designed to highlight the spectacular $1.5 million 69.42-carat diamond necklace given to Taylor by Burton, which she wore that evening. "The dress also accentuated Taylor's hand-span waist, voluptuous bosom and with its soft tonal play of hydrangea-blue mauves, her legendary violet eyes," commented fashion authority Hamish Bowles. "Head and Taylor had collaborated on a visual projection of what the actress represented then as now—the paradigm of the great Hollywood star." That night—as part of her politicking to help Burton win the Oscar—she agreed to present the Best Picture award, which went to *Midnight Cowboy*. That evening marked her first Oscar appearance since she had won for *BUtterfield 8*. Burton lost the award, however, to John Wayne for *True Grit*.

During these years, Elizabeth made three films without Burton that stood out from the others. John Huston's *Reflections in a Golden Eye*, based on a story by Carson McCullers, was originally planned for Taylor and Montgomery Clift. In fact, one of her primary interests in the film, aside from the material and working with director Huston, was to act again with Clift. By now, Clift was a shell of his former self, addicted to painkillers, never having fully recovered from the car accident and emotionally something of a wreck. No insurance company would cover him for *Reflections*, in which he would have played a repressed homosexual military officer. Aware that Clift longed to do the film, Elizabeth put up her salary as insurance to get him cast. But not long before production began, Clift suddenly died of a heart attack at age forty-five. Clift's death marked for Taylor the end of a chapter in her life, perhaps the end of a more optimistic time. He had been her soul mate and closest friend who had helped her to look more seriously at what it meant to be an actress. Afterward, Marlon Brando hoped to play the role, but the studios mistakenly thought that because of a series of flops, his career was nearing its end. But Taylor used her clout to get Brando hired. The critics pounced on the film. In later years, *Reflections in a Golden Eye* managed to acquire a status as an offbeat classic.

In 1972, *X, Y & Zee* was released, a tale by Edna O'Brien of a troubled marriage that Taylor may have thought would be a critical and commercial hit along the lines of *Who's Afraid of Virginia Woolf?* Mostly, the lukewarm notices failed to note her powerful star performance. Pauline Kael, however, wrote a glowing review that praised Taylor's "all-out, let-it-bleed performance that shows her talent for comic toughness. She appears to be having a roaring good time on camera and she's so energetic that Michael Caine and Susannah York (it's a triangle movie) have to work hard to hold their own."

A third film, *Ash Wednesday*, directed by Larry Peerce, and focusing on an aging woman who undergoes a face-lift in hopes of recapturing the affections of her husband, costarred Henry Fonda. Surprisingly similar to the reactions of audiences to seeing Taylor's earlier films *Rhapsody* and *The Last Time I Saw Paris*, in *Ash Wednesday* she was again so breathtakingly beautiful that it was impossible for the audience to take their eyes off her. Once again it wasn't simply her physical beauty but the emotional inner life that

411

made her so striking, a work of art unto herself. Again Pauline Kael took notice, writing that "she's absolutely ravishing, in an unearthly, ageless way."

But her film career was never the same. A new generation did not appear to think of her as Elizabeth Taylor, the actress. Instead she became Elizabeth Taylor, the celebrity.

"A star since childhood, she has sustained a long record," said Irene Sharaff, "and despite several quite dismal films continues to interest and attract a worldwide audience." Cover portraits of either Elizabeth alone or with Burton continued: on *Life, Look, McCall's, Ladies' Home Journal*, and as those fan magazines like *Photoplay* and *Modern Screen* died out, on the covers of their replacements, such publications as *People* and *Us Weekly*—and the new tabloid sheets: *National Enquirer, The Globe*, and *Examiner*. Publicity was often devoted to the extraordinary jewels that Burton bought for Taylor: the Taj Mahal diamond; the Krupp Diamond (a 69.42-carat pearl-shaped diamond); La Peregrina; a Bulgari sapphire neck-lace, to name just a few of the exquisite pieces of jewelry. Most publicity also centered on the couple's ups and downs, their minor spats, their major quarrels, their drinking, their over-the-top extravagant lifestyle with yachts, lavish hotel suites, a steady retinue trailing behind them. The strain showed on her. She had also endured great sadness in 1968 when her father Francis Taylor died. Her health deteriorated even more.

Each was complicated. Each had demons. Burton was viewed as a Faustian figure who had sold himself out, the man who looked destined to become England's next great stage actor, instead was making movies—some shockingly bad—and basking in a lifestyle that didn't seem to have a place for high art. Yet he enjoyed the sometimes maddening years with Elizabeth and the media attention. "Unlike his wary, media-bruised wife, Richard *loved* the press!" recalled columnist Liz Smith. "And, he loved to talk." Few things seemed to please Burton more than having an audience offstage and -screen as he gave another kind of performance, in an attempt sometimes to *justify* his life's choices to everyone, including himself. But he also didn't seem able to shake his guilt, not only about some aspects of his career but also for having hurt Sybil and his children. That explained part of the reason for his excessive drinking.

But the drinking, which Burton knew was part of his public image—he was the lusty manly man who drank hard and lived hard—had also been a way of life for him for far too long. The British writer Michael Thornton recalled that when he first glimpsed Burton on location at Heathrow Airport for a scene to be shot for *The V.I.P.s*, Burton was "wild-eyed and red in the face" and was "punching the air like a boxer who had lost coordination." Thornton thought he might be filming a drunk scene. But that wasn't the case. In actuality, he *was* drunk. Thornton "discovered that he had consumed 14 Bloody Marys before lunch, then moved on to a neat vodka in the afternoon." In his diaries, Burton once wrote: "Drank enormously and cheated when E. [Elizabeth] wasn't looking. Don't remember much except falling a lot and suggesting divorce. Can't control my hands, so cannot write any more. Very silly. Booze!" The next day he wrote: "Having been so drunk yesterday, felt terrible in morning and was desperately ill. Went quietly at 9:30 to find a double brandy. Bar closed until 10. Asked for Fritz (manager). Reluctantly, he opened bar for me and suggested vodka as it wouldn't be so smelly when E had morning kiss. Drank it with very shaking hands. Have become a 'falling-down' [drunk]. My handwriting indicative of the shakes. Painful knee, bottom, right elbow, back of head, right ear."

During the years of her marriage to Burton, Elizabeth's consumption of alcohol grew even more. The constant round of social engagements —where the alcohol flowed—did not help matters. The booze helped enliven their luncheons, their dinners, their afternoons, their evenings, their late nights. Neither gave their drinking serious thought. For too long, neither considered the effect it had on their health and their relationship. Sometimes Elizabeth appeared to be drinking to keep up with Richard, although she handled the booze better. And Burton himself became self-conscious—when with Elizabeth—about his huge alcohol intake. "I started drinking with Burton in 1949," recalled columnist James Bacon. "He could outdrink anyone but Elizabeth Taylor. I have always thought that is why their marriage broke up. Who wants to be a legendary drinker married to a wife who can drink you under the table?"

Taylor's complications were not as obvious. Columnist Smith, who began writing about Taylor in 1965, observed that thirty years later Elizabeth was her "most mentioned subject." "The star was frosty at first, but eventually thawed out," Smith recalled. "Richard Burton helped a lot." The two had the remarkable gift of knocking one another off his or her high horse. Smith commented: "Elizabeth can be an elegant, distant icy creature when she wants to use her MGM-trained goddess stuff. Burton liked to joke how she could turn on 'the frost in her eyes.'" Smith became friends with Taylor—one of the few people in the media Elizabeth appeared to genuinely like. Smith saw beneath that glacial facade. "The real ET is a rowdy, raunchy earthy profane dame. Of course, she is also very spoiled—she wants what she wants when she wants it, and she wants what she wants right away! But that's been as much a part of her life as those incredible eyes. The girl can't help it." That aspect of Taylor—the star with demands, the star who in some respects, but not all, believed the world revolved around her, the star who delighted in her material possessions—never really changed. But Taylor was always looking for something larger than herself, something she could give herself to that would have meaning. In some instances, it was other people, their work, their careers, their aspirations. That clearly was the case with her husbands Todd and Burton. That clearly was the case with her children; her brother, Howard; her family life. That clearly would be the case with Michael.

For Taylor and Burton—the tabloids' and the public's beloved *Liz and Dick*—there came the tumultuous breakups. In 1974, they divorced. In 1975, they remarried in Botswana. A year later they divorced again. Afterward Taylor seemed at loose ends, emotionally adrift, her weight fluctuating, her drinking increasing. A visit to Washington, DC, where she was hosted by the Iranian ambassador Ardeshir Zahedi with whom it was rumored she had an affair, ultimately led to a romance and then a surprising marriage to the Republican former Secretary of the Navy John Warner of Virginia in 1976.

If Elizabeth Taylor ever fully emerged out of the cocoon she had lived in all her life, certainly it was during this time. With senatorial aspirations, Warner campaigned with Elizabeth by his side. She attended barbecues, lunches, banquets, fund raisers. On one occasion, so many people rushed to shake her hand that blood vessels were broken. On another occasion, when their campaign vehicle broke down, she and Warner boarded a public bus where passengers were startled to see her. Her chum during this time was the ultimate political wife, first lady Nancy Reagan. "She was 'my partner' in what appeared to be an impossible challenge—for the United States senate," recalled Senator Warner. "Hand in hand we marched off with no campaign staff, no funds were raised, and we had but nine weeks to put together a campaign which we did. And won." In many respects, Elizabeth Taylor won John Warner his seat in the United States Senate.

During this time, many were shocked because she often didn't seem to care about her appearance; if anything, she seemed psychologically angered by the beauty. Was she not valued for something more than her face? Heavier than ever, puffy, looking middle-aged in a way Hollywood stars were not supposed to age, the question asked was: "What has happened to the onetime most beautiful woman in the world?" With unflattering cover portraits on such publications as *People* and *Us Weekly*, she endured the fat jokes of comedians, the gossip of the tabloids, the maddening, nonstop scrutiny of the media.

A period of deep loneliness followed Warner's election to the senate. Warner proved to be a hardworking, dedicated senator, often away from home, leaving Elizabeth alone. Still accustomed to an environment in which she resided at the center, she seemed disoriented and restless. Politically, she also struck many as being the polar opposite of the conservative Warner. Eventually, she returned to acting in a 1981 Broadway revival of Lillian Hellman's *The Little Foxes*. On the day the play was announced, it sold out. A slimmed-down Taylor triumphed and won a Tony nomination for a performance that Frank Rich called a "black and thunderous storm that just may knock you out of your seat." Not long after-ward she divorced Warner.

"She has everything: magic, money, beauty, intelligence," Andy Warhol reportedly said. "Why can't she be happy?"

Returning to Broadway in 1983, she starred opposite Burton in a revival of Noel Coward's *Private Lives*. Burton's life and career had had a wildly fluctuating set of ups and downs. During these years, he had starred in a series of terrible movies such as *Exorcist II: The Heretic* and *The Klansman*. While Burton filmed *The Klansman*, columnist James Bacon said the actor drank vodka from a coffee cup during the day. In the evenings he had double martinis most of the night, said Bacon. After his second divorce from Elizabeth, Burton wed Suzy Hunt. He also returned to theater where he gave a fine performance in the drama *Equus*. He starred in the 1977 Sidney Lumet film version for which Burton won his seventh and final Oscar nomination. In 1980, he appeared in a revival of the musical *Camelot*, the very play that had marked such a dramatic change in his life after Joseph L. Mankiewicz had seen his performance and offered him the role of Marc Antony in *Cleopatra*. But now he was in a declining physical state, suffering from bursitis and disintegrating vertebrae. He left the production to have surgery for his condition. Elizabeth had urged him to do *Private Lives*. By now, she had divorced John Warner. It looked as if she hoped to rekindle her romance with Burton and perhaps try marriage with him for a third time. Taylor herself had romances with Henry Wynberg and Victor Luna. Later she would briefly be engaged to Dennis Stein. *Private Lives* was panned by the critics; Burton lost patience with her; her drinking continued. At the end of the play's run, a commercial hit despite the critics, she and Burton parted, though neither could ever get the other out of their systems. Burton married

Sally Hay, a thirty-four-year-old former BBC production aide. He had met her on the set of the television film *Wagner*, in which he had starred.

Having bought a home in Bel Air, Elizabeth returned to the sunshine and blue skies and promise of California. Embarking on new ventures, she starred in the HBO movie *Between Friends* with Carol Burnett. But much to the distress of those close to her, her drinking veered out of control. One night in her Bel Air home, she collapsed in a hallway. During a hospital stay for a bowel obstruction, her children; her brother, Howard, and his wife; and her friend Roddy McDowall had an intervention.

"I was in such a drugged stupor that when they filed into my room I thought, 'Oh, how nice, my family are all here to visit,' " she recalled. "Then they sat down and each read from the papers they had prepared, each saying they loved me, each describing incidents they'd witnessed of my debilitation, and each saying that if I kept on the way I was with drugs, I would die."

They had been brutally honest with her. In turn, she became brutally honest with herself.

"For 35 years, I couldn't go to sleep without at least two sleeping pills. I'm a genuine insomniac. And I'd always taken a lot of medication for pain. I'd had 19 major operations, and drugs had become a crutch. I wouldn't take them only when

I was in pain. I was taking a lot of Percodan. I'd take Percodan and a couple of drinks before I would go out. I just felt I had to get stoned to get over my shyness. I needed oblivion, escape.

"Not being a drunk is the only way I'm going to say alive," she realized. "Drunk is a hard word, but I've had to be hard with myself to face it. A drunk is a drunk. Somebody who drinks too much is a drunk. Somebody that takes too many pills is a junkie. There's no polite way of saying it."

In December 1983, she entered the Betty Ford Center in Rancho Mirage, California, to undergo treatment for her alcoholism and her dependence on pain medication, the first celebrity to do so. Like all patients at the center, she had to be up by six thirty, do chores, and attend lectures, meetings, and also group therapy sessions in which patients had to openly discuss their problems and backgrounds. For a world-famous woman, this was a particularly difficult form of treatment. But she endured it. On January 20, 1984—after seven weeks—she left the facility and began a new life. Having lost eleven pounds, she dieted to lose more.

Her life was transformed in another dramatic way. When she learned her former *Giant* costar and her close friend Rock Hudson was ill because of a "new" disease called AIDS that was affecting the world's gay community as well as drug addicts, she realized AIDS was considered a "gay disease," a "gay plague," not worthy of much discussion. Even in the entertainment community that had lost any number of people to the disease, most show business people also avoided the topic. Nothing was being done. Someone had to step forward and do something. And so she did. Organizing and hosting Hollywood's first fund raiser for the disease in 1985, she raised $648,000 for AIDS research. Now she had embarked on an odyssey for research into the disease, to fight it, to turn the tide, but also to make the public more aware of it. A movement within the entertainment industry was afoot, led by Elizabeth. In 1985, the same year Rock Hudson died from AIDS complications, she cofounded amfAR with Dr. Mathilde Krim.

For yet another new generation, she also reconfigured the concept of stardom: the idea of using one's fame to help others, to become involved in national/international causes. Audrey Hepburn began to work diligently with UNICEF. Other stars, past and present, had lent their time, their energies, and their names to charitable causes. But none worked as tirelessly for a controversial issue—an unpopular cause—that some in Hollywood feared could wreck their careers by association.

Not only had Elizabeth Taylor reinvented herself and the definition of stardom, but she also underwent a physical transformation. Following her strict diet—after leaving the Betty Ford Center—she shed an additional forty-five pounds and also had cosmetic surgery. It appeared as if she had a well-executed face-lift with results that were dazzling. "She was beautiful again," commented *People*. With George Hamilton often as an escort, she elicited the oohs and ahs of the past as people fought to catch a glimpse of her. For a spell, she also went blond.

This was the Elizabeth Taylor—in all her glorious yet unfinished history—that Michael observed, was even somewhat obsessed with, and who he set out not only to meet but also to win over. What she represented to him was not just classic iconic stardom but on a personal level, someone who had endured physical and emotional pain.

In the mid-1980s, he finally touched base with her. But at first the going would be rocky for their evolving friendship. Ironically, it would blossom, though at a crucial time in his life—his most difficult emotionally and professionally— a time he could never have anticipated. But first came the courtship, and it was Michael who clearly did the courting and, like a young lover in pursuit, there would be moments of romantic agonizing about her yet he would come to treasure every minute of it.

Chapter 14

MICHAEL HAD BEEN waiting to meet Elizabeth, waiting too long. Not just to meet her in the ordinary sense, at a Hollywood opening. Or at a charity event. Or at a big dinner. Not just to say hello and tell her, "I love you. I love everything you've done." Not just then to say good night and give a kiss and then she'd go her way and not really think about him again. No, that wasn't what he wanted. He wanted to *really* meet her, to make a connection, then to see her again and again and to get to know her and for her to get to know him. That was what he wanted. Something deep inside Michael Jackson needed Elizabeth Taylor —even if it was just an acknowledgment that she knew who he was. Though he probably couldn't articulate what he wanted from her (who could?), she was both a star goddess and even then a mother goddess.

She, of course, was aware of him, had seen photographs, had heard stories, knew his importance. But apparently she had never seriously thought about him, certainly not the way he thought about her. She was a part of his dreams, and with his love of show business history, she was the embodiment of Hollywood history as well as the embodiment of what it meant—the bad mixed with the good—to be a star. She was indeed as Liz Smith liked to say, "The Star of Stars."

He knew that she liked to keep up with the current scene and enjoyed meeting a new generation of performers whose talents she admired. A close friend was songwriter Carole Bayer Sager, who had written for Michael. Sager remembered Taylor's interest in Stevie Wonder. It was Sager who arranged for Elizabeth to meet Wonder when he was recording "That's What Friends Are For" with Dionne Warwick in 1985. Sager and her husband, Burt Bacharach, had written the song. The proceeds of the recording— Elton John and Gladys Knight also sang on it— went to AIDS research. Elizabeth seemed intrigued by the new popular music stars, so different from those of her generation. Later, Elizabeth would spend time with Bob Dylan, who in his 1963 song "I Shall Be Free" had written a lyric about making love to Elizabeth Taylor and catching hell from Richard Burton. As entranced by Taylor as the men in her earlier life, Dylan was said to have written the song "Emotionally Yours" for her. Yet with all that said and done, Elizabeth didn't seem to be panting to meet anyone.

In 1984, Michael broke ground when he stayed at the Helmsley Palace Hotel in New York. Located in midtown Manhattan, the Helmsley

Palace was one of the city's most luxurious five-star hotels, with elegant suites and a staff that made sure every need or whim of a guest was met. The Helmsley accommodated the rich, the famous, the privileged, the pampered. The general manager of the hotel's suites was Dominic Cascio, an affable, very likable professional who was well attuned to dealing with famous people.

When traveling, Michael found himself often alone—and lonely—during his downtime. On one visit to the Helmsley, he struck up a conversation with Dominic Cascio, and in time the two became friendly, so much so that Michael visited Cascio's home in Hawthorne, New Jersey. By now, Michael was cautious with most people he met. His security man Bill Bray, who had watched over Michael since the days of the Jackson 5, was accustomed to checking out people and places. The Cascios were deemed fine, and in time, the family helped ward off Michael's loneliness. He became something of a surrogate member of the Cascio clan. Dominic's wife, Connie, was a wonderful cook who prepared special meals. Michael became friendly with the Cascio children, Frank and Eddie. Said Frank Cascio, who first met Michael at age five in 1984: "The doorbell would ring at night, and Eddie and I would know it was Michael." Eventually, Frank Cascio traveled with Michael and, atanother point, worked for him. So did his younger brother, Eddie.

One thing that Frank Cascio's father, Dominic, was well aware of was Michael's burning desire to meet Elizabeth Taylor.

"My father was actually the man who arranged for Michael and Elizabeth Taylor to meet for the first time. It happened when one of Elizabeth's daughters [Liza Todd] was getting married and she was staying at the Helmsley Palace at the same time as Michael," recalled Frank Cascio. Though Michael was about to check out of the hotel, he called Dominic to his room when he learned Elizabeth was there. "Dominic, please give this note to Elizabeth Taylor. I'd really love to meet her." It was delivered to Elizabeth. Nothing was said. Nor did she respond to the note.

"When Michael came back to the hotel, two or three months later, he kept asking my father, 'Did you give the letter to Elizabeth? Are you sure she got it?' He couldn't believe she hadn't been in touch with him."

Though his big attempt to meet her went nowhere, Michael was unwilling to give up the chase. He pursued her in a way he had not had to pursue the other great stars with whom he became friends. He knew the key would be to meet up with her when they both were in the same place at the same time. Given his touring schedule and given her schedule, he knew that wouldn't be easy.

Elizabeth Taylor was still going full steam. But

she was also undergoing new trying times. After leaving the Betty Ford Center, she worked hard to keep her life in order. She would also soon agree to write a book on her dramatic weight loss. She filmed an episode of the TV series *Hotel* with her long time friend Roddy McDowall. Then came the devastating news that Richard Burton had died on August 5, 1984. Perhaps it was all the more shocking to the world because the marriage to Sally Hay appeared to calm him. During these years, he filmed the miniseries *Ellis Island* in which his daughter Kate Burton, now an accomplished actress, also appeared. He starred in an adaptation of George Orwell's *1984* with actor John Hurt. Burton also spent time with Hay in a home he had maintained for twenty-six years in the Swiss village Celigny on Lake Geneva. Mainly, in Celigny—with a population of 620 townspeople—Burton sought a settled life, away from the fanfare and the bright lights. And he hoped to regain his health. Hay helped him watch his diet—and his drinking. In August 1984, his costar Hurt was a houseguest of Burton and Hay. They dined casually at one of the village's two restaurants. All seemed fine. But two nights later, Burton suffered a massive stroke and died. He was fifty-eight. Sally contacted Burton's remaining seven siblings with whom he had remained close all his life. She also called Elizabeth. Hurt announced the death to the press.

Because she believed her appearance might turn the solemn occasion into a media circus, Taylor did not attend his funeral out of respect for his widow. Afterward, she privately visited his grave. Cameras, however, snapped the grief-stricken Taylor standing by the gravesite.

Like everyone else, Michael was aware of this new sadness and tragedy in her life. When he learned, however, that she was back at her home in Los Angeles—at the same time he was winding up the *Victory* tour, which was scheduled to play Dodger Stadium at the end of November and the first two days in December—he sent word that he'd provide tickets to his concert, as many as she wanted for herself and her party. By one count, it was fifteen seats; by another, it was thirty.

That night, as he performed, he was on pins and needles just at the thought that she was watching him. From his perspective, however, the evening ended disastrously. She had left the stadium midway during his performance.

"I went to a concert and I couldn't see a thing. I was way up," Elizabeth recalled, "in a stadium." Actually, she was seated in a special glass-enclosed VIP section that apparently didn't give her the best sight lines. "I couldn't see a thing and I brought thirty people, and we couldn't even hear. So we went home to watch it on television by disc.

"Michael heard that I had left halfway through

and called me the next day and was like in tears 'cause he'd heard I had walked out," Taylor said. "I hadn't walked out. I just couldn't see anything. And then we talked on the phone for about three hours. From there on in, we talked more and more on the phone."

"After that, we talked on the phone every day," Michael said. "She somehow got my schedule. . . . I thought, Wow. Doesn't she have other things to do? After all, she's Elizabeth Taylor." Something magical happened during those phone conversa-tions. Michael and Elizabeth became hooked on each other.

Once back in LA, Michael asked her if he could come to tea—and if he could bring Bubbles, his frisky chimpanzee. At this point, Michael took Bubbles just about everywhere, introducing him to the media and a range of celebrities. Of course, Bubbles was a safety net for him, a personal security blanket, a way of blocking out his fears of the world by focusing on something else. Taylor understood. "Sure," Elizabeth told him. "I love animals."

"Then we met and spent more and more time with each other," said Taylor. "Just became really good friends. Told each other everything."

Told each other everything.

That was the essential comment. What indeed was *everything?* Certainly, that meant long discussions of their childhoods, the loss of innocence, the responsibilities of a child being a professional in an adult world, the demands of being bread-winners for their families, the relentless schedules, the discipline and focus it required, and the stamina, drive, and talent it took to make the transition from child star to major adult super-star. But Elizabeth provided Michael with something else. For someone who had grown up fascinated by entertainment history, Michael heard first-hand stories of the days at MGM, the greatest of Hollywood studios, when Louis B. Mayer reigned supreme; of a galaxy of stars who resided at the studio; of everything from the commissary at MGM to the huge wardrobe and makeup departments to the vast back lots. "I get to learn so much from her," he said. "She'll tell me about James Dean and Clark Gable and Spencer Tracy and Montgomery Clift," he said. "She tells me what they were really like." He also found that she liked children, loved toys and games, and cartoons. "She's playful and youthful and happy and finds a way to laugh and giggle even when she's in pain."

Michael told her tales of life on the road when as a child he had been exposed to a seamy side of show business but also when he came face-to-face with those African American legends he admired. Surely, she was hearing some names for the first time. For a woman always eager to learn more, to move outside of the cocoon that MGM as well as her handlers—the agents, the managers, the publicists—had locked her in, she no doubt found it enlightening to hear his stories.

But on another level, she sought to help him cope better with fame—and the media. He was struck by the way she handled her fame. In the past, he had seen Diana Ross navigate her way through fame, refusing to let it restrict her but so much. On one occasion "Diana Ross marched bravely into a Manhattan shoe store with her three daughters and had them fitted for running shoes, despite the crowd of 200 that convened on the sidewalk. Michael, who's been a boy in a bubble since the age of reason, would find that intolerable," commented writer Gerri Hirshey. Of course, Ross had lived her very early years without mass attention. Growing up in Detroit's Brewster projects, she pushed her way onto the world stage, not only through her talent but also through her fierce ambition, which was always a part of her appeal. But those early Detroit years grounded her in the basics of "ordinary life." Elizabeth Taylor had never had an "ordinary life" during her childhood years, except perhaps that brief period in her beloved England. Like Michael, she had a dim memory of a childhood. Otherwise it was all work, all discipline, all adhering to the rules of entertainment culture. Yet she had done something Michael believed he hadn't mastered. Some things she obviously couldn't do because of her fame. But some things she would not let her fame stop her from doing, especially during her marriage to Mike Todd and later on the political trail with John Warner. Surely, all this fascinated Michael. "One night Michael, Elizabeth and I went out to dinner," Lionel Richie recalled. "Because she was also a child star, Elizabeth could relate to him. They talked about isolation and what you do when you're lonely. It was good for Michael to hear that Elizabeth often went out of the house without security guards. The idea that you could live without them was a revelation to him."

Told each other everything.
Certainly, that meant discussions about their families, especially their parents and the relationship of their parents. Taylor learned about Joe Jackson's unruly temper, about the beatings he gave his children, about his philandering, about his insensitivity to Michael. She also heard of Katherine's loving, warm nature, of the comfort she had provided Michael and her other children. But no doubt she also heard some of Michael's conflicting feelings. Why had Katherine never left Joseph? Why had she endured so much from him? In turn, Michael learned about Elizabeth's family life: the distant, sometimes abusive father; the assertive mother. Interestingly, she had come

to the point where she understood her parents, had reconciled any conflicting feelings about them. Interestingly also, she had made no public complaints about her mother, whom she appeared to love deeply. She also appeared to love her brother, Howard, deeply. And in time, she would make public comments only about her father's temper and abuse to illustrate aspects of her life and Michael's that drew them to each other. Otherwise she had a rather stoic, philosophical attitude about the meaning of her past, including her childhood. "Even though I missed out on a lot," she said, "I wouldn't change anything."

Told each other everything.
Certainly, racial and cultural differences and distinctions were a part of their developing friendship. Perhaps they didn't have protracted, heavy-duty discussions about the nation's racial history. Or its sexual history and its gender inequalities. But they must have discussed such topics at times because such topics were always there in the sense of how each viewed the struggles of one another. And each was keenly aware of racial and social inequities and bigotry. Michael never forgot the incident when Katherine had been racially insulted when driving her Mercedes. His entire family had witnessed the civil rights movement. So had Elizabeth, who had always been liberal and

progressive. At the same time, Elizabeth most likely discussed in some way women's issues, especially in her recollections about her experiences in show business. In any kind of interracial relationship or friendship, there are always racial or cultural bridges that are established and crossed. Usually, the parties involved enjoy learning something about the other's culture: the customs, the traditions, the histories, the esthetics, the use of language, everything from holiday celebrations to foods to religious observances. So it was with the two of them. The topic of race was never something ignored with Elizabeth and Michael.

Told each other everything.

Certainly, that involved health issues. Her ongoing back problems. The medication to ease some of the constant pain. The unending trips in and out of hospitals. For him, there remained the still-fresh pain from the burns during the filming of the Pepsi commercial. He also had other ailments and saw the prominent Beverly Hills dermatologist Arnold Klein, who examined splotches on Michael's skin and would conclude in 1986 that Michael was suffering from vitiligo: a skin condition that causes discoloration over the body, which is due to a lack of pigmentation. Michael also would later suffer from lupus. Elizabeth, too, would have a bout with skin cancer.

In time, medication for both would be something neither would seriously think about twice. Medication was essential just to keep them functioning.

But for Elizabeth there was something else about Michael that appealed strongly to her. He brought out the nurturing side of her personality. She had always loved focusing on loved ones, whether it'd been Mike Todd, during those days when he was promoting *Around the World in 80 Days* in the States and abroad; or Richard Burton during those years when she seemed determined that Burton get the big movie roles and when she herself was sometimes not working in order to push his career; or John Warner when she campaigned relentlessly to get him elected to the United States Senate. Of course, Michael was such a huge star that she knew there was nothing she could do to advance his career. But she could provide him with a comfort that might have been missing in his life.

With his lost-boy quality, with his heightened sensitivity, with his Pepsi accident, even with his use of drugs to dull his physical pain, he was reminiscent of Monty Clift, with whom she shared so much, and perhaps of James Dean and Rock Hudson, all troubled, all conflicted, all trying to come to grips with their childhoods and their fame. With each of them, she had felt there were no secrets. For her, they perhaps all called to mind those closing lines of Maggie in

436

the Broadway version of *Cat on a Hot Tin Roof*, although not in the movie: "Oh, you weak, beautiful people who give up with such grace. What you need is someone to take hold of ou—gently, with love, and hand your life back to you, like something gold you let go of—and I can! I'm determined to do it—and nothing's more determined than a cat on a tin roof—is there? Is there, baby." Though Elizabeth never thought of Michael or the others as weak, she clearly believed she could save people, and perhaps she believed she could help Michael to save himself.

She hadn't been able to do that with Monty. But maybe with Michael. Coming from different generations, from different classes, and from different races, they crossed those lines—as well as gender lines—without much to-do.

Michael would be more forthcoming about details of their friendship and their times spent together. Elizabeth would be reticent. For a woman whose life had been so hotly discussed, dissected, analyzed, criticized, and exploited by the media, notably the tabloid press, she was still a private person who kept the door shut on her experiences. Though she wrote four books about her life (including *Nibbles and Me*), and though she gave countless interviews to magazines and newspapers, which as a child of Hollywood she had been bred to do, there was much she refused to share, especially as she grew older. Once, when

Barbara Walters asked her about her memories of life with Richard Burton she responded that she had many memories and that they were *her* memories. She turned down pleas to write a formal autobiography. Always she kept guarded her experiences with Michael. In the years to come when she was asked about the friendship by such skilled interviewers as Oprah Winfrey, Larry King, and Johnny Carson, she seemed to have a response set in stone: she referred to the demands and pressures of their professional childhoods and the things they had missed. Occasionally, something more personal would be discussed but not at length. Her children also helped maintain their mother's privacy. They understood she needed room to breathe.

Michael, however, in time would discuss their times at Neverland or at the movies. He would also comment on the fact that both had tough, brutal fathers. And he would speak of her survival instincts in a general way. He, too, would only go but so far, aware that her need for privacy was greater than his.

When together, Elizabeth and Michael were clearly in their own world, one that few could understand. Or enter.

Then word of their budding friendship leaked out to the press. Michael's friendships with other former child stars were nothing new. Nor were his relationships with older women, from Ross to Minnelli, from Fonda to Sophia Loren to Katharine Hepburn. Michael Jackson himself may have assumed at first it would just be such another one of those friendships. But she was different: warmer, more willing to listen, more simpatico, willing to devote more time to him. Having been under her sway *from afar,* now he was under her spell *up close.* The media took note in a way it hadn't with those other women, except for Ross. For the media, Taylor was *the* deluxe item; so was he, which obviously accounted for the publicity they generated.

Soon they were seen together publicly at events. One evening they might turn up at a Liza Minnelli concert. Another evening they might be spotted at one of Bruce Springsteen's concerts. Or later they might attend opening night of the Los Angeles Ballet with Lionel Richie and Mikhail Baryshnikov. Sometimes there was more excite-ment at watching the two of them than at seeing the performers onstage. When Michael signed to star in a special seventeen-minute 3-D science fiction film *Captain EO*—shown only at Disney theme parks from 1986 into the 1990s—directed by Francis Ford Coppola and produced by George Lucas, with costars Anjelica Huston and Dick Shawn, Michael saw it as a chance to continue a film career that until then had not progressed anywhere. With a cost of $30 million, maybe *Captain EO* would change things. He even wrote two songs for it. His costar was Anjelica Huston. Celebrity friends visited him on the set: Sophia Loren, Warren Beatty, and Barbra Streisand. Elizabeth also visited Jackson for several days. Sitting in his trailer, they were like two kids playing hooky, having food fights, gossiping, horsing around, being children all over again during those off-hours on the movie set.

Soon their trips to the races also turned heads and drew stares, with the media following and recording their every move. On Christmas Day 1985, they watched as Elizabeth's racehorse, Basic Image—with jockey Willie Shoemaker astride him—came in next to last. Passersby heard Elizabeth unleash a stream of expletives, which seemed to embarrass Michael. He would need to get used to it, and soon he did. For Michael, who rarely cursed (at this point) and who, because of his religious upbringing, seemed to feel it "sinful" for people to beat on horses or casually curse up a storm, here was another kind of education. Soon the press was on the lookout for them at the track.

But the big event that seemed to certify that Michael and Elizabeth were a "couple"—and which drew a horde of photographers, videographers, reporters, and onlookers was the 1986 American Music Awards ceremony, held on January 27.

Hosting the ceremony was a ravishing Diana Ross. That night, Michael, Lionel Richie, and Quincy Jones walked off with awards for their 1985 recording "We Are the World," recorded to raise funds for African relief during a devastating famine. The showstopper, however, was the appearance of Elizabeth—lustrous in a blue chiffon dress—on the arm of Michael, dressed in quasi-military regalia. The media had a field day. "Michael Jackson who nearly swept the awards two years ago when the *Thriller* album was hot, showed up backstage about midway through the show with friend Elizabeth Taylor. When photographers learned of the couple's presence, several people were nearly trampled in the stampede to catch a shot of the pair," wrote one reporter. "The couple also livened up things backstage in the crowded media area," another breathlessly recounted. "When they appeared briefly, the area, which had been calm all evening suddenly turned into a madhouse. Photographers stampeded to a designated security line near the stage entrance. It was one of those frantic paparazzi scenes, with photographers jockeying for position, shoving their colleagues."

With friends, the two continued hopping off to the tracks. So did the media. "The opening of Hollywood Park on Wednesday brought out all the potential winners, including this year's really fun couple—the devastatingly slim and pretty

Elizabeth Taylor and her buddy, pretty and slim Michael Jackson," it was reported. "The yellow and black dress La Liz was wearing gave clear evidence that she is once again a knockout—and the best advertisement for the beauty book she is currently writing. In great spirits, Taylor . . . even kiddingly bopped Jackson on the head with her program for some laughing remark. It was a big day for that table." Also in the group were Carole Bayer Sager, her husband Burt Bacharach, and Elizabeth's lawyer Neil Papiano.

Other times, even when on a date, Elizabeth wanted Michael by her side. That occurred on another day at the racetrack with other friends, including her boyfriend, actor George Hamilton, who, like many, noted not only Michael's delight in being with Elizabeth but also his boyish charm. During a day at the racetrack with Elizabeth and Michael, Hamilton asked Michael to pick a horse. Because he was still a Jehovah's Witness, Michael refused. Hamilton suggested that he simply put his hand down on the racing form and select a horse, which he did. The horse won a race. According to Hamilton, it had been a 30-1 shot. Hamilton tried to give Michael his winnings. But Michael refused and ran off.

During the early years of their friendship, Michael—like the typical Taylor suitor—obviously loved playing the part of the gentleman escort, at her beck and call, making sure she was comfortable, making sure any request to a waiter or whomever was taken care of. Yes, she was high maintenance. Yes, he was, too. Still, when with her, he enjoyed keeping that high maintenance high. Michael's friend, producer David Gest, recalled the time they were having dinner at La Scala in Beverly Hills. As people flocked around Elizabeth, Michael realized he wasn't the center of attention, which he didn't mind at all. "I remember he leaned over and whispered to me, 'Now that's what you call royalty.'" He also knew that she loved gifts, and like Fisher, Todd, Burton, and others, he would eventually lavish her with jewelry.

When Michael gave her a huge diamond ring, he urged her, "Put it on, put it on. Look at the way it sparkles. I bet it's bigger than the Krupp." Said Elizabeth: "So I asked innocently, 'Really? How many carats is it, Michael?' 'Seventeen,' he answered. I embraced him and whispered in his ear, 'My honey darling, you missed.'" No one could ever really duplicate the jewels of Todd and Burton.

"Another time we were at an auction together and I was getting excited about bidding on a pair of long shaggy Marina B diamond earrings, so I told him that he had to buy something, too," she recalled. "I showed him this delightful monkey necklace made up of diamonds, emeralds, and rubies with matching earrings. He probably thought I had something like 'auction fever' when I pointed out that the two monkeys symbolized us, bonded in friendship. In hindsight, I must have made some sense, because these little monkeys are perfectly at home with all my other beloved jewelry."

Public appearances with Elizabeth—even their private times together—were for Michael a glorious wish-fulfillment, being part of classic old/mid-century Hollywood with its greatest star. Understanding what he was experiencing, Elizabeth appeared amused and delighted. For her, all the really big-time spenders had vanished. So had the grand gestures. Both she and young Michael were the last signs of larger-than-life stardom.

Special occasions were also spent at the Encino home. La Toya remembered that several times a week, Michael invited famous stars to the home, sometimes for what Katherine called his "star-studded dinners": along with Elizabeth there were such other classic Hollywood stars as Gregory Peck, Cary Grant, Marlon Brando, Sophia Loren, Yul Brynner, Jane Fonda, and Muhammad Ali. Often at the homes of the stars or in their trailers, Michael tape-recorded the conversations, even of Elizabeth. "I think he was so enraptured by being with them," Jermaine recalled, "that he wanted to make sure that he never missed a word they said. At night, back at

Hayvenhurst, he played back those conversations, listened, and took notes. Michael was a prolific note-taker and note-sender."

During the 1980s into the 1990s, other glittering evenings followed for Elizabeth and Michael. A special evening for Michael occurred on the occasion of Elizabeth's fifty-fifth birthday party, held on February 28, 1987, one day after her birthday, at the home of her then married friends Carole Bayer Sager and Burt Bacharach. Elizabeth was escorted by George Hamilton. But she paid close attention to Michael. As Michael expected, it was a glamorous gathering. In attendance was a heady mix of stars: Stevie Wonder, Bob Dylan, Dionne Warwick, Joan Collins, Shirley MacLaine, Whoopi Goldberg, Bette Midler, Charles Bronson, and Barry Manilow. For Michael, a memorable moment was meeting actress Bette Davis. At the end of the evening, he excitedly asked Elizabeth to take a picture of him with Davis. But perhaps the highlight was when Elizabeth introduced him to another woman. It was her mother, Sara.

On another occasion in New York, Michael and Elizabeth attended a benefit at the Sheraton Hotel for the United Negro College Fund, where Michael was honored—and they posed for pictures with Liza Minnelli and Whitney Houston. All four stars—along with Quincy Jones—seemed giddy just to be in one another's company, to be a part of an elite club, reserved only for the major players. One star's appearance with the other certified megastardom. And there was the occasion of the 1989 Soul Train Awards, when Elizabeth stood at the podium with Eddie Murphy to present Michael with the evening's Heritage Award. That night she called him the King of Pop—Rock and Soul. Michael's publicist Bob Jones has said that he came up with the title; regardless, when Queen Elizabeth publicly anointed him the King of Pop, the title stuck. For Michael, it was all the more potent a certification of pop legendry because Elizabeth had done the honors.

Never could the media get enough of the pair. Carrie Fisher recalled an evening when Elizabeth and Michael attended an AIDS benefit at the Beverly Hilton hotel. Fisher accompanied the two, as did actress Shirley MacLaine. Fisher described it as a double date. Both she and MacLaine were obviously famous, each with adoring followings of her own. But when they arrived with Elizabeth and Michael at the Beverly Hilton to face a horde of paparazzi, Fisher said that she and MacLaine were "instantly rendered invisible . . . unrecognizable." The two ended up being "spectators to the spectacle of Michael and Elizabeth. All you can really do in a situation like that is watch."

As much aware as everyone else of the frenzied coverage they generated when together, Elizabeth and Michael could hardly have been said to be upset or annoyed by it—as they could be with other intrusions of the media into their individual lives. Instead, they seemed to delight as much in the coverage as in each other's company. During this period, each looked downright radiant. Though the public would always be fascinated by Elizabeth, no one had appeared wildly excited by seeing John Warner on her arm. Most fans couldn't wait for her to get out of that marriage and back to Hollywood. With George Hamilton, there was mild interest primarily because they looked good together. But not wild enthusiasm. Nor was there much excitement at seeing her with Victor Luna and Dennis Stein, her various fiancées to come.

Indeed, the media coverage was the third party in their relationship.

For Taylor, some of the relentless attention with Michael must have called to mind the Todd and Burton days, although less intense. For Michael, it may have brought to mind his appearances with Brooke Shields—and even other evenings in 1991 with Madonna. He and Madonna were all smiles on those occasions. He confided to his friend Rabbi Shmuley Boteach that on one evening before they went out, she told him they were not going to Disneyland. "But I didn't ask you to go to Disneyland." She told him that they'd go to a restaurant and then a strip bar. "I am not going to a strip bar," he told her. They ended up at the

Ivy restaurant and a few nights later they attended the Oscars together. The paparazzi loved it. But Michael was not thrilled on either occasion nor when the two attended a birthday party for producer David Geffen nor when they dined at Spago. "She is not a nice person," he said. He also called her a "nasty witch." He most objected to her reaction when some little kids asked for their autographs. "Get out of here," he said she told the kids. "Don't ever talk to children like that." "Shut up," she told him. "You shut up," he said. But he also said, oddly enough, inexplicably, he believed she was "sincerely in love with me and I was not in love with her." He added: "I knew we had nothing in common." But it was a different world with Elizabeth. Surely, it was no secret—nor did it go unnoticed that Elizabeth and Michael loved the glamour and megawattage stardom.

At the same time, some members of the Jackson family may not have felt completely happy about Michael's relationship with Taylor. The parents had always been wary of outsiders. Joe Jackson discouraged his sons from having friends in their Gary, Indiana, neighborhood and later in Los Angeles. He didn't even like the idea of his daughter Rebbie marrying. The same was true of Katherine. And he wasn't overjoyed when his sons married. Jermaine recalled that once Tito married, Joe "thought he was losing us. . . .

Bottom line in our house: marriage wasn't celebrated as the joy of two people coming together, it was initially viewed as a wedge driving apart a winning team of brothers." Their Encino compound was maintained like a family fortress that others could never really penetrate, perhaps never really comprehend.

As uncomfortable as the parents may have felt with outsiders—including the brothers' wives—they also knew when they had to back off. When Michael was younger, Joe and Katherine had to deal with his fixation on Diana Ross. All the family was awed by her glamour, her talent, by her ability to transfix an audience, by her coverage in the press. The family accepted his infatuation with Ross no doubt as a boyhood fantasy. The family also knew that Ross had a full, busy life, touring and then raising her own family. So Ross ultimately did not pose a great threat.

But perhaps now came a combatant (from their vantage point) they could in no way battle. Or ignore. Elizabeth Taylor was simply too great a star, too great an international phenomenon. Like the rest of America, Joe and Katherine, while still in Gary, had read of her scandalous romances and marriages to Mike Todd, Eddie Fisher, and Richard Burton. In Hollywood, she was considered the queen, one of those rare stars who turned the heads of other stars; who, whether young or older, slim or heavy, still could enter a room and have every eye focused on her. Even Diana Ross probably didn't relish the idea of Elizabeth as a rival for Michael's attentions. A story made the rounds of an evening when Michael planned to have dinner with Ross—until he heard from Elizabeth, who also wanted to have dinner. Not quite knowing how to handle the situation, Michael was advised by Elizabeth to invite Ross to join Michael and her at a restaurant. When Michael told Ross, she was reportedly not pleased. "This is not the way to do things, Michael," Ross told him. In the end, she reportedly told him they'd have to do dinner another time *without* Elizabeth Taylor. For Michael, it had to have been a thrill to have two high-voltage, high-powered women vying for him.

Like everyone else, Joe and Katherine might have preferred for Elizabeth to go away, that she not in any way influence Michael. It was said that they even blamed Michael's reliance on medication on Elizabeth. Joe and Katherine might not have wanted Michael to spend too much time with her—or worse, to share secrets with her.

Still, special as Elizabeth and Michael's times together were, everyone knew that such occasions were not everyday occurrences. Both had full schedules. In some ways again, it was like Elizabeth's days with Montgomery Clift—periods when they couldn't get together, then intense reunions.

Chapter 15

THE YEAR 1987 was a great one for Michael. His album *Bad* was released in August and was another sensation. Again he had worked with Quincy Jones, exploring themes of paranoia, racism, the media, and world peace. Though he hoped to see it shoot past the sales of *Thriller*, that didn't happen. Still, *Bad* was hugely successful, with five number one singles: "I Just Can't Stop Loving You," "Bad," "The Way You Make Me Feel," "The Man in the Mirror," and "Dirty Diana." The album shot to number one in the United States and twenty-seven other countries. During its first year, *Bad* sold seventeen million copies. In short, the album certified again that he was the most important artist in music. He also shot videos for it, two of which had a particularly personal significance.

The first was the video for "Smooth Criminal," a song he'd written. The video was shot between February and April in 1987. Directed by Colin Chilvers as a gangster-style movie with Michael dressed in a white suit and hat, "Smooth Criminal" had a breathtaking sequence in which Michael and the dancers around him stood erect as they leaned forward almost to the floor in a feat that seemed to defy gravity. It was actually the result of a special device that Michael co-patented: the dancers were hitched to a mechanism with pegs that rose from the floor and shoes with ankle supports that slid over the pegs. In "Smooth Criminal," Michael also held a machine gun and fired shots. It was a real firearm he had been trained to use by experts on the set.

Also on the set were two Jehovah's Witnesses who were there to "monitor" Michael—just as there had been on the set of the video "Thriller." Touching a firearm was prohibited by their faith. Michael had to explain himself. Ultimately, he was told to decide between his faith and his profession, actually his art. Pushed to a breaking point and no longer accepting the pressure of the Witnesses to oversee his work, he officially broke off from the Jehovah's Witnesses. It was not an easy decision to make, especially because of his mother. But upset as Katherine was, she understood Michael and the importance of his art. She stood by him. Though free of the restrictions and prohibitions of the organization, Michael had been too indoctrinated in the church to ever leave its dictates entirely behind. He still felt uneasy about sex, even discussing it. He also missed the calm relief the services at Kingdom Hall had afforded him, the chance simply to be normal.

The other video, which was released in 1989, was for the song "Leave Me Alone," in which he gave advice to a media that hounded and distorted him. Stories had turned up that he slept in a special hyperbaric chamber; that he sought to buy the bones of the severely deformed Joseph Merrick (sometimes referred to incorrectly as John), known in the nineteenth century as the Elephant Man; and that he had proposed to Elizabeth. Included in the "Leave Me Alone" video was footage of a young Elizabeth. He poked fun at all the rumors as well as the tabloid press description of him as Wacko Jacko. Of course, Michael himself was reported to have contributed to some of the rumors and outrageous stories as a diversion, a way of keeping the media at bay and manipulating them, and showman that he was, of keeping the public interested. With his soft public speaking voice and his charitable acts, his public image was that of both an eccentric—or a weirdo as the tabloid press viewed him—and an innocent, a kind generous soul with a heart.

With *Bad*, he also began his first solo tour, which proved an extraordinary success, totaling 123 concerts in fifteen countries over four continents. Traveling on the tour was Bubbles as well as an entourage of some 132 people. Crowds greeted him on his arrival in different cities. More than six hundred journalists turned up at

Tokyo's Narita International Airport on the first leg of the tour that began in September 1987 in Japan. Next on the first leg of the tour was Australia. The second leg picked up in February 1988, and took him to cities in the United States, then parts of continental Europe, England, then back to the States, back to Japan into 1989. Everywhere he went, he met and was often wined and dined by the rich, the famous, the powerful. During the European dates, he visited Oona O'Neill, the widow of Charlie Chaplin, in the town of Vevey in Switzerland. Afterward he proclaimed he had fulfilled a childhood dream. At London's Wembley Stadium, he had seven sold-out shows, one of which was attended by Princess Diana and Prince Charles. There he broke the attendance records of such stars as Madonna and Bruce Springsteen. Performing in total for an audience of 4.5 million, his concert tour grossed $125 million. Had any music star in the world ever had this kind of success?

During this period, time was also spent with lawyers, managers, and corporate people, to help him manage his career and his vast fortune. But he understood the demands of his position, and contrary to that image of him as the soft-spoken boy who hadn't grown up, the other Michael, with the more commanding voice, exhibited a decisiveness that let it be known that he expected his orders to be carried out. Among his chief officers were John Branca and Frank DiLeo. Formerly at Epic Records at the time of *Thriller*'s release, DiLeo had headed promotions. Once with Michael, he served as his manager; he co-executive produced Michael's film *Moonwalker*; he also managed the *Bad* tour. DiLeo had been hired in 1983, after Michael had decided he no longer wanted Freddy DeMann and Ron Weisner to manage him. Michael's new legal counsel John Branca—a former corporate tax attorney—had drafted the termination papers. Branca also negotiated Michael's $47 million acquisition of the ATV Music Publishing catalog, which included the rights for thousands of songs—including those of the Beatles. There was the thrill of all these negotiations and the unprecedented deals, yet Michael also retreated from the pressures, especially when it might cause a confrontation or a decision about which he had conflicting feelings.

Time was spent on charitable works. But, ironically, raising funds for AIDS was at first not on his agenda. He was late in publicly commenting on AIDS. No doubt Elizabeth spurred him forward. The turning point came when Michael learned that a teenager named Ryan White from Kokomo, Indiana, had been expelled from his middle school nearby in Russiaville because he was HIV infected. Much was not known at the time about the causes of

HIV/AIDS. A hemophiliac, White was diagnosed in 1984 as having become infected from a contaminated blood infusion. A court battle ensued over his right to attend school. Michael spoke out in defense of the boy and befriended him.

In 1987, Michael also made a bold personal move. Finally deciding to leave his family home in Encino, a decision that may well have been influenced by Elizabeth, he purchased—for the sum of $17 million—twenty-seven hundred sweeping acres of land about six miles from the town of Los Olivos (which had a population of 250) in California's Santa Ynez Valley. Then he spent $55 million to reconstruct the property, creating his own Shangri-la: a sprawling luxurious playground known as the Neverland Valley Ranch—but usually referred to simply as Neverland—after the magical kingdom in which Peter Pan, Wendy, and the gang resided. When Michael moved there in 1988, it marked his first time living on his own.

Neverland was a child's dream of paradise. (A security team checked every guest who arrived.) Walking through its magical portals, visitors saw neon lights that read *Michael Jackson's Neverland.* Two railroads ran on the property, one called the Neverland Valley Railroad—with a steam locomotive named Katherine, after his mother. At the train station itself were candy and fresh pastries. On the property, there was also a Sea Dragon ride, a carousel, a Ferris wheel, a roller coaster, bumper cars, a private zoo, and a private theater that seated about one hundred, plus an amusement arcade. Near the theater entrance were animatronic characters from *Pinocchio*, as well as an animatronic Michael that could moonwalk in a circle, all especially designed by artists at Disney. A private bedroom sat on each of the two sides of the theater. Perched high up on the grounds was a sky gazebo with spectacular views where Michael might dine with guests. A bridge led to the main Tudor-style house, where his Bentley might be parked. In the circular drive in front of the house, there stood a thirty-foot-high statue of Mercury with winged helmet and caduceus. Inside the house, there was his personal library— said to number some ten thousand volumes— and his art collection. There were also images of Diana Ross, Marilyn Monroe, Charlie Chaplin, and of course, Elizabeth—as well as Mickey Mouse and Peter Pan. Also there were guest bungalows that were actually four separate units in a ranch-style house. The Elizabeth Taylor Suite was known for its huge king-size bed. At one point, Michael wanted a room painted the color of her violet eyes. But painters couldn't get the color right. Throughout were beautifully landscaped and manicured grounds with bushes trimmed and shaped to look like animals. Bronze statues of children adorned areas. Surrounding it all were glorious mountains. All of this was conceived by Michael, which revealed another side of his creativity.

Michael soon opened the gates of the Neverland Valley Ranch to children and their families, especially children who were ill, including Ryan White. Once past security, visitors were greeted by lined-up members of his staff. He brought in kids from tough areas of Los Angeles, giving them a taste of pop splendor. Also coming to Neverland were children of his brothers, especially the sons of Tito, with whom Michael grew close; he encouraged their musical group 3T. Over time, other guests walked through the magic gates of Neverland: Chris Tucker, Mike Tyson, Nick Carter, the Cascio family, dermatologist Arnold Klein, who invited Carrie Fisher and her daughter, Billie, to join him there; and a boy named Jordan Chandler, who came with his mother and half-sister.

By now, Arnold Klein had become a relatively close friend of Michael's. Born in Mount Clemens, Michigan, and the son of an Orthodox rabbi, Klein earned both his bachelor of science and doctor of medicine degrees from the prestigious University of Pennsylvania. Eventually, he had headed west, where he established his thriving office in Beverly Hills.

Klein had big-name, often wealthy patients. Appearing to love the LA scene, he was as enamored by Hollywood culture as anyone else in the town. Outgoing and good-humored, he had developed a friendship with Michael, whom he treated for various skin ailments, including vitiligo. He also was thrilled to meet Elizabeth. Involved in the fight against AIDS, Klein helped raise a great deal of money for the cause, which led to a kind of friendship with Elizabeth, who then occasionally socialized with Klein.

With her weight still under control and having taken care to preserve her spectacular looks, Elizabeth launched her perfume line in 1987, starting with Passion—an apt name. Making television commercials, posing for print ads, agreeing to interviews, she traversed the country and did the unthinkable: she appeared at department stores, where crowds lined up to see her. She also answered questions from the crowds, albeit questions that had been screened beforehand. Accompanying Elizabeth on her first perfume press tours, in 1987, was her hairstylist José Eber. "It was beyond what you would see in your life," he said. "Five to ten thousand people in department stores. It was unbelievable." He also said that at each stop she'd slip away to visit a hospice for HIV/AIDS patients, unknown to the press. All the promotion got the brand off to a spectacular start. Later she launched Black Pearls and White Diamonds. In time, hers became the most successful celebrity perfume in the industry's history. In fact, the first of the million-dollar movie stars was actually said to have made even more money from her perfume empire than she had from her films.

During this time, she also began a friendship with New York multimillionaire Malcolm Forbes, the owner of the monthly business publication *Forbes*. Clearly, he adored her. A motorcycle enthusiast, he once presented her with a purple Harley Davidson in tribute to her eyes—and her Passion perfume line. When she attended the seventieth anniversary bash of *Forbes* magazine, he presented her with a check for $1 million for amfAR. Time was spent on the back of Forbes's motorcycle as he joined buddies for rallies; on Forbes's yacht for trips to Thailand and Tahiti; and later in Tangier, Morocco, where she was his hostess as he celebrated his seventieth birthday. He had flown some eight hundred friends in for the occasion. The media loved seeing her with Forbes almost as much as with Michael. Completely enjoying her renaissance, she also spent much of her time raising funds for AIDS research. The year 1987 also marked the publication of her book *Elizabeth Takes Off*. She would later write *My Love Affair with Jewelry*, a dazzling look at her extraordinary jewel collection, published in 2002.

But the Forbes relationship would take a backseat to another one that slowly began in 1988. At that time, she had slipped back into alcohol and prescription drug abuse: a drug combo that included Demerol, Percodan, Xanax, Zantac, Ativan, and Tylenol with codeine for her back pain. Her weight had ballooned again. She returned to the Betty Ford Center in July. There, she met a rugged former construction worker named Larry Fortensky, also a patient. Liz Smith observed: "When they met, Elizabeth was overweight, wracked with pain from a fractured vertebrae in her back and more depressed than she's ever been. It was her second stay at Betty Ford, and she was ashamed that she had fallen off the wagon. Larry's first glimpse of Elizabeth was in stark contrast to her glamorous, movie-queen persona. She was simply a vulnerable woman in emotional and physical pain. From this, they built a solid, refreshingly realistic relationship."

On April 11, 1990, a saddened Michael attended the funeral of Ryan White, who had died of AIDS at age eighteen, in Indianapolis. That year, he lost his maternal grandmother. Sammy Davis Jr. died, too. All three deaths affected him deeply. That same year he was set to begin work on his eighth studio album *Dangerous*. Pressures were mounting. On June 3 Michael collapsed and was taken to Saint John's Health Center in Santa Monica, where he was treated for chest pains. (His publicist Bob Jones later said that Michael had actually faked this illness in order to avoid making a decision about a business matter.)

Elizabeth was then a patient at the same hospital —with yet another very serious life-threatening health crisis. Once again a seemingly mild (sinus) infection had developed into a 104-degree fever, which led to pneumonia. "Within two weeks, Elizabeth Taylor was fighting for her life in

the intensive care unit of St. John's," *People* reported. "It was by far her gravest illness since she suffered a near-fatal bout of pneumonia while filming *Cleopatra* in 1961. Coming after more than 30 years of drug and alcohol abuse and aggravated by persistent, if apparently unfounded rumors of AIDS, it was also the most alarmingly mysterious. As her family gathered by her bedside, concern for the star escalated." The media rumors that the woman who had fought so hard for AIDS was suffering from the malady itself appeared to be a cruel way of undercutting her battles for others.

But the seemingly indestructible phoenix slowly rose again. Margaret Maldonado Jackson, then the spouse of Jermaine, had visited Michael at the hospital with Jermaine. Michael sat in his hospital bed wearing his black fedora and a hospital gown. When she realized that he had no bathrobe, underwear, or slippers, she went shopping to pick up some items for him. When she returned, Michael didn't want Margaret or Jermaine to stay. Why? He was expecting Elizabeth. Recovering but still weakened and in the hospital, she'd learned that Michael was a patient there and went to comfort him. Elizabeth's visits lifted his spirits, although some family members once again may have felt Michael was becoming too close to her, especially when Michael preferred time alone with her.

"Elizabeth Taylor was going to visit and Michael wanted some privacy," recalled Margaret Maldonado Jackson. "Jermaine made a wisecrack about Elizabeth and was quickly put in his place. 'Don't ever talk bad about Elizabeth Taylor to me, Jermaine,' Michael said softly. 'She's beautiful. The most beautiful woman I've ever met.'"

Said Maldonado: "By this time Michael and Elizabeth were already well acquainted, but their friendship would grow during this brief stay in the hospital. She came for visits several times a day and sometimes brought him violets, which stood in sweet contrast to the dozen black roses La Toya had had delivered from London."

On June 8, Michael was released from the hospital. Immediately, he resumed preparations for recording his new album *Dangerous*. No longer did he work with producer Quincy Jones. Perhaps he believed that without Jones he was stretching himself creatively. But it was hard to find a talent as formidable as Jones—or someone who understood Michael artistically *and* music itself as well as Jones. Nonetheless, he produced the album himself along with such fine talents as Teddy Riley, Bill Bottrell, and Bruce Swedien. Of the fourteen songs on the album, he wrote or cowrote twelve, including "Remember the Time," "Give In to Me" (which featured Slash), "Heal the World," "In the Closet" (which featured Princess Stéphanie of Monaco and was about two lovers in a clandestine affair), and "Jam" (which featured rapper Heavy D). For this album he recorded ballads. But he also included social commentary with the song "Heal the World" as well as commentary on the racial situation with "Black or White." Aware that musical tastes were always changing, he now sought an edgier, hard-hitting sound on some songs. He explored rap with "Jam," with the help of Heavy D. With writer/producer Teddy Riley on such songs as "Why You Wanna Trip on Me" and "She Drives Me Wild" (featuring Wreckx-n-Effect), he recorded a genre known as new jack swing. On the completed album, there would also be his tribute to Ryan White, "Gone Too Soon." It was an ambitious, daring undertaking that proved to be a long and demanding process that took more than a year. *Dangerous* was completed October 29, 1991. The album was set to be released in November.

By this time, there had been a significant shift with his record label Epic. In 1988, Sony Music had bought CBS Records. Henceforth Michael's music would be distributed by Sony. In 1989, Branca negotiated Michael's contract with Sony Music Entertainment, which was now the parent company of CBS/Epic. For each album that Michael would do in the future, he would receive an advance of $15 million. Michael's new royalty rate would be 25 percent. In March 1991, he had also negotiated a $50 million contract with Sony, then the biggest deal in music history. He was committed to do three studio albums (which included *Dangerous*) as well as a remix album and two compilations of his greatest hits. Still at the forefront of the music industry, he intended to remain in that position with the belief that no one could top him but himself.

Interestingly, at this point his sister Janet had made extraordinary inroads in popular music with songs—a mixture of pop, funk, rhythm and blues—that were socially relevant and in time sexually daring. She had come a long way from the start of her career in the 1976 television variety show *The Jacksons*. Under the management and tutelage of her father, Joe, she had signed a contract with A&M Records at age sixteen in 1982. After her first two albums— *Janet Jackson* in 1982 and *Dream Street* in 1984—had gone nowhere, she ventured into new musical territory. Working with producers Jimmy Jam and Terry Lewis, she recorded *Control,* released in 1986. The title song applied to Janet herself, taking control of her life, living on her terms. Her theme of personal self-empowerment was present in such songs as "What Have You Done for Me Lately," "Nasty," "When I Think of You," and "Let's Wait Awhile," all of which, along with the title song, became top five singles. Her next album *Janet Jackson's Rhythm Nation 1814*, released in 1989, also soared to the top of the charts and scored fifteen Billboard Music Awards. Now a social consciousness was a part of her music. The song "Love Will Never Do (Without You)" and its video also revealed a more sexual, adult Janet as she was seen seductively on a beach dancing and in the arms of actor Antonio Sabato Jr. In 1991, she signed a huge $32 million contract with Virgin Records— just days before Michael made his deal with Sony.

Michael once said Janet was his best friend in the family. But now gossip circulated that there was a complicated competitive edge in their relationship—on Michael's part. La Toya Jackson recalled an earlier time when Michael had helped her record a number. Unsatisfied with the results, he wanted changes. In the end, La Toya felt the changes suggested by Michael were not for the best. She said her mother told her that Michael did not want her to do better than him. Nonetheless, Janet Jackson had emerged, steadily becoming a major recording star. She also had hugely successful tours and eventually appeared in such films as *Poetic Justice*, *The Nutty Professor II*, and *Why Did I Get Married?* In time, such albums as *Janet* in 1993, *The Velvet Rope*, *All for You*, and *Damita Jo* would simply extend her remarkable impact in popular music.

Once Elizabeth had left Saint John's Health Center, she had been back on the move. She shed pounds again, resumed her nonstop schedule, and was ready to give life another full-blast try. When she announced plans to marry Larry Fortensky, the former construction worker twenty years younger (she was fifty-nine; he was thirty-nine), whom she had met during her second stay at the Betty Ford Center, most of the media and the public were skeptical. How could a woman who had socialized with royalty, who hobnobbed with the likes of everyone from Robert Kennedy to Malcolm Forbes to Aristotle Onassis to Henry Kissinger, who from the time she was a teenager had enjoyed the high life on the international stage, now just pick up with an ordinary joe? Had she gone bonkers? But Elizabeth had made up her mind about Fortensky, and of course, no one could change it. Surely, her mother and her brother, Howard, knew it was pointless to talk to her about it.

Michael seemed delighted that she had found love again. If Elizabeth loved this man, then he would, too. He decided to host the wedding at the most idyllic setting either he or Elizabeth could think of: his Neverland Valley Ranch. Though neither Elizabeth nor Michael ever publicly commented, the plan for a Neverland wedding was a stroke of PR magic, which sent the media into frenzy. Neverland, however, would be closed off to everyone except the very exclusive list of guests.

Elaborate plans were made to dress up Neverland in a special way for the occasion. A tent—draped in ivory silk—was erected for the wedding reception. The ranch's flower beds were pulled out, replaced by white blooming plants. Security would be provided by a one-hundred-man force, led by a former Israeli army officer, Moshe Alon. Arriving limousines with guests would be searched—except for the one that would carry former first lady Nancy Reagan. The bride would wear a $25,000 yellow wedding gown—a gift from its designer, Valentino. Following the ceremony, the bridal bouquet of roses and lilies would later be frozen and donated for an auction for AIDS research. To help ensure all went well were Elizabeth's assistant Jorjett Strumme and Michael's assistant Norma Staikos. After all, this was to be a wedding made as much in Hollywood as in heaven. And not only did Elizabeth have to be guarded but also her host, Michael, had to be.

On the morning of the wedding, October 6, 1991, as the gazebo was being bedecked with gardenias, so excited was Elizabeth that she rose early—still in her nightgown—to watch the florist David Jones at work. "She was like a little girl at her first party," said Jones.

Estimated cost of the wedding: $1.5 million. Michael insisted upon footing the bill.

Invitations were limited to some 160 guests, including Nancy Reagan, Quincy Jones, Elizabeth's longtime friend Sydney Guilaroff, Carole Bayer Sager, Barry Diller, Diane von Furstenberg, Barbara Davis, Merv Griffin, Eva Gabor, designer Valentino, and Brooke Shields, who was Michael's date. Touchingly among the most honored guests were Elizabeth's frail ninety-five-year-old mother, Sara, and her big brother, Howard, as well as Elizabeth's children and three granddaughters. Members of the groom's family were also present. The only journalist invited was columnist Liz Smith, who had become the most important celebrity/entertainment columnist of the time. By now, columnists Hedda Hopper and Louella Parsons were long gone. No longer was the old-style gossip columnist needed to get the big scoops. Television programs such as *Entertainment Tonight* covered movies, TV, music, theater—and dished out some of the dirt on stars. "Page Six" in the *New York Post* and later the television show *TMZ* also provided information on celebrity doings—and *un*doings. But Smith maintained her position as a reliable, perceptive, and balanced insider whom some stars such as Elizabeth still "confided" in to break stories. Of course, as Smith herself knew, Elizabeth was quite skillful at knowing what to divulge and what to still keep under wraps.

The ceremony itself was delayed for an hour and a half by the bride, as might have been expected. Escorting her down the aisle were her oldest son, Michael Wilding Jr., and Michael himself. The best man was Elizabeth's hairstylist José Eber; matron of honor was Elizabeth's longtime friend Norma Heyman. Her grand-daughters were among the bridesmaids. For decades now, Elizabeth's children had "shared" their famous mother with the adoring, curious masses—and with her close friends and her husbands. Sometimes it may not have been easy for them. In the case of Michael—a surrogate son for their mother—here was someone close to them in age. But the children seemed to accept him without any problems. In the midst of the ceremony, helicopters buzzed above, filled with photographers hoping to snap pictures. One photographer on a glider landed on the property and was promptly escorted off. After the exchange of vows, the bride and groom took their first dance. They were cut in by Brooke Shields and, of course, Michael. Over the years, Shields and Michael had maintained a warm friendship. Toasting her host with mineral water, Elizabeth said: "You've been so generous, it makes me want to cry. I'll never forget it as long as I live." The wedding may well have symbolized the optimistic high point of Elizabeth and Michael's friendship. "I couldn't think of what to give Michael to show my undying thanks," she later said.

A few days later, Elizabeth—with Larry by her side—began a two-day promotional tour for her new perfume, White Diamonds. Michael resumed preparations for the release of the new album, *Dangerous*. Not long afterward, he received a call from Elizabeth, who planned to drop by with a gift. He awaited her, and true to Elizabeth Taylor, she arrived in her own special way—by helicopter. The gift? "I had been trying to think of a truly meaningful way to thank him," she said. "Then I got an idea: Michael has a zoo. I'll get him an elephant! That clinched it. I got him a great big Asian elephant [named] Gypsy."

That same day, he presented her with a gift: a huge wall-sized tapestry of Elizabeth, patterned after a photograph of her. Michael had the whole incident filmed for posterity.

Some years later, a replay of the elephant gift occurred when Elizabeth and Michael, along with others, including dermatologist Arnold Klein, were in Las Vegas for Elizabeth's birthday. "We stayed at the incredibly beautiful Bellagio, where we had dinner and watched the fountains. The whole thing was just perfect for me because I've grown tired of big-deal birthdays. At one point, I turned to Michael and said, 'All right, where's my present?' Well, he looked at the ground, he looked around the room, he looked at our friend Arnie Klein, but they didn't really say anything. So I said, 'Michael, I know they have great jewelry shops in the lobby, I can't believe you haven't noticed.' Michael and Arnie start giggling. I continued, 'This is really breaking my heart, Michael, I'm not sure I can go on.' You know, I was really hamming it up. Finally, Michael and Arnie excused themselves and returned to the table some time later with a perfectly interesting-sized box." Inside she found "the most exquisite titanium elephant evening bag" with an elephant "saddle of rubies and pearls." She saw that "the dear little creature had huge diamond eyes" and was "the most unusual thing I'd ever seen."

She admitted: "I was also a little embarrassed that he had actually gone and gotten me something this amazing. But Michael and I do kid around a lot, and I knew I hadn't really overstepped my place in our relationship."

But that was not the end of the story. Once she was back at her Bel Air home, she discovered her "*real* birthday present from Michael," one of the then new flat-screen television sets. "Truly, the biggest one I've ever seen. I was the innocent in all this, the most happy innocent. And Michael played it totally straight." But the elephant evening bag brought back memories of her helicopter visit to Neverland with her special gift of Gypsy. "I guess you could say we exchanged elephants."

"Over the years Michael has given me some truly incredible jewelry," Elizabeth said.

Indeed he had. Other jewelry given to Elizabeth by Michael: A diamond bracelet. A colored-diamond pendant necklace. A suite of diamond, emerald, and ruby jewelry by Massoni. A diamond and gold "Lord Kalla" bracelet watch by Vacheron Constantin. A ruby, sapphire, and diamond bracelet. A ruby and diamond bracelet. A diamond and emerald necklace. A diamond and gold bangle bracelet. A diamond gold bow brooch. A diamond necklace. An emerald and diamond necklace by Oscar Heyman and Brothers. A diamond and colored-diamond line bracelet. And at least three rings: a diamond ring, a diamond and sapphire ring, and a ruby and diamond ring.

And so it went for the two for many years—extravagant gifts, laughter, exchanging stories and secrets, during times spent together whenever possible and many such times coming not too long before the darkness set in.

But now and in the years to come, there were also quiet times, away from the spotlight. Michael loved to have egg sandwiches some afternoons at her home. There were also still those picnics at Neverland. On Thursdays, the two would slip off to a movie together. Originally, Michael wanted to head to the Warner Bros. studio—for private viewings. But Elizabeth wouldn't hear of it. "No, I'm getting you out," she told him. "So we go right into this area, which I can't say, and walk right in. And it's usually empty because people are working at the time. [The theater employees] go 'Wow, come on in,' and we never really pay. And we're the ones who can afford it." Other times the two would wear disguises when they went to movie theaters. They'd sit in the back and hold hands. He recalled her excitement at viewing the animated film *A Bug's Life*, which she playfully had hounded him time and again to see with her.

Once, when she was asked if she saw much of Michael, she answered: "More of him than people realize—more than I realize." When he was asked to describe her, Michael answered: "She's a warm cuddly blanket that I love to snuggle up to and cover myself with. I can confide in her and trust her. In my business, you can't trust anyone. . . . Because you don't know who's your friend. Because you're so popular, and there's so many people around you. You're isolated, too. Becoming successful means that you become a prisoner. You can't go out and do normal things." He added: "But Elizabeth is also like a mother—and more than that. She's a friend. She's Mother Teresa, Princess Diana, the Queen of England and Wendy [the soul mate of Peter Pan]. We have great picnics. It's so wonderful to be with her. I can really relax with her because we've lived the same life and experienced the same thing." And he said that they liked the same things: the circus, amusement parks, and animals. At Neverland, she loved the carousel and Ferris wheel, but she steered clear of the "scary rides."

Chapter 16

THE PERIOD FROM 1984 to early 1993 marked the good years for the two. Elizabeth's perfume empire grew. Her acting career continued, primarily in television films. Most important, her work for AIDS gave her something to fight for, in a sense to deal with something bigger than herself and her own health issues. "You know, I was always famous, so it didn't have meaning to me," she confided to Liz Smith. "But when I saw that my fame could help in my fight against AIDS, I thought, Bring it on! If people wanted to come to an AIDS event to see whether I was fat or thin, pretty or not, or really had violet eyes, then great —just come. My fame finally made sense to me. I'd always loved my life—the parties and jewels and clothes . . . and the men. But that was all just a warm up." She added: "That was off the record, Liz. It sounded like I was ready for my halo or my grave, and I'm not ready for either."

Michael remained in full gear with his career, possibly the most successful in the history of popular music. His new album, *Dangerous*, was released on November 26, 1991. The reviews were basically good, with some critics calling attention to the Michael of music and the Michael of the headlines. In the January 1, 1992, issue of *Rolling Stone*, Alan Light wrote: "*Dangerous* might seem to be a chance to separate this dancer—the 'eccentric' Michael of the chimps, the Elephant Man bones, the hyperbaric chamber —from his dancing and singing, which remain among the wonders of the performance world and, lest we forget, were the real reason we paid so much attention to Jackson in the first place. . . . But of course this polarity between Jackson's on- and offstage lives is exactly what makes him so fascinating, and the triumph of *Dangerous* is that it doesn't hide from the fears and contradictions of a lifetime spent under a spotlight." Light added: "The aggressive yet fluid dance grooves Riley helped construct—and his emphasis is on writing grooves, not traditional songs— prove a perfect match for Jackson's clipped, breathy up-tempo voice." He also commented: "Exactly half of *Dangerous* is concerned with affairs of the heart, and Jackson's greatest fears are brought right up front—there's not a single straightforward love song in the bunch. Instead we get betrayal in 'Who Is It' and repressed lust in the titillatingly titled (and determinedly heterosexual) 'In the Closet.' "

Though *Dangerous* would ultimately not top *Thriller*'s commercial success, Michael nonetheless had another successful piece of work. He also had his ATV catalog, which seemed to assure him of a lifetime of financial security. Its value had escalated. But troubled times began not too long after Taylor's Neverland nuptials—after the release of *Dangerous*.

Now that Michael was out of the Encino home, his relations with his family—with the exception of his mother, Katherine—grew distant. His sister La Toya had also left home but under far different circumstances. Described by most as basically a sweet-tempered, perhaps slightly spacey young woman, she had run off with a onetime family friend Jack Gordon, who managed—or most would say mismanaged—her career, much to the grief of the Jackson clan. In 1989, she posed nude for *Playboy*, which became one of the best-selling issues in the magazine's history. In 1991, she posed again for *Playboy* and also published a book simply called *La Toya*, which recounted the torments of growing up Jackson under the dominating and brutal hand of Joseph. *Family secrets should remain family issues,* the Jackson family (like most others) felt. Katherine and Joseph were convinced their daughter had been brainwashed by Gordon, which may have been partially the case. Some years later, La Toya revealed that she had gone from one domineering man (her father) to another (Gordon). Interestingly, in her book, she spoke warmly of her siblings and took pride in their accom-plishments. But the aspect of the book that drew the most attention was its portrait of a dysfunctional family. It was a horrifying tale that no doubt forever tarnished the Jackson family's image. Later La Toya made public statements that distressed the family all the more. In an interview in Tokyo, La Toya accused her father of having incestuous encounters with his daughter Rebbie and herself. "She says her father regularly came to the bedroom she shared with her older sister, Rebbie, and violated the older daughter while La Toya lay terrified in the same bed," the *Chicago Tribune* reported on November 3, 1991. "When Rebbie left home to live with another family as a teenager, [La Toya] Jackson says, her father began to molest her." It was all sordid stuff that frankly no one knew whether or not to believe. But it had been put into the public arena.

Though Michael appeared above the fray, he was certainly troubled and hurt by the comments of a sister to whom he had been so close. The family had been damaged, especially Katherine, who valued privacy for her children and even Joe. Michael also grew alienated from brother Jermaine, for whom he seemed now to have a great disdain. When Jermaine was set to work on music for his album *You Said* with L. A. Reid and Kenny "Babyface" Edmonds, he was later stunned to learn that Michael "offered them *very* substantial amounts of money to work on songs for his new album," recalled Clive Davis, "and surprisingly they had agreed to do it. Everything they wrote during this immediate, well-defined period of a couple of weeks would be for Michael to use." At this time, Davis recalled having dinner with a "totally disconsolate" Jermaine in Paris. "He was crying, indeed sobbing at times, so deeply hurt that his brother would do this to him."

Upset, angered, and feeling betrayed, Jermaine wrote the song "Word to the Badd!!" which accused Michael of lightening his skin, of undergoing plastic surgery, of being a "child," not a "man," in essence of forgetting who he was. Before the release of Jermaine's album, the song was leaked to radio stations. It was an attack on Michael that Jermaine defended by saying: "I know people are going to go off on a tangent and say that Jermaine is jealous. But it's not true. Michael and I have never feuded. The only reason I wrote this song—and it came from the bottom of my heart—was to help my little brother get a grip on reality. I never meant to discredit him." No one believed that. As Clive Davis said of Jermaine, "He came off as petty and desperate. Of course, no one knew about the dramatic situation that had triggered his anger and generated the song in the first place."

When Michael learned the song was set to go onto Jermaine's album *You Said*, to be released on the LaFace Records label in which music mogul Clive Davis had an interest and which was distributed by Davis's Arista Records, he called Davis. "How could you let my brother do this? I don't want you to release that record." Davis recalled that he "felt it would be wrong for me to tell an artist to take a song off his album." He told Michael that it was really a problem between the two brothers. "You've got to deal with him directly." Later Jermaine told Davis that Michael "confronted me with the problem. We really had it out."

Some years later the *New York Post* reported that Jermaine had tried to sell a proposal for a tell-all book about Michael. "Jermaine waxes lyrical on all aspects of Michael's life, including how the family has always been suspicious of the singer's feelings for boys," wrote the *New York Post*, which had seen a copy of the proposal. "Jermaine also says that he suspects that his younger brother may have been a victim of sexual abuse by their dad, Joseph. 'There were times when Joseph and some of these men he'd describe as "very important business people," would meet late at night in our hotel suite with Michael, and Michael alone,' Jermaine writes. 'I always felt something was wrong with that and Michael would always be sick for days after these "meetings." ' " In an unexpected way, one might feel sympathy for Joe Jackson, as two of his children were so eager to depict him in such a way—and as one questioned if there was veracity in the accounts. In any case, the proposal did not sell. Still, later Jermaine would write a book with a more sensitive portrait of Michael in which Jermaine also defended him. La Toya would also write another book with a different perspective. But certainly word of Jermaine's proposal had to have upset Michael.

The days of that hip and fun-loving guy with the quick boyish smile and jaunty manner from *Off the Wall* and *Thriller* were gone. The emotional strain was evident. Now he had an almost ghostly appearance, partly because of his vitiligo. Using a special makeup to cover the splotches and give his skin an overall even color, he looked much lighter. Later, additional plastic surgery gave his nose an eerie look, almost as if it were not a nose at all. His lips were redder, and his eyes had been darkly lined or tattooed. Because of the chronic pain from the burn injury, he still took medication that could make him seem spacey, and he also continued to wear hairpieces to hide a scalp that looked raw and was bald. In time, the hairpieces became long and very dark, giving him almost the look of Elizabeth in posters for her movie *Suddenly, Last Summer*. Often he wore hats as well. Stories circulated that he was denying his race, that he wanted not only to be white but also to be a white *woman,* which hurt him more than was realized. But as a friend commented: "To Michael, Elizabeth was a saint, a goddess. And it's tragic— all those surgeries [Michael had]. If you look closely, in the beginning, he's trying to look like Elizabeth. His ruined face, his appearance, was a tribute to Elizabeth gone terribly wrong. I think he wanted it to be the greatest fan letter ever written."

He was seen in the company of children more and more, both at Neverland and on the road. The Cascio children frequently were by his side, even traveling with him. Such children as Macaulay Culkin and Corey Feldman were guests at Neverland. He also spent time with the young teenager Jordan Chandler, whom he called Jordie, the boy's mother, and his half sister. Other children visited Neverland, usually accompanied by their parents. For a long time, the public at large seemed willing to overlook his time spent with children. It was accepted as the case of a great artist who marched to the beat of his own drum. Michael Jackson, however, was rarely thought of as merely eccentric. He was Wacko Jacko, as the tabloids had dubbed him.

On February 3, 1992, Michael announced at a press conference his plans for an ambitious four-part *Dangerous* tour that would carry him through Europe, Asia, South America, and North America.

It would raise funds for his newly established Heal the World Foundation, an international children's charity. With hopes of raising $100 million by Christmas 1993, he planned for some of the money to go to pediatric AIDS "in honor of my friend, Ryan White," Michael said. "I am looking forward to this tour because it will allow me to devote time to visiting children all around the world, as well as spread the message of global love, in the hope that others will be moved to do their share to help heal the world." It was a pretty lofty endeavor and a sincere one. At that very press conference, Pepsi—yes, *Pepsi*—announced it would donate a reported $20 million to sponsor the tour.

The first leg of the *Dangerous* tour, from June through December, carried him throughout Germany, the Netherlands, Italy, Norway, Sweden, Belgium, the United Kingdom, Austria, Switzerland, France, Spain, Portugal, Romania, and Japan. Fans expected a Michael Jackson concert to be almost exclusively Michael Jackson. Yes, there would be opening acts, background singers, and backup dancers. But mainly it was Michael singing and dancing, going almost nonstop throughout the show. For Michael, there could be no compromises, no shortcuts. At the end of a performance, with his adrenaline still pumping, it could take hours for him to come down. He said: "Your adrenaline is at the zenith of the universe after a concert—you can't sleep. It's maybe two in the morning and you're wide awake. After coming offstage, you're floating." Once he did come down, he was soon preparing for the next evening's show. There were also the public appearances—for the benefit of the fans. "I loved being onstage. I loved doing the shows," he said. But it could be difficult to relate to people who came up to him afterward. "I've never liked people-contact. Even to this day, after a show. I hate it, meeting people. It makes me shy. I don't know what to say." Aside from the performances, the traveling itself, with the different time zones and the climate changes, proved grueling and exhausting, enough to wipe out the sturdiest of performers. Always contending with anxieties and preperformance tensions, he held himself together remarkably well. In turn, there had been record turnouts to see him. The film rights to the concert were sold to HBO for $21 million in 1992. It received HBO's highest ratings and was shown in sixty-one countries. He took medication to ward off his anxieties, to preserve his energy, but the medication took its toll.

Upon his return to the States in December, he was exhausted.

Once back in California, he didn't have much downtime, but still he tried to unwind. Aware that Michael was now free to celebrate holidays, birthdays, and other special occasions now that he was no longer a member of the Jehovah's Witnesses, in early January 1993 Elizabeth arrived at Neverland with husband Larry to give Michael his first real Christmas celebration. Toys and games were exchanged—in front of video cameras. Later, that videotaped Christmas would be shown publicly when his home movies aired on television.

Then came a whirlwind of other activities. On January 31, 1993, his spectacular performance at halftime during the Super Bowl game actually increased the halftime ratings of the broadcast by 8.6 percent over the previous year, reported *Forbes*. "Since that 1993 show, the halftime performance has become a huge part of the game," wrote Gordon Block in *Bleacher Report*, "and made the game much bigger than the sport of football. It's a cultural event and one that is almost impossible to miss." At Michael's request, the National Football League donated $100,000 to Jackson's Heal the World Foundation.

Soon afterward, about ninety million television viewers around the world tuned in to see him interviewed by Oprah Winfrey at Neverland. Earlier in the day, Elizabeth had been interviewed by Winfrey. During Michael's interview, she appeared by his side. Michael agreed to the interview mainly as a way to kick off the next leg of the *Dangerous* tour. But Winfrey managed to ask questions that made the interview more than a promo piece. Michael revealed his father's brutality. Elizabeth also, by way of explaining what drew Michael and her together, briefly referred to her father's physical abuse. This was quite a public revelation, though viewers didn't seem to realize this. Michael also discussed his plastic surgery and his vitiligo, explaining that he wore heavy makeup to disguise it. Viewers might not have believed him and may have dismissed it as just an excuse to be lighter, but his brother Jermaine later spoke of having splotches of discolored skin as well. Still, Michael had been guardedly forthcoming. When asked by Oprah what about Michael was most misunderstood, Elizabeth made the statement that many would question but which she had no doubts about. "He is the least weird man I have ever known," she said emphatically.

Michael had accomplished what he wanted, not only stating facts about himself that he could control but also creating a buzz that was sure to help his *Dangerous* tour.

The year was off to a spectacular start.

Not scheduled to continue the *Dangerous* tour until August, he again spent time with Elizabeth, although arranging occasions together could be difficult for both. His health was as fragile as hers. Both continued to medicate themselves with high doses of painkillers. When Elizabeth was honored by the American Film Institute with its Lifetime Achievement Award on March 11, 1993, Michael arrived on crutches. A few months later, the two were together to meet Nelson Mandela on the occasion of his seventy-fifth birthday celebration in Culver City. Shortly afterward, Michael arrived on the set of *The Flintstones*, in which Elizabeth was appearing. It would be her last feature film. Photographs of the two reveal beaming smiles—and for Michael there was a sweet contentment in his eyes.

But suddenly everything changed as he continued preparations in the States for the next leg of the tour—scheduled to begin in Bangkok on August 24 and later to hit Singapore on August 29. He learned that he was accused of having molested thirteen-year-old Jordan Chandler. Though Jackson consulted his lawyers, he appeared not to understand the gravity of the situation. "Michael dismissed the demands as extortion and left the country to begin his *Dangerous* tour in Bangkok," said Margaret Maldonado. The American public also learned of the accusations as the tabloids went into overdrive to report on the case. Maldonado said: "The fact that the American press was having a field day was kept from my brother-in-law by a tight net of advisers who closed him off from outside contact." On August 18, Los Angeles's Police Department's Sexually Exploited

Child Unit began an investigation of Michael.

On August 21, three days before his Bangkok opening, a search warrant was issued, permitting police to search Neverland. The Jackson family, which at first may have also dismissed the accusations, was now shaken by the search of Neverland and then a lawsuit.

The details of the allegations against Michael were not pretty. In fact, they were shocking, chilling, and disturbing.

According to Jordan Chandler, he was five years old when he first met Michael at a restaurant that Chandler, his mother, and stepfather frequented. The next meeting occurred when Michael, having car problems, went to the car rental company owned by Chandler's stepfather. Aware that Jordan was a great Jackson fan, the stepfather called the boy and suggested he should come to the car rental place to see Jackson. Chandler got to speak to Michael that day. Afterward, he received phone calls from Michael, who was on tour part of the time. According to Chandler, the calls some-times lasted three hours. Then came trips to Neverland for Jordan; his half-sister, Lily; and his mother, June. The family slept in guest quarters. There was a trip to a Toys R Us store where "we were allowed to get anything we wanted. Although the store was closed, it was opened just for our visit." On another occasion, Jordan, Lily, and their mother were flown on a private plane to Las Vegas as guests of Michael's. They stayed at the Mirage. June and Lily shared a bedroom. Jordan ended up sleeping in the same bed with Michael but "there was no physical contact." Afterward, on trips to Neverland and at Jordan's family home and at hotels in New York, Florida, and Europe, Chandler said he slept again with Michael. Then there were innocent kisses, then kisses on the lips. Eventually, there was, according to Chandler, sexual contact, initiated by Michael.

The court papers stated: "These sexually offensive contacts include but are not limited to defendant Michael Jackson orally copulating plaintiff, defendant Michael Jackson masturbating plaintiff, defendant Michael Jackson eating the semen of plaintiff, and defendant Michael Jackson having plaintiff fondle and manipulate the breasts and nipples of defendant Michael Jackson while defendant Michael Jackson would masturbate."

But there were aspects of the backstory of the case that made the lawsuit that eventually followed highly questionable. Jordan Chandler's father, Evan Chandler, who lodged the lawsuit, was divorced from June. A dentist with aspirations for a screenwriting career, Evan had already collaborated on the screenplay for *Robin Hood: Men in Tights*. When he learned of his son's meeting and friendship with Jackson, Evan

Chandler was pleased, even boasted of the friendship to patients. Carrie Fisher, who was one of Chandler's patients, said he was known as the "Dentist to the Stars." She remembered that he frequently talked about how much he and Michael liked each other. "And the most disturbing thing I remember him saying was, 'You know, my son is *very* good-looking.' Now I ask you—what father talks about his child that way?" He also told Fisher about the fabulous trips Michael and his son went on—and that they were "sleeping in the same bed." That comment stopped Fisher cold. He explained that his wife was always around, so things were fine.

Evan Chandler also tried to pitch his new screenplay to Michael. But nothing came of that. During Jordan's visits to his father's home, Michael was occasionally a guest. It was then that Evan Chandler—observing his son and the singer together and actually sharing a bed together—grew suspicious and questioned his former wife about the Jordan-Jackson friendship. She dismissed any ideas of inappropriate behavior. At one point, Evan reportedly confronted Jackson, asking if he was having sex with his son, which Michael denied. Rather than going to the police, Evan eventually consulted an attorney. Ultimately, rather than taking the case to criminal court, Evan wanted some kind of settlement worked out. What he reportedly wanted was a screenwriting deal from Jackson. Then his legal team wanted a $20 million settlement. That didn't happen. An offer was made for $1 million, which Evan refused. Then Evan lowered the settlement to $15 million. Michael's counteroffer was $350,000. It was then that both Evan and June, as the guardians of Jordan, a minor, decided to go to civil court with a lawsuit.

Carrie Fisher recalled the night Evan came to her home and let her know that he and his ex-wife were suing Michael—because the pop star was sleeping in the same bed with his son. "I know for a fact that when this first started happening the good doctor saw no problem with this odd bunking!" Fisher never thought Michael's relationship with kids was sexual. "Never. Granted, it was miles from appropriate, but just because it wasn't normal doesn't mean that it had to be perverse." Fisher also believed that Michael was not sexual at all. She saw him as talented, childlike, and "pathologically kind, absolutely." How could anyone, she asked, be stupid enough to have sex with kids he was hanging out with? "And Michael was not stupid." Perhaps naïve. And now the prey for someone out for money.

On September 14, 1993, a civil lawsuit was filed against Michael in the Superior Court of the State of California. Michael's attorneys Howard Weitzman and Bert Fields said it was all a case of extortion. But they were faced with defending Michael against Jordan Chandler's accusations.

By then in Singapore for the *Dangerous* tour, Michael could neither ignore nor evade the inevitable: that the allegations might lead to criminal charges. Hearing the news, his family defended and tried to rally round him. But the Jacksons were confronted with a wall that was around Michael, created by his staff, his publicists —or his "handlers" as the Jackson family referred to them—that prevented anyone from getting through to the superstar. "Katherine tried in vain to reach her son to tell him what he must have already known: that she supported him completely," Maldonado recalled. "One person who did penetrate the security net was Elizabeth Taylor. Michael had telephoned her soon after the story broke and asked her to come and stand by his side. It was a familiar role for Elizabeth, who also had stood by her friend Rock Hudson as he told the world he was dying of AIDS. She wanted nothing other than to help a friend in need."

Michael asked Elizabeth to come to Singapore. From some accounts, he sounded as if he were at the breaking point. Elizabeth knew she had to make the trip. Certainly, her doctors would have advised her not to go. Having recovered from the near-fatal pneumonia that kept her hospitalized for weeks in 1990, she had been stricken in 1992 with that severe upper respiratory tract infection that had led to hospitalization again. Now she was about to embark on a twenty-hour flight that could cause more medical problems. There was always the issue of her back. But whatever medical advice was given was ignored. Before departing, she became the first of Michael's friends to publicly support him—and *unequivocally*. "I totally believe 100% in Michael's integrity. He'd rather cut his own wrist than harm a child. He worships children."

With husband Larry, Taylor endured the long flight, arrived in Singapore, and checked into the Raffles hotel, where Michael was staying. In her hotel suite, Taylor reportedly gave him a belated birthday dinner. They also went to the zoo together. "And we hung out and had our own private tour and had fun," Michael recalled—without discussing the fact that emotionally he was in terrible shape.

Word of Elizabeth's arrival in Singapore would not please some members of the Jackson family. They felt no more comfortable with the presence of Elizabeth Taylor in his life than before.

Shortly afterward, Taylor and Fortensky traveled with Michael to Taipei, Taiwan, where he performed on September 4–6. Jackson family members—which included Katherine, Joe, Rebbie, Jackie, Jermaine, and Randy—also traveled to Taipei. "When the Jacksons arrived, they stayed in the same hotel as Michael, Elizabeth Taylor, and her husband Larry Fortensky," recalled Michael's publicist Bob Jones, who was traveling with him. "Michael didn't want his mother, Katherine, to come ver, but she eventually did, along with Rebbie and Jermaine."

"Just what I need," Michael was reported to have told Elizabeth when he learned of his family's arrival. "Why do they have to come?"

"They are your family, Michael. You must put up with them."

"My father, I can't even stand to be in the same room with that man," he said.

"Neither can I, dear," Elizabeth reportedly told him.

According to Bob Jones, Katherine "was angry, too." "Why does Elizabeth Taylor get to see him any time she wants, but I have to make an appointment to see him for five minutes," she reportedly said. According to Bob Jones, she later commented: "I'm his mother, not Elizabeth Taylor." Of course, her feelings were understandable. He would always be her son, and she wanted to comfort him.

The fact that Michael had often spent so much time with Elizabeth appeared to gnaw at Katherine. The writer Stacy Brown, who knew the entire family for more than two decades, but who reportedly was never close to Michael, recalled that on visits to Neverland, Katherine "would decide where she'd have lunch or dinner depending upon whether or not Liz had ever used the spot."

"I'm not sitting where she sat," Katherine was reported to have said, according to Brown. "She's stolen my son away." Brown said that Joe Jackson had similar feelings about Berry Gordy Jr. "Michael better realize, it's my blood running through his veins. Mine and nobody else's. I'm his father. Katie is his mother."

At one point, Brown said, Janet Jackson had been concerned about her family's psychological well-being and paid for the family to undergo therapy. When they repeatedly complained about Michael, the therapist finally told them in essence to forget about Michael, their brother. "Michael is not your family in his mind. Elizabeth Taylor is his mom, and you guys should move on."

"Michael's handlers don't want us to get to him," Jermaine later said publicly about their time in Taipei. But it wasn't that simple. By most accounts, Michael gave explicit instructions to his staff regarding his family. Almost always, Katherine was the only person he was willing to see whenever *she* wanted. But this situation was different.

Michael still preferred the company of Elizabeth, who mothered him tirelessly, especially during a time of crisis such as the one during the *Dangerous* tour. Tormented by the child molestation allegations, he had stopped eating while in Taipei. But Elizabeth was insistent. "She took the spoon and opened my mouth and made me eat," Michael recalled. She also had a sense of humor. When she tried to persuade him to eat a piece of cake, he refused. "Take it away," he told her. Finally, she reportedly told him, "Michael, if you don't eat this cake, I swear to God, I will call your family in here and let them have a go at you. And you know I'll do it, too." "Give me that goddamn cake," he said. The two laughed.

Finally, Michael saw his family.

What Michael may have tried to hide from his mother, which may explain why he didn't want to see her, he could not hide from Elizabeth, who realized he was in terrible shape. "The *Dangerous* tour was doomed from the start," said publicist Jones. "Michael was in no condition to do the shows, and drugs became an issue." Taylor knew something had to be done to save him from himself. Tour dates were canceled, and Elizabeth made arrangements for Michael to stay at her chalet in Switzerland. Traveling with him was the Cascio family. A story circulated that he underwent drug treatment while in Switzerland.

But his stay in Switzerland was not long. On October 7, Jackson resumed the *Dangerous* tour, now scheduled for South America from late October to early November.

• • •

Once back in Los Angeles, Elizabeth took an active role in Michael's defense. Several times a week, she held strategy meetings at her Bel Air home with Michael's defense team, which included Michael's attorneys Weitzman and Fields, his manager Sandy Gallin, and the well-known controversial private investigator Anthony Pellicano, who ultimately refused to attend the meetings with a "movie star." Little did he realize that Elizabeth Taylor was not a *mere* movie star. Also involved in the defense strategy was a newcomer to the group: Lisa Marie Presley. For some time now, she and Michael had been quietly seeing each other, and it became apparent that theirs was a significant relationship for the King of Pop. Having first met years earlier in Las Vegas, when she was seven and Michael, still with the Jackson 5, was seventeen, they met again as adults at a dinner party in Los Angeles.

Born in 1968 and heir to an estimated $150 million estate, Lisa Marie was famous as the only child of Elvis and Priscilla Presley. Everyone agreed that she had her father's sensual mouth—and sometimes that oddly seductive sullen stare. Known for being outspoken, hip, cool, confident, and sometimes bluntly honest—and described by a writer as being "reclusive and idiosyncratic"—she already had shown her marks as a rebel. She had quit high school. Then in 1988, she had married the rocker Danny Keough, with whom she later had two young children, a daughter and a son. (Their daughter, Riley Keough, would eventually go on to become an actress.) By this time, the marriage was in trouble and would soon end. Like Michael and Elizabeth, she also had ties with a nontraditional, actually controversial, religious organization. Hers was the Church of Scientology, which she joined as a teenager. Her mother was also a member. Lisa Marie had sometimes lived at the Scientology Celebrity Centre in Hollywood. Through the years, she had also taken her children to the Scientology retreat in Clearwater, Florida. "It's the best thing I've ever been involved in," she once said.

Now she was clearly becoming devoted to Michael, "showering him with notes, balloons, and gifts." Said a Presley friend: "Lisa Marie wanted to help Michael with his life. She fell in love with him."

During strategy sessions for Michael's defense, Elizabeth and Lisa Marie reportedly were at odds with each other. To some, Elizabeth appeared unwilling to share Michael. Perhaps Lisa Marie didn't want to share him, either. But the women also had entirely different styles. Elizabeth evoked old-school Hollywood: always made-up; always coiffed; often dripping with plenty of bling—rings, bracelets, necklaces, dangling earrings; forever dramatic and aware of an audience. Lisa Marie looked like a rocker: hair that just hung, though casually styled on purpose; makeup, subtly applied to give her the look of not wearing makeup, although it, too, had its dramatic points; clothes that were casual, jeans and tank tops. Both women, however, were earthy and true to themselves. Neither really gave a damn what other people thought of them. Still, both women were convinced of Michael's innocence and were eager to have the best defense team possible. Yet not enough progress was being made in Michael's defense. A grand jury had heard testimony from members of Michael's staff, especially damaging comments made by one of Michael's maids who said she had seen the singer nude with naked boys. Another maid would later say that she left his employ after he made advances toward her seven-year-old son. The offices of two of Michael's doctors, Arnold Klein and Steve Hoefflin, had been raided by the Los Angeles police. Medical records and files were taken. Dermatologist Klein had also been forced to testify.

But something about the defense team itself made Michael look out of touch. Geri Branton, the wife of Leo Branton Jr., one of Los Angeles's leading African American attorneys, always felt that it was Elizabeth who determined that Michael should have an African American on the team. Already too many stories circulated that Michael was denying his blackness, trying to wipe it out with his nose jobs and his skin lighteners. Surrounded by white lawyers, he looked all the more like someone living in a white bubble. That did neither his image nor his defense much good in the realm of public opinion. A decision was made to bring in the African American attorney Johnnie Cochran. Shrewd, sophisticated, highly intelligent, and blessed with street smarts, Cochran's presence alone, aside from his astute legal logistics, helped Michael's case. (Taylor also apparently wanted to bring in her tough-minded attorney Neil Papiano, but that idea was scratched.)

"Every day seemed to bring new drama, none more unexpected than the surprise incident that occurred on November 8, 1993, while the family was in Phoenix, Arizona, for the funeral of Joseph's father," recalled Margaret Maldonado. "Without warning, the gates were opened and sixteen undercover police officers stormed the Hayvenhurst house, armed with a search warrant. They went to work sifting through drawers, closets, and cupboards, but concentrated their search in Michael's room." Maldonado added: "The men proceeded to tear through his belongings, which Katherine had carefully preserved exactly as Michael had left the room." Upon learning of the police search, "Katherine was in a rage." Boxes of items were now in the possession of the police. On November 11, the

New York Post reported that Taylor was in a crisis session talking with Michael on the phone.

According to writer Maureen Orth, a panicky Jackson called a friend in the States on November 18. "I'm never coming back. All my money is being taken over here. We're cleaning out all my assets, my accounts. I'm selling all my holdings. . . . My lawyers are going to get me out of it. It's nothing but scandal. They want my money. . . . I wake up every day and think I'm in hell. I don't even want to be alive. . . . I can't come back and face that. I can't. I can't. I can't." According to Maldonado: "Michael heard about the search while he was in Mexico. He reacted with what the media described as a breakdown that sent Elizabeth Taylor back to his side."

Uppermost in Elizabeth's mind—and in the minds of others—was Michael's drug problems. His use of prescription drugs—of antianxiety medication, of high-powered pain medication— was out of control, which Elizabeth well understood. She herself still relied on painkillers. But Taylor had learned to manage the addiction to painkillers without being overwhelmed by them, although actor Robert Wagner said that when he saw Elizabeth, she often enough had a "buzz," due to the medication he believed she was on. For Michael, it was quite different. He had not grown up living with constant pain, as

Elizabeth had. Having undergone additional surgery on his scalp some months earlier, he was frantic for relief. Complicating Michael's use of prescription drugs was treatment for a new condition with which he had been diagnosed—lupus—of which the public was not yet aware. By then, he was using medication for his depression.

The decision was made that Michael needed to go into rehab, and probably the only person who could convince him to do so was Elizabeth. Once again, she took a medically ill-advised flight to be by his side in Mexico City. Also on the flight were her husband Larry Fortensky and Michael's attorneys. "I thought Michael was fine," said Frank Cascio, who was traveling with Michael, "until, before one of the concerts in Mexico City, Elizabeth Taylor suddenly showed up."

In Mexico, an argument broke out between Bert Fields and Michael's longstanding security man Bill Bray, who felt the attorneys weren't handling the case properly and that Michael might end up in jail. Elizabeth sided with Bray.

"You need to get out there and start deposing these people. They are liars all over the place, and they need to be revealed for who they are . . . all these housekeepers and maids and butlers," Elizabeth said. Then she told Michael: "I know good help is hard to find, Michael, but where did you find *these* people? Look at how they turned on you."

"What am I going to do?" an obviously distraught Michael asked.

"We're fighting, Michael," she told him, "but it's because we love you."

Elizabeth persuaded Michael—after completing his Mexico concerts—to undergo treatment at the well-known Nightingale Hospital in England. "On November 12, we learned that Michael had canceled the remainder of his *Dangerous* tour because of an addiction to painkillers," recalled Maldonado. Later Jackson was sued by a promoter for $20 million. The suit stated that "Jackson fraudulently concealed his drug addiction and that the police were investigating charges he sexually molested a 13-year-old boy." It also alleged that "the singer only performed 24 dates of a 43-date schedule for which he had already been paid a $900,000 fee." "Even when he performed," the promoter stated, "Jackson wasn't Jackson. The singer was so preoccupied with his problems that he often had long pauses in between songs and disappeared from the stage for long periods of time."

Getting Jackson to the Nightingale Hospital was an ordeal. Once the flight touched ground in England, everything had to be done rapidly. The last thing anyone wanted was for the media to learn what was happening. Customs and immigration officials apparently checked documents on board. Two rented mini-buses stood on the tarmac, ready for the passengers, which included Taylor, Fortensky, and Michael's physician David Forecast. Bodyguard Steve Tarling was assigned to quickly get Jackson off the flight and into a mini-bus. "He was sitting alone and seemed to be asleep. A red tartan blanket was wrapped over his legs and a black hat was titled over his eyes," recalled Tarling. "Michael, you have to get off now," Elizabeth aid as she shook him awake. But it wasn't easy.

"He was completely out of it. He was so drugged up he was like a zombie. He just looked like a lost soul," said Tarling. "When his hat came off and I saw his whole face for the first time I was physically shocked. I had this image of Michael Jackson the performer in my mind, but the sight I saw was nothing like that—he looked terrible. He wore full make-up with smudged red lipstick and eyeliner. His face was covered in white paste like a clown. He looked as if he had been wearing the same make-up for a couple of weeks. What shocked me most was the tip of his nose—it was jet black. His whole face was white except for his nose which was like an open cut goes when it congeals over into a scab. It looked awfully painful."

Tarling also remembered: "I wanted to get him off immediately because the longer we stayed there, the more vulnerable we were. It was pandemonium on the plane, security men and airport ground staff were unloading baggage, but Jackson was oblivious to it all."

Elizabeth, however, was completely alert. She had her two dogs with her, and aware that Britain's quarantine laws forbade pets from entering the country for a period of time, she wanted her animals smuggled off the plane. Tarling refused. He said she then told Fortensky to stay on the flight with the dogs. He did not seem pleased.

Tarling had to carry Michael off the plane. At the same time, a Michael Jackson "lookalike was smuggled on to the plane and curled up on his seat pretending to sleep. The decoy worked and as far as the passport control officers were concerned, Jackson had never left the plane."

Waiting in one mini-bus was the therapist Beauchamp Colclough, who questioned Michael: Did he understand "why he was there and did he know he had a problem." The rules of the clinic were explained. Michael seemed to have no problem when told he'd have to make his own bed and wash his dishes. Or perhaps he was too out of it to understood what was being said. But when he was informed that phone calls would not be allowed, Michael snapped to attention. "Suddenly Jackson said very calmly and coherently, 'Excuse me, can you turn this bus around and take me back? If I can't use a telephone, I'm calling the whole thing off.'" Said Tarling: "It made everyone realize that he wasn't such a spaced-out idiot after all." It was agreed that he could use the phone.

In the van, Taylor's temper flared when she learned that Michael could not immediately go to the clinic because of concern about the media. "This is bull shit," she said, then proceeded to ask Tarling about his credentials. In the van, her fragile physical condition became apparent to the bodyguard. "As I drove around, she screamed out hysterically. Apparently, the movement had hurt her back." Once again, she was exerting herself in a way that would have appalled her physicians.

Michael was first taken to the home of Elton John's manager John Reid. "Within an hour, Taylor insisted Jackson be taken to the clinic. She felt he would react better to treatment in a hospital environment and the doctors agreed." In the early morning hours, he was secretly moved to the clinic. Taylor reboarded the plane, which then flew to Switzerland.

Michael's stay at the clinic was difficult for him—and the staff. "I felt sorry for him. You could tell he was determined to get out and was ready to walk on to the streets of London in the freezing cold. Half the world's media were searching for this man and he nearly walked right out into the open—on his own." But he somehow stuck it out. At one therapy session, Michael, with other patients, introduced himself. "Hi, I'm Michael, and I'm addicted to drugs." It was no different from Elizabeth's group therapy sessions at the Betty Ford Center. Not long afterward, the decision was made to take Michael back to the home of John Reid where, under staff supervision and along with nurses, doctors, and fellow patients, his treatment continued. When Jackson had to wear a disguise—"baggy tracksuit pants, a long coat, scarf and an old baseball cap"—to leave the clinic, Tarling remembered: "Jackson was as cool as you like. He waited for my signal, then walked to the car just outside and I drove off. He liked the disguise but refused to change his shoes." Both the disguise and the Jackson lookalike on the flight seemed to spring from old-school Hollywood, which surely pleased Michael, subterfuges worthy of Howard Hughes or Garbo or even Elizabeth.

On December 10, Michael was discharged from the clinic and returned to the United States.

In the States, he returned to what, for him, was a nightmarish media circus. He was also confronted with a long-running suit from songwriters who accused him of using their material on *Thriller*. Both Bert Fields and security consultant Anthony Pellicano left his defense team. So intense and pervasive was the coverage that the NAACP accused the media of being "excessive and too negative." "There have been no charges filed and if they are filed, they will be filed in the court-room—not the newsroom," the organization's West Coast region director said. "We are sick of watching negative news stories."

By January 1, 1994, $2 million had been spent on the investigation. "Two grand juries had questioned more than two hundred witnesses, including thirty children who had been friends of Michael's over the years. Not one witness could be found who could corroborate Jordie Chandler's story," it was reported.

But the worst was yet to come. Because Jordan Chandler's deposition had described distinguishing marks on Michael's genitalia, the prosecution ordered Michael to undergo a strip search, which would be photographed, to see if such marks existed. Fortunately, his attorneys arranged for the procedure to be performed at Neverland. But it was still psychologically painful. On the day of the strip search, Michael protested that he couldn't leave his room. According to J. Randy Taraborrelli, it took about an hour for attorneys Cochran and Weitzman to coax Michael to come out of his bedroom and into the parlor. Also present was Santa Barbara's District Attorney Thomas Sneddon Jr. As the search was about to begin, Sneddon left the room, as did Michael's attorneys. "Bodyguard Bill Bray was allowed to remain, as would the two detectives and two photographers and two doctors." Wearing a robe, an angry, frazzled, and humiliated Michael shouted at one of the detectives: "You!

Get out! I don't want you here for this. Get out!"
A doctor calmed him down. Hearing the commotion, Cochran and Weitzman returned to the room. "Get these sons of bitches out of here," Michael shouted.

Finally, he stood on a platform and was photographed by a DA's photographer.

Afterward, an outraged Michael addressed the public in a taped video that was broadcast on CNN. "Don't treat me like a criminal," he said, and thereafter described the complete body examination by investigators. "It was the most humiliating ordeal of my life." A cry from the heart, his words appeared true, emotional, and perhaps for some surprisingly heart-wrenching.

His attorneys apparently questioned if he could endure a trial, now set for March 1994. Discussions ensued about his welfare, his state of mind, his emotional state. Finally, it was suggested he settle out of court and be done with the whole experience. Who knew what else might be revealed or distorted during a trial. The scrutiny could break him. But Michael was adamant. Not a penny would go to Evan Chandler, whom he believed had put Jordie up to the allegations. From most accounts, he never spoke ill of the boy. He could never understand why, from his perspective, Jordie had turned against him.

In the midst of the media frenzy and the

defense team's maneuvers, Michael had a party for two hundred underprivileged children at Neverland on January 16. One could only wonder what he was thinking. But Michael remained in many respects naïve, an innocent.

Michael was finally persuaded to settle the case rather than endure the continued media frenzy—and also a trial that would leave him even more emotionally battered and drained.

"Michael Jackson Settles Suit For Sum Said to Be in Millions," read the front-page headline in the *New York Times* on January 26, 1994. "In return for the financial settlement the boy, who is unidentified, dropped the civil lawsuit he had instituted against Mr. Jackson. But a separate criminal investigation will continue." Los Angeles's District Attorney Gil Garcetti said: "The criminal investigation of singer Michael Jackson is ongoing and will not be affected by the announcement of the civil case." Johnnie Cochran read a statement, however, stating: "In short, he is an innocent man who does not intend to have his career and his life destroyed by rumors and innuendo." "With the civil case ended, legal experts said a criminal investigation of Mr. Jackson might collapse," the *New York Times* reported. "Under a California law adopted two years ago, a victim of sexual abuse cannot be compelled to testify against his or her assailant." The *New York Times* also stated: "But legal experts said the settlement had left Mr. Jackson open to similar suits." The *New York Times* would be right on both counts.

Estimates of the settlement ran as high as $22 million, of which $20 million would be put in trust for Jordan; one million each would go to his parents, Evan and June. Additional sums would be paid to Chandler's attorney Larry Feldman for contingency fees. One estimate of those fees was $5 million.

Ironically, before the settlement, the results of a poll conducted earlier by the tabloid television show *A Current Affair* indicated that 75 percent of people felt Jackson was innocent. But if anything, the settlement led many to believe Michael was indeed guilty. Afterward, it was said by those close to him that he regretted the settlement for the rest of his life.

His image never fully recovered. Henceforth, the media depicted him primarily as Wacko Jacko. His look itself would undergo further changes. The skin lotion seemed to be even lighter, the hairpieces even more extreme, and the nose looked even more as if it were about to fall apart.

"On the professional front, Jackson has become a bad risk, both as a pitchman (Pepsi parted ways with him in November)," reported *Newsweek*, "and as an entertainer (he is being sued for more than $20 million in a fraud and breach-of-contract suit due to his canceled world tour). And he seems to have lost every supporter but Elizabeth Taylor, who proclaimed his innocence again last week."

"Thank God this case is being dismissed," Elizabeth informed the media. "Michael's love of children is one of the purest things I have ever seen, it shines like an extra sun, despite the media's distorted lens. I always knew this would be thrown out of court, and I am so grateful." But, in reality, the case had not been thrown out of court. Michael's attorneys had prevented it from ever getting there.

In some circles, Elizabeth was criticized, labeled an enabler. But generally she was considered a loyal friend. Within the African American community, where it was often believed, as the NAACP had indicated, that Michael was being persecuted by the media, Taylor was viewed as a heroine, the one person he seemed to believe in during these troubled times. Columnist Liz Smith reminded her readers: *"USA Today's* Jeannie Williams made the significant point that no member of Jackson's family has really comforted him during this latest crisis—only Elizabeth." Perhaps it is best to add that although Katherine Jackson and other family members *tried* to comfort him, he didn't find relief in their arms. He still had too many conflicting feelings about his family. Liz Smith also pointed out that Elizabeth's die-hard support of Michael could be expected of this "maternal and nurturing woman. She loves Michael as she loves her own children. No further explanation needed. She is the original hand-in-the-fire-for-a-friend gal."

As for the public's opinion of Taylor, Smith added: "There *has* been some question of Elizabeth's reputation being harmed by her steadfast loyalty to Michael. But this movie queen-turned-AIDS-crusader-and-perfume mogul occupies an untouchable position in the celebrity pantheon. Elizabeth today is eons removed from the home-wrecking femme fatale who once brought the wrath of the Vatican down on her head. Her strenuous efforts on behalf of Jackson —putting her own fragile health in peril—have only solidified her current, very positive, loyal public image."

Of course, about those who remained critical of her, Elizabeth Taylor frankly didn't care one iota. Most important to her, she had saved Michael in Mexico City. She had fought to ensure he had the proper defense. Despite her own physical maladies, none of which was helped by the traveling and by the stress, she had stuck by him to the end of the nightmare. Yet her frailty and poor health would very soon be apparent.

As for Michael, he would never forget her loyalty and support, her fundamental kindness.

Chapter 17

PUTTING THE PIECES of his life back together, Michael spent time with Lisa Marie Presley, his staunchest ally, second to Elizabeth. Neverland functioned just about as it always had. Resuming his social activities, he also set out to rehabilitate his image.

In February 1994, he participated in a television special: *The Jackson Family Honors*, reportedly the brainchild of Jermaine, who was the program's executive producer. Televised from the MGM Grand hotel in Las Vegas, the special also seemed partly an attempt to rewrite the family's dysfunctional reputation. Honoring Berry Gordy *and* Elizabeth for their achievements, the program featured performances by such stars as Gladys Knight and the Pips, Smokey Robinson, and Dionne Warwick. Also present at the taped broadcast was Louis Farrakhan, the minister of the Nation of Islam, once critical of Michael but now seemingly a fan. During the taping of the special, there was also a threat that La Toya "would sneak in disguised as an Arab and disrupt the event," reported the *New York Times*. No one seemed to know why she would don such a disguise. But the threat that she would do so was made by her manager, Jack Gordon. "That was how I planned it," Gordon informed the *New York Times*. "When La Toya goes to Europe, we dress her like an Arab. We put a thing around her face. She goes like an Arabic woman from the Mideast." Fortunately, or perhaps unfortunately, in terms of the public's response to the program, she was a no-show. But, regarding the makeup of the audience to see Michael that night, the *New York Times* pointed out: "There were no Hollywood power brokers, no movie stars, and few, if any, representatives of Sony Music Entertainment, which has a contract with Michael Jackson worth $50 million to $65 million, and the Creative Artists Agency, which represents the performer."

Introduced by Michael, who looked sleek and dapper in all black with long hair, Elizabeth accepted her award—mostly by praising Michael. "Michael is a remarkable human being. He has a commitment to others beyond compare. We have suffered with you, Michael. From the depths of our deepest anguish we knew you would emerge victorious—bruised but magically untouched by the malicious tongues of the world." She added: "Enough of tabloid media. Enough of tabloid television." Those comments received a thundering ovation. But the atmosphere changed as younger audience members called out Michael's name. They wanted to see the King of Pop onstage—*in action*. When Elizabeth said that he would not be performing, the mood of the audience quickly changed—as shouts and boos were heard throughout the theater. "Don't boo," she said. "That's an ugly sound." She then cut her speech short.

Actually, earlier backstage Elizabeth had tried to persuade Michael to perform, using her world-famous charms. But also present was Lisa Marie, who put her foot down. "Look, he's not going to perform, so you might as well just leave it alone." Elizabeth Taylor was not accustomed to being spoken to in this way, especially by a woman young enough to be her daughter. Michael apparently said nothing. "Well, you're the boss, I guess," said Taylor to Presley. Then she walked off.

But of great interest to television viewers was Elizabeth's appearance—"ailing and enormous," commented columnist Linda Stasi. "The actress, reportedly about to have hip surgery, was seen being transported to the hotel earlier in the day by ambulance and was obviously in a great deal of pain. Her weight seemed to have ballooned from a few months ago." Clearly, she should not have attended the event. Heavily medicated, her weight gain may have been the result of steroids administered to combat the pain. Before the year was out, the results of an investigation of her pain medication prescriptions would be published in the *Los Angeles Times*: "Three prominent Los Angeles physicians have been publicly reprimanded by the California Medical Board for falsifying patient records to cover up the massive amounts of addictive drugs they prescribed to actress Elizabeth Taylor. The action, yet to be publicly announced, finally brings to a close the accusations filed against the doctors in 1990 by the California attorney general's office, alleging that the physicians prescribed excessive doses of painkillers for Taylor during the 1980s."

Most significant, by the time *The Jackson Family Honors* aired in late February, Taylor had entered the hospital and undergone hip replacement surgery, the result of years of suffering from osteoarthritis of the left hip. The expected period of recuperation was eight weeks.

With the exception of Katherine, Michael didn't seem interested in saying much to other family members at *The Jackson Family Honors*. Nor did his sister Janet, who performed at the event and then quickly exited. Like Michael, she also appeared to keep her distance from her family, save for her mother. In Las Vegas, family members were booked into the MGM Grand; Janet chose to stay at the Luxor. Michael opted for the Mirage.

The show did nothing to alter the public's

perception of the Jacksons. "Family reunions are often strange affairs. But the public reunion of the performing Jackson clan on Saturday night was, even by Las Vegas standards, one of the strangest spectacles in theatrical history," commented Bernard Weinraub in the *New York Times*. "Part soap opera, part tragedy and part weird comedy, the Jackson family epic took another turn in a reunion (minus one outcast daughter) before 15,000 people." The newspaper also commented: "But most of the real-life drama actually took place offstage. Certainly the most pointed comment of the reunion came, unexpectedly, from Katherine Jackson, the matriarch. Several hours before the stage reunion, Mrs. Jackson appeared at a news conference with her husband, Joseph, and their son Jermaine. . . Mrs. Jackson was asked if her family, with all its wealth and fame, was living the American dream. 'It's been an American nightmare in the last six months,' she said tartly. No one would dispute her."

Following the taping of the special, Michael and Lisa Marie went to Neverland.

Chapter 18

AFTER HAVING DATED for four months, Michael had a question for Lisa Marie, "What would you do if I asked you to marry me?" Of course, there would be a little stumbling block once Lisa answered yes. She was still married to someone else. That issue was soon resolved. On May 6, Lisa Marie's husband Danny Keough flew with her to the Dominican Republic to finalize their divorce. They both quickly left the island. It all called to mind the arrival of Michael Wilding in Mexico to provide Elizabeth with a quick divorce so that she could quickly marry Mike Todd. On May 26, Lisa Marie returned to the Dominican Republic, where she and Michael were married by a judge in a secret ceremony without family or friends in attendance. For months, nothing about the Jackson-Presley nuptials was revealed to the press. When rumors floated about the marriage, there were denials. Like just about everyone else, Lisa Marie's mother, Priscilla Presley, was left in the dark until a phone conversation with her daughter. With helicopters hovering over her home, Priscilla reportedly told her daughter that she was hearing strange news reports that Lisa Marie had married Jackson. She was ready to laugh the story off, thinking it was one more media fabrication.

But when nothing was said on the other end of the phone, Priscilla realized the story was true. A distressed Priscilla reportedly feared Michael might be using her daughter to clean up his image after the molestation case. "Can't you see what he's up to? It's so obvious," she reportedly said.

A friend of Priscilla's, who saw her about a month after the wedding, commented: "She looked downright terrible. It was obvious she was very preoccupied."

Apparently, Michael also had not told Elizabeth about his plans to marry Lisa Marie. He waited until afterward—to call her. An upset Elizabeth reportedly asked a friend: "What has he done? *What has he done?*" This may have marked a shift in their relationship. But, still dealing with the aftermath of her hip replacement surgery, she also hadn't much time to fret about it. She still had pain and problems walking. As it turned out, she would eventually have two more hip surgeries.

"Lisa Marie: I Married Michael: Call Me Mrs. Jackson" read the *New York Post* headline on August 2, 1994.

Michael's publicist Bob Jones, vice president of MJJ Productions, had faxed an announcement of the wedding to the Associated Press. The media swung into action with reports on the nuptials of the couple.

At the time, the two were tucked away in a $110,000-a-month twelve-room duplex penthouse at Manhattan's Trump Tower. "I am very much in love with Michael. I dedicate my life to being his wife," Lisa told the press. For a young woman known for being tough-minded, even cynical, Lisa Marie's proclamations about her love for Michael were unexpectedly giddy. "I've never seen her look so happy. They have fun together," said Jerry Schilling, her former manager. "There was a lot of teasing, a lot of kidding around, like any other newlywed couple," said Jackson's family friend and former publicist Steve Manning.

Initially, the Jackson family had no comment. But in a short time, they appeared to accept and like Lisa Marie, who spoke on the phone with Katherine and Janet. Part of the positive response may have been that she was Elvis's daughter. The daughter of the King was surely a fit spouse/companion for the King of Pop. But part of their response was also due to Lisa Marie's down-to-earth personality. Michael's interests were her interests. Katherine's reaction to Lisa Marie was vastly different from her feelings about Elizabeth. Michael seemed to want Lisa Marie to be friendly with some family members, but he had mostly kept Elizabeth to himself. The family may have also believed that finally with the marriage those rumors about Michael being gay were put to rest. But that was wishful thinking.

In her August 4, 1994 column, Liz Smith asked: "And how long will it be before Elizabeth Taylor descends on New York personally to congratulate her dear friend? This would come on the heels of her joyful public statement wishing the newlyweds happiness—a statement much more effusive than the one issued by the bride's mother."

Though Elizabeth's feelings may not have been too different from Priscilla's but for other reasons, this was a key moment in Michael's life that she had to support.

At her Bel Air home, Elizabeth hosted a dinner for Michael and Lisa Marie and friends, which no doubt pleased Michael. Elizabeth and Lisa Marie would still have differences, especially when Elizabeth was reported to have given Lisa Marie some marital advice: She should always look her best. "He's into glamour, and you must be into it, too. And if you don't like the jewelry he gives you, fake it; act like you do. And keep separate bedrooms to keep him guessing. Also find the right colors and wear the hell out of them." Apparently, Lisa Marie later told Michael: "What era is *she* living in? No wonder she's been divorced seven times!" "Now, Lisa," Michael was reported to have told his wife. "Be nice." Much of the public didn't appear to take the marriage seriously—or to believe that Michael had any sexual interest in Lisa Marie. Some even suggested she should be careful of her children around him. But Presley maintained that theirs was a normal, healthy sex life, though she noted his eccentricities. He liked her to wear jewelry in bed. He didn't want her to see him without his makeup.

There were also nights when he struggled with insomnia. Sometimes he would wake her up to talk. He also moved around the room. Much of his behavior she found "endearing." He also wanted her to have children. Part of her still wanted to save him. Part of her was mesmerized by him.

"He was an incredible, an incredibly dynamic person," she later said. "He had something so intoxicating about him, and when he was ready to share with you and be himself—I don't know if I've ever been that intoxicated by anything. He was like a drug for me." She enjoyed spending husband-and-wife time with him. But she also understood and accepted the demands of his career—though with Michael there rarely seemed to be a period of calm. Always some new issue had to be addressed. On June 20, 1995, his new album *HIStory: Past, Present, and Future, Book I* was released, amid controversy that the lyrics in the song "They Don't Care About Us" were anti-Semitic. Michael denied the charges without appearing to have given the lyrics much thought.

Before the public, Lisa appeared to take the constant media attention in stride, but the public glare could be blinding. Hovering over their marriage and Michael's career were still the child molestation charges. At Neverland, Lisa Marie also saw up close his fascination with children. In time, rumors circulated that Michael had settled other cases involving children. She said she never saw any inappropriate conduct.

When Michael and Lisa Marie were interviewed by Diane Sawyer for ABC's *Primetime* in 1995, Michael was asked about the Jordan Chandler accusations. They were "lies, lies, lies." But Michael did not discuss the monetary settlement of the case. "He's been barred to discuss it," said Lisa Marie. "The specific terms, *and* the specific amounts." Still, a consequence of his "lies, lies, lies" comment was that Evan Chandler sued Michael *again,* this time for $60 million for violating the confidentiality agreement of the settlement. He also charged that the anti-Semitic lyrics in "They Don't Care About Us" (which were later changed) had been aimed at Jordie and himself. The case was thrown out of court. Michael also told Sawyer: "I could never harm a child or anyone. It's not in my heart. It's not who I am and it's not what I'm even interested in." Lisa Marie appeared uneasy when Sawyer asked: "What's a thirty-six-year-old man doing sleeping with a twelve-year-old boy, or a series of them?" Yet she rushed to his defense. "Let me just say that I've seen these children. They don't let him go to the bathroom without running in there with him. They won't let him out of their sight. So when he jumps in the bed, I'm even out . . . you know? *They* jump in bed with *him*."

Still, despite her defense of Michael and despite the appearance of a lovey-dovey, happily-ever-after married couple, the marriage started to unravel in a very short time. "I loved taking care of him. It was one of the highest points in my life when things were going really well, and he and I were united. It was a very profound time of my life," Lisa Marie said. With Lisa Marie, he had no trouble discussing the usual Jackson tropes: the loss of his childhood, the abusive father, the loving mother. But otherwise he obviously had problems opening up. "If he didn't want you around, if you were going to make him confront something he didn't want to confront, he could make you go away," she said. "I think that was a train heading in a certain direction that no one could have stopped. I've had to really get my head around that in order to stop the pain."

Lisa Marie realized he couldn't completely share himself. In this respect, he was the polar opposite of Elizabeth, who readily shared with her husbands and friends and her children. Her declaration, though—*We told each other everything*—leaves open a question: Was he able to share more with Elizabeth, his idealized mother figure, than with the woman who became his wife?

A crisis occurred not long after the Diane Sawyer interview. "We were really on shaky ground," recalled Lisa Marie. He was also on drugs. She remembered the times she would pick him up from a doctor's office and Michael "would not be coherent." "I knew that that was, because of injections because they were painful and he would need certain things." Other problems fractured the marriage, especially his mysterious absences. "There would be periods of time where I had no idea where he was—only by the press. He would just disappear."

For about six weeks before the 1995 MTV Video Music Awards, she heard nothing from him. Then a month before the broadcast, she received calls from his people who stressed that it was important that she attend the ceremony.

She agreed but only if she did not have to walk the red carpet. That would be fine, she was told. But that evening, she was led down the carpet. "I was pissed," she said. "I just felt like I was being used." Told that Michael would sing to her onstage while she sat in the audience, her anger grew. She glared at him as he performed onstage. "I remember my whole look was: 'Don't you come anywhere fucking near me—we haven't spoken in a month.'" In the end, Michael did not come over to her. Later when they talked, he told her, "I saw the look on your face, and I knew that if I walked up to you, I didn't know what you were going to do to me."

Later, her anger flared up again when he gave an interview to *TV Guide* in which he had said that she told him her father had had a nose job. "He was quoting me," she said, "which was absolute bullshit. I think it justified something in his mind—they were asking him about his plastic surgery. I read that, and I threw it [the publication] across the kitchen."

It was also the drugs that led her to decide "to walk when I saw the drugs and the doctors walk in and they scared me and put me right back to what I went through with my father." Interestingly, during the marriage, Lisa Marie maintained a $2.6 million apartment in a gated community with patrol guards in Hidden Hills, about ninety miles from Neverland. Perhaps it was her place of refuge when Michael disappeared or when she needed some space.

The breaking point occurred in December 1995 when there was another crisis. While at a rehearsal for an HBO special in New York, Michael collapsed and was rushed to Beth Israel Medical Center. During a five-day stay, he suffered from dehydration, low blood pressure, exhaustion, and a virus. "I couldn't really get a straight answer as to what was happening," Lisa Marie later told Oprah Winfrey. But she believed he was on drugs. Visiting Michael at the hospital, Lisa Marie informed him that the marriage was over. "Once she makes up her mind, she doesn't look back," said a friend of hers. Yet oddly enough, the two later saw each other and sometimes spent time together. "I was still flying all over the world still with him," she later said. She recalled that the two of them "spent four more years after we'd divorced getting back together and breaking up and talking about getting back together and breaking up." But there would be no reconcilia-tion.

The press had a field day with the dissolution of the marriage. Why had it failed? What hope had there been in the first place? "Irreconcilable differences. Which means nothing and everything," said Lisa's lawyer John Coale. "They fell out of love. Anything she feels is going to remain private."

Michael appeared to have no second thoughts about her decision. Not long after leaving the hospital, he hopped on the Concorde to Paris, where he stayed at his usual haunt—the Sleeping Beauty suite at Euro Disney's Disneyland Hotel.

Not much was heard from Elizabeth, often confined to her Bel Air home. A second hip replacement operation occurred in 1995. The rehabilitation was especially hard on her. For a time, she walked with a cane. "Elizabeth spent almost two years attempting to recover from these operations, procedures that were supposed to improve the quality of her life," said Liz Smith. Her physicians eventually discovered that the second surgery had not gone well. One leg was shorter than the other. Advised to have a third operation to correct the problem, she refused to endure the physical agony again—that was, until her then-present agony left her no choice. With all the medical problems, she also saw her marriage to Larry Fortensky crumbling. On August 31, 1995, the *New York Post* ran a front-page story with the headline: "Splitsville For Liz: Taylor and 7th hubby separate." Taylor informed columnist Liz Smith that she and Fortensky were separating but hoped to work things out. That didn't happen; they later divorced. The month after the separation announcement, she entered St. John's Hospital in Santa Monica because of an irregular heartbeat. Then, in late September, as she hosted a barbecue at her home for family and friends—that included her son Christopher, several grandchildren, as well as writer Dominick Dunne, Mrs. Adnan Khashoggi, columnist Liz Smith, and others—she revealed that she would undergo the third hip operation in a few weeks. For the woman who had loved wearing spiked high heels, there was the realization ultimately that she would never walk again in the same way. .

Chapter 19

MICHAEL'S IMPATIENCE TO have children was thought to be a real problem for his marriage to Lisa Marie. She had not appeared to be in a rush. A story circulated that Michael, even before the marriage ended, had already found a solution to his fatherhood quest. That solution's name was Debbie Rowe. For a hopped-up media eager for any wild story possible about Wacko Jacko, the saga of Michael and Debbie Rowe soon proved perfect.

Friendly, feisty, bubbly, quick to use an expletive, Debbie Rowe was in some ways a child of Hollywood, at least psychologically. Born in 1958 in Spokane, Washington, she had been taken to live in Los Angeles by her mother after she and Debbie's father divorced. Her father, who once served in the air force, was said to have gone to work in the Middle East, and contrary to some reports that her family didn't have much money, other reports suggested that her father was financially quite comfortable. Graduating from Hollywood High School in 1977, Debbie was something of a good-natured rebel who was willing to break the rules to live as she saw fit.

People remembered the way she rode through town on her Harley-Davidson or in a truck. If people didn't like it or think it was ladylike, that was their problem. She raised eyebrows when she married a teacher from her high school in 1982. The couple moved to a condo in Van Nuys. In 1988, they separated and divorced. Afterward she worked as a nurse in the office of Michael's dermatologist, Arnold Klein.

Klein liked Debbie Rowe, who, in key respects, kept things moving in the office and was adept at dealing with patients. During a treatment at Klein's office in the early 1980s, Michael got a taste of Rowe's pleasantly blunt personality. "I go 'Hi,' " Rowe recalled of her initial meeting with Jackson. "And he goes 'Hi,' and I said, 'You know what? Nobody does what you do better, and nobody does what I do better. Let's get this over with.' " Contrary to what most might have assumed, Debbie Rowe fit a pattern of the kind of women Michael favored, if he was to have an important relationship with them. Like Diana Ross, Elizabeth, and Lisa Marie, she was strong and direct. Michael also liked protective women, which indeed Debbie was. She was also understanding of his vulnerabilities and eccentricities—and, of course, she wanted to save him.

As their friendship developed, Rowe and Michael had late-night phone calls with discussions about whatever interested them. Along with

Klein, Rowe traveled on various world tours with Michael. Often he seemed surprised that, as one of Rowe's friends said, she "used language like a trooper." "I had a very 'colorful' language, and every time I went to say something," said Rowe, "Michael would cut me off with words like 'shoot' and 'fudge.' He didn't think it was necessary when other words would do." But by now Michael was clearly accustomed to women with salty language.

During the breakup of his marriage to Lisa Marie, Debbie comforted him. "I was trying to console him, because he was really upset," Rowe recalled. Michael confessed his desire to have children. "He was upset because he really wanted to be a dad. I said, 'So be a dad.' He looked at me puzzled. That is when I looked at him and said, 'Let me do this. I want to do this. You have been so good to me. You are such a great friend. Please let me do this. You need to be a dad, and I want you to be.' "

At one point, he had told Lisa Marie—while they were still married—that if she would not have his child that Debbie Rowe would. Later Lisa Marie told Oprah Winfrey that she always believed that *that* was a retaliatory act by Michael.

Thereafter it was Rowe's mission to be the mother of his children. It became his mission to let her do so. "I believe there are people who should be parents," she said at that time, "and he's one of them. And he is such a fabulous man, and such a good friend, and he's always been there for me, always, from the day I met him."

Her first pregnancy ended in a miscarriage. During her next pregnancy, when she was six months pregnant, she left her one-bedroom, $840 a month apartment, deposited her dogs with a friend in Van Nuys, and boarded a fourteen-hour flight to Sydney, Australia, where Michael was on his *HIStory* tour. In Sydney, she was met at the airport and thereafter was promptly ensconced in the $2,750-a-night presidential suite at the Sheraton on the Park. An elated Michael confirmed they were expecting. Ten days later, on November 14, 1996, the two married.

His nurse makes amazing claim:
I'm having Jacko's baby
NEW YORK POST
NOVEMBER 3, 1996

What Friends Are For: Debbie Rowe may not be the love of Michael Jackson's peculiar life—but she's a good enough pal to bear his child and to marry him
PEOPLE
DECEMBER 2, 1996

On February 13, 1997, Debbie gave birth to Michael Joseph Jackson at Cedars-Sinai Medical

Center in Beverly Hills. The baby henceforth was called Prince, certainly not in honor of the pop star Prince—still not one of Michael's favorites—but of Michael's maternal grandfather. Debates will rage forever about the matter of conception, whether it was through artificial insemination or hot lovemaking. Michael and Rowe ignored the talk. By the end of the year, Debbie was pregnant again. On April 3, 1998, Rowe gave birth to a daughter, Paris-Michael Katherine. "Though the rumors are persistent," the *New York Post* reported, "Jackson and his wife deny they are making babies the artificial (insemination) way, and insist they enjoy passion and romance." Elizabeth was the godmother to the children, and though the media didn't cover her relationship with them, she clearly was happy for Michael. Her relationship with Debbie Rowe was another matter. Before Debbie's pregnancy, Michael had not introduced Elizabeth to her. His attitude apparently was that if Debbie wanted to meet Elizabeth, she couldgo do it on her own. Rowe told the story that she called Elizabeth's office and even left her address. In return, she received a signed photograph from Elizabeth, thanking her for being such a supportive fan. Rowe took it with humor. Still, the story indicated a basic fact: close as Elizabeth and Michael were, they also had very separate lives. Elizabeth had her own family, to whom she was close.

Following the birth of Paris, Rowe's days with Michael basically came to an end. They "never shared a home," she later said. "We never shared an apartment." Soon afterward the couple divorced. "I'm not into changing diapers," said Rowe as she relinquished custody of Prince and Paris to Michael. Later it was revealed that after she and Michael were divorced, she was permitted only brief visits with her children. Specifically, she was limited to seeing her children for eight hours every forty-five days. "The meetings were held in hotels, under the watchful eye of a stern, overprotective nanny who didn't want them to finger-paint because she feared they'd get dirty," reported the *New York Post*. "The environment was sterile. It wasn't a quality relationship," said Rowe at one point.

Questions about Michael's sexuality never went away. Stories ran rampant that not only was Rowe artificially inseminated but not even with Michael's semen. At one point former child star Mark Lester was assumed to be the children's father. Another day it was Arnold Klein.

In 1997, Elizabeth faced yet another threatening health crisis. When her lifelong migraines and blinding headaches became more frequent and more intense, she underwent tests that determined that she had a benign brain tumor. The surgery for its removal was scheduled. But Elizabeth had already committed to ABC for the broadcast of a celebrity-laden tribute of her sixty-fifth birthday, *Happy Birthday Elizabeth . . . A Celebration of Life*. The TV special would raise money for AIDS. "Elizabeth told me that her thoughts weren't very clear and it probably wouldn't be a good idea for her to do the celebration," said her friend Carole Bayer Sager. "I asked her to cancel. I told her now is the time to take care of herself." But whatever second thoughts she had, she decided to tape the television special first and enter the hospital the next day. Michael would be her escort at the event.

On February 16, the stars, the fans, the media were all on hand for one of the most glamorous and dramatically intense of Elizabeth and Michael's public appearances. Exiting a limousine, she was resplendent in a green gown, her hair dark and lustrous, her smile dazzling. With the focus on Elizabeth and with Michael serving mainly as her gallant escort, he looked wide-eyed and jubilant with excitement as if it were his first noncontroversial public appearance in, well, a lifetime. For those standing behind the barricades and for those with the cameras and mikes, it was yet another drama in the incredible life of Elizabeth Taylor. Inside the auditorium, such stars as Madonna, John Travolta, Shirley MacLaine, Cher, Carol Burnett, Dennis Hopper, Patti LaBelle, Drew Barrymore, Roseanne Barr,

Alec Baldwin, Kathy Bates, Hugh Grant, Arsenio Hall, and Paul Reiser all paid tribute. Michael performed a song he had written for Elizabeth, titled simply "Elizabeth I Love You." Film clips showed her in classic roles and at the height of her celebrated beauty.

Yet there was a silent, interior drama that evening, and it was all within Elizabeth. For a woman who preferred not to look back, past memories were inevitable. Her father, Francis, had died in 1968. Her mother, Sara, had also died, at age ninety-nine in 1994. Her close friend and publicist Chen Sam had died in 1996, the year before the televised special. Underneath the optimistic facade, most likely there was doubt and apprehension. Despite her physicians' assurances, she had absolutely no idea what lay ahead. Rarely did those watching her consider the realities she had to live with. Though composed and smiling, she may well have wanted the evening to end.

"I wasn't ready to face this latest thing," she later said.

"I haven't lived a quiet life. I've lived dangerously. Sometimes disaster has come at me like a train. There have been times when I've almost drunk myself to death. . . . Yet some instinct, some inner force, has always saved me, dragging me back just as the train whooshed past."

She also commented: "I sometimes give way to panic but not to despair. I never think of giving up. . . . I believe in life and I'll fight for it."

Most important, she said: "If the knife slips while I'm on that operating table tomorrow and I never wake up in this world again, I'll die knowing I've had an extraordinary life."

Elizabeth's brain surgery was a success. Within the pages of *Life*'s cover story on her, she posed with her head shaven and her eyes all the more magnetic. For a time, she kept her head shaven, then let her hair grow in almost completely white, similar to her father's. But her recuperation took time. Frightening dizzy spells occurred. Medica-tion had to be changed. Quiet as it was kept, she suffered a minor stroke. There was concern about her traveling, especially by air. If any one medical crisis permanently altered Elizabeth Taylor's life, it was the brain surgery. Frankly, her life would never be the same. Nor would Michael's.

Chapter 20

MICHAEL'S LIFE WAS soon to take an irreversible turn. Living extravagantly, he had spent wildly over the years—on antiques, on art objects, on hotel suites. His expenses were staggering. He struggled to hold on to Neverland and eventually took out a $23 million mortgage on the home. He also supported Katherine, and in essence, some of his siblings. But his bank accounts were drained, and with mounting debts, he faced possible financial ruin. A battery of lawyers and accountants struggled to keep his lifestyle afloat or at least to prevent collapse. He also would hire a new brigade of attorneys, advisers, and financial investors. Frank DiLeo had been fired in 1989. By 2003, John Branca would be gone. In 1995, he sold Sony a 50 percent stake in the ATV music catalog for $100 million. In 1998, the year of Paris's birth, he used his share of the catalog as collateral for a $140 million loan from Bank of America. But he continued to spend. In 1999, he paid $1.54 million for David O. Selznick's Oscar for Outstanding Production (now known as Best Picture) for *Gone With the Wind*—simply a trifle.

By 2000, his credit line at Bank of America was

up to $200 million. He was also in serious debt to Sony, which had advanced him large sums of money against future earnings of his albums. Though *HIStory* was commercially successful, by Michael's standards and those of Sony executives, it was not the success they had hoped for. In time, Michael—to clear the debt—would pay $4 million a month to Sony. In time, Bank of America sold Michael's loan to the Fortress Investment Group. With his creditors demanding money, he understood that they may also have had their eyes on his half of the ATV catalog, which was worth an estimated $1 billion.

Still, he often lived as if he didn't have a financial care in the world.

In early May 2000, Michael traveled with his children; their nanny, Grace Rwaramba; and others to Monaco for the World Music Awards. There Prince Albert presented him with the Male Artist of the Millennium Award. Afterward, he went to London, where he visited his friend, actor Mark Lester, giving rise to stories again that Lester might be the biological father of his children. He was also in London because of Elizabeth.

With her four children, Elizabeth had flown to England, where she was honored by the queen (one Elizabeth honoring another Elizabeth) at Buckingham Palace. Elizabeth had been named a

Dame Commander of the British Empire for "her services to acting and charity, recognizing her fundraising for AIDS research." "This is the greatest honor of my life," she said. "I didn't think I was eligible, as I've lived in America for such a long time, but I've always felt I've taken my Britishness with me." Other ceremonies followed. She was also honored by the British Film Institute with a BFI Fellowship at a dinner at the Dorchester, where she was staying. Two days later, on May 26, a musical tribute to her —called *Dame Elizabeth Taylor: A Musical Celebration*, with proceeds to go to AIDS research —was scheduled at Royal Albert Hall. The day before, Michael arrived at the Dorchester in a black van with blacked-out windows. Having heard that he'd be checking into the hotel, fans waited for hours outside the Dorchester to catch sight of him. At yet another of the big events in Elizabeth's life, he was her escort at the musical tribute. As the two sat in a first-tier box near the stage, every eye in the concert hall focused on them. Onstage, such stars as Tony Bennett, Charles Aznavour, Debbie Harry, and Andrea Bocelli performed. As the evening drew to a close, Joan Collins stood onstage and introduced Elizabeth. The crowd rose to its feet at Elizabeth's arrival. She spoke of the fight to continue to raise AIDS awareness. Then Michael walked onstage to present her with a lavish bouquet of white flowers. He did not perform. Instead, he hugged her and simply stood by her side on *her* night.

Afterward, Elizabeth and Michael returned to the Dorchester, where they spent time in the hotel's shopping gallery, doing what else but perusing the jewelry showcases. Then they retired to their separate suites. Around 2:00 a.m. Michael left the hotel to go to Harrods. The department store opened especially for him. There he shopped for presents for Elizabeth. Upon returning to the Dorchester, he threw several written messages from the balcony of his suite to the enthusiastic fans, still gathered outside the hotel. The messages read:

Make sure all fans read this. Let s [sic] have a tabloid burning.

I love you. I miss you all. Let s [sic] destroy all tabloid [sic]. I hate them.
Burn them.

Later that day, Michael left the Dorchester.

For Elizabeth, the festivities in London, especially her investiture by the queen, had indeed been glorious in the most personal sense. England remained her "old country." Yet the celebrations took a toll on her. Though in good spirits, she had looked heavier, puffy, fragile, and not entirely comfortable. In all likelihood, she also realized Michael was not well, either.

• • •

In March 2001, Michael returned to England, where he was set to speak at the University of Oxford. The engagement had been arranged by Michael's friend Rabbi Shmuley Boteach. Respected, lively, and knowledgeable, Boteach had previously served as a rabbi to Oxford's students. He had met Michael in the summer of 1999 through a mutual friend, the Israeli illusionist and psychic Uri Geller. Becoming friends with Boteach and his wife and family, he spent two Thanksgivings holidays with them at their home in New Jersey. The Boteach family had visited Michael at Neverland during the summer of 2000. In some respects, Boteach had become a spiritual adviser, helping Michael put his life back in order. Michael also wanted the rabbi to help him in his efforts to improve the lives of children. The two had long conversations. Most significant, Michael agreed to let Boteach tape him in an extensive series of discussions— covering a range of topics about the pop star's life and career. On the tapes, Michael often appeared genuine, earnest, perhaps a bit anxious to explain himself. Michael believed his love and concern for children was pure and innocent. The tapes might one day be used for a book. Obviously, he still sought to rehabilitate himself in the eyes of the public after the child molestation case. The speech at Oxford was part of those rehabilitation efforts.

A few weeks before he came to England, Michael had called Boteach, informing him that he had broken his foot while practicing a dance number. He was in pain. Upon arriving in England, Michael was accompanied by a physician as well as the adult Frank Cascio, who was now managing some of Michael's affairs and was known as Frank Tyson. Michael was on crutches, and his foot was in a cast.

At Oxford, Michael, despite the injury, gave a very moving talk about love between parents and children—and the power of forgiving one another. He spoke of his own father, and the time when he realized he must forgive Joe for past behavior. Most touchingly, he remembered the occasion when—at a little carnival—Joe had lifted him and put him on a pony. For Michael it was an expression of his father's love, a time when his father was gentle and caring with him. It was an impassioned speech, actually written by Boteach, that ended with the audience giving Michael a standing ovation.

In line with the message of the Oxford speech, shortly before Michael spoke, Boteach had urged Michael to call his father and say that he loved him. Using his cell phone, Michael reached Joe in Las Vegas and indeed did precisely that.

During the Oxford visit, Boteach became concerned about Michael's well-being. Boteach noticed that Michael and his physician "would go together into his [Michael's] room and emerge, about a half-hour later, with Michael looking glassy-eyed."

The day following the speech, Michael—still in England—was best man at Uri Geller's wedding, at which Rabbi Boteach officiated. Michael had arrived three hours late for the wedding. Otherwise, all seemed fine. But later, when Boteach was about to take his flight back to the States, he received a call from Michael, who was slurring his words. Boteach felt he was on something very strong. Thinking about other incidents, he recalled that Michael often had injuries, often complained of pain and seemed in need of medication. Sometimes he was woozy. On one occasion, his head drooped while at the home of a friend of Boteach's. Because Michael often seemed spacey, the idea that some of this behavior was the result of possible medication or drugs had been ignored. In the months to come, Boteach observed Michael more closely, and he believed indeed that the superstar was on drugs. His conclusion was no different from Lisa Marie Presley's. Nor was it different from Elizabeth's observations when she had persuaded Michael to go into rehab. In all likelihood, Elizabeth detected Michael's possible drug usage again when at the tribute to her in London in May.

Katherine and Joe expressed their concern, too, when they invited Boteach to their Encino home to discuss Michael's drug problem.

Still the consummate showman with a maddening desire now to revitalize his career and reline his dwindling coffers, he pulled together a major event: a two-part thirtieth-anniversary concert at New York's Madison Square Garden, to be produced by his friend David Gest, set for September 7 and September 10, 2001, and scheduled to air later on CBS. It was also a way to promote his first—and long delayed—album in seven years, *Invincible*, due to be released on October 30. But before the actual concerts, behind-the-scenes problems flared up. Joe and Katherine again pushed for his brothers to be part of the celebration, but that wasn't the only hassle for Michael. Set to address the audience, at Michael's request, was his friend Marlon Brando, who reportedly asked for $1 million to be present. Though Michael had asked Elizabeth to be his date, she declined. There didn't seem to be any way to convince her to appear.

But Michael was determined to persuade her to come. Said Cascio: "He never had to buy Elizabeth's friendship or lobby for her presence at public events but when the spirit didn't move her, Michael had a little trick up his sleeve, and it wasn't rocket science. All it took was . . . you guessed it . . . diamonds. When Michael wanted Elizabeth to join him for an award show, or in this case, his thirtieth anniversary special, she was there for him contingent upon receipt of a diamond."

What Cascio probably did not realize, nor even did Michael, was that she was in such poor health that it was ever harder to make public appearances. Since her trip to London for her investiture as a Dame Commander, she remained weak and fragile. In June, she had flown to Philadelphia to accept the Marian Anderson Award—named after the great African American contralto who had broken down racial barriers from the 1930s through the 1950s—for her work with AIDS. But now a flight from Los Angeles to New York would be difficult for her.

Nonetheless, Michael picked out a $200,000 necklace from the jeweler David Orgell in Los Angeles. She agreed to come. "I absolutely love the necklace, Michael. And of course I will come to your show," she told him. The jeweler also provided Michael with a diamond watch— valued at almost $2 million—to wear on the show. Both Taylor and Brando no doubt also assumed the tab for their "expenses" would be paid by Michael's record company.

In many respects, the concerts went off without a hitch. Among the performers and presenters were Whitney Houston; Beyoncé with the group Destiny's Child; Justin Timberlake with the boy band *NSYNC; Liza Minnelli; Britney Spears; James Ingram; Gloria Estefan; Marc Anthony;

Chris Tucker; Slash; Usher; and Samuel L. Jackson. Also on the bill were Michael's brothers. In the audience, so the press release boasted, were "50 Legendary Ladies of the Silver Screen" that included Janet Leigh, Esther Williams, Debbie Reynolds, Margaret O'Brien, and Ann Miller.

But before the first evening of the concert, Michael's drug problems nearly wrecked the show. Still in pain and heavily medicating himself, he may have fallen victim to a severe case of nerves just before the concert. At his hotel earlier in the day, Michael had locked himself in the bedroom of his suite. Now working as an assistant for Michael since 1990, the adult Frank Cascio broke in. He saw Michael lying in bed. "All at once I knew what had happened," Cascio recalled, "and just like that, my naïve belief that Michael wouldn't let his medicine interfere with the show blew up in my face. I can't begin to describe my feeling of disappointment and panic."

Cascio asked if one of Michael's physicians had been there. "In a very slow voice, he said, 'Yeah, Frank. I was in so much pain. I couldn't do it.' "

Cascio said that never in the past had Michael taken medication before a performance. Was this a sign of future problems, perhaps even an emotional collapse? To revive Michael, Cascio got him to drink Gatorade and to take vitamin C pills. Finally, he was about ready to appear before the public.

Once Michael had his hair and makeup done, he rode with Elizabeth to Madison Square Garden. As the two exited the limousine, once again it was pandemonium with fans screaming and crying while photographers snapped pictures and cameras recorded their arrival. Though she sometimes appeared to have trouble walking, a blond Elizabeth, looking rested and slimmer, exuded the glamour she knew Michael thrived on. Michael cut a splashy figure, decked out in a silver-sequined jacket. Yet at times he looked disoriented.

But other problems arose. Wearing a dark suit and dark wraparound glasses, Brando opened the show, referring to himself as a "fat fuck," then proceeded with a rambling, windy speech about humanitarianism, which led to boos from the audience. Britney Spears was reportedly in a panic about performing "The Way You Make Me Feel" with Michael, who had to reassure her that she would be fine. Whitney Houston, skeletal and drawn, led many to believe she was on drugs, which indeed she was; already there were murmurs she was headed for a bad end.

Onstage Michael performed as brilliantly as ever, without any sign of his earlier distress and disorientation. Once again, his rendition of "Billie Jean" stole the show. The second concert on September 10 went even better.

But the next day—September 11, when two

planes crashed into New York's World Trade Center—was terrifying. At the hotel, everyone was in a panic. All the bridges and tunnels into and out of the city were closed. Everyone feared America was under an ongoing terrorist attack. A story made the rounds that Michael gathered Elizabeth and Brando and managed to get them temporarily to New Jersey. Then the three took to the road—in a car they themselves drove! Along the way, Brando was said to have wanted to stop at every McDonald's and Burger King that he saw. Such stops did not sit well with Elizabeth and Michael. It was a funny story—a warm fantasy about three of the greatest pop icons of the twentieth century off on a road trip through America. Of course, it wasn't true. But in other respects, the fantasy trivialized the fears and sadness Elizabeth and Michael experienced in the aftermath of September 11.

Debbie Reynolds recalled the events before and immediately following the destruction of the World Trade Center. When Michael's anniversary concert had first been announced, Reynolds, then in Los Angeles, contacted Elizabeth's assistant Tim Mendelson to request a single ticket for herself. Seeing Elizabeth's arrival at the concert that night, Reynolds had waved to her. Afterward, having loved the show and as dazzled as ever by Michael's talents as well as those of the other performers, she returned to her midtown hotel.

There Reynolds later learned of the terrorist plane crashes. A call came to her from Mendelson. Aware that Reynolds was in New York by herself, Elizabeth—ensconced in a huge suite at the Hotel Pierre—invited Reynolds to be a guest in her suite, rather than stay alone at her own hotel. Elizabeth's children, who had also attended the concert, left the city before the tragedy struck. So there was plenty of room for Reynolds. Also staying in the suite were Mendelson and Elizabeth's hair stylist and friend José Eber as well as Elizabeth's masseur and his young daughter. Because Elizabeth was experiencing severe back pain, her physician was tending to her in the suite.

Reynolds recalled that Elizabeth was crying, saddened and shocked by the events as well as the mayhem. Everyone sat watching the television for information on exactly what was happening. There were reports of people jumping from the Twin Towers in desperation. They also were aware of the plane crashes at the Pentagon and on a field in Pennsylvania. Debbie was fearful of what the future might hold. It was a gathering of a stunned group. "Her French butler took very good care of us as we watched the TV in disbelief, all of us sitting and crying together. When it became too much, we'd go to our rooms and try to rest," Reynolds recalled. There was nothing frivolous or fantastical about the time they spent together. Reynolds also informed Elizabeth that she was scheduled soon to appear at a sold-out performance outside San Diego. But there was no way she could get out of New York. To Reynolds's surprise, Elizabeth told her she would call John—to see what could be done. John? Yes, it was Elizabeth's former husband Senator John Warner. Arrangements were made for them to go to Teterboro Airport in New Jersey where a private plane carried them all back to the West Coast. It was a solemn journey. "As we flew over the crash site we saw the heartbreaking devastation below us," Reynolds recalled.

Michael, his children, and their nanny Grace did indeed go to New Jersey. Through connections with the police department, Frank Cascio was able to secure permission to leave the city by the George Washington Bridge. They headed to his family's home in New Jersey. As in earlier years, Michael once again found comfort with the Cascios. Later, Michael helped organize a special benefit concert for the victims of the September 11 attacks. Called *United We Stand: What More Can I Give* was held on October 21, 2001, at RFK Stadium in Washington, DC. Michael performed along with such stars as Mariah Carey, Al Green, Destiny's Child, Jennifer Lopez, *NSYNC, P. Diddy, Train, James Brown, Usher, Bette Midler, and the Backstreet Boys. Several days later, an edited version of the concert aired on ABC. But there was no mention of Jackson's name. For his thirtieth anniversary show, he had signed a contract with CBS that prohibited him from appearing under his name in any other program at the time. Thus neither his rendition of "Man in the Mirror" nor of "What More Can I Give" (which he had written) was broadcast. Instead, he was only seen singing with other performers.

Michael had yet worse financial/legal problems, one of which led to a misunderstanding with Elizabeth that he feared might damage their friendship. The $2 million watch that jeweler David Orgell in Los Angeles had *lent* Michael for the performance at the anniversary concert had not been returned. Nor had Orgell been paid for the necklace that Michael had given Elizabeth. When a lawsuit was threatened, Cascio said that Michael decided to return everything. That included Elizabeth's necklace. A call was made to Taylor by one of Michael's lawyers, asking for the necklace. Apparently, Taylor was enraged, not so much by the request for the return of the necklace, which she had indeed assumed was a gift, but that she was treated in such an impersonal way by one of Michael's attorneys. Cascio said that "it bothered her that Michael hadn't made the call himself." She had the necklace returned, but she wouldn't speak to Michael for months, said Cascio. This clearly distressed him. Later he wrote her an apology and asked to be forgiven. He blamed his handlers for the mix-up. In time, Elizabeth forgave him.

On February 9, Elizabeth and Michael drew crowds when they appeared at a joint fund raiser sponsored by the Laguna Art Museum and the AIDS Services Foundation Orange County. The event was "Art for AIDS, a Tribute to Rock Hudson." Cochair of the event was dermatologist Arnold Klein. The first part of the evening was a $2,500-per-plate sit-down dinner in the art-filled home of Barbara Alexander Stiles and Thomas B. Stiles II. As with such other evenings, guests were fraught with anticipation—at the prospect of seeing Elizabeth and Michael. Everyone patiently waited—and *waited*—for the two to arrive. Once they *finally* entered the home and mingled with guests, Taylor's friend Merv Griffin quipped: "Elizabeth, the party was *last* night."

Shortly after the dinner, the crowd headed to the museum for a sold-out auction attended by hundreds. Praising her friend Rock Hudson, Elizabeth vowed: "I, for one, will never stop my personal fight against AIDS, and I ask the same of you." The event raised $200,000. But otherwise it didn't look like a good night for either Taylor or Jackson. Both appeared as if it had been an effort to pull themselves together. Dressed in a dark, military-style jacket and wearing a not very becoming hairpiece, Jackson looked wan, glassy-eyed, a bit disoriented. With her blond hair spiked to the max and with an overload of her famous jewels, Taylor looked pale and puffy. As so often was the case, she was putting up a brave front. Her chronic pain had become more intense.

On February 21, 2002, Michael became a father for the third time with the birth of his son Prince Michael Jackson II, called Blanket because it meant covering someone with great love. Again the question was raised about his child's biological parents. For most it was a total mystery. The mother's identity was never revealed. For others, Michael's friend Miko Brando might be the father. About the only story that appeared certain was that immediately after Blanket's birth, Michael wrapped the child, held him in his arms, and departed the hospital. Most likely the mother had been paid for her time and effort. Everything had been carried out with a secrecy worthy of Howard Hughes.

A little more than a month later—on March 16—Elizabeth and Michael made one of their last public appearances and one of their most discussed. Liza Minnelli was marrying Michael's childhood friend, producer David Gest, at the Marble Collegiate Church in downtown New York. Elizabeth agreed to be one of Liza's matrons of honor, while Michael was to be David's co-best man along with his brother Tito. The whole star-filled event, extravagantly stage-managed by Gest, looked like an attempt to recapture the glamour of Hollywood past. Among the guests: Lauren Bacall, Mickey Rooney, Kirk Douglas, Joan Collins, Gina Lollobrigida, Mia Farrow, Lee Grant, Martha Stewart, Natalie Cole, Robert Wagner and his wife Jill St. John, Turner Classic Movies host Robert Osborne, columnists Liz Smith and Cindy Adams, along with about 842 close friends of Liza and David. Also present was Diana Ross. But the actual exchange of vows was over an *hour* behind schedule, not because of jitters of the bride- and groom-to-be but because of—one can imagine—Elizabeth.

"No surprise there," recalled Robert Wagner, who had known her for years and once, as he said, had a "fling" with her. "Elizabeth was always—and I do mean *always* late." Delayed leaving her hotel to get to the ceremony, she discovered, upon her arrival at the church, that she was wearing slippers, not her shoes. Someone had to rush back to her hotel to pick up the shoes. Meanwhile, guests were getting antsy.

"Unless she really, really liked you, Elizabeth was always late," Wagner recalled. "And sometimes she was incredibly late even if she did like you." Once Elizabeth's assistant returned with the shoes, everyone assumed the proceedings would begin. But still there was no Elizabeth.

Where was she?

Finally, David Gest asked Michael to find her and see what the hold-up was. But then guests were left waiting for Elizabeth *and* Michael. Recalled Wagner: "Because I knew Elizabeth so well, I was finally deputized to get Michael away from her so the wedding could proceed."

Walking past the bodyguard stationed outside the room where the two were ensconced, Wagner caught the sight of them during one of their rare moments of real privacy. "Elizabeth was sitting there, gazing at Michael. Michael was on his knees, gazing at Elizabeth. He was holding her hand. Nothing was being said. He was besotted with her; he was drinking her in."

When Wagner told Michael that the wedding had to start, Michael seemed still too transfixed by Elizabeth to fully comprehend what Wagner said. "I want to be with Elizabeth," Michael said. "I *love* Elizabeth."

Said Wagner: "Talking to Michael when he was in one of his reveries was exactly like talking to a six-year-old waiting up for Santa Claus. You didn't want to disabuse him of his fantasy, but you had to firmly lead him away from the Christmas tree so that the presents could be put out."

Finally, the two came out of the room. But there was another delay, though minor, when Elizabeth walked on the wrong side of the church and then had to walk around to the correct side. "Since Elizabeth was fairly immobile and walked with difficulty—part of it was her back, part of it was the medication for her back, which always gave her a buzz—she had to be helped onto the altar," recalled Wagner.

For many that day, it must have been sad to see her. She was heavy, looked pasty, and wore a small black hat with a rather strange black veil on it, looking like a relic from the 1940s. Michael also appeared waxy and again glassy-eyed. Neither seemed to be in the room. They had the appearance of being far, far away. Both also were in physical pain. Afterward, at the reception, Andy Williams and Gloria Gaynor sang. A toast was proposed by Michael to the couple. But Elizabeth had left.

Liza and David separated about a year and a half later. The real stars of the wedding had been Elizabeth and Michael. No one had been able *not* to gaze at the two. Recalling the delays, the shoes, the whole bizarre event, Lee Grant remembered looking over at Elizabeth at one point. "She and Michael were whispering to each other. They broke the mold, folks."

But for Elizabeth and Michael, their fun-filled days at the racetrack, at the big benefits, at the receptions, at the awards shows, had really now come to an end. Trouble lay ahead for both of them.

Chapter 21

FOR MICHAEL, PROFESSIONAL headaches and disappointments consumed him.

He drew criticism and mockery for his public outings with his children, who wore masks to hide their faces, their very identity. What few understood was that he wanted the children to have freedom from the burden of his fame. When not with him, the children and their nanny, Grace, did the typical things kids would do: go to stores, playgrounds, events, *without* masks. Generally, no one even knew who they were on those occasions. A public outcry—or perhaps more of a media one—shot up when Michael, showing his child Blanket to adoring fans, held the boy over a balcony in his hotel in Berlin. In his public appearances, Michael often looked more dis-oriented than ever.

His paranoia grew. Apparently, so did his use of drugs. Writer Stacy Brown recalled having been invited to Neverland with his family in 1997. Though they stayed there four days, not once did they see Michael. "But I'm sure he saw us," said Brown. Guests at Neverland, according to Brown, had to sign waivers. In the end, Michael was free "to eavesdrop on telephone calls, video tape comings and goings, and spy on those on the grounds." Even Elizabeth was said to have once stayed for three weeks at Neverland without seeing much of him. They had dinner only once.

His family attempted a drug intervention "no less than a half-dozen times." "Three months after the 2001 concerts, at a hotel in New York, Janet, Randy and others attempted to rid him of dependence," said writer Brown. "Leave me alone, mind your business," Jackson reportedly told them. "I'll be dead in one year anyway." Said Brown: "Michael had cut them off, one by one. He preferred to stay locked inside his rooms, watching the world through cameras."

The disappointing sales of *Invincible* cemented the general worry that his glory days had ended and were a thing of the past. Those low sales also led to a public clash with Sony executive Tommy Mottola, whom Michael referred to as "the devil." Michael felt strongly that Mottola had failed to do enough to push his album *Invincible*, despite the fact that Sony had spent an estimated $25 million in promotion. Michael lambasted Mottola when he spoke in Harlem at Reverend Al Sharpton's National Action Network, a coalition that had been formed by Sharpton and Michael's former attorney Johnnie Cochran. The coalition sought "to investigate whether artists are being financially exploited by record labels," *Billboard* reported. "Michael Jackson, already feuding with his record company, charged Saturday that the recording industry was a racist conspiracy that turns profits at the expense of performers—particularly minority artists. 'The recording companies really, really do conspire against the artists—they steal, they cheat, they do everything they can,' Jackson said in a rare public appearance."

Billboard also commented: "Jackson, who records for Sony Music Entertainment's Epic label, also singled out company chairman Tommy Mottola, saying he was 'mean, he's a racist, and he's very, very, very devilish.' " The publication added: "Jackson also accused Mottola of using 'the n-word' when speaking about an unidentified black Sony artist."

This type of public feud was something Michael had always avoided in the past.

He also now believed that the media's criticism of him grew out of its racism. He told his friend Shmuley Boteach that the white press didn't like the fact that white girls the world over screamed and cried in adoration of him, shouting out: "I am in love with you." "That's what has made it hard for me, because I was the pioneer and that's why they started the stories. 'He's weird.' 'He's gay' . . . anything that turns people against me. They tried their hardest. And anybody else would be dead as a junkie right now, who's been through what I've been through."

Still seeking to rectify his image, to reveal to the public that he was not Wacko Jacko, Michael granted an extended interview to British journalist Martin Bashir for a TV quasi-documentary *Living with Michael Jackson*. No doubt for Michael, part of the appeal of the interview was that Bashir had conducted a widely seen interview with Princess Diana. That alone perhaps validated Bashir's credentials as a serious journalist. Over a period of eight months, cameras and Bashir followed Michael on his shopping trips with his masked children, on his spending sprees in Las Vegas. The cameras also trailed him to Berlin and later Miami. But of most interest was his life at Neverland. Seen with Michael were a thirteen-year-old cancer victim Gavin Arvizo and his younger brother, both of whom had been guests at Neverland. So was their mother. During the interview, Michael held Gavin's hand, and Gavin put his head on the singer's shoulder. When Bashir, who must have realized that he had hit a jackpot in "exposing" the King of Pop, questioned Michael's comment that the child slept in his bed at Neverland, Michael replied with a naïveté and innocence that might have been touching had it not led to such serious repercussions. "Why can't you share your bed? The most loving thing to do is share your bed with someone," he said. "When you say 'bed,' you're thinking sexual. They make that sexual. It's not sexual. We're going to sleep." Overlooked was the fact that Michael stated that while Gavin and his brother slept in the bed, Michael himself slept on the floor. Michael also said that at other times other children such as child star Macaulay Culkin, Macaulay's younger brother Kieran, and his sisters had also slept in his bed. He refused to see how anyone might view it as anything other than innocent.

Shortly after *Living with Michael Jackson* aired in the United Kingdom on February 3, 2003, then in the United States on February 6, 2003, Jackson was engulfed in an uproar that seemed to bewilder him. His appearance with Gavin Arvizo coupled with some of his comments confirmed for some that he was "overly fond of young boys." When Lisa Marie watched the program, she cringed. "I had the same reaction everybody else had—it was like watching a train wreck. It seemed like it was overly cruel—the guy [Bashir] had his agenda and was after him," she recalled. "It honestly looked to me like, it would be like somebody walking into a convalescent home and just antagonizing someone and having it on film the whole time." She also believed Michael was again on drugs. "I didn't see the Michael that I knew in that Martin Bashir interview. He was high as a kite, from what I saw and from what I knew."

But now the child molestation claims that had

dogged him resurfaced. Because Jackson shrewdly had his own camera crew filming at the same time as Bashir's, Michael used his footage—*The Michael Jackson Interview: The Footage You Were Never Meant to See*—as a rebuttal to Bashir's interview. Frank Cascio believed that in the larger context, the unedited tapes revealed "how opportunistic Bashir had been, editing the material in the most sensationalist way imaginable." But such damage control did not help the situation in which Michael found himself.

On February 20, the mother of Gavin Arvizo was interviewed by the Sensitive Case Unit of the Los Angeles Department of Children and Family Services. She was suspected of neglect. At that time, she stated—the entire family did, in fact—that there had been no inappropriate contact between Michael and her son. *That* comment, however, later changed. Nonetheless, the children made other trips to Neverland, as did their mother. At one point, the mother spoke to an attorney about Bashir. She said she'd never given permission for her children to be on the show. But somehow the focus shifted to Michael Jackson. It was then, despite the mother's earlier protesta-tions, that charges of child molestation began. She also consulted the same attorney who had obtained the settlement in the Chandler case.

In June 2003, a criminal investigation began. In November 2003, a search warrant was issued for the Neverland ranch. Seventy investigators were on the scene. A warrant was also issued for Michael's arrest. On November 20, Michael flew from Las Vegas—where he was shooting a music video for a song from his new album, *Number Ones*, a compilation of his greatest hits— to Santa Barbara, where he surrendered to police. Handcuffed, booked, and charged with child molestation, he posted a $3 million bail.

In December, there was reported to be much discussion and dissension within Michael's staff about the security force provided for the singer by the Nation of Islam. "Officials from the Nation of Islam, a separatist African-American Muslim group," reported the *New York Times* on December 30, 2003, "have moved in with Michael Jackson and are asserting control over the singer's business affairs, friends, employees, and business associates of Mr. Jackson said." The paper also reported that while members of the organization had been invited to Neverland to provide security some weeks earlier, those members were "now restricting access to him and have begun making decisions for him related to the news media, his business affairs and even his legal strategy." Such claims were denied by Michael's lawyer (in the child molestation case) Mark Geragos as well as by *The Final Call*, the Nation of Islam's newspaper. But the *New York Times* reported that one senior

Jackson employee, who spoke on condition of anonymity, said emphatically: "The Nation of Islam and Louis Farrakhan's son-in-law [Leonard Muhammad] have taken over completely and are in full and total charge."

Mark Geragos informed the *New York Times* that some members of the security force were Muslim but that that didn't mean they were members of the Nation of Islam. Still, two of Michael's top business partners stated they had been unable to reach him for the past two weeks.

It was also reported that Geragos and Leonard Muhammad had negotiated an interview that Michael had just given to television's *60 Minutes*. Interestingly enough, the *New York Times* reported: "Mr. Jackson was introduced to the Nation of Islam through his nanny, Grace Rwarmba [sic], who is a member of the group, and through Mr. Jackson's brother Jermaine, several people close to Mr. Jackson said."

Controversies continued to swirl around Michael. In time, Mark Geragos left his defense team.

In January 2004, Michael was arraigned in court at Santa Maria. Late for the arraignment, he was chastised by the judge. But he was also out of it. With hundreds of fans looking on, he danced to his music atop his SUV, which of course drew media attention. "It was more apparent than ever that Michael had become delusional," recalled his publicist Bob Jones. "He seemed to think the 2,000 or so fans and hordes of media in attendance at the arraignment were gathered for a concert rather than a criminal proceeding. The entire day was nothing short of a circus." In April 2004, Santa Barbara District Attorney Thomas Sneddon convened a grand jury, which indicted Jackson. For millions around the world reading about the case or watching reports on the evening news or reading accounts online, it seemed a shocking replay of the Chandler accusations. Even ardent Jackson supporters asked had he not learned anything—about appearances, if nothing else. In January 2005, the case went to trial. Michael was charged on fourteen counts: four charges of child molestation; one charge of attempted child molestation; one conspiracy charge; eight possible charges of providing minors with alcohol.

Forming a united front in his defense, showing up daily in the courtroom, were members of the Jackson family, including La Toya, now back in the family fold. One day his sisters displayed a dazzling dash of show biz in the courtroom: each was dressed in white. But the entire family looked genuinely distressed, especially Katherine. Michael himself—sometimes late for court, another time wearing pajama bottoms when he arrived—often appeared disoriented. But daily he sat through the proceedings.

The trial drew worldwide media attention. Michael's legal team had undergone a change. In the end, Tom Mesereau led the defense of Michael. Michael's brother Randy took an active role in the defense too. Reporters, photographers, and videographers packed the area, although no cameras were permitted inside the courtroom. As it turned out, the trial was a show unto itself.

Not attending the trial and seemingly silent— in comparison with her vigorous defense of Michael in the Chandler case—was Elizabeth. Nor was much heard from Lisa Marie, who later said that at the time she still felt distanced from Michael. Yet she remained convinced that Michael had been misled by Bashir during the interview. Some questioned Elizabeth's silence. But the truth was that she was now greatly incapacitated. In 2002, she had undergone radiation therapy for basal cell carcinoma. Two years later she underwent spinal surgery to repair seven compression fractures. Suffering from osteoporosis, she was also diagnosed with congestive heart failure in 2004. The pain now was crippling. Much time was spent in bed—with her dog Sugar nearby. Her great solace were her children and grandchildren.

Many of the prosecution's efforts seemed to backfire. Actor Macaulay Culkin, Brett Barnes, and Wade Robson were cited by the prosecution as having been molested by Jackson in the past.

There were witnesses who were set to attest to the molestations of the three. But all three appeared in court and testified that they had slept in Jackson's bed but he had never molested them. Nor had he done anything sexual to them.[*]

Called to testify by the prosecution was the mother of Jordan Chandler, who stated that Jackson and Jordan had slept in the same room on various occasions. But she denied ever having seen any molestation. She also testified that though she was listed as plaintiff and received settlement money in the first molestation case, she herself had not sued Jackson; instead, it was her former husband and her son. She also stated that she had not seen her son, Jordan, since 1994.

The prosecution called Debbie Rowe, assuming she would testify "that a videotaped statement in early 2003 supporting Mr. Jackson had been enticed from her and that her answers to questions then had been heavily scripted to favor him." At the time of the trial, she was seeking to have her custody rights over her children, which she had relinquished in 2001, reinstated. Most were convinced that perhaps she would put a nail in Michael's coffin. But Rowe testified "that she had refused to even look at the questions in advance of the taping and that she had been eager to give

---

[*]In 2013, Wade Robson filed a lawsuit saying he had been molested. In May 2015, the lawsuit was dismissed in court.

answers largely supportive of Jackson." She also stated that three of Jackson's business and public relations associates were "liars and thieves who worked together to exploit his fame and steal his money." When asked to describe Michael, reported the *New York Times*, Debbie "looked affectionately at her former husband . . . and began to cry" as she said: "There's two Michaels: there's like my Michael. And then Michael that everyone else sees. Michael the entertainer." Also reported: "Mr. Jackson at that moment dabbed at his own eyes with a tissue." In the end, many in the courtroom felt her testimony was "highly favorable to the defense." She helped save Michael.

The testimony from the prosecution witnesses was sometimes ludicrous, and some of the facts about the Arvizo family threw the entire case into question. The mother's checkered past was revealed. In August 1998, the family had been accused of shoplifting at a JCPenney store in West Covina, California. She sued JCPenney saying she had been roughed up—"viciously beaten"—by the store's security officers. Two years later she accused a male officer of sexually fondling her breasts and pelvis area for "up to seven minutes." JCPenney had settled the case out of court for the amount of $152,000. Throughout the mother's testimony, she sounded confused and erratic, and jurors were not pleased when she snapped her fingers at them. The paper quoted one female juror: "I disliked it intensely when she snapped her fingers at us. I thought, 'Don't snap your fingers at me, lady.'"

"Their mother, a difficult witness for the prosecution," reported the *New York Times*, "testified that Mr. Jackson had held the family captive and that he had forced them to make a video testimonial to rebut a documentary in which he had acknowledged sleeping with young boys. The mother appeared to lose the jury with her rambling, incoherent and at times combative testimony. She argued with Mr. Jackson's lawyer and delivered lectures to the jury, even as she wove a tale of mistreatment at the hands of Mr. Jackson's minions."

The defense put actor Chris Tucker, a friend of Michael's, on the stand to testify that he had known the Arvizo family, and that in essence, the Arvizo family had tried to hustle him for money.

But most confounding was the fact that, according to testimony of the Arvizo boy, there had been no molestation *before* the time of the Bashir broadcast. Commented the *New York Times*: "The timeline of the accusations, for example, was problematic, because the molesting was said to have taken place after the broadcast of the documentary, when the world's attention was focused on Mr. Jackson and the boy." Why would

Michael Jackson, once he was suspected of having molested a child who he previously had *not* molested, suddenly begin molesting him? None of it made sense.

Later, in November of 2005, defense attorney Thomas Mesereau spoke to an audience at Harvard Law School. Mesereau stated that at the time of the trial, he heard "the prosecutors tried to get [Jordan Chandler] to show up, and he wouldn't. If he had, I had witnesses who were going to come in and say he told them it [Michael's reported molestation of him] never happened and that he would never talk to his parents again for what they made him say. It turned out he'd gone into court and got legal emancipation from his parents." In 2009, Jordan Chandler's father, Evan Chandler, would commit suicide with a self-inflicted gunshot wound to his head.

In the end, some of the trial seemed a travesty. And in the end, Michael Jackson was found innocent of all fourteen of the initial charges. After a two-year investigation and a six-month trial, the jury unanimously acquitted Michael on June 13, 2005. His family was jubilant. Michael himself was relieved. But the ordeal had drained him. Bruised and battered by the accusations and the trial, he became, if anything, less trusting and more paranoid. Michael would never again be the same person. He was a broken man. Six days later—on June 19th—Michael left the United States with his children by private jet. Ten days later he arrived on the remote island of Bahrain in the Persian Gulf, the guest of Sheikh Abdullah bin Hamad bin Isa Al Khalifa, the wealthy second son of the king of Bahrain. Originally a friend of Jermaine, the sheikh had musical aspirations with hopes that Michael might be of help. With Michael, he made plans to form a music company called Two Seas Records. In Bahrain, the sheikh wined and dined Michael in sumptuous high style. A palatial home was provided for Jackson and his family. Land was provided for Michael to build an even more lavish home. A Bentley, a Maybach, and a Rolls-Royce were also available for the singer. But professional ties were soon broken. "Michael abruptly abandoned Bahrain—and his royal partner's plans for a record company after signing a contract promising half of everything he [Michael] created going forward," reported Zack O'Malley Greenburg. With his children and their nanny, he departed for London, and later Ireland where he stayed for the next six months. In Ireland, he collaborated on new music with will.i.am of the group the Black Eyed Peas. But the sheikh had no intention of letting the matter just pass. He took legal action against Michael. "When Jackson's erstwhile business partner later sued," said Greenburg, "the singer claimed he had no idea that [half of everything he created going forward] was part of the deal but subsequently settled for more than $5 million." Obviously, it was money the singer did not have. Dejected and dispirited, Michael decided to return to the States—where other lawsuits and legal entanglements awaited him. But he had no choice. Finding himself in a precarious financial position, one that he could no longer deny, he had to pull things back together and also somehow work his way through his mountains of debts—for the future of his children as well as himself. He also hoped to perform at one of the big hotels in Las Vegas.

Chapter 22

ON DECEMBER 22, 2006, Michael Jackson returned by private jet to the United States. His plane touched down at McCarran International Airport in Las Vegas late in the evening. With him were his three children; their nanny, Grace; and an assistant. Waiting to take the passengers to a home where they would reside was bodyguard Bill Whitfield. Having been recently hired by an associate, Whitfield had not been told who his new client at the Las Vegas airport would be. He was surprised when he realized the slender man dressed in black who had gotten off the plane was indeed Jackson. Nor did Jackson know Whitfield, who was part of a motorcade of four Cadillac Escalades. But according to Whitfield, it "was not the same Michael Jackson who'd left the country the year before. There was no entourage nor a security team that night because there was *nobody,* period. He was all alone." All the passengers were driven by Whitfield to a home at 2785 Monte Cristo Way.

A second bodyguard, Javon Beard, was also hired to stand on watch for the King of Pop. Michael's long stay in Vegas was a time of isolation and loneliness. Scattered visitors came to see him, including will.i.am, who had worked with Michael in a studio in Ireland—and who now worked with him on plans for a twenty-fifth anniversary edition of *Thriller*. Michael's friend Miko Brando visited with his children. A school-teacher conducted classes for the children. His mother, Katherine, came. But, according to the bodyguards, other family members were not welcomed. When Joe Jackson unexpectedly showed up, Michael refused to see him. "I'm working. I cannot be disturbed when I'm being creative. Tell him he has to come back and make an appointment." Siblings Jackie, Rebbie, and Randy also tried to see him, according to Michael's bodyguards. Michael was especially adamant about not seeing Randy. Oddly enough, his bodyguards said at that time he wouldn't see Janet. Long discussions were also conducted between Michael and his lawyers, between Michael and various managers. But his children were his priority. When his daughter, Paris, was ill, it was arranged for a doctor to come to the Vegas home to see her. Polite and professional and evidently making a good impression on Michael, the physician was Dr. Conrad Murray.

Others who came in contact with Jackson, such as a repairman working on the Vegas home, had to sign confidentiality agreements. Cell phones were not permitted. His every move was one of secrecy. He was suspicious of every camera he saw. "The man was paranoid, very paranoid. Didn't sleep much. He was always going around the house at three, four in the morning, checking the locks on all the doors," Bill Whitfield recalled. "Mr. Jackson trusted no one."

There were forays out of the Vegas home—to FAO Schwarz with the children, to shows with the children, also a trip to Virginia for a vacation of sorts, originally intended to be three weeks, but it went longer. Making a trip to Washington, DC, he visited the Smithsonian with his children. Whenever he ventured other places, security measures were always taken. He used disguises in order not to be recognized. Obviously, he didn't want a stampede of excited fans. But also in the back of his mind was a fear that he might be denounced by onlookers as a pedophile. Sometimes those disguises drew suspicion. The fake mustaches and beards. The unusual clothing. At a large store in Virginia, the bodyguards said the store's security people thought he was there to rob the place.

During his stay in Virginia, Michael was also visited by two young attractive women. The bodyguards were never informed of their names. The first was a petite, dark-haired woman with an eastern European accent whom Michael personally asked the bodyguards to pick up at Dulles International Airport. She was taken to a hotel in Chantilly, Virginia. On several occasions during her visit of approximately a week, Michael was driven to see her. He had gifts bought for her, was openly affectionate with her, and on such occasions, he might spend several hours with her in her hotel room. But his bodyguards said he never spent the night. After her first visit, she returned a few weeks later. The other woman was a curly haired blond who flew in from Europe and stayed at a hotel in Middleburg, Virginia. Michael visited her but he appeared closer and more flirtatious with the first woman. The bodyguards knew little else about either woman.

Except for his children, not much seemed to bring him great joy. The one occasion when he registered great excitement centered on Elizabeth. Michael had been contacted by Elizabeth's people, who informed him there was to be a seventy-fifth birthday party for her, to be held in Las Vegas. It would be wonderful if he could surprise her on that evening. Some months earlier, she had spoken in his defense—when he was still abroad—on *Larry King Live*.

When asked by King what she thought of the charges against him, she answered, "I've never been so angry in my life."

"But don't you think it strange, Dame Elizabeth, to have someone in his forties spend the night with children?"

"All right I'll answer that," she said, "because I've been there when his young nephews were there and we were all in the bed watching television. There was nothing abnormal about it. There was no touchy-feely going on. We laughed like children. And we watched a lot of Walt Disney. There was nothing odd about it."

"So you think they were out after him?"

"I think the paparazzi started it, not the paparazzi, the press."

"Is he going to come back to work?"

"I don't think so, except maybe in Europe."

"You don't think he'll ever live in the United States again?"

"Well, really, why should he? He's been treated like dirt here."

Michael made great preparations for the birthday party. To see Elizabeth, to spend some precious time with her, to gaze into her eyes, to hear her laughter, to make plans to see her again made him so excited. But also he could be part of a world again, where he felt safe and cared for. It had been too long. The designer Roberto Cavalli was flown in to create a special outfit. So were Michael's hairstylist and his makeup artist. The bodyguards were instructed to buy new suits for the evening. Michael also informed them that the cars were to be cleaned and waxed. "Make sure your shoes are shined like mirrors," he told them. "You guys have to look great. I want everybody to look great." "He never did that kind of thing before," recalled Javon.

But on the very day of the party—just as everyone was almost ready to walk out the door—there was a crash of a gray Mercedes SUV into the gate that kept trespassers from getting near the house. The driver was Michael's brother Randy. Told that Michael would not see him and told to leave, he refused. He said Michael owed him money. "I want my fuckin' money!" Randy was reported to have said. According to Stacy Brown, Randy had "persuaded several friends to remortgage their homes" and "used the cash to help pay Michael's legal and other expenses." Now that Michael was back in the States, Randy wanted the repayment. "Randy tried to confront him, but Michael would not have it," recalled Brown. It was then that a "desperate Randy charged the compound housing Michael. He sat in the driveway for another two hours," recalled Bill Whitfield. "We had to call his father."

But even before Joe arrived, a dejected Michael decided not to go to the party. "He'll just find out how to follow us to Liz's party and cause a huge scene; she doesn't deserve that."

Elizabeth arrived at her party in a wheelchair, which she would be confined to for the rest of her life. Surrounded by her children—her two sons, Michael Wilding Jr. and Christopher Wilding (whose birthday was the same day), and her two daughters, Liza Todd and Maria Burton—she still evoked an old Hollywood glamorous aura as she smiled, laughed, and chatted with guests that included Debbie Reynolds and her daughter, Carrie Fisher; dermatologist Arnold Klein; Vegas hotel/casino mogul Steve Wynn; and former Vegas headliners Siegfried Fischbacher and Roy Horn. Also there was former model Kathy Ireland, who was Elizabeth's business partner at House of Taylor, which manufactured, marketed, and distributed jewelry. The cameras clicked as reporters rushed to Elizabeth for comments. When asked about Michael, she said she had spoken to him earlier in the day. But he did not get to see her. She left Las Vegas the next morning.

In 2007, Michael also traveled to New York for two photo shoots: one for Italian *Vogue*, the other for *Ebony*, to commemorate the twenty-fifth anniversary of *Thriller*. Italian *Vogue* put him into the posh Carlyle hotel on New York's Upper East Side, the kind of luxurious setting he always enjoyed. He also relished all the attention: the makeup artists and hairstylists assuring that he looked just right; the stylists checking out every fold of his clothing; the lighting people; the various crew members all focused on him. Here he seemed safe and secure, his paranoia and fears temporarily put at bay.

During this time in the east, he and his children also stayed at the home of the Cascio family in New Jersey. Frank Cascio recalled that on the evening of August 19, 2007, after a surprise birthday party was thrown for his mother at the family's home in New Jersey, most guests had left when Michael arrived—with his children, his dog Kenya, and a cat. Frank suggested that Michael should make use of the studio in the Cascio home. "Start working, start writing, start producing," Frank told him. He ended up taking residence at the Cascio home, longer than had been expected, for several months.

Having long felt secure with the Cascio family, Michael's stay was no doubt pleasant and refreshing. A classroom was set up for the children in one of bedrooms. Daily a tutor came. Michael worked with Eddie Cascio in the studio in the Cascio home. He also celebrated his forty-ninth birthday there. Between Michael and Frank, who were no longer working together, there had been tensions, differences, and then an estrangement. During conversations with Michael at this time, Frank felt old issues had been resolved. Though it was evident the trial had affected Michael, Frank believed Michael would rebound. He also observed: "There was no sign that he was on any sort of medicine. He was back to being Michael."

Back to being Michael also meant back to tough realities and back to ways to circumvent his pressures. For Michael's bodyguards, Michael's excursions and travels were all an adventure, but there was a nagging, ongoing problem: often the bodyguards were not being paid. Once they finally received some form of payment, it might be only half the amount due to them. At other times, they lived off their per diems. As aware as the men were of Michael's financial problems—credit card payments were declined—they were puzzled by his behavior. Dire as Michael's financial straits were, he still went on lavish spending sprees. He visited antiques shops in New York. He talked of moving into a $55 million estate in the area. Once, he saw a Ferris wheel at the Mall at Short Hills in New Jersey and wanted to buy it. But its cost of $300,000 made that purchase clearly out of the question. At the same time, he also could be generous. His bodyguard Bill Whitfield remembered a badly scarred man who as a child had been set on fire by his father. Michael knew the man and kept in touch with him. One day, he asked Whitfield to deliver a package—a carefully wrapped large sum of money—to the man.

• • •

Returning to Vegas, Michael made a brief trip to Los Angeles. Afterward, he moved into the Green Valley Ranch in nearby Henderson, Nevada, for a couple of weeks. But finances forced him to move. Arrangements were made through an attorney in the music business for Michael and family to stay at the luxurious Palms. There, Michael worked again on *Thriller 25*. Later, he returned to Los Angeles again. Michael knew the inevitable had to occur: he had to generate an income, and so, in time, he would have to get back to work. Negotiations had begun.

Chapter 23

IN SEPTEMBER 2008, a deal was being set up between Michael and the Anschutz Entertainment Group (AEG) for Michael to perform a series of concerts at O2 arena in London in 2009. The news spread like wildfire throughout the entertainment industry. Now a whole new cast of players, including a battery of lawyers and advisers, rushed onto the scene, some of whom had been around in the past. Back on the team was Frank DiLeo. Michael's father, Joseph—with *his* people—was also around again, ready to launch a reunion tour for Michael and his brothers. Clearly, Joseph Jackson—even at this late date— was still unable to accept Michael as anything other than part of a family affair. Along with the new personalities, often warring with one another for the King of Pop's attention—and warring among themselves for the huge amount of money that would come from the concerts—there was also a new round of lawsuits about music rights, about managerial rights, about broken deals, about whatever. Michael's former attorney Tom Mesereau said that Jackson was "the greatest target for civil lawsuits I've ever, ever experienced. He's literally been sued thousands of times by people he hasn't met, people he knows nothing about." Mesereau added: "And, yes, there are people who would like to obtain his property, including his interests in the Beatles catalogue." Referring to Michael's trial, Mesereau added: "And their desire to obtain his assets would have significantly been enhanced if he had been convicted." Seeing dollar signs, everyone wanted a piece of the action.

Though feeling the old pressures, Michael also enjoyed the old perks and privileges. A healthy $6.2 million advance from AEG would provide Michael with some much-needed cash. At the same time, an agreement had been worked out with billionaire Tom Barrack Jr., the CEO of Colony Capital, to halt foreclosure proceedings on Neverland. Capital also poured in to restore Neverland. His estate had been saved, although it would now be jointly owned by Colony Capital with plans to later sell it. In fact, it was Tom Barrack who had initially put Michael in contact with Philip Anschutz for the AEG deal.

Once back in Los Angeles, Michael was first ensconced with his children in posh digs at the deluxe Hotel Bel-Air. In December 2008, AEG agreed to move Michael and his family to a luxurious home at 100 North Carolwood Drive in Los Angeles's exclusive Holmby Hills. The cost of $100,000 a month for the home would later be deducted from his earnings. A staff was provided at the home to keep Michael hopefully content and calm during the arduous rehearsal period for the concerts. The nanny, Grace Rwaramba, was at the home. So were the expected servants. So was a security detail. Eventually, so were a personal chef and a trainer. Also eventually added to the staff was Dr. Conrad Murray, who had been hired by AEG at Michael's insistence to ensure he was in the best of shape. It was old-style Hollywood extravagance, and though frail and brooding, Michael had to have loved it.

His last Christmas Eve, in 2008, was spent with his children and guests on Carolwood Drive. Arnold Klein arrived with friends. Michael also invited Carrie Fisher to the home. In some respects, because he would always think of her as Princess Leia from *Star Wars*, Michael asked Fisher to read the hologram speech from *Star Wars* for his children.

Still, there were demands to be met. No doubt with great physical effort and with mixed feelings, Michael flew to London for a press conference on March 5, 2009. At O2 arena, he stepped onstage to announce the show—called *This Is It*—to some four hundred journalists, as well as about seven thousand wildly enthusiastic fans. There would be ten performances. Count-less times before, he had launched shows, speaking with enthusiasm and optimism, smiling broadly, never letting his fatigue or anxieties show. Always mindful of old-style PR, he understood that he had to present an image that would excite the fans and get them rushing out to buy tickets to see him. As in the past, he pulled it off. But there was another tone within the enthusiasm and optimism. "And *This Is It* really means this is it," he told the excited crowd. "This will be the final curtain call. I love you. I love you all."

Not long after Jackson's announcement, the tickets sold out. Then came a change in the concert schedule. Rather than ten concerts, there would be fifty. "When they upped it to fifty shows, he was livid," recalled bodyguard Bill Whitfield. "Fifty was the original number, because that was how many shows he really needed to do to make this big money they were waving in his face." But Michael had been adamant about limiting the number of shows. "They want me to do fifty shows," he had said. "I *can't* do fifty shows." "And it wasn't just the physical aspect," recalled bodyguard Javon Beard. "It was his demeanor. Some days he was upbeat, other days he was down. Like with Elizabeth Taylor's birthday. He could be up, totally in a good mood, ready to go, but if one little thing threw off his day, that was it. He'd shut down."

As could be expected, neither Michael nor Elizabeth was in the best of health. In Vegas,

Michael had been seen in a wheelchair. Unknown to most, he had problems with his knees and ankles, a curse for a dancer. Elizabeth's work for AIDS continued, but in 2004, she was reported to have broken her spine, and what with her other ailments, she was increasingly confined to her Bel Air home, just as Michael, in so many ways, was confined to his in Holmby Hills.

Yet, though reclusive, Elizabeth was not the regular, everyday kind of recluse. Occasionally, there was a touch of Norma Desmond about her. Actor Frank Langella, who became friendly with her during the new millennium, recalled a very strange Oscar night at Taylor's home. Guests had been invited, none of whom knew her, none of whom she knew. "They were a motley crew of friends of her housekeeper, someone's cousin, some agent's secretary," recalled Langella. "None of them appeared to know each other and were hanging out in little groups of twos and threes." Seated to watch the televised broadcast of the awards, the group was fed, and no doubt thrilled to be in her home. Yet when she entered the room once the proceedings were under way, she spoke to none of these guests, simply sat in her chair, briefly watched the show. When it ended, her guests headed out the door. "She acknowledged no one's presence but mine," said Langella. The only exception was her hair stylist José Eber.

Most times, Elizabeth entertained friends and

family, inviting guests over for barbecues and poolside parties. Her spirits could be high on these occasions. Carrie Fisher, Elizabeth's former stepdaughter, recalled a party at which Elizabeth warned that she would push Carrie, fully clothed, into the swimming pool. Then she did so. It seemed to clear the air finally of any tension there might have been about the fact that Elizabeth had walked off with Carrie's father. The two became friends. Carrie also wrote the 2001 TV movie *These Old Broads*, which starred Elizabeth with Shirley MacLaine, Joan Collins, *and* Debbie Reynolds. Talk about letting bygones be bygones! It was not an easy shoot. Suffering from arthritis in her spine, Elizabeth struggled to walk and was in constant pain. Her doctors had advised her not to accept the role. But Reynolds believed that this also "was an attempt to make amends to Carrie and me for her part in my first divorce decades before."

Now a family matriarch, Elizabeth had gatherings for her children and grandchildren. Her son Michael's daughters, Naomi and Laela, who lived with their mother in Wales, would visit her twice a year in Los Angeles. Later, Naomi stayed with her for a spell. Sometimes sitting with her granddaughters, Elizabeth would discuss—what else but, she joked—*boys!* At Thanksgiving, a table might be set for fifty. At Easter, she relished Easter egg hunts with lots of children at her home. Dogs, cats, birds were part of the place, too. Sometimes performers from Cirque du Soleil did acrobatics outdoors. "Of course when she had to appear at an important event, she would put on the most beautiful dress and the most amazing jewelry and become Elizabeth Taylor the star," fashion designer Valentino recalled. "But at home she liked a cozy life, friends, good food."

Interestingly, during her later years, Elizabeth appeared to have come to terms with her life— and its meaning. After her brain surgery, she had given an interview to Barbara Walters in which she explained publicly her relationship with her father —and the physical abuse she had suffered yet come to understand. It was something she had referred to but without giving any specifics during Michael's interview at Neverland with Oprah Winfrey. Now she gave some details and revealed how she came to understand her father. "When I was a little girl, my father was abusive when he drank and seemed to like to bat me around a bit," she said. "But when I left home and had my own child, I started thinking about my father and how it must have felt for him to have his 9-year-old daughter making more money than he was, all of a sudden shoot to fame when he had been this very proud, beautiful, dignified man. And I don't blame him at all. I know he was drunk when he did it. I know he didn't mean to do it. He didn't know what he was doing." She remembered that she had called him and asked him to come to her home. There the two discussed her early years. "I put my arms around him and buried my head in his neck, and we both sobbed . . . and we bonded for the first time since I was nine. And it was until he died." She still maintained a certain privacy. But she had been willing to discuss publicly something she and Michael most likely discussed in the initial years of their friendship.

"Despite compulsive addictions, and addictive compulsions, Elizabeth was not a tragic victim like Marilyn Monroe or Judy Garland, nor was she an empty shell like Lana Turner," commented Liz Smith. "She did not lash out uncontrollably like Ava Gardner. She did not escape, unhappily, like Grace Kelly. No, Elizabeth did not have any tortured ambivalence about fame or privilege. She accepted it. Fame was all she knew." But she had channeled that fame for the benefit of others into the AIDS battle, which had given her life a new meaning.

In March 2009, she gave an interview to Kim Kardashian for *Harper's Bazaar* in which she had told the young woman who idolized her, "I never planned to acquire a lot of jewels or a lot of husbands. For me, life happened, just as it does for everyone else. I have been extremely lucky in my life in that I have known great love, and of course, I am the temporary custodian of some incredible and beautiful things. But I have never felt more alive than when I have watched my children delight in something, never more alive than when I have watched some great artist perform, and never richer than when I have scored a big check for AIDS. Follow your passion, follow your heart, and the things you need will come."

On April 12, 2009—just a little over a month since announcing the AEG concerts—Michael and his children attended Elizabeth's Easter party. Among the guests, there was much talk about Michael's forthcoming concerts. Elizabeth herself was making plans to attend. For Michael, there was the pleasure of Elizabeth's company: the laughter, the warmth, the bravery amid so much discomfort.

There now seemed to be a calm within her that Michael no doubt detected that Easter. He himself had not yet arrived at that point. He had tried to move forward by focusing on his family. But still bruised by the scandals and now struggling with finances, he had to find a way to keep himself afloat. Elizabeth's friendship helped.

Tito Jackson remarked on "her steadfast loyalty and unwavering friendship" to Michael. "Liz provided a sense of relief and comfort to my brother at various difficult times in his life."

In May, Michael took his children to an Indian restaurant in Beverly Hills to be a part of the

Jacksons' "Family Day," a festive time when the brothers and their large families gathered with their parents to celebrate. This year it was a celebration of the sixty-year marriage of Katherine and Joseph—but with a surprise. Katherine and Joseph were told they would be dining with their children. Unknown to them was the fact that in the restaurant was the *entire* family, which included not only the children with their spouses but also the grandchildren. Janet had arranged the special gathering. When Katherine first entered a private room of the restaurant, she was greeted by the cheers of everyone. Her face lit up with joy. Michael stood with the rest of the family as happy about the family gathering as everyone else. No matter what, he still loved them all. He and his three children were at brother Jackie's table. At one point, Jermaine recalled that Janet—seated on the other side of the room—started making strange sounds that were "half scream, half cackle." Suddenly, Michael burst into laughter. It was a private joke, a special moment, between Michael and Janet, the sister to whom he had felt closest when growing up. It didn't matter that no one else seemed to be in on the joke. For Michael and Janet, it apparently meant much. That evening, Jermaine said, was the last time the family saw Michael alive.

Chapter 24

AS HE BRACED himself for the performances, Michael began rehearsals at Los Angeles's Staples Center under the direction of choreographer Kenny Ortega, who had an impressive list of credits stretching back to 1980, when he had worked with the legendary Gene Kelly in the film *Xanadu*. Later Ortega did the choreography for the 1987 hit movie *Dirty Dancing*. He also choreographed music videos, including Madonna's "Material Girl." On television, he directed and choreographed a trio of deliriously impassioned teen singing-and-dancing spectaculars: *High School Musical*, *High School Musical 2*, and *High School Musical 3: Senior Year*. Imaginative and masterful at capturing the attitudes, rhythms, and energies of youth, he had also worked with Michael on the *Dangerous* and *HIStory* tours and was sensitive to Michael's artistic needs and his methods of expression. He also understood Michael well enough that if there should be personal or health issues, Ortega could navigate his way around them. In turn, Michael appeared to trust Ortega. The *This Is It* show grew to some twenty production numbers, reportedly running up a tab of $30 million. For the dancers, the musicians, the crew, and the countless behind-the-scenes staffers, the preparations for the concert were certainly a once-in-a-lifetime experience. Some had grown up watching the King of Pop. Others had gazed at him from afar. Now just catching a glimpse of him at the Staples Center during rehearsals was enough to cause goose bumps, to stop people in their tracks.

The long rehearsals, sometimes running for eight hours, could be tough and certainly grueling. Suffering from insomnia and the long-standing anxieties, the now fifty-year-old Jackson fought to maintain his stamina. Some days everything went well, and as was later seen in the posthumously released film of rehearsals titled *Michael Jackson's This Is It*, a thin, rather vague and wan Jackson nonetheless remained a fascinating perfectionist, the consummate performing artist, who worked strenuously, demanding the utmost from the musicians, the dancers, and of course, himself. With his magic undiminished, he was a marvel to behold. But other days, things didn't go well. "He wasn't himself today," was what bodyguard Bill Whitfield said he heard about some rehearsals. Very soon there were problems. Shortened rehearsals. Missed rehearsals.

Not long before Michael was to fly to England for the shows, his former manager and television producer Ron Weisner met with him at the Staples Center and was shocked by what he saw. "He hadn't looked *really* healthy for a good long while, but this was at a whole other level. The first thing I thought when I saw him was, *He looks like a goddamn prisoner of war.*" Weisner believed that Michael weighed about a hundred pounds. After watching Michael struggle through a rehearsal, Weisner concluded: "I knew there was no way he'd get to England. No way. For that matter, I knew that was the last time I'd see him." In Michael's eyes, Weisner saw "a look I've seen too many times in my life, a look of resignation, a look that said, *It's over,* and it broke my heart, because up until things headed south in the early 2000s, he had it all." Few knew about Michael's "fearlessness," Weisner said. "There's nothing, *nothing* he wouldn't try in order to entertain a crowd of 100 or 100,000."

During long conversations with Dr. Conrad Murray, Michael discussed his family, his troubles, his life, and his feelings for Elizabeth. "His father Joe Jackson was one of the destroyers of Michael, and Michael told me his mother was an enabler," Murray said. "Michael told me that Liz Taylor was more of a mother to him than Katherine ever was." Harsh as it sounded, Michael no doubt still had conflicting feelings and perhaps even harbored resentment because his mother agreed to so much that Joseph wanted. Concerned that fifty concerts would destroy Michael's health, Katherine reportedly was persuaded to push for a reunion tour in which Michael's brothers would be there to help carry the weight, and of course, from the family's vantage point, ensure a fabulously entertaining show. Much as he loved his mother, he was adamant that there would be no reunion tour. With Elizabeth, he never had to deal with conflicting emotions, never felt torn, which no doubt accounts for his comment about Katherine to Murray. Regardless, Michael appeared always to love his mother profoundly.

Disoriented and struggling to focus, his problems were exacerbated by his chronic insomnia. When desperation set in, he was vocal about his need for sleep medication, mainly the drug propofol—a high-powered sedative used in surgeries to numb patients to pain. But propofol had to be administered under tight security. A nurse Michael met said he pleaded with her for the drug. She declined to help.

Michael was on a frantic search for relief from the pain and his insomnia. He apparently turned to his friend Arnold Klein for help. During this time (roughly from February to May), "Klein had injected Jackson with Demerol fifty-one times in the three months prior to his death," TMZ later reported. "Klein also took Jackson to various surgery centers to put him under with propofol, the drug that killed the singer. On one occasion Klein took Jackson to the gynecologist next door to his office and put him under with anesthesia which one doctor said was propofol under the pretext it was for an acne treatment. Klein denied it was propofol. Klein gave Jackson prescriptions for various narcotic drugs including Demerol under a variety of aliases, including Omar Arnold, Fernand Diaz, Peter Madonie and Josephine Baker."

Kenny Ortega became alarmed by the missed rehearsals and by Michael's state of mind. On June 19, Ortega sent Michael home from a dismal rehearsal. Afterward, Ortega e-mailed an AEG executive: "He appeared quite weak and fatigued this evening. He had a terrible case of the chills, was trembling, rambling, and obsessing. Everything in me says he should be psychologically evaluated. If we have any chance at all to get him back in the light, it's going to take a strong therapist to help him through this as well as immediate physical nurturing." Ortega added: "I believe that he really wants this. It would shatter him, break his heart if we pulled the plug. He's terribly frightened it's all going to go away. He asked me repeatedly tonight if I was going to leave him. He was practically begging for my confidence. It broke my heart. He was like a lost boy. There may still be a chance he can rise to the occasion if we get him the help he needs." But on June 24, Michael was back in action at the Staples Center for a dress rehearsal.

That night at home, Michael turned to Dr. Murray for help with sleeping. Murray gave him the sedatives lorazepam and midazolam. But nothing helped. After ten in the morning on June 25, Murray gave him twenty-five milligrams of propofol. Later, Murray realized Michael was not breathing. After administering CPR, Murray ran downstairs. He called for help. Michael's children Prince and Paris went into their father's bedroom. After almost a half hour, 911 was finally called.

An ambulance rushed Michael to the UCLA Medical Center. Hearing the news, Katherine Jackson rushed to the hospital. Other family members soon congregated at the hospital. La Toya. Randy. Janet called from New York. But it was too late. En route to the hospital, Jermaine received a call on his cell phone from his mother, who said, "He's *dead!*" Once at UCLA Medical Center, Jermaine recalled: "I walked over, knelt beside her and hugged her as tight as I could. She was rigid and didn't even flinch, such was the strength of her daze. I kept holding her, gaining comfort as much as giving." Later Jermaine met with the press to announce: "My brother, the legendary King of Pop, Michael Jackson, passed away Thursday, June 25, 2009, at 2:26 p.m. It is believed he suffered cardiac arrest in his home. However, the cause of his death is unknown until the results of the autopsy are known." According to Jermaine, Michael had stopped breathing in his bedroom around 12:05.

Once TMZ's website broke the news, social media—Google, Twitter, the website of the *Los Angeles Times*—went into a frenzy as fans and others, unable to fathom what had happened, feverishly searched for information. (That same day, actress Farrah Fawcett also died.) Later they expressed their shock and their grief. At New York's Apollo Theater, distraught fans gathered outside in tribute to Michael. Around the world, there were candlelight vigils. At London's O2 arena, where Michael was to have performed, fans gathered, many dressed in sequined military jackets and one single white glove. The next day, newspapers around the country ran front-page stories on his death. Network broadcasts opened with the story. Social media continued to relay an outpouring of grief.

When word first broke of Michael's death, Elizabeth was in the bedroom of her Bel Air home, where her staff was preparing for her trip to London. Upon hearing the devastating news, Elizabeth was said to have let out a piercing cry and shrieks that could be heard throughout the house. What had happened? How could this be?

Having opened a Twitter account, she expressed her sorrow the day after Michael's death:

My heart . . . my mind . . . are broken. I loved Michael with all my soul and I can't imagine life without him.

We had so much in common and we had such loving fun together.

I was packing up my clothes to go to London for his opening when I heard the news. I still can't believe it. I don't want to believe it.

It can't be so. He will live in my heart forever but it's not enough. My life feels so empty.

I don't think anyone knew how much we loved each other. The purest most giving love I've ever known. Oh God! I'm going to miss him.

I can't imagine life without him. But I guess with God's help I'll learn.

On July 7, 2009, a tribute was held at the Staples Center with Michael's children, his family, and a host of celebrities that included Brooke Shields, Berry Gordy Jr., Stevie Wonder, Usher, Mariah Carey, Lionel Richie, Jennifer Hudson, Queen Latifah, and John Mayer. Michael's daughter, Paris, broke down as she paid tribute to him. More than thirty-one million in the United States watched the televised event. Millions of others watched in England, Brazil, and other countries. Some thirty-seven million streamed it on their computers.

But Elizabeth was nowhere in sight.

On Twitter on July 6, Dame Elizabeth had announced:

I've been asked to speak at the Staples Center. I will not be a part of the hoopla.

And I cannot guarantee that I would be coherent to say a word.

I just don't believe that Michael would want me to share my grief with millions of others. How I feel is between us. Not a public event.

I said I wouldn't go to the Staples Center and I certainly don't want to be a part of it. I love him too much.

My heart goes out to Katherine and Michael's beloved children.

But columnist Cindy Adams believed the family did not want her at the tribute. "Michael Jackson's twists and turns in death mirror those in his life," Adams commented. "Ever wonder why two bold-faced names, topping any list of those who crept closest to him, were not among those who cried for the cameras? Debbie Rowe ostensibly shunned that media attention? Really? Why? . . . Elizabeth Taylor, Krazy Glued to him forever as his closest, truest friend, ostensibly preferred to mourn privately? Really? Why?" Adams added: "About Debbie, who knows? Who cares? About Elizabeth, I know. I also know both sides will deny this and issue press releases saying I'm an imbecile, I'm babbling, I should be committed. OK, now that that's out of the way. Elizabeth Taylor was snubbed. Not accidentally. Deliberately. Willfully. Given short shrift. Put on the B-Minus list." Adams also commented: "The family purposefully dissed her. Didn't want her. Offered her a seat someplace in the Staples Center, but not with them. Not near them. Nor was the world's most famous name given an invite or access to any of their private events. Not one. Why? Because she was always Michael's friend. Not the family's. Michael's. They resented her. Elizabeth Taylor was crushed. She's still crying."

On September 3, 2009, Elizabeth did, however, attend Michael's private funeral at Forest Lawn Memorial Park, along with the Jackson family and various friends that included Lisa Marie Presley, Macaulay Culkin, Quincy Jones, Corey Feldman, and many more, in total about two hundred people for the private ninety-minute service. Gladys Knight sang "His Eye Is on the Sparrow." The pallbearers were Michael's five brothers—Jackie, Tito, Jermaine, Marlon, and Randy. Michael's children placed a crown on his coffin. The family had hoped Michael might be buried at Neverland. But because of red tape that would have entailed for months, it was decided to bury him in the Great Mausoleum at Forest Lawn Memorial Cemetery. Frail and in a wheelchair, Elizabeth looked as if struggling against pain. Yet she was as magnetic as ever, her eyes still drawing the world in. There she saw Tito Jackson and his son TJ, Michael's beloved nephew, as well as other members of the family.

Like everyone else, Elizabeth endured the endless media stories about his death. Pictures turned up of the deceased Michael lying on a hospital gurney—violating him now in death. On August 27, the Los Angeles Coroner's Office had ruled that Michael's death was a homicide due to "acute propofol intoxication with benzodiazepine effect." Charged with involuntary manslaughter in February 2010, Dr. Murray went on trial in the fall of 2011 and was found guilty on November 7. He was sentenced to four years in prison. AEG was also sued by Katherine Jackson, but she lost the suit.

Some controversy sprang up about Michael's will, dated July 7, 2002. Earlier versions of his will had essentially specified the same disbursements. A Michael Jackson Family Trust had been established to control funds of Michael's estate. Twenty percent of his estate was to go to charity. The remainder of his estate was to be divided equally between a lifetime trust for his mother, Katherine, and a trust to be divided among Michael's three children. Upon the death of Katherine, any remaining funds from her portion would revert to Michael's children. Katherine was also designated to be the guardian of Michael's children. Should Katherine not survive, then Diana Ross was nominated as the children's guardian. He stipulated in the will: "I have intentionally omitted to provide for my former wife Deborah Jean Rowe Jackson." Named as the coexecutors of the estate were John Branca and John McClain. Originally, Barry Siegel had also been a coexecutor, but he had resigned as a cotrustee.

Not mentioned in the will was Joseph Jackson or any of Michael's siblings. Katherine Jackson objected to the appointment of Branca and McClain as coexecutors. But later she accepted them. As it had been pointed out, why raise any issues about a will in which she was named a chief beneficiary? But Joseph and Randy Jackson were not satisfied. Joseph challenged the will. In court in 2009, Judge Mitchell Beckloff stated emphatically: "Joseph Jackson takes none of this estate." He added: "This is a decision his son made." In time, Joseph and Randy, as well as others, had to accept the terms of the will. Creditors stepped in for payment of debts of over $400 million. Still a part of Michael's estate was his share of the Sony/ATV catalog, which in time would be worth about $2 billion. Branca and McClain were able to refinance Jackson's debts. They also generated new income, new projects. In time, a $250 million recording contract was sealed. A joint venture endeavor was established between the estate and Cirque du Soleil for a spectacular *Michael Jackson The Immortal World Tour.* Michael would be represented onstage performing. The Soleil troupe would also entertain. In the first part of 2012, the show grossed $75 million. The film *Michael Jackson's This Is It*, a record of Michael in rehearsal for his tour directed by Kenny Ortega, was released, and became a hit that grossed $261 million.

Stories again focused on the biological parent-hood of Michael's three children. Mark Lester's name came up again as the father. Dermatologist Arnold Klein joined in the fray with suggestions that he was possibly the father of the first two children.

On October 6, Elizabeth returned to the hospital for a heart procedure that she announced on her Twitter account. Now she seemed to prefer Twitter as a direct, controlled way of communicating that could not be distorted or sensationalized by the media.

In her wheelchair, she made a visit to Universal Studios with Michael's children and their nanny, Grace, as well as Miko Brando, and Michael's nephews, including TJ.

Once Elizabeth had seen *This Is It*, she took to Twitter to praise the film, to praise Ortega, and again to praise Michael.

She continued to protect and defend Michael. In May 2010, Elizabeth took to Twitter to express her feelings about dermatologist Klein's assertion that Michael had a homosexual affair with someone from his office.

Dr. Arnie Klein declared on May 2 that he did not betray Michael Jackson by saying publicly that he had a homosexual relationship.

With someone in "Arnie's" office. It seems he supplies not only women (Debbie Rowe), but men too . . . how convenient.

Just what we want in our doctors. And then to say he did not betray Michael's confidence. No wonder he has death threats.

I thought doctors, like priests took an oath of confidentiality. May God have mercy on his soul.

Elizabeth's days now were long.

Still, she never lost her interest in life and in the lives of others. When her assistant Tim Mendelson's mother was dying of liver cancer, the biographer Sam Kashner reported, "Elizabeth virtually turned part of her home into a hospice for her." She had once done the same for her assistant Chen Sam. She had not lost her passion for new experiences and for travel. Accompanied by a nurse or friends and in her wheelchair, she sometimes went to a gay bar in West Hollywood called the Abbey. She got to know its owner and sometimes enjoyed conversations with patrons. She had also traveled to the Hawaiian home of her friends Jason Winters and Erik Sterling. Their personal-management company Sterling Winters Management represented her as well as Janet Jackson, Kathy Ireland, and others. Later she described the African American Winters as her dearest friend. There had even been rumors that she and Winters would marry, which both Elizabeth and Winters denied. While in Hawaii in 2006, the seventy-four-year-old Elizabeth, dressed in a bathing suit with a T-shirt on top, had herself lowered in a Plexiglas cage into the Pacific Ocean so she could swim with the sharks. No one seemed eager to watch her do so. She was also advised to remove some of her jewelry that might catch the eyes of the sharks, but she reportedly answered, "Isn't that the fucking point!" In 2007, she performed, seated in a wheelchair, with actor James Earl Jones in a special stage presentation of A. R. Gurney's play *Love Letters*. It was a charity event to raise money for mobile AIDS units for patients. The audience gave her a standing ovation for her performance.

In 2010, she had a photo shoot with Firooz Zahedi, the cousin of former Iranian ambassador Ardeshir Zahedi. She had known Firooz for twenty-five years. Reportedly, she had almost backed out of the photo session at her home. But after she was shown a rare photograph of Burton that Firooz had brought as a gift, she decided to move ahead with the shoot.

Shortly afterward, she made another trip. With her children and Tim Mendelson, she flew to London where, as a guest of Prince Charles, she attended a ceremony honoring Burton at Buckingham Palace. The Richard Burton Theatre at the Royal Welsh College of Music and Drama in Cardiff, Wales, had been established. During her time in London, she stayed at the Dorchester, where she and Burton had resided in the heady, delirious years of their marriage. It was also where she and her mother had stayed upon her return to London in 1948. Other occasions had been spent there. It was a kind of second home for her. And, of course, she was back in her beloved

England, the country she had never been able to leave behind. Had those childhood years in England truly been her happiest? This visit proved to be her last stay at the Dorchester and her last trip to England.

Back in Bel Air, her condition worsened. Family and friends saw her further steady physical decline. "I think the last few years didn't bring her as much joy because her body was failing. And she wasn't. Her spirit wasn't," Carole Bayer Sager remembered. "But her body was. It had lived a lot and suffered a lot." Elizabeth had "fractured both of her knees, and literally had to be carried out of the wheelchair and hospital bed. She couldn't do the things she had. She was so brave. Most of her life she endured chronic back pain and she brought all this light and love and generosity to this world despite the fact, often she was in pain."

Perhaps believing the worst just might happen, she held her seventy-ninth birthday party early, in January. Her family and friends celebrated with her. In February, she entered Cedars-Sinai Medical Center in Los Angeles. Her congestive heart failure had weakened her even more. Daily, family and friends gathered by her bedside. Press releases seemed to indicate she was progressing well but slowly. But several weeks after entering the hospital, Elizabeth took a turn for the worse. Carole Bayer Sager visited "to say goodbye and I knew she was going and I hated that she'd been in hospital for seven weeks, but she wasn't in pain . . . and she wasn't really conscious when I saw her. I was there with Liza and Maria, her two daughters, and I was able to say goodbye." On March 23, 2011, Elizabeth Taylor, surrounded by her four children, died.

Newspapers around the country ran front-page stories on her. Nightly news shows opened with accounts of her extraordinary life and death. Online social media went into overtime drive with an outpouring of grief and tributes. Said TJ Jackson, Michael's nephew: "RIP, Elizabeth, I'll never forget the love and support you gave my Uncle and our family. Your heart was good." La Toya described Elizabeth "as an incredible friend to my brother, at his side through some of his most difficult times, and, of course loved by his children and our family." She added: "She will live on in our hearts forever."

Later, news came of the fortune she had left. It was estimated at $1 billion. Reportedly, each of her children would receive $100 million. Money was also left to AIDS research. An auction at Christie's of her belongings and notably of her world-famous jewels shattered records. The sale of her jewels alone brought in $116 million.

Within forty-eight hours of her death, her

funeral was held at Forest Lawn Memorial Cemetery, where Michael had been interred almost two years earlier. Colin Farrell, whom Elizabeth had befriended, read Gerard Manley Hopkins's poem "The Leaden Echo and the Golden Echo." As family and friends had gathered to say good-bye, they realized the service had been delayed. According to Elizabeth's specifications, her casket was to arrive fifteen minutes late. Ah, late for her own funeral.

After Richard Burton's death, she had said she wished to be buried next to him in Celigny, Switzerland. But *that* she realized might cause long-standing and unresolved complications. At the end, she had requested to be buried close to Michael in the Great Mausoleum in Forest Lawn Memorial Cemetery.

Theirs had been a friendship we might never really understand. These were large talents and large personalities who occupied a world all of their own, both individually and when together.

They had met at just the right time, as if their meeting had been decreed by destiny. At the peak of his fame, Michael had been searching for someone to open up to, confide in, laugh with; someone who would not judge him, who he could trust, and who would understand him. From those early years as a kid who missed his mother as he traversed the world on tour with his brothers, when his tutor Rose Fine had comforted him during those airline flights that frightened him, who would have warm milk for him and read to him in the evenings, and who would tell him the door was open, this was yet another aspect of childhood he truly hoped to recapture; someone who helped ward off his fears, his loneliness, his demons. He had looked for someone who would glance into his eyes and be ready to reassure him everything would be all right. He had had other friendships with other stars he had adored, and in the case of Diana Ross, he'd had a friendship not only with someone he could learn from but have fun with too; a star with a blazing talent and a bold sense of style and glamour. But still his search was on. Gazing at Elizabeth from afar, he had sensed that Elizabeth might be someone he could connect to and someone different from other stars, a survivor who had endured, living by her own rules, reaching out to help others. Thus he had invited her to see him in concert; when he knew he would be at his best, at his most confident, and perhaps at his most appealing. Then after she had left the concert before it ended, he had been in a panic and had called her and cried. He had opened himself up to her completely at that point, revealing his vulner-abilities and insecurities, putting them front and center, not holding back. And then as he opened up to her, she had neither mocked nor dismissed his vulnerability or his tears.

For Elizabeth, Michael had come at the right time. Her children were grown. She had lost Richard Burton. Though she still had a flourishing career, she didn't feel as challenged by it as in the past. She also battled addictions. She stood at an unacknowledged crossroads in her life as she too still searched—in her case, for something larger than herself. Then she saw him in concert and then she had heard him on the phone and then he had showed up at her home with his chimp Bubbles by his side. Almost nothing had to be said. But as she was quick to reveal, they told each other everything.

Perhaps she was saying in her heart to him those lines she had said to Montgomery Clift in *A Place in the Sun*: "Tell Mama. Tell Mama all." For Elizabeth, he probably was like Monty in many ways: extraordinarily talented, heartbreakingly sensitive, and in need of someone who understood his torment and his search. Away from one another, each had families, careers, obligations, commitments, demanding schedules, and other important relationships. But when they were together, each moment had its magic.

Their private times together would remain private. But then there were their forays into the outside world that fascinated the public as the two navigated their way through Hollywood, Las

Vegas, New York, London, and even Singapore in the midst of such tribulations. These were days of adventure and fun. Jaunts to the racetrack. Appearances at award shows and tributes. Afternoons at the movies. Trips to Neverland where for Elizabeth, there was the joy of having Michael show her this other realm he resided in. For Michael, there was the joy of seeing Elizabeth on the carousel or Elizabeth sitting in the gazebo or Elizabeth refusing to go on the scary rides or Elizabeth presenting Michael with Gypsy, the elephant, with Elizabeth herself dressed like a gypsy. It was great fun for two who had missed such times during childhood. Then came the dark days when Elizabeth defended Michael, when she saw that Michael was injured in a way from which there would never be a full recovery. He never forgot though that she had stood by him. It had deepened their relationship.

Loving Michael seemed to have given Elizabeth another chance in life and in turn, it gave her life another dimension. Loving Elizabeth had given Michael a chance to be a kid again and also a man of the world.

And so now all of that had ended, the magical times, the maddening times. Their experiences together were now all a memory, glorious and otherwise, links to each of their powerful legends.

Now both were at rest in Forest Lawn.

Elizabeth and Michael together again.

Acknowledgments

WRITING *ELIZABETH AND MICHAEL* has been a challenging and often daunting but exhilarating experience. In some respects, it is a different book from my original conception. In other respects, it has been similar to writing three interconnecting books in one. The individual sections on Elizabeth and Michael are not full-scale biographies. But the research entailed in writing those sections has often been far more encompassing than I had planned. Initially, I had not intended to write extensively about the early lives of Elizabeth Taylor and Michael Jackson. But as I started researching and developing the book, I realized it was crucial to draw on their early experiences as children operating professionally in adult worlds and the toll that had taken on both. Their early professional as well as personal lives were also the foundation on which their extraordinary friendship was built. With Elizabeth, I wanted very much to unearth the recollections, memories, and "voices" of people who knew her when she was very young—when her view of the world was taking shape and when the warm yet strong-willed personality was formed and still evolving. With the spirit of a true rebel-individualist, Elizabeth Taylor lived by her own rules and her own code. That individuality—coupled with her strength and endurance—would enable her to survive in a film industry in which so many of her contemporaries did not. Discovering the young Elizabeth meant digging for the up close observations of those then around her. Frankly, I was surprised to see how important such MGM associates as the great hair stylist Sydney Guilaroff and the remarkable (and perhaps underrated) designer Helen Rose were to her. I had interviewed Guilaroff while researching my book *Dorothy Dandridge: A Biography*. He had been immensely helpful, and I delighted in all his stories and observations on classic Old Hollywood. Sydney had great discretion yet at times he was surprisingly open about his experiences with famous stars. Consequently, significant glimpses into Elizabeth's early life were provided by Guilaroff's memoir *Crowning Glory: Reflections of Hollywood's Favorite Confidant* and also Helen Rose's *Just Make Them Beautiful*. Both understood Taylor and were keenly aware of her life away from the studio. With Rose, I also was fortunate in locating a rare documentary-style television special, *Elizabeth Taylor: An Intimate Portrait*. Here Rose spoke warmly of Elizabeth as did Sam Marx, the producer who cast Taylor in her first important film, *Lassie Come Home*. Also interviewed was Elizabeth's mother Sara Taylor who was then as devoted to her daughter and her daughter's career as she had been during those early years when she was at Elizabeth's side at MGM. She read a letter from the teenage Elizabeth, written at a time when her daughter had debated whether or not to remain in films. Also important to understanding the child and then young adult Elizabeth was Hollywood gossip columnist Hedda Hopper. Her columns as well as her book *The Whole Truth and Nothing But* charted Taylor's career and her evolving personality. Interestingly enough, the columns and articles of a perceptive chronicler of a later time, Liz Smith, provided insights into Elizabeth (young and older) and the marriage of Taylor to Richard Burton. I also combed through numerous biographies on Taylor. One of the earliest biographies was Ruth Waterbury's *Elizabeth Taylor*, which was just what I wanted: again an account by someone from an earlier period in the actress's life. Of the biographies, Alexander Walker's *Elizabeth* was an especially reasoned, balanced account that did not sensationalize Taylor's life. Of course, Elizabeth Taylor herself authored four books: *Nibbles and Me, Elizabeth Taylor: An Informal Memoir, Elizabeth Takes Off*, and *My Love Affair with Jewelry*. Taylor was a master at knowing what to say and what to keep private. Yet there are insights and surprising information in all four books. The same is true of the countless interviews Elizabeth Taylor granted to the media throughout her career. Having been bred by both Sara Taylor and MGM to understand the importance of the press, she knew an actress must be visible, must share herself with the legions fascinated by her. Yet again she withheld a part of herself and her experiences. That would be true even when she publicly discussed Michael Jackson. There was much she would not comment on.

With Michael, I was surprised by the sometimes frank recollections of Jermaine Jackson's *You Are Not Alone* and La Toya Jackson's *La Toya.* Though La Toya Jackson was often criticized for her memoir, it struck me as an honest view of her very famous family, which was crucial to understanding Michael's childhood and early adulthood. Both Jermaine and La Toya were fairly protective of their brother as have been their other siblings. Digging more into Michael's life, the public interviews and recollections of Michael's parents, Katherine and the much criticized Joseph Jackson, also provided insights not only into Michael but also into the parents themselves. Margaret Maldonado Jackson's *Jackson Family Values* was a real eye-opener and said much about the family's tangled relationships. Perhaps nothing could have prepared the family for the extraordinary fame

Michael attained—and for the effects his fame (as well as that of his brothers early on) would have on the family unit. The Jacksons are often viewed as a dysfunctional family. Yet in all truthfulness, the Jacksons are indeed a family, and ultimately, their loyalty to Michael proved important. J. Randy Taraborrelli's *Michael Jackson: The Magic and the Madness* also provided significant information on Michael's early years, notably when he and his brothers were signed by Motown, as well as his later career and also his family life. Then there was Michael Jackson's *Moonwalk*. In some respects, it too was frank although there was, of course, much he did not discuss and much that was glossed over. Yet in *Moonwalk*, he presented himself from *his* point of view. The same could be said of Michael's comments in Shmuley Boteach's collection *The Michael Jackson Tapes*.

And thus my intense period of research had begun. Exploring the experiences of both stars seemed to take forever. Quite challenging was to establish individual chronologies—not an easy task because both had such unbelievable schedules. Then a joint chronology had to be established of those periods in which their lives intersected. The archives of the *Los Angeles Times* provided extraordinary information and details. My own personal archives, with material from the *New York Times*, the *New York Post*, and a vast array of publications, proved extremely useful. YouTube also was helpful in viewing the interviews that the two stars granted (especially Elizabeth) during their careers.

Also important to this book have been the many public recollections, memories, and insights of innumerable people in the lives of Michael and Elizabeth: Carrie Fisher, Elizabeth's stepdaughter for a time, who developed an unexpected friendship with the woman most felt had broken up the marriage of her parents Eddie Fisher and Debbie Reynolds, and who also had a friendship with Michael, provided thoughtful observations, not only in her memoir *Shockaholic* but also in her public interviews. Debbie Reynolds herself revealed an ever-changing relationship with Elizabeth in her memoir *Unsinkable*. Eddie Fisher as well authored two books in which he rather honestly wrote about his life with Elizabeth and drew a fascinating portrait of her during the years when her image was changing and when she was about to peak in her worldwide fame. Richard Burton's *Diaries* revealed the day-to-day doings of a couple living in the storm of unending media coverage. Frank Cascio's *My Friend Michael* brought into perspective Michael's close relationship with the Cascio family. Biographer A. Scott Berg, in his book *Kate Remembered*, recalled a fascinating evening when Michael came to Katharine Hepburn's home. In *Remember the Time*, Michael's body-guards Bill Whitfield and Javon Beard proved to be of great help in discussing Michael's return to the United States in 2006 when he briefly resided in Las Vegas, as he was solemnly approaching the end of his life, although no one at the time could have imagined just how soon that demise would be. Also of great value were the public interviews of Carole Bayer Sager, who spoke so poignantly of the final period of Elizabeth's life, and touchingly, the rare but frank public interviews that Lisa Marie Presley granted, especially after Michael's death. These were just some of the recollections that were so important to me as I wove together the stories of the lives, the careers, and the destinies of Elizabeth and Michael.

It is a pleasure to acknowledge the many individuals and the research resources, aside from those already mentioned, that proved important during the lengthy period of writing *Elizabeth and Michael*. My former teaching assistant at New York University's Tisch School of the Arts, Mia Kai Moody, gathered information in Los Angeles, notably at the Margaret Herrick Library of the Academy of Motion Picture Arts and Sciences. The staff at the library was very helpful. Mia also established a chronology of the touring schedules of the Jackson 5 and of Michael on his solo tours. At the beginning of this project, David Aglow located valuable material on the joint public appearances of Elizabeth and Michael. Toward the end of the project, he helped prepare the notes for the book and offered important suggestions. I have to express my appreciation to my former researcher, now a director, Phil Bertelsen, with whom it was always good to exchange ideas. He would often come up with material he thought might prove useful. It has also always been a terrific experience to talk to my dear friend the producer Debra Martin Chase about the inner workings of the entertainment industry. My friend, the writer Allison Samuels, formerly of *Newsweek* and *The Daily Beast*, is another entertainment expert with whom it has been greatly valuable to discuss the music world and the Jackson family. Jerald Silverhardt has come to the rescue on occasions when I have put in a call to the West Coast to check on some detail. Bruce Goldstein of Film Forum has been helpful. The great drama coach and acting teacher Janet Alhanti, who also resides in Los Angeles, has always been insightful. I want to thank such friends at Turner Classic Movies as Darcy Hettrich, Dori Stegman, Genevieve McGillicuddy, and of course, the astute host of TCM, Robert Osborne. Most of all, I have to express my gratitude to my great friend Charlie Tabesh, the Vice President of Programming at TCM, who has helped me track down rare films to screen—and with whom it is always a pleasure and an enlightened experience to discuss film history and popular culture as well as politics and current events.

There have been many remarkable friends and associates who have provided great assistance and have been far more helpful with this book than they may realize. My gratitude goes to Emery Wimbish, Grace Frankowsky, Sarah Orrick, Carol Scott Leonard, Catherine Nelson, Ronald Mason, Kim Mason, Deesha Hill, Martin Radburd (who has always come to the rescue when there have been computer problems), Alan Sukoenig, Hiroko Hatanaka, Billie Johnson, Rae Rossini, Nels Johnson, Cathie Nelson, film historian Ed Mapp, Tony and Vanita Nicholas, Keith Holman, Jean Franz, Clerio Demoraes, Gloria Hopkins Buck, Pat Faison, Jane Rappaport, Mary Sue Price, Joerg Klebe of German Educational Television, Rigmor Newman, Robert Katz of K2 Pictures, Jeanne Moutoussamy Ashe, Susan Peterson, Tink Alexander, Linda Doll Tarrant, Marie Orlanti, Judith Osborne, Fotini Lomke, Arthur and Joanie Rossi, the Lagow family—Barbara, Ellen, and James—Margaret McDowell, Ben Armento, Barbara Reynolds, Herma Ross Shorty, Clifford Laurent, Peg Henehan, Loan Le, Rachel Gold, Franklin Lara, Doug Rossini, Liza Rossini, Meghan Rossini, Brett Haber, Todd Hoellerman, dear Sally Placksin, Heidi Stack, Elsa Aglow (a true die-hard Taylor fan), Hamida Belkadi, and the fantastic entertainment reporter Marian Etoile Watson, who had covered the Jackson 5 during their time in Senegal.

Family and friends who gave great support include some of my favorite people: Jacqueline Bogle Mosley; Robert Bogle Sr., publisher of the *Philadelphia Tribune*; Roslynne Bogle; Jeanne Bogle Charleston; Janet Bogle Schenck and her husband, Jerry Schenck; the ever-resourceful Roger Bogle; Gerald Grant Bogle; Jay Bogle; Mariska Bogle; Robert Bogle Jr.; Luellen Fletcher; Fred Charleston; Fred Charleston Jr.; Lori Stimpson Guile; Ayana Charleston; Hassan Charleston; Denise Charleston; Mechelle Mosley Palmer; Hermond Palmer; Mark Mosley; Sylvia Gholston Mosley; dear Bettina Batchleor; Karin Leake; Alex Bogle; Aminata Diabate; Clarence Edwards; Kevin Guile; my good friend Enrico Pellegrini; Katrina Pavlos; Sean Batchleor; Shaaron Boykin; and my colleagues at the University of Pennsylvania Gale Garrison and Carol Davis as well as to my colleagues at New York University's Tisch School of the Arts Janet Neipris, Richard Wesley, David Rhangelli, and Patricia Ione Lloyd. My gratitude is extended to my round table of former Penn students with whom I frequently have lunch to catch up on films and television: Gigi Kwon, Raj Gopal, Jake Stock, and Nadine Zylberberg. Special thanks also go to my former students Marcel Salas, Kyle

Webster, Wesley Barrow, Robin Williams, and especially to Laurence Coman. My gratitude also goes to Yemaya Bogle.

Finally, my great appreciation and gratitude are extended to the always perceptive Marie Dutton Brown; to my former editor (on another book) Evander Lomke, with whom it was great to discuss *Elizabeth and Michael*; to another former editor, the fantastic Elisabeth Dyssegaard.

I also have to thank my agent Jennifer Lyons, who steadfastly offered advice and assistance and who provided feedback on the book in its early drafts. I will forever be grateful to my other agent, the late Bob Silverstein, who urged me to do this book. He was also a wonderful friend. The original editor on *Elizabeth and Michael* was Malaika Adero, who was consistently insightful, encouraging, and enthusiastic. Later Leslie Meredith briefly was my editor and also proved helpful. Rakesh Satyal was my editor as the book took further shape and finally was completed. Always he provided terrific observations, and his editorial comments were extremely important as I restructured the book. Also significant was his remarkable enthusiasm. He has been a huge fan of both Elizabeth and Michael. It always meant much to know that he saw the importance of this book—and wanted the best for it.

Selected Bibliography

Baker, Carroll. *Baby Doll: An Autobiography.* New York: Arbor House, 1983.

Berg, A. Scott. *Kate Remembered.* New York: G. P. Putnam's Sons, 2003.

Bergman, Ingrid, and Alan Burgess, *Ingrid Bergman: My Story.* New York: Delacorte Press, 1980.

Birkin, Andrew. *J. M. Barrie & the Lost Boys.* New Haven, CT: Yale University Press, 2003.

Biskind, Peter, ed. *Lunches with Orson: Conversations Between Henry Jaglom and Orson Welles.* New York: Metropolitan Books/Henry Holt and Company, 2013.

Bogle, Donald. *Bright Boulevards, Bold Dreams: The Story of Black Hollywood.* New York: One World/Ballantine, 2006.

_____. *Dorothy Dandridge: A Biography.* New York: Berkley Publishing Group.

_____. *Heat Wave: The Life and Career of Ethel Waters.* New York: HarperCollins, 2012.

Boteach, Shmuley. *The Michael Jackson Tapes.* New York: Vanguard Press, 2009.

Bosworth, Patricia. *Montgomery Clift: A Biography.* New York: Harcourt Brace Jovanovich, 1978.

Burton, Richard. *The Richard Burton Diaries.* Edited by Chris Williams. New Haven: Yale University Press, 2012.

Cascio, Frank with Hilary Liftin. *My Friend Michael: An Extraordinary Friendship With An Extraordinary Man.* New York: William Morrow, 2011.

Christie's Catalogue: *Unforgettable: Fashions of the Oscars.* New York: Christie's, 1999.

Davis, Clive with Anthony DeCurtis. *The Soundtrack of My Life.* New York: Simon & Schuster, 2013.

Dunne, Dominick. *The Way We Lived Then: Recollections of a Well-Known Name Dropper.* New York: Crown Publishers, 1999.

Fisher, Carrie. *Shockaholic.* New York: Simon & Schuster, 2011.

Fisher, Eddie, with David Fisher. *Been There, Done That.* New York: St. Martin's Press, 1999.

Fisher, Eddie. *Eddie: My Life, My Loves.* New York: Harper & Row Publishers, 1981.

Gates, Phyllis and Bob Thomas. *My Husband Rock Hudson.* Garden City, NY: Doubleday & Company, Inc., 1987.

Gordy, Berry. *To Be Loved: The Music, The Magic, The Memories of Motown: An Auto-biography.* New York: Warner Books, 1994.

Grant, Lee. *I Said Yes to Everything.* New York: Blue Rider Press, 2014.

Greenburg, Zack O'Malley. *Michael Jackson, Inc.: The Rise, Fall, and Rebirth of a Billion-Dollar Empire*. Atria: New York, 2014.

Guilaroff, Sydney, as told to Cathy Griffin. *Crowning Glory: Reflections of Hollywood's Favorite Confidant*. Santa Monica, CA: General Publishing Group, Inc., 1996

Harris, Mark. *Pictures at a Revolution: Five Movies and the Birth of the New Hollywood*. New York: Penguin Press, 2008.

Heymann, David C. *Liz: An Intimate Biography of Elizabeth Taylor*. New York: Birch Lane Press, 1995.

Hopper, Hedda, and James Brough. *The Whole Truth and Nothing But*. Garden City, NY: Doubleday & Company, Inc., 1962, 1963.

Jackson, Jermaine. *You Are Not Alone: Michael Through A Brother's Eyes*. New York: Touchstone, 2011.

Jackson, La Toya with Patricia Romanowski. *La Toya: Growing Up in the Jackson Family*. Dutton: New York, 1991.

Jackson, La Toya with Jeffré Phillips. *Starting Over*. New York: Gallery Books, 2011.

Jackson, Margaret Maldonado with Richard Hack. *Jackson Family Values*. Dove Books: Beverly Hills, 1995.

Jackson, Michael. *Moonwalk*. New York: Doubleday & Company, Inc., 1988.

Jones, Bob with Stacy Brown. *Michael Jackson:*

The Man Behind the Mask. New York: SelectBooks Inc., 2009.

Kael, Pauline. *5001 Nights at the Movies.* New York: Henry Holt and Company, 1991.

Kashner, Sam, and Nancy Schoenberger. *Furious Love: Elizabeth Taylor, Richard Burton, and the Marriage of the Century.* New York: HarperCollins Publishers, 2010.

Langella, Frank. *Dropped Names: Famous Men and Women As I Knew Them, A Memoir.* New York: Harper, 2012.

Lawrence, Greg. *Jackie as Editor: The Literary Life of Jacqueline Kennedy Onassis.* New York: Thomas Dunne Books/St. Martin's Press, 2011.

Morley, Sheridan. *Elizabeth Taylor: A Celebration.* London: Pavilion Books Limited, 1989.

Opie, Catherine, with contributions by Hilton Als, Tim Mendelson, and Ingrid Sischy. *700 Nimes Road.* New York: DelMonico Books/Prestel, 2015.

Reynolds, Debbie, and Dorian Hannaway. *Unsinkable: A Memoir.* New York: William Morrow, 2014.

Rose, Helen and Sidney Sheldon. *Just Make Them Beautiful: The Many Worlds of a Designing Woman.* Santa Monica, CA: Dennis-Landman, 1976.

Sharaff, Irene. *Broadway & Hollywood: Costumes*

Designed by Irene Sharaff. New York: Van Nostrand Reinhold Company, 1976.

Sheppard, Dick. *Elizabeth: The Life and Career of Elizabeth Taylor.* Doubleday & Company, Inc.: Garden City, NY, 1974.

Spada, James. *Peter Lawford: The Man Who Kept the Secrets.* New York: Bantam Books, 1991.

Stevens Jr., George. *Conversations with The Great Moviemakers of Hollywood Golden Age at the American Film Institute.* New York: Vintage, 2007.

Sullivan, Randall. *Untouchable: The Strange Life and Tragic Death of Michael Jackson.* New York: Grove Press, 2012.

Taraborrelli, J. Randy. *Call Her Miss Ross: The Unauthorized Biography of Diana Ross.* New York: Birch Lane Press, 1989.

_____. *Elizabeth.* New York: Warner Books, 2006.

_____. *Michael Jackson: The Magic and the Madness.* New York: Birch Lane Press, 1991.

_____. *Michael Jackson: The Magic, the Madness, the Whole Story 1958-2009.* New York: Grand Central Publishing, 2009.

Taylor, Elizabeth. *Elizabeth Takes Off.* New York: G.P. Putnam's Sons, 1988.

_____. *Elizabeth Taylor: An Informal Memoir.* New York: Harper & Row Publishers, 1964, 1965.

_____. *My Love Affair with Jewelry*. New York: Simon & Schuster, 2002.

_____. *Nibbles and Me*. New York: Duell, Sloan, and Pearcek Inc., 1946, 1974. Also: Simon & Schuster with Introduction and Additional Illustrations by Elizabeth Taylor, 2002.

Tiel, Vicky. *It's All About the Dress: What I Learned in Forty Years About Men, Women, Sex, and Fashion*. New York: St. Martin's Press, 2011.

Wagner, Robert with Scott Eyman. *You Must Remember This: Life and Style in Hollywood's Golden Age*. New York: Viking, 2014.

Walker, Alexander. *Elizabeth: The Life of Elizabeth Taylor*. New York: Grove Press, 1997.

Wanger, Walter and Joe Hyams. *My Life with Cleopatra: The Making of a Hollywood Classic*. New York: Vintage Books, 2013.

Waterbury, Ruth. *Elizabeth Taylor*. New York: Appleton-Century, 1964.

Weisner, Ron. *Listen Out Loud: A Life in Music —Managing McCartney, Madonna, and Michael Jackson*. Guilford, CT: Lyons Press, 2014.

Whitfield, Bill, and Javon Beard with Tanner Colby. *Remember the Time: Protecting Michael Jackson in His Final Days*. New York: Weinstein Books, 2014.

Wiley, Mason, and Damien Bona. *Inside Oscar:*

The Unofficial History of the Academy Awards. New York: Ballantine Books, 1987.

Wilson, Mary with Patricia Romanowski and Argus Juilliard. *Dreamgirl: My Life as a Supreme*. New York: St. Martin's Press, 1986.

Winters, Shelley. *Shelley: Also Known As Shirley*. New York: William Morrow, 1980.

Elizabeth Taylor: An Intimate Portrait, Jack Haley Jr. Productions, 1975.

About the Author

DONALD BOGLE, ONE of the foremost authorities on African Americans in film and in entertainment history, is the author of eight books, including the classic *Toms, Coons, Mulattoes, Mammies, and Bucks: An Interpretive History of Blacks in American Films* as well as two highly acclaimed, groundbreaking biographies: the bestseller *Dorothy Dandridge: A Biography* and *Heat Wave: The Life and Career of Ethel Waters.* His social history *Bright Boulevards, Bold Dreams: The Story of Black Hollywood* looks at the early years of African Americans in Los Angeles as they struggled to make a place for themselves in the film industry. He adapted his book *Brown Sugar: Over One Hundred Years of America's Black Female Superstars* into a four-part documentary series for PBS. Bogle has also appeared on numerous television and radio programs. He was a special commentator and consultant for Turner Classic Movies' award-winning *Race and Hollywood* series. He teaches at both the University of Pennsylvania and New York University's Tisch School of the Arts.

Center Point Large Print
600 Brooks Road / PO Box 1
Thorndike, ME 04986-0001 USA

(207) 568-3717

US & Canada:
1 800 929-9108
www.centerpointlargeprint.com